[illegible]

JOURNAL FOR THE STUDY OF THE NEW TESTAMENT SUPPLEMENT SERIES

87

Executive Editor
Stanley E. Porter

Editorial Board
Richard Bauckham, David Catchpole, R. Alan Culpepper, Joanna Dewey, James D.G. Dunn, Robert Fowler, Robert Jewett, Elizabeth Struthers Malbon, Dan O. Via

JSOT Press
Sheffield

Worship, Theology and Ministry in the Early Church

Essays in Honor of Ralph P. Martin

Edited by
Michael J. Wilkins
and
Terence Paige

Journal for the Study of the New Testament
Supplement Series 87

BS
2395
.W660
1992

Copyright © 1992 Sheffield Academic Press

Published by JSOT Press
JSOT Press is an imprint of
Sheffield Academic Press Ltd
343 Fulwood Road
Sheffield S10 3BP
England

Typeset by Sheffield Academic Press
and
Printed on acid-free paper in Great Britain
by Biddles Ltd
Guildford

British Library Cataloguing in Publication Data

A catalogue record for this book is available
from the British Library

ISBN 1-85075-417-9

JESUIT - KRAUSS - McCORMICK - LIBRARY
1100 EAST 55th STREET
CHICAGO, ILLINOIS 60615

RALPH PHILIP MARTIN

PRAECEPTORI ET MINISTRO FIDELI IN CHRISTO
HUNC LIBRUM DEDICAVIMUS

CONTENTS

PART III
MINISTRY

PREFACE

In his 'Occasional Bulletin' to graduate students at Fuller Theological Seminary, the director once brought to the light a dilemma which is recurrent for theological students:

> A perennial question that is sure to surface in an institution of academic research and study such as Fuller (especially in the Graduate Studies Program) is one that runs like this: how does the student strike a balance between scholarship and spirituality? With a rightful concern with rigorously technical and academic pursuits, how may we attend to the needs of spiritual development and nurture?[1]

This present volume honors the person who penned those words—Professor Ralph P. Martin. The question he raised reveals a distinguishing characteristic of his own career, as is evidenced by the testimony of his colleagues, students, and friends. A recurring theme echoes from those who have had the privilege of being acquainted with Professor Martin during his distinguished career: each attests to a remarkable synthesis in his life of extraordinary scholarship, sincere devotion, and pastoral concern.

That synthesis forms the basis for this volume of essays. The title, *Worship, Theology and Ministry in the Early Church*, is deliberately broad—as broad as Professor Martin's own interests. Professor Martin's research, writing and teaching has provided leadership in the exploration of each of these areas of study for over thirty years.

A chord often struck in his writings is the link between biblical studies and the living faith of the contemporary church. Perhaps because of his own involvement in the life of the church during much of his career, Professor Martin has a sensitivity for the concrete applications—or the dangers of misapplication—of biblical theology to the

---

[1] 'Occasional Bulletin of the Graduate Studies Program', Fuller Theological Seminary (Vol. 7, no. 2; January, 1986), p. 1.

church today. Those of us who have had the pleasure of knowing Professor Martin as his students admire the way he models the faith he teaches. In his patience, his catholicity of spirit, his humility, and his sharing of his home—as well as in his demands for academic excellence on his students' part—he has shown that he holds sincerely the faith about which he teaches others.

The essays collected here come from a variety of theological perspectives from several different countries, representing Professor Martin's own widespread interest and influence. The articles come from people he has worked with throughout his career: from London Bible College (Leslie Allen and Donald Guthrie) to Fuller Theological Seminary (Leslie Allen, Colin Brown and Donald Hagner) to the University of Sheffield (Andrew Lincoln). They come both from former students (Donald Hagner, Colin Kruse, Lynn Losie, Peter O'Brien, Terence Paige, Marianne Thompson, Michael Wilkins) and from colleagues in scholarship (Ernest Best, James Dunn, Earle Ellis, Gerald Hawthorne, Howard Marshall, Leon Morris, Graham Stanton, and Eduard Schweizer).

We wish to recognize two of the original contributors who were unable to complete their essays. One contributor in particular must be noted as sadly missing. F.F. Bruce, with whom Professor Martin taught at the University of Manchester, had hoped to contribute an article on 'Ministry and Worship in the Roman Church'. Upon receiving our invitation to be a contributor, he wrote to us:

> I habitually decline such invitations nowadays, because I find that it takes me much longer to produce less than it formerly did; but as I considered your letter I felt that I must make an exception in favor of Ralph. I am delighted that he is being honored in this way.

Unfortunately Professor Bruce passed away before he could complete the essay, but we include his good wishes, as good as the deed in this case.

Another original contributor—George R. Beasley-Murray—suffered a bad fall while lecturing in the USA which occasioned the breaking of an arm, one or two lesser bones, and severely injuring one of his legs. Professor Beasley-Murray had a very slow recovery with complications developing. He was, therefore, unable to submit his contribution, but asked that we extend with apologies his congratulations to his good friend, Ralph Martin.

The editors wish to acknowledge the many people who have assisted in the publication of this volume. Although we cannot mention all by name, we wish to single out some who have given special assistance. First, great debt is owed to the contributors, all of whom assented so eagerly to this project. Each has been a model of the highest standards of scholarly excellence. Second, heartfelt thanks must go to Sheffield Academic Press for their enthusiastic support in making this volume possible, especially David Hill and Philip R. Davies. Third, special appreciation is extended to our teaching institutions—Talbot School of Theology and Belfast Bible College—for their support and encouragement. A publishing grant from Talbot School of Theology, Biola University helped make it possible to put this volume together, but the secretarial assistance and costs of intercontinental communication were also largely defrayed by our institutions. We also wish to thank Kathryn Rhodes, a teaching assistant who helped format several of the essays, Professors Clinton Arnold and Walter Russell who helped proof-read several essays, and Mrs. Joan Anderson who helped in a variety of valuable ways. Finally, we wish to thank our families for their support during the months we have attended to this most worthy project.

We join a host of colleagues, students, friends and family in celebrating the distinguished career of Professor Ralph P. Martin. Our hope is that his unique synthesis of scholarship, devotion, and ministry will continue be an inspiration to us for many years to come.

MICHAEL J. WILKINS
TERENCE PAIGE

The Contributors

Leslie C. Allen
Professor of Old Testament, Fuller Theological Seminary, Pasadena, California, USA.

Ernest Best
Professor Emeritus of Divinity and Biblical Criticism, University of Glasgow, Scotland.

Colin Brown
Professor of Systematic Theology and Associate Dean for Advanced Theological Studies, Center for Advanced Theological Studies, Fuller Theological Seminary, Pasadena, California, USA.

James D. G. Dunn
Professor of Divinity, Department of Theology, University of Durham, England.

E. Earle Ellis
Research Professor of Theology, Southwestern Baptist Theological Seminary, Ft. Worth, Texas, USA.

Donald Guthrie
President, London Bible College, London, England.

Donald A. Hagner
Professor of New Testament, Fuller Theological Seminary, Pasadena, California, USA.

Gerald F. Hawthorne
Professor of Greek and New Testament Exegesis, Wheaton College, Wheaton, Illinois, USA.

Colin G. Kruse
Senior Lecturer in New Testament, Ridley College, University of Melbourne, Victoria, Australia.

ANDREW T. LINCOLN
Senior Lecturer in New Testament, University of Sheffield, Sheffield, England.

LYNN A. LOSIE
Associate Professor of New Testament, C.P. Haggard School of Theology, Azusa Pacific University, Azusa, California, USA.

I. HOWARD MARSHALL
Professor of New Testament Exegesis, University of Aberdeen, Scotland.

LEON MORRIS
Principal Emeritus, Ridley College, University of Melbourne, Victoria, Australia.

PETER T. O'BRIEN
Vice Principal and Head of New Testament Department, Moore Theological College, Newtown, New South Wales, Australia.

TERENCE PAIGE
Lecturer in Biblical Studies, Belfast Bible College, Belfast, Northern Ireland.

EDUARD SCHWEIZER
Retired Professor of New Testament, University of Zürich, Zürich, Switzerland.

GRAHAM STANTON
Professor of New Testament Studies, King's College, University of London, London, England.

MARIANNE MEYE THOMPSON
Associate Professor of New Testament Interpretation, Fuller Theological Seminary, Pasadena, California, USA.

MICHAEL J. WILKINS
Chair and Professor of New Testament Language and Literature, Talbot School of Theology, Biola University, La Mirada, California, USA.

ABBREVIATIONS

Ancient Works

Diogn.	*The Epistle to Diognetus*
D.L.	Diogenes Laertius, *Lives of the Philosophers*
Euseb.	Eusebius of Caesarea
Hist. Ecc.	Eusebius, *Historia Ecclesiastica*
Praep. Evang.	Eusebius, *Praeparatio Evangelica*
Ign.	Ignatius of Antioch
Ign. *Eph.*	Ignatius, *Letter to the Ephesians*
Magn.	Ignatius, *Letter to the Magnesians*
Phld.	Ignatius, *Letter to the Philadelphians*
Pol.	Ignatius, *Letter to Polycarp*
Rom.	Ignatius, *Letter to the Romans*
Smyrn.	Ignatius, *Letter to the Smyrnaeans*
Trall.	Ignatius, *Letter to the Trallians*
Mart. Pol.	*Martyrdom of Polycarp*
Philo	
Leg.	*Legatio ad Gaium*
Vit. Cont.	*De Vita Contemplativa*
Vit. Mos.	*De Vita Mosis*
Plut.	Plutarch of Chaeronea
Comm. not.	*De communibus notitiis*
Stoic. absurd.	*Compendium argumenti Stoicos absurdiora poetis dicere*
Stoic. repug.	*De Stoicorum repugnantiis*
Conj. praec.	*Conjugalia praecepta*
Pol. *Phil.*	Polycarp, *Philippians*

Modern Works

AB	Anchor Bible
AusBR	*Australian Biblical Review*
AnBib	Analecta biblica
ANRW	*Aufstieg und Niedergang der römischen Welt*
ASTI	*Annual of the Swedish Theological Institute*
ATR	*Anglican Theological Review*

BAGD	W. Bauer, W.F. Arndt, F.W. Gingrich, and F.W. Danker, *Greek-English Lexicon of the New Testament and other Early Christian Literature.*
Bib	*Biblica*
BHT	Beiträge zur historischen Theologie
BT	*The Bible Translator*
BU	Biblische Untersuchungen
BZ	*Biblische Zeitschrift*
CBQ	*Catholic Biblical Quarterly*
EDNT	H. Balz and G. Schneider (eds.), *Exegetical Dictionary of the New Testament*
EKKNT	Evangelisches-Katholischer Kommentar zum Neuen Testament
EncJud	*Encyclopaedia Judaica*
ETL	*Ephemerides theologicae lovanienses*
EvT	*Evangelische Theologie*
EvQ	*Evangelical Quarterly*
EBC	Expositor's Bible Commentary
ExpTim	*Expository Times*
FRLANT	Forschungen zur Religion und Literatur des Alten und Neuen Testaments
GNB	*Good News Bible = Today's English Version*
GNC	Good News Commentaries
GrOrthThR	*Greek Orthodox Theological Review*
HTKNT	Herders theologischer Kommentar zum Neuen Testament
ICC	International Critical Commentary
Int	*Interpretation*
JAC	*Jahrbuch für Antike und Christentum*
JAAR	*Journal of the American Academy of Religion*
JBL	*Journal of Biblical Literature*
JQR	*Jewish Quarterly Review*
JR	*Journal of Religion*
JSJ	*Journal for the Study of Judaism in the Persian, Hellenistic and Roman Period*
JSNT	*Journal for the Study of the New Testament*
JSNTSup	*Journal for the Study of the New Testament*, Supplement Series
JSOTSup	*Journal for the Study of the Old Testament*, Supplement Series
JTC	*Journal for Theology and the Church*
JTS	*Journal of Theological Studies*
KJV	King James Version
KEK	Kritisch-exegetischer Kommentar über das Neue Testament
LCL	Loeb Classical Library
LUA	Lunds universitets årsskrift
MNTC	Moffatt New Testament Commentary
NASB	*New American Standard Bible*
NCB	New Century Bible

NEB	*New English Bible*
NICNT	New International Commentary on the New Testament
NIDNTT	C. Brown (ed.), *The New International Dictionary of New Testament Theology*
NIGTC	The New International Greek Testament Commentary
NIV	New International Version
NovT	*Novum Testamentum*
NovTSup	*Novum Testamentum* Supplements
NRSV	New Revised Standard Version
NTS	*New Testament Studies*
ÖTKNT	Ökumenischer Taschenbuch-Kommentar zum Neuen Testament
RB	*Revue biblique*
RelS	*Religious Studies*
RevExp	*Review and Expositor*
RNT	Regensburger Neues Testament
RSR	*Recherches de science religieuse*
RSV	Revised Standard Version
SANT	Studien zum Alten und Neuen Testament
SBFLA	*Studii biblici franciscani liber annuus*
SBLDS	Society of Biblical Literature Dissertation Series
SBLSP	Society of Biblical Literature Seminar Papers
SE	*Studia Evangelica*
SJT	*Scottish Journal of Theology*
SNTSMS	Society for New Testament Studies Monograph Series
ST	*Studia theologica*
SVF	*Stoicorum Veterum Fragmenta*, ed. Johann von Arnim
TDNT	G. Kittel and G. Friedrich (eds.), *Theological Dictionary of the New Testament*
TLG	*Thesaurus Linguae Graecae*
TLZ	*Theologische Literaturzeitung*
TNTC	Tyndale New Testament Commentaries
TS	*Theological Studies*
TZ	*Theologische Zeitschrift*
UBSGNT	United Bible Societies' *Greek New Testament*
VC	*Vigiliae christianae*
WA	M. Luther, *Kritische Gesamtausgabe* (='Weimar' edition)
WBC	Word Biblical Commentary
WTJ	*Westminster Theological Journal*
WUNT	Wissenschaftliche Untersuchungen zum Neuen Testament
ZNW	*Zeitschrift für die neutestamentliche Wissenschaft*
ZTK	*Zeitschrift für Theologie und Kirche*
ZWT	*Zeitschrift für wissenschaftliche Theologie*

Ralph Philip Martin: *Curriculum Vitae*

Compiled by Lynn A. Losie

*Background**

Ralph Philip Martin was born in Anfield, Liverpool, England, on August 4, 1925, to Philip and Ada Martin. His father was a printer, and young Ralph received his early education first at the Anfield Road School and then at The Liverpool Collegiate, located in the city. As war broke out in 1939, Ralph was evacuated along with his classmates to Bangor, North Wales, for several months, and in a little over a year after returning to Liverpool, he left school at sixteen to work in an insurance office.

About this time, two young women, Lily Nelson and her sister Eva, began attending the Anfield Methodist Church, which Ralph had attended since childhood, and invited Ralph and his best friend, James Tootill, to the monthly Saturday evening 'squash meetings' of the Young Life Campaign. On February 6, 1943, after four months of exposure to the simple gospel message proclaimed at these meetings and through the guidance of an older man, W.J. Wilson, Ralph and James made a public profession of faith in Jesus Christ as their Savior. Ralph soon felt God's call to the ministry, and began preparing to attend Manchester Methodist College. But a growing conviction concerning the doctrine of believers' baptism led him to consider affiliating with the Baptists. Called up to serve the war effort as a 'Bevin boy' in the coal mines of Lancashire, Ralph made his decision to join the Baptists and was baptized by the Rev. H.S. Phillips at the Aenon Baptist Church, Burnley.

*The Rev. James Tootill, a longtime friend of Ralph Martin just recently retired from service as a missionary in Thailand, kindly supplied much of this biographical information.

After three years of service in the mines, Ralph was released and began training for the pastorate at Manchester Baptist College, earning a degree in theology from the University of Manchester (with Distinction). Unaware of a scholarship to the University of Cambridge through an administrative oversight, Ralph entered the Baptist ministry in 1949 and was ordained at the Kendal Road Baptist Church, Gloucester, inaugurating his ministry with a sermon on the 'unswerving conviction', 'unfailing communion', and 'unshakeable confidence' expressed in Psalm 16.8. It was at this time, also, that he married Lily Nelson, through whose influence he had come to a deeper spiritual commitment and who shared his desire for Christian service. In time the family expanded to four, with the birth of two daughters, Patricia and Elizabeth. After four years in Gloucester, Ralph moved to another pastorate at the West Street Baptist Church in Dunstable, Bedfordshire (abbreviated 'Beds.'). At the induction service, the secretary of Ralph's former church in Gloucester remarked, 'He'll soon get you out of your beds!'

During ten years of faithful pastoral work, Ralph continued to develop his academic gifts, and in his leisure hours he was able to earn an M.A. in Pauline studies from the University of Manchester and complete a commentary on the New Testament book of Philippians (still in print as the Tyndale New Testament Commentary 11). These accomplishments did not go unnoticed, and in 1959 Ralph was invited to become a lecturer in theology at the London Bible College.

Throughout the illustrious academic career that has ensued both in England and in the United States, Ralph has continued to minister in local churches. Although a stimulating lecturer, prolific writer, and generous supervisor of post-graduate students, Ralph has found time to serve as interim pastor of a number of churches, most notably the Sale Baptist Church (Sale, Cheshire, England), the Altadena (California) Baptist Church, and the Eagle Rock Covenant Church (Los Angeles), and he has been constantly in demand as a teacher of adult Bible classes. His popular commentary on the Gospel of Mark (*Where the Action Is* [1977]), dedicated to the adult Bible class of the Eagle Rock Covenant Church, exemplifies this helpful ministry. Now having returned to his native England, occupying his time in semi-retirement with part-time pastoral and professorial duties, Ralph Philip Martin continues a life which has truly been characterized by scholarship in the service of the church.

Education

B.A.	University of Manchester, 1949 (with Distinction, and with pastoral training at Manchester Baptist College)
M.A.	University of Manchester, 1956 (by thesis, 'Eucharistic Teaching in 1 Corinthians', Supervisor: Professor T.W. Manson)
Ph.D.	King's College, University of London, 1963 (by thesis, 'Philippians ii.5-11 in Recent Interpretation and in the Setting of Early Christian Worship', published as *Carmen Christi: Philippians ii.5-11 in Recent Interpretation and in the Setting of Early Christian Worship* [SNTSMS 4; Cambridge: Cambridge University Press, 1967], Supervisor: Professor D.E. Nineham)

Pastoral and Teaching Posts

1949-53	Pastor, Kendal Road Baptist Church Gloucester, Gloucestershire, England
1953-59	Pastor, West Street Baptist Church Dunstable, Bedfordshire, England
1959-65	Lecturer in Theology London Bible College, London, England
1964-65	Visiting Professor of Biblical Literature Bethel College and Seminary, St. Paul, Minnesota
1965-69	Lecturer in New Testament University of Manchester, Manchester, England
1969-88	Professor of New Testament Fuller Theological Seminary, Pasadena, California
1979-88	Director of the Graduate Studies Program Fuller Theological Seminary, Pasadena, California
1988-	Pastor, Norwood Avenue Baptist Church Southport, Lancashire, England
1988-	Professor Associate in Biblical Studies University of Sheffield, Sheffield, England

Professional Societies

Studiorum Novi Testamenti Societas
The Society of Biblical Literature
Institute for Biblical Research
Baptist Professors of Religion

Lectureships, Editorships, and Honors

1959	Tyndale New Testament Lecture
1962-64	Editor, *Vox Evangelica*
1968	Visiting Professor of New Testament Fuller Theological Seminary, Pasadena, California
1970	Editor (with W. Ward Gasque) *Apostolic History and the Gospel: Biblical and Historical Essays Presented to F.F. Bruce on His 60th Birthday.* Exeter: Paternoster/Grand Rapids: Eerdmans
1972-87	Advisory Editor, *Studia Biblica et Theologica*
1975	Visiting Lecturer Spurgeon's College, London
1977-78	Biblical Editor, Marshalls Theological Library Marshall, Morgan and Scott, London
1977-	New Testament Editor Word Biblical Commentary, Word Books, Waco, Texas
1978	Visiting Lecturer Institute of Holy Land Studies, Jerusalem
1978	Visiting Lecturer New College, Berkeley, California
1978-79	Consultant Editor, Marshalls Theological Library Marshall, Morgan and Scott, London
1979-80	Consultant Editor, New Foundations Theological Library John Knox Press, Atlanta, Georgia
1981	Weyerhauser Award Fuller Theological Seminary, Pasadena, California
1981	Visiting Lecturer Moore Theological College, Sydney, Australia
1981	Visiting Lecturer Ridley College, Melbourne, Australia

1982 Derward W. Deere Lectures
Golden Gate Baptist Theological Seminary, Mill Valley, California

1990 Huber L. Drumwright Lectures
Southwestern Baptist Theological Seminary, Fort Worth, Texas

Select Publications

1959

The Epistle of Paul to the Philippians: An Introduction and Commentary. The Tyndale New Testament Commentaries. London: Tyndale/Grand Rapids: Eerdmans.

'Μορφή in Philippians 2^6'. *The Expository Times* 70, pp. 183-84.

1960

An Early Christian Confession: Philippians ii.5-11 in Recent Interpretation. Tyndale New Testament Lecture, 1959. London: Tyndale.

The Lord's Supper. London: Crusade.

1962

'Blasphemy', 'Bride, Bridegroom', 'Communion', 'Idols, Meat Offered to', 'Judas Iscariot', 'Lord's Supper, The', 'Philippians, Epistle to the', 'Trial of Jesus'. In *The New Bible Dictionary*, ed. J.D. Douglas. London: Inter-Varsity/Grand Rapids: Eerdmans.

'The Composition of I Peter in Recent Study'. *Vox Evangelica* 1, pp. 29-42.

1963

'Aspects of Worship in the New Testament Church'. *Vox Evangelica* 2, pp. 6-32.

1964

'An Early Christian Hymn (Col. 1.15-20)'. *Evangelical Quarterly* 36, pp. 195-205.

'A Footnote to Pliny's Account of Christian Worship'. *Vox Evangelica* 3, pp. 51-57.

'The Form-Analysis of Philippians ii, 5-11'. In *Studia Evangelica* II/III, ed. F.L. Cross. Texte und Untersuchungen 87-88. Berlin: Akademie, pp. 611-20.

'The Kingdom of God in Recent Writing'. *Christianity Today* 8, pp. 5-7.

Worship in the Early Church. London: Marshall, Morgan and Scott/ Westwood, New Jersey: Revell.

1966

'The Bithynian Christians' *Carmen Christo*'. *Studia Patristica* 8, pp. 259-65.

'The New Quest of the Historical Jesus'. In *Jesus of Nazareth: Saviour and Lord*, ed. C.F.H. Henry. London: Marshall, Morgan and Scott/Grand Rapids: Eerdmans, pp. 25-45.

1967

Acts. Scripture Union Bible Study Books. London: Scripture Union/ Grand Rapids: Eerdmans.

Carmen Christi: Philippians ii.5-11 in Recent Interpretation and in the Setting of Early Christian Worship. Society for New Testament Studies Monograph Series 4. Cambridge: Cambridge University Press.

1968

'Authority in the Light of the Apostolate, Tradition and the Canon'. *Evangelical Quarterly* 40, pp. 66-82.

1 and 2 Corinthians, Galatians. Scripture Union Bible Study Books. London: Scripture Union/Grand Rapids: Eerdmans.

'An Epistle in Search of a Life-Setting'. *The Expository Times* 79, pp. 296-302.

'A Mediocre Year for New Testament Volumes'. *Christianity Today* 12, pp. 10-12.

1969

'A Brighter Outlook for New Testament Volumes'. *Christianity Today* 13, pp. 6-8.

'A Gospel in Search of a Life-Setting'. *The Expository Times* 80, pp. 361-64.

'St. Matthew's Gospel in Recent Study'. *The Expository Times* 80, pp. 132-36.

1970

'Ephesians'. In *The New Bible Commentary, Revised.* Eds. D. Guthrie and J. A. Motyer. London: Inter-Varsity/Grand Rapids: Eerdmans, pp. 1105-24.

'Romans' (with F. Davidson). In *The New Bible Commentary, Revised.* Eds. D. Guthrie and J. A. Motyer. London: Inter-Varsity/Grand Rapids: Eerdmans, pp. 1012-48.

'Some New Directions in New Testament Study'. *Christianity Today* 14, pp. 10-13.

'A Suggested Exegesis of I Corinthians 13^{13}'. *The Expository Times* 82, pp. 119-20.

1971

'Ephesians'. In *The Broadman Bible Commentary. Vol. 11: 2 Corinthians-Philemon,* ed. C.J. Allen, et al. Nashville: Broadman, pp. 125-77.

1972

Colossians: The Church's Lord and the Christian's Liberty: An Expository Commentary with a Present-Day Application. Exeter: Paternoster/Grand Rapids: Zondervan.

Mark: Evangelist and Theologian. Exeter: Paternoster/Grand Rapids: Zondervan.

1973

'The Authority of the Preacher'. *Christianity Today* 17, pp. 10-14.

'Cremation', 'Exogamy', 'Foolishness', 'Koinonia', 'Purity'. In *Baker's Dictionary of Christian Ethics*, ed. C.F.H. Henry. Grand Rapids: Baker.

1974

Colossians and Philemon. New Century Bible. London: Oliphants.

'Reconciliation and Forgiveness in Colossians'. In *Reconciliation and Hope: New Testament Essays on Atonement and Eschatology Presented to L.L. Morris on His 60th Birthday*, ed. R. Banks. Exeter: Paternoster/Grand Rapids: Eerdmans, pp. 104-24.

'Worship, Early Church'. In *The New International Dictionary of the Christian Church*, ed. J.D. Douglas, et al. Grand Rapids: Zondervan.

Worship in the Early Church. Revised Edition. London: Marshall, Morgan and Scott/Grand Rapids: Eerdmans.

1975

'Colossians, The Epistle to the'. In *The Zondervan Pictorial Encyclopedia of the Bible*, ed. M.C. Tenney. Grand Rapids: Zondervan.

New Testament Foundations: A Guide for Christian Students. Vol. 1: The Four Gospels. Exeter: Paternoster/Grand Rapids: Eerdmans.

1976

'Example', 'Mark, Brand'. In *The New International Dictionary of New Testament Theology. Vol. 2: G-Pre*, ed. C. Brown. Grand Rapids: Zondervan.

'Liturgical Materials, NT'. In *The Interpreter's Dictionary of the Bible: An Illustrated Encyclopedia. Supplementary Volume,* ed. K. Crim, et al. Nashville: Abingdon.

Philippians. New Century Bible. London: Oliphants.

'Salvation and Discipleship in Luke's Gospel'. *Interpretation* 30, pp. 366-80.

1977

'Approaches to New Testament Exegesis'. In *New Testament Interpretation: Essays on Principles and Methods,* ed. I.H. Marshall. Exeter: Paternoster/Grand Rapids: Eerdmans, pp. 220-51.

'How the First Christians Worshipped'. In *[Eerdman's Handbook to the] History of Christianity*, ed. T. Dowley. Berkhampstead: Lion/Grand Rapids: Eerdmans, pp. 122-28.

Where the Action Is. A Bible Commentary for Laymen/Mark. Glendale, California: Regal Books.

1978

'*Haustafeln*' [under 'Virtue']. In *The New International Dictionary of New Testament Theology. Vol. 3: Pri-Z*, ed. C. Brown. Grand Rapids: Zondervan.

'The Life-Setting of the Epistle of James in the Light of Jewish History'. In *Biblical and Near Eastern Studies: Essays in Honour of William Sanford LaSor*, ed. G.A. Tuttle. Grand Rapids: Eerdmans, pp. 97-103.

New Testament Foundations: A Guide for Christian Students. Vol. 2: The Acts, The Letters, The Apocalypse. Exeter: Paternoster/ Grand Rapids: Eerdmans.

'The Pericope of the Healing of the "Centurion's" Servant/Son (Matt. 8:5-13 par. Luke 7:1-10): Some Exegetical Notes'. In *Unity and Diversity in New Testament Theology: Essays in Honor of George E. Ladd*, ed. R.A. Guelich. Grand Rapids: Eerdmans, pp. 14-22.

'The Theology of Mark's Gospel'. *Southwestern Journal of Theology* 21, pp. 23-36.

1979

The Family and the Fellowship: New Testament Images of the Church. Exeter: Paternoster/Grand Rapids: Eerdmans.

1980

'Blasphemy', etc. [see under *The New Bible Dictionary*, 1962]. In *The Illustrated Bible Dictionary*, ed. J.D. Douglas and N. Hillyer. Leicester: Inter-Varsity/Wheaton: Tyndale.

'New Testament Theology: A Proposal: The Theme of Reconciliation'. *The Expository Times* 91, pp. 364-68.

'New Testament Theology: Impasse and Exit: The Issues'. *The Expository Times* 91, pp. 264-69.

Philippians. New Century Bible Commentary. Revised Edition. Grand Rapids: Eerdmans.

1981

Colossians and Philemon. New Century Bible Commentary. Grand Rapids: Eerdmans [reprint].

Mark. Knox Preaching Guides. Atlanta: John Knox.

Reconciliation: A Study of Paul's Theology. Marshalls Theological Library/New Foundations Theological Library. London: Marshall, Morgan and Scott/Atlanta: John Knox.

'Salvation and Discipleship in Luke's Gospel'. In *Interpreting the Gospels*, ed. J. L. Mays. Philadelphia: Fortress, pp. 214-30.

1982

Adoração na igreja primitiva. Sao Paulo, Brazil: Sociedade Religiosa Edições Vida Nova [Portuguese translation of *Worship in the Early Church*, 1974].

'Blasphemy', etc. [see under *The New Bible Dictionary*, 1962]. In *The New Bible Dictionary.* Second Edition, ed. J. D. Douglas and N. Hillyer. Leicester: Inter-Varsity/Wheaton: Tyndale.

'Gospel', 'Jesus Christ'. In *The International Standard Bible Encyclopedia. Vol. 2: E-J*, ed. G. W. Bromiley. Grand Rapids: Eerdmans.

'Some Reflections on New Testament Hymns'. In *Christ the Lord: Essays on Christology Presented to Donald Guthrie*, ed. H.H. Rowdon. Leicester: Inter-Varsity/Downers Grove, Illinois: Inter-Varsity, pp. 37-49.

The Worship of God: Some Theological, Pastoral, and Practical Reflections. Grand Rapids: Eerdmans.

1983

Carmen Christi: Philippians ii.5-11 in Recent Interpretation and in the Setting of Early Christian Worship. Revised Edition. Grand Rapids: Eerdmans.

'New Testament Hymns: Background and Development'. *The Expository Times* 94, pp. 132-36.

1984

Colossenses e Filemon. Sao Paulo, Brazil: Sociedade Religiosa Edições Vida Nova [Portuguese translation of Colossians and Philemon, 1974].

New Testament Books for Pastor and Teacher. Philadelphia: Westminster.

The Spirit and the Congregation: Studies in 1 Corinthians 12-15. The Derward W. Deere Lectures, 1982. Grand Rapids: Eerdmans.

1986

'Acts, Apocryphal', 'Colossians', 'Galatians, Letter to the', 'Gospel', 'Greece', 'Hebrews, Letter to the', 'John, Apostle', 'John, Gospel of', 'Josephus, Flavius', 'Luke, Gospel of', 'Mark, Gospel of', 'Paul, Apostle', 'Peter, Apostle', 'Peter, Epistles of',

'Philemon', 'Philip, Apostle', 'Romans, Letter to the', 'Timothy, First and Second Letters to', 'Titus'. In *The Dictionary of Bible and Religion*, ed. W.H. Gentz. Nashville: Abingdon.

2 Corinthians. Word Biblical Commentary 40. Waco: Word Books.

'Mark, Gospel According to', 'Mark, John', 'Peter', 'Peter, First Epistle of'. In *The International Standard Bible Encyclopedia. Vol. 3: K-P*, ed. G. W. Bromiley. Grand Rapids: Eerdmans.

'The Setting of 2 Corinthians'. *Tyndale Bulletin* 37, pp. 3-19.

1987

The Epistle of Paul to the Philippians: An Introduction and Commentary. Tyndale New Testament Commentaries 11. Second Edition. Leicester: Inter-Varsity/Grand Rapids: Eerdmans.

New Testament Foundations: A Guide for Christian Students. Vol. 2: The Acts, The Letters, The Apocalypse. Revised Edition. Exeter: Paternoster/Grand Rapids: Eerdmans.

'The Opponents of Paul in 2 Corinthians: An Old Issue Revisited'. In *Tradition and Interpretation in the New Testament: Essays in Honor of E. Earle Ellis for His 60th Birthday*, ed. G.F. Hawthorne with O. Betz. Tübingen: J.C.B. Mohr [Paul Siebeck]/Grand Rapids: Eerdmans, pp. 279-89.

1988

1, 2 Corinthians. Word Biblical Themes. Waco: Word Books.

James. Word Biblical Commentary 48. Waco: Word Books.

'The Spirit in 2 Corinthians in Light of the "Fellowship of the Holy Spirit"'. In *Eschatology and the New Testament: Essays in Honor of George Raymond Beasley-Murray*, ed. W.H. Gloer. Peabody, Massachusetts: Hendrickson, pp. 113-28.

'1, 2 Timothy and Titus'. In *Harper's Bible Commentary*, ed. J.L. Mays, et al. San Francisco: Harper and Row, pp. 1237-44.

'Worship'. In *The International Standard Bible Encyclopedia. Vol. 4: Q-Z*. G.W. Bromiley, ed. Grand Rapids: Eerdmans.

1989

'Patterns of Worship in New Testament Churches'. *Journal for the Study of the New Testament* 37, pp. 59-85.

1990

'Paradoxes of Ministry'. *The Expository Times* 102, pp. 82-84.

'Theological Perspectives in 2 Corinthians: Some Notes'. *Society of Biblical Literature: 1990 Seminar Papers*, ed. D.J. Lull. Atlanta: Scholars Press, pp. 240-56.

1992

Ephesians, Colossians, and Philemon. Interpretation: A Bible Commentary for Teaching and Preaching. Louisville: Westminster/John Knox.

Forthcoming

The Theology of the Epistles of Peter and Jude. New Testament Theology. Cambridge: Cambridge University Press.

PERSONAL REMINISCENCES

Leslie C. Allen

In my seminary office two of the photographs on the walls feature the scholar we are honoring by this Festschrift. One is in color and shows Ralph Martin and me looking slightly bored and standing together in academic regalia, obviously as part of a Fuller faculty line that would sooner or later process into chapel. Since our University of London regalia matched, we liked to walk together as a pair. That photograph must have been taken in 1987. The other one is much older. It is a black and white, horizontal picture of the robed students and faculty of London Bible College in September 1963. He and I are sitting with our colleagues in the front row, with rows of standing students towering behind us.

The two photographs indicate the parameters of our association. When I joined the LBC faculty in 1960 as an ex-student just down from Cambridge, Ralph had already been there a year, having left his pastorate at Dunstable Baptist Church. He was wrapping up his Ph.D. dissertation on the hymn in Philippians 2. Although his heart was in the New Testament, unfortunately there was no opportunity to teach it at that time. He taught Systematic Theology. It was rumored that he had mistaken his assignment for Historical Theology. Students groaned under the papers on Luther and Calvin they had to produce. The subject was a supposedly easier 'college' course rather than part of the academic curriculum they had to take for their University of London degree, but it was difficult for them to spot the difference. However, they grudgingly acknowledged that Dr. Martin got to the root of the matter and that it was doing them good. If he has made heavy demands on his students, it is because he has always made such demands on himself as a perpetual student.

We all had administrative duties, and Ralph was college librarian. A constant feature of faculty meetings during his period at LBC was a 'k-k-k' sound as he slit open the uncut pages of French books he had ordered for the library. The meetings tended to be tedious, and the rest of us rather envied his productivity. If you were to go today to the library in the present, resplendent premises of London Bible College at Northwood and penetrated to the periodicals room, you would notice instance after instance where the runs of theological journals go back to the year 1960. *Si monumentum requiris, respice!* His labors of love gradually built up the library into a repository of academic scholarship, from the new catalogs and used book lists he assiduously sent for and scoured.

Faculty meetings were once in a while hotbeds of controversy and accusation. I well remember the time when a colleague concernedly reported that he had seen Ralph gardening in his front yard on his weekly study day. In the minds of the rest of us the one who voiced the accusation was the loser, for the academic output of the accused was well substantiated. He, of all people, should never have been accused of shirking. He was—and is—never one to pursue a safe path because it was the right view for conservatives to hold, but would leave no stone unturned in his quest for exegetical truth and in his fair assessment of any proposal, irrespective of its source. That, of course, was the real charge behind the accusation of the gardening.

I appreciated his blend of faith and scholarship. He became an academic role model for me. He introduced me to Dr. Williams' Library, a well-stocked theological library in Bloomsbury, the first of countless visits for me in the next twenty years. It was a few miles from the college, which was then a couple of blocks east of Baker Street, and I recall that he took me on the back of his motorcycle through busy London streets.

Ralph has always been known for his flashes of quirky humor that catch us off guard. It fell to our lot as faculty members to conduct morning prayers and to preach now and then at the weekly service. On one such occasion Ralph preached on Psalm 40 in the college chapel, where in facing front rows the choir sat on one side and the faculty on the other. He warmed to his theme, how we like the Psalmist had been brought up out of the miry clay and given a new song. With a gesture of his hand from one side to the other, he triumphantly summed up the message: 'out of the mire into the choir!'

My own chief memories of those days concern how I fell in love with a student and secretly wooed her. In the Upstairs Downstairs atmosphere of those days, after our engagement was announced at a college breakfast one morning, she became something of an embarrassment to her fellow students, and to a lesser extent I to my colleagues. Ralph was one of the few who sensitively appreciated our predicament and sought to ease it. Elizabeth and I well remember how he and his dear wife Lily invited us out to their home and made us feel like an ordinary couple.

Ralph duly moved to Manchester, to teach at last his beloved New Testament in Professor F.F. Bruce's department. Thereafter I heard of him only through the grapevine and via his books and articles, since in Britain there are no professional meetings for both Old and New Testament studies. Eventually he moved to California, to become Professor of New Testament at Fuller, and he served as director of the graduate program. Our association was renewed when I was invited to be visiting professor at Fuller for a term in 1982, to investigate and be investigated in connection with a vacancy. I have always suspected that Ralph had a hand in that invitation. While we were there as a family, the British colony at Fuller looked after us well. Especially Ralph and Lily put themselves out to show us around and make us feel at home. They it was who fetched us from the airport, installed us in our apartment and took us out to breakfast—a most un-English thing to do—next morning. Then, when I came for good with my daughter in October 1983 and my wife, having finally sold our London home, with our son on the last day of the year, again it was Ralph who transported us. He and Lily were a tower of strength in their companionship and in their patient explanations of an alien culture. They would take us to Santa Monica, where we could pretend we were strolling along an English seaside promenade. They counseled us in our search for a home in the Altadena area they knew so well. Nor were we the only ones to be on the receiving end of such loving concern.

There followed years of collegiality as Ralph and I had adjacent offices and shared a secretary. Eventually Lily's illhealth hastened their return to the England that has always been home to their hearts. We still see him as he returns to Fuller as visiting professor, squeezing time from his Southport pastorate and his professorial post at Sheffield.

May this quintessential Englishman long thrive and contribute to the Church and to theological scholarship!

PART I

WORSHIP

The Saints and the Synagogue

Leon Morris

Jesus worshipped regularly in the synagogue and temple as did his disciples. Not long after the close of his earthly life his followers were seen as 'the sect' of the Nazarenes (Acts 24.5), i.e. as part of Judaism. There is every reason for holding accordingly that the worship of the early Christians would have been influenced by Jewish worship. This would enable us to say much about the connection between the two were it not for two important facts: we do not know for certain what was done in the synagogue in the first century AD and we do not know for certain how the early Christians worshipped. For these reasons we must always exercise a certain caution when we discuss the subject.

The Synagogue

George Foot Moore begins his treatment of the synagogue by saying, 'A consequence of the idea of revealed religion which was of the utmost moment in all the subsequent history of Judaism was the endeavor to educate the whole people in its religion'.[1] We do not always appreciate how revolutionary this was. In the religions of the peoples round the Mediterranean there were priesthoods who knew what had to be known and who told the worshippers what it was necessary for them to know. Worship was apparently largely concentrated on great state occasions, on set religious feasts and on important family dates. At such times the worshippers would simply make the offerings and follow the ritual as the priests directed. They would also be expected

[1]*Judaism* (Cambridge, Mass., 1958), I, p. 281.

to observe any taboos their religion laid down and to live with a due respect for the deities they acknowledged.

But there was no equivalent of the Jewish idea of a body of revealed truth which it was the business of everybody to know and practice. The Jews believed that God had spoken and that what he had said was contained in the Law and the Prophets and the Writings. When they worshipped they saw it as important that they give good heed to what God had said and this meant that in the synagogue Scripture had a very special place. At Sinai the people had said, 'Everything that the Lord has spoken we will do' (Exod. 19.8), a vow which meant that the people had to know what the Lord had spoken. By New Testament times the development of this idea meant that worship and instruction in Scripture went hand in hand. The synagogue was a place of instruction (Philo calls synagogues 'schools', *Vit. Mos.* ii.216) as well as a place of worship (it was also a centre of community life; cf. Mt. 10.17; Lk. 12.11; Acts 26.11; but that is not our present concern). Instruction in what God has made known was an integral part of Jewish worship.[1] It is instructive to reflect on the different places occupied by the temple and the synagogue. All Jews paid great respect to the temple; it was built according to the instructions God had given and worship was carried out in it according to divine directions. It was the one place where sacrifice could be offered and it was in a special sense the holy place for all Jews. But unless they lived in Jerusalem they could participate in its worship but rarely. Synagogues, however, were everywhere. For most Jews it was the synagogue that was the real centre of the Jewish religion.

The origins of the synagogue are shrouded in mystery. Some take the institution back into a remote antiquity, while others see it as having appeared not long before New Testament days.[2] The oldest mention of a synagogue so far known appears to be in an inscription in Egypt dated some time after 247 BC[3] It is generally agreed that the synagogue appeared in Palestine somewhat later than in the Diaspora, but how much later is uncertain. A. Deissmann argued for a syna-

[1]W. Schrage can say, 'The meaning and purpose of the synagogue derive from the central importance the Torah and Halachah came to have in Judaism. Without the Law there would have been no synagogues . . . . The synagogue is undoubtedly many other things, but it is primarily the place of the Torah, which is to be read and taught, heard and learned there' (*TDNT*, VII, p. 821).

[2]H.H. Rowley has a good summary, *Worship in Ancient Israel* (London, 1967), ch. 7. He sees it as having appeared first in Babylon among the exiles (p. 224).

[3]It comes from the reign of Ptolemy Euergetes, 246-221 BC (*NTS* 36 [1990], p. 2, n. 4).

gogue in Jerusalem before AD 70,[1] but H.C. Kee can say, 'there is simply no evidence to speak of synagogues in Palestine as architecturally distinguishable edifices prior to 200 C.E.'[2] Kee holds that there were gatherings in private homes and in public buildings, but not in buildings that may properly be called 'synagogues'. Sidney B. Hoenig earlier argued that 'the beginnings of synagogue ritual and liturgy are to be dated after 70 CE—not before'.[3] But we must bear in mind Luke's reference to a synagogue or synagogues in Jerusalem (Acts 6.9).

All this means that we should not overlook the fact that there is a good deal of uncertainty about the antiquity of the synagogue. And there is little information about the order of service as it was practised in New Testament times.[4] The Gospels and Acts make it clear that there were many synagogues in the New Testament period (cf. Acts 15.21), but they do not tell us as much as we should like about what went on in those assemblies. We can certainly learn some important truths about the background to Christian worship, though we must also bear in mind Levertoff's warning that in looking for 'the Jewish background of the Christian liturgy' we should not overlook 'the Christian influence on the Jewish Liturgy'.[5] Influence went both ways.

The oldest account of a synagogue service in existence is that in Luke 4.16-30.[6] This does not tell us in detail how the service was

---

[1] A. Deissmann, *Light from the Ancient East* (London, 1927), pp. 439-41.

[2] *NTS* 36 (1990), p. 9. He further says, 'Several responsible archaeologists and epigraphers who saw it [i.e. the inscription cited by Deissmann] prior to publication dated it to the time of Trajan or of Hadrian in the second quarter of the second century C.E.' Deissmann, he thinks, 'arbitrarily assigned the inscription to a pre-70 date' (p. 7).

[3] *JQR* 54 (1963), p. 129. Hoenig further says, 'Archaeological findings too have not uncovered any synagogues in Judea of the period before 70 CE' (p. 130).

[4] P.P. Levertoff remarks on 'how difficult it is to visualise an early Synagogue service, especially the manner in which it took place before the destruction of the Temple in the year A.D. 70. *The only certain data* are found in St. Luke' (W.K. Lowther Clarke, ed., *Liturgy and Worship* [London, 1932], p. 73; Levertoff's italics).

[5] *Liturgy and Worship*, p. 68.

[6] Eusebius has preserved a description of a synagogue service from Philo's *Hypothetica:* 'He required them to assemble in the same place, and to sit down one with another in reverent and orderly manner, and listen to the laws, in order that none might be ignorant of them. And so in fact they do always meet together and sit down one with another, most of them in silence, except when it is customary to add a word of good omen to what is being read. But some priest who is present, or one of the old men, reads to them the holy laws, and explains each separately till nearly eventide: and after that they are allowed to depart with a knowledge of their holy laws, and with great improvement in

conducted. It does not mention, for example, the *Shema'* nor the reading from the Law, which were so basic to Judaism that both must have been used. Jesus stood for the reading, a mark of respect for Scripture, and sat for the sermon, the customary posture of a teacher. Luke does not say so explicitly, but it would appear that there was no fixed preacher and that anyone might be invited to give the sermon (if there was one; a sermon seems not to have been obligatory). Thus Jesus was invited to preach at Nazareth and from Acts we find that Paul and Barnabas frequently spoke in synagogues as they travelled about. There is no mention of any regular 'minister' to conduct the services and apparently any qualified man might do this.

It seems that the service consisted of five parts: the *Shema'*,[1] the prayers,[2] (by the end of the first century the prayers were those known as the Eighteen Benedictions, but we cannot be sure that these were used in the New Testament period),[3] the reading from the Law, the reading from the Prophets, and the sermon. If a priest were present he would pronounce the benediction (Num. 6.24-27); this did not come at the end of the service as we might perhaps expect, but during the prayers.[4] Presumably the leader of the service would say a prayer to end the service, or there may have been some other form of dismissal. The Talmud tells us that 'they recited the Ten Commandments, the *Shema'*...' but that the commandments were

---

piety' (*Praep. Evang.* viii.7.12-13, trans. by E.H. Gifford [Oxford, 1903], pp. 389-90). This is interesting but tells us little about the order of service in synagogue worship.

[1]'The first duty' in connection with gatherings for the reading of the Law 'was the recitation of the *Shema...*' which every individual Israelite was obliged to perform twice daily, and which consisted mainly of the Deuteronomic sections vi.4-9; xi.13-21' (G. Dalman, *Jesus-Jeshua* [London, 1929], p. 38).

[2]At least in later times, 'A man should always first recount the praise of the Holy One, blessed be He, and then pray' (*Ber.* 32a). J.S. McEwen remarks, 'By the influence of the local synagogues prayer began to permeate the daily life of the people. Every Jew (ideally at any rate) prayed thrice daily (Ps. 55.17, Dan. 6.10). There were family prayers at the beginning and ending of the Sabbath, before and after meat, at the Passover, and a general custom of invoking God's name before any special task or enjoyment' though he adds, 'but how far vital, and how far merely formal, it would be hard to decide' (A. Richardson, ed., *A Theological Word Book of the Bible* [London, 1950], p. 170).

[3]Moore says 'All forms of the Tefillah that are known to us in the past or the present go back to this redaction by the authority of Gamaliel II about the end of the first century of our era' (*Judaism*, I, p. 292). The dates of the prayers are thus uncertain, but Moore points out that the second benediction refers to the resurrection of the dead and this 'is specific Pharisaic doctrine, and cannot well have got into the synagogue prayers till the Pharisees obtained control of the synagogue' (*ibid.*, p. 293).

[4]Dalman says it took place between the sixth and seventh part of the prayers (*Jesus-Jeshua*, p. 39), but H. Danby places it between the eighteenth and nineteenth benedictions (*The Mishnah* [Oxford, 1933], p. 6, n. 9).

stopped 'on account of the insinuations of the *Minim*' (*Ber*. 12a). This is usually taken to mean that Jews stopped the recital of the Ten Commandments because the Christians held that this was the only valid part of the Law. Which in turn means that the Ten Commandments were prob-ably in the synagogue service at the time the Christians first made their appearance.

It must be insisted that this is about all that we know for certain about the worship of the synagogue in New Testament times. The synagogue continued to be important in Judaism, both for worship and as a centre for community life and what is attested for later periods is often said to have happened in New Testament times. As our information for the earlier period is so meagre such reasoning cannot be ruled out: more must have happened in synagogue worship than our early sources tell us. But it is well to keep separate what we know from these sources and what we infer from later sources. The two are not necessarily the same.

An example of our ignorance is the use of the Psalms. These have been highly valued by Jews and Christians alike and they have been greatly used in worship. But how they were used in the first century is unknown. Rowley cites N.H. Snaith for the view that by New Testament times there was a triennial cycle for the Psalter in Palestine, so that all the Psalms were read each three years.[1] But G. Foot Moore is uncertain whether 'the use of select Psalms' had become the practice by New Testament times. He thinks that as late as 'the middle of the second century the daily repetition of these Psalms (i.e. Psalms 145-150) was a pious practice of individuals rather than a regular observance of the congregation'.[2] We may believe that some at any rate of the Psalms were used in worship, but that is a theory we must hold in the light of our view of the probabilities; it is not supported by evidence.

From all this it seems clear that the synagogue was a place of worship that stressed the importance of the Law. The Law was read and its content explained and applied. With that went the reading of other parts of Scripture and the offering of prayer. It is unfortunate that we lack information on many of the details, but the main outline seems clear enough.

---

1 *Worship in Ancient Israel*, p. 237.

2 *Judaism*, I, p. 296.

Worship in the New Testament

Jesus was brought up as a Jew and throughout his life he seems to have retained his links with the synagogue (Lk. 4.16). He observed at any rate some of the Jewish feasts (Lk. 22.15; Jn 2.23) and he taught in the Temple courts (Mk 12.35). There is no record of his ever offering a sacrifice, but he suggested that others do this (Mt. 5.23-4; Mk 1.44). The cleansing of the Temple seems to have sprung from a passionate desire that it be put to its right use, not a wish to do away with it.

But Jesus was a long way from being a conventional Jewish worshipper. His attitude to the Sabbath caused great offence to the religious establishment of his day and he was in frequent conflict with the Pharisees, the guardians of orthodoxy. His teaching that 'defilement' comes from the heart, not physical contact with 'unclean' objects was very different from that of ordinary Jewish worshippers (Mk 7.14-23). He did not denounce the synagogue or the temple as far as we know, but his attitude towards the worshipping practices of his day was one of sovereign freedom. 'His proclamation cannot be fitted into the existing order', writes Ferdinand Hahn, 'and is associated with radical criticism of traditional worship'.[1]

His followers worshipped at the temple at any rate to the degree of observing hours of prayer (Acts 3.1). Paul is noteworthy for worshipping regularly in synagogues as he travelled. On at least one occasion a Christian assembly is referred to as a synagogue (Jas 2.2). It is not unlikely that at first Christian assemblies were in fact synagogues, for any ten Jewish men could form a synagogue. There was nothing schismatic about doing this and we read of a synagogue or synagogues in Jerusalem (Acts 6.9).[2] There are also references to the Christians as a 'sect' (Acts 24.14; 28.22), specifically as 'the sect of the Nazarenes' (Acts 24.5); the same word is applied to the Sadducees in Acts 5.17 and to the Pharisees in Acts 15.5; 26.5.[3] There is a teas-

---

[1] *The Worship of the Early Church* (Philadelphia, 1973), p. 14.

[2] I.H. Marshall remarks, 'It was natural for national groups to form their own synagogues for worship in Jerusalem, and they would be attended both by immigrants settled in Jerusalem and by casual visitors' (*The Acts of the Apostles* [Leicester, 1980], p. 129).

[3] F.J. Foakes Jackson and K. Lake think it probable that Christians were known as 'the Synagogue of the Nazarenes' and draw attention to Acts 6.9 with its reference to the synagogue of the Libertini, etc. (*The Beginnings of Christianity* [London, 1920], I, p. 304). F.F. Bruce holds that the use of the term αἵρεσις in Acts 24.5 'implies that by the Jews the Christians were still regarded as a heretical Jewish sect' (*The Acts of the Apostles* [London, 1951], p. 422).

ing little problem in the way we should understand Acts 1.14, for the word generally translated 'prayer' was in common use with the meaning 'synagogue' (cf. Acts 16.13) and the meaning here may be 'they continued at their synagogue'.

C.W. Dugmore reasons from all this that 'we are forced to conclude that the Synagogue worship was the norm of Christian worship in the days of the Apostles, even to the response "Amen" by the people at the close of every thanksgiving'.[1] From the same data, however, Gerhard Delling comes to the opposite conclusion: 'It is amazing how few elements of Jewish Worship survive the scrutiny of the primitive Christians'; 'The order of the synagogue service has obviously not influenced the early Christian one'.[2]

Clearly we must take care when such opposite conclusions can be reached and we must not read too much into the data. But certainly the Christians took over from the synagogue the basic pattern of worship with its concentration on the reading of Scripture together with exposition of its content and prayer, and this on one day each week. The weekly gathering for worship was a distinctive of the Jews and of the Christians; no other religion seems to have had anything to compare with this.[3]

The Lord's Worship on the Lord's Day

But each of those characteristics was given a distinctively different emphasis by the Christians. They worshipped on a different day and perhaps this helps us see that in their worship they had distinctive ideas of their own.[4] They worshipped on the first day of the week

---

[1]*The Influence of the Synagogue upon the Divine Office* (London, 1964), p. 8. W.D. Maxwell can say, 'Christian worship, as a distinctive, indigenous thing, arose from the fusion, in the crucible of Christian experience, of the Synagogue and the Upper Room' (*An Outline of Christian Worship* [London, 1945], p. 5).

[2]*Worship in the New Testament* (London, 1962), pp. 7, 42. Similarly F. Hahn rejects dependence on the Jewish synagogue: 'Synagogue worship was related to the temple cult, consisted preeminently in legal instruction, and was bound to fixed traditions of prayer; it could therefore hardly have furnished a model for the worship, in the Spirit, of the community assembled in the name of Jesus Christ' (*The Worship of the Early Church*, p. 52).

[3]'The Christians, like the Jews, ascribed special religious significance to one day of the week by making it a day of assembly. No other religious cult in the ancient world shared this practice' (H.C. Kee and F.W. Young, *The Living World of the New Testament* [London, 1971], p. 371).

[4]'Christian worship, like Christian literature, was continuous with, and yet in marked contrast to, Jewish worship... Christian worship was continuous with Jewish worship and yet, even from the first, distinctive' (C.F.D. Moule, *Worship in the New Testament* [London, 1961], pp. 9-10).

rather than the Sabbath (Acts 20.7; 1 Cor. 16.2), for this was the day when Jesus rose from the dead. They called it 'the Lord's day' (Rev. 1.10). Sunday worship was a weekly reminder of the centrality of Christ's resurrection.

Again, they remembered that Jesus had said, 'Where two or three are met together in my name, there I am in the middle of them' (Mt. 18.20). They recalled that this followed a statement in which he said that he would answer their prayers. Their prayer 'in the name of Jesus' was different from any other form of prayer because of the place they ascribed to their Lord. Central to their worship was the fact that they broke bread together in a sacred meal that reminded them that Jesus had died for them, died to put away their sins and make a way of approach to God for them. J.A.T. Robinson goes so far as to say that the gathering for the Holy Communion 'was the gathering for which the Lord's Day existed, and by which alone it was for hundreds of years distinguished from any other working day'.[1]

This meant a radically different approach to worship and to the whole liturgical year. While Christians might worship from time to time in the Jewish synagogues, from the beginning they had their own gatherings (Acts 2.42) and as these included 'the teaching of the apostles' and 'the breaking of the bread' it is clear that they were distinctively Christian, not pale imitations of Jewish worship. The Christians saw these gatherings as important (Heb. 10.25). They had no special buildings in which to assemble, but apparently met in homes (cf. the references to house churches, Rom. 16.5 etc.). It is recorded that Paul taught in the house of Titius Justus (Acts 18.7) and in the hall of Tyrannus (Acts 19.9) and such places may have been used for worship as well.

As to the nature of services we have very little to go on. The Christians knew how they worshipped and saw no reason to write it down. In the synagogues the most significant item was the reading of the Law and the Christians followed this at least to the extent that they made the reading of Scripture a very important part of their assemblies. It is not likely that they concentrated on the Law because they were more interested in gospel than law and for them other parts of

---

[1] *Liturgy Coming to Life* (London, 1960), p. 28. He further comments on 'the equivalence of "When you come together" (1 Cor. xi.17), "When you assemble as a church" (xi.18), and "When you meet together, it is not the Lord's supper than you eat" (xi.20)' (*Liturgy Coming to Life*, p. 28, n. 1). J.-J.von Allmen argues that the early church understood Sunday as 'the eucharistic day' (*Worship its Theology and Practice* [London, 1965], p. 226).

the Old Testament were very significant (for example the psalms and the prophets).[1] But they did read Scripture and there is an exhortation to Timothy, 'Give attention to the reading' (1 Tim. 4.13; NRSV reads, 'give attention to the public reading of scripture'). Linked as it is to exhortation and teaching this clearly refers to reading in the services of worship, not to private study. Reading from a first century manuscript was not as straightforward as we might think, for manuscripts were written entirely in capital letters, there was practically no punctuation, there were no spaces between words, and there were quite a few abbreviations. We can understand that the readers would do well to 'give attention' to reading from a manuscript.[2] Most people could not read for themselves (and would not have been able to afford manuscripts if they could) so public reading was very important.

It is generally agreed that the Christians read passages from the Old Testament Scriptures,[3] though Delling argues strongly that they read only their own writings at their worship.[4] But they accepted the Old Testament as sacred Scripture and from the first appearance of lectionaries which list passages to be read we find that the Old Testament was included. Despite Delling's hesitation it is perhaps better to see Old Testament lections behind such New Testament passages as 1 Timothy 4.13. But we must bear in mind the fact that Paul's writings are classed with 'the other scriptures' as early as 2 Peter 3.16, and the further fact that we know that Paul's letters were read when the believers assembled (Col. 4.16; 1 Thess. 5.27), which in all probability was when they came together for worship. Our best

---

[1] In the Index of Quotations to the Greek New Testament in *UBSGNT*³, 157 passages are listed where the Law is cited, 79 of the Psalms and 108 from the prophets. By contrast, in the Index to H. Danby's translation of the Mishnah there are almost six columns of quotations from the Law, but just over three for all the rest of the Old Testament.

[2] Cf. D. Guthrie, 'The public reading of Scripture was important because it was the means of a large number of people being able to hear the text, whereas only a few would have had personal access to the text, or have been able to read it. For a considerable time to come the scarcity of manuscripts would make the public reading of Scripture essential to the life of the church' (*The Pastoral Epistles: An Introduction and Commentary*² [Leicester/Grand Rapids, 1990], p. 109). Guthrie thinks that in this passage the reading of the Old Testament is in mind, but J.N.D. Kelly holds that specifically Christian writings, like the letters of Paul were also included (*A Commentary on the Pastoral Epistles* [London, 1963], p. 105).

[3] Cf. Massey H. Shepherd, the Christians 'had taken over from the synagogue the regular reading of the Old Testament and some of its familiar prayers and hymns' (*The Worship of the Church* [Greenwich, 1952], p. 72).

[4] *Worship in the New Testament*, p. 92.

understanding is that as early as New Testament times apostolic writings were read along with the Old Testament scriptures in Christian worship.

An integral part of synagogue worship was teaching. Devout Jews met to hear the Law not only read but expounded. There is not the slightest doubt that Christians took over this aspect of worship from the synagogues. As far as we know regular instruction was no part of the worship of the multiplicity of deities honored in the first century Roman Empire. But for the Christians instruction in the faith was of central importance. Paul's instructions in 1 Corinthians 14 make it clear that many people made their contribution to worship and that this included teaching, revelation, speaking in tongues, and interpretation. Paul himself is recorded as having preached until midnight at one meeting of Christians on the first day of the week (Acts 20.7-12; there were unfortunate results for Eutychus!). There are many references to the importance of teaching and clearly instruction about Christian doctrine and the way believers should live out their faith formed significant parts of early Christian worship.

Teaching in the Christian assemblies was not merely an intellectual exercise; it was essentially devotional. 1 Corinthians 14 makes it clear that there was the 'real presence' of God in the assembly, for the outsider who hears prophesying will fall on his face and worship, acknowledging that 'truly God is among you' (1 Cor. 14.25).[1]

Delling finds evidence of the use of fixed forms from the Pauline letters. Thus he argues from the references to grace and peace in the openings of these letters that these salutations marked the beginning of the services of worship.[2] Similarly he sees in the doxologies in a number of letters evidence for the liturgical use of doxologies.[3]

Against such views there is the fact that some New Testament references indicate the use of free and unstructured forms. Thus Paul writes, 'When you come together, each has a psalm, has a teaching, has a revelation, has a tongue, has an interpretation' (1 Cor. 14.26).

[1]W. Hahn says, 'In Christ we see the God who reveals Himself, the God who speaks to us' and he quotes V. Vajta, 'The means whereby God has revealed Himself is the Word, which includes both preaching and worship' (*Worship and Congregation* [London, 1963], p. 25).

[2]'It is probable that in the greeting "Grace to you and peace . . ." we have a formula of introduction to the service' (*Worship in the New Testament*, p. 49).

[3]'The usage was thus not invented, presumably, in the letter-writing of the primitive Church, but was imported from elsewhere. And the most obvious place of origin is in Worship: for rounding off teaching, exhortation and prepared discourses, an expression of praise was most suitable' (*Worship in the New Testament*, p. 64).

It seems from this chapter that in worship any member of the congregation might make a contribution and that the contributions varied. There is no suggestion here of a fixed liturgy of any sort. Paul apparently thinks of the Spirit as directing the whole and we should understand this as a most important and distinctive feature of Christian worship. As far as we know no other religion had the idea that the divinity might take charge of everything that was done and everyone who did it and direct it all into unexpected but edifying channels. But the Spirit might lead any member of a Christian congregation to take the initiative. Indeed someone who had expected to speak in the assembly might have to keep silent because of a later revelation made to someone else (1 Cor. 14.30). But Paul is not writing of liturgical chaos, for he rounds it off with 'Let all things be done decently and in order' (v. 40).

We saw that the offering of prayer was an integral part of synagogue worship and naturally this was just as important for the early Christians. But there were significant differences. Very important is the difference in the place ascribed to Jesus. Jesus had told them that when they met in his name he was there, in their midst (Mt. 18.19-20) and this must have been the most important thing for them for the whole of their worship and not only for their prayers. But it was important for prayer, for it contained the assurance that Christian prayers would be heard and answered. Further, John records that Jesus had told his followers to pray in his name (Jn 14.13-14; 16.23-24). The dying Stephen prayed 'Lord Jesus, receive my spirit' (Acts 7.59) and the Christians generally spoke of 'calling upon the name of the Lord' (Acts 9.14; 22.16). Paul can almost define Christians as those who 'call upon the name of our Lord Jesus Christ' (1 Cor. 1.2; cf. Jas 2.7).

In all this we see a resemblance to the synagogue in that prayer was very important. But there was also a significant difference, for the Jews would have regarded what the Christians saw as central in their praying as nothing less than blasphemy. In the Aramaic word *Maranatha* (1 Cor. 16.22) we have the oldest recorded Christian prayer form, and significantly it is a prayer addressed to the Lord Jesus (cf. Rev. 22.20). It is probably significant also that there is no trace in Christian worship of such characteristic Jewish forms as the *Shema'* and the Eighteen Benedictions. There is every reason for holding that at the time the Church appeared these were important features of Jewish worship. But the Christians overlooked them and went their own way.

It seems that the early Christians loved to sing.[1] Jesus and his disciples sang in the upper room (Mk 14.26), and even in prison in Philippi Paul and Silas added the singing of hymns to their prayers (Acts 16.25). Believers sang 'psalms and hymns and spiritual songs, singing and making melody to the Lord in (their) heart' (Eph. 5.19; cf. Col. 3.16). The New Testament leaves the impression that their worship was a very joyful affair. Luke records a number of hymns, the *Benedictus*, the *Magnificat* and the *Nunc Dimittis*. Most scholars point to the Jewish content in these songs; they are suitable for Christian use, but for the most part the words would be acceptable also to Jews. But there also seem to be specifically Christian hymns (e.g. Rev. 19.6-8; cf. also Eph. 5.14; Phil. 2.6-11; 1 Tim. 3.16, etc.). There is an objection that such passages are not specifically designated 'hymns' and there can be disagreement; is 1 Peter 1.3ff. a hymn or not? The trouble is, as C.F.D. Moule puts it, 'the criteria are inconclusive'.[2] What is beyond doubt is that the early Christians loved to sing and that singing formed part of their worship even if we cannot identify with any certainty what it was that they sang.

We know that prominent in the church's worship was the celebration of the Holy Communion. We have accounts of the institution in all three Synoptists (cf. 1 Cor. 10.16-17; 11.20-26). But this is an unambiguously Christian observance, one that derived from the giving up of Jesus to death, and it cannot be connected with synagogal practices, so that, important as it was for the early Christians, it can scarcely form part of this discussion.

We should notice the use of some liturgical terms, though there are not many of these. But some Aramaic terms used in the New Testament appear to go back to the earliest days of the faith and to have been used in a liturgical way. These include *Abba* 'Father', *Alleluia* 'Praise the Lord', *Amen*, the response of a congregation to a prayer voiced on its behalf by one leading the service, and *Maranatha* 'Our Lord, come' which has been called 'the oldest Christian prayer'. They indicate that the early Christians were not averse to the use of their own liturgical terms, even if they found little use for those more

---

[1] Dr. Martin has an excellent chapter on 'Hymns and Spiritual Songs' (Ch. 4 in his *Worship in the Early Church* [London, 1974]). He begins it with 'The Christian Church was born in song'.

[2] *The Birth of the New Testament* (London, 1962), p. 25.

usual in the Temple and the synagogue. F. Hahn has drawn attention to the fact that 'Almost none of the traditional concepts occur in the New Testament; and where they do, they are unmistakably used metaphorically'. From this he draws the conclusions that 'The terminological evidence means not only that any cultic understanding of Christian worship is out of the question, but also that there is no longer any distinction in principle between assembly for worship and the service of Christians in the world'.[1] Liturgical terms were known to believers from their use in the Temple and the synagogue, but they apparently did not find them very useful in a Christian context, presumably because Christian worship was so different from that to which the terms referred.

Conclusion

What are we to make of all this? First, I think, that there is a straight line from the worship of the synagogue to that of the early church. We must bear in mind that the synagogue represented something new in the religions of the Mediterranean world. It was new that worship should be on a regular weekly basis, that it should be dominated by the reading of Scripture and that instruction in the tenets of the religion should be an integral part of the worship. And the synagogue was a layman's movement. While no doubt priests would be given honored places when they attended synagogues, they were not necessary to the function of the synagogal system and their office gave them no special privileges in that system. Indeed priests, as priests, had no place in it at all.

In all this the church followed the practice of the synagogue. There can be no doubt that the early Christian assemblies were modelled on the synagogue rather than on the temple in Jerusalem or those other temples in which idols were worshipped. The idea of worship on a regular weekly basis comes from the synagogue, as do the ideas that the reading of Scripture was central and that instruction in the faith was critically important. In both synagogue and church the place of lay people was significant. There is no indication in the New Testament that anything resembling the Jewish priesthood developed; worship in the church was the concern of all the people of God and

---

1 *The Worship of the Early Church*, pp. 35-36, 38.

any of them might be expected to take a significant part in its leadership.[1] In such ways the Christian churches took over the practices of the synagogue.

But there was a fundamental difference. For the synagogue the Law was the central thing and everything followed from that. In the worship of the Sabbath day the high point was the reading from the Law. There was not always a sermon but when there was it served to bring out the meaning of some aspect of the Law. The Law was seen as having relevance to the whole of life and instruction in the Law was accordingly of the first importance. The Christians, of course, revered the Law as part of sacred scripture. But for them it was of the first importance that, when they met, Christ was in their very midst. They gloried in the gospel and Christianity was from the very first a religion of the gospel rather than a religion of the Law. Thus the reading of the Christian writings and the understanding of the implications of the gospel took centre stage. This represented a fundamental difference from the synagogue. While the early church was clearly indebted to the synagogue, equally clearly Christian worship was something essentially new.

[1] I am not unmindful of the importance of apostles and elders in the early church, nor of the gallons of ink that have been expended on the development of the ministry in the early church. But it seems to me beyond doubt that in the earliest days any Christian might perform some function in the worship service.

The Use of Credal and Liturgical Material in Ephesians

Ernest Best

This is not another attempt to isolate credal and liturgical material in Ephesians but an examination of the material that various scholars have isolated in order to inquire after the way in which the author in using it has modified it and to discern if possible his reasons for doing so. I assume that Paul was not the author but there would be little need to modify any of my argument if in fact he were. It is difficult to draw precise lines between credal, liturgical and catechetical material since the same material may have been used for more than one purpose, but by limiting our examination to credal and liturgical we mean to exclude catechetical material intended primarily for ethical instruction. Credal material would certainly have been used when catechumens were taught.

When Paul quoted the little creed of 1 Cor. 15.3-5 he did so because it was one known to his readers and therefore could form a basis for an argument. But it was not merely one known to his readers which he may have created for them when he was with them; it was a creed belonging to the early church and carrying therefore an authority wider than Paul's personal authority. What he quoted was both known to his readers and was accepted by them as authoritative. When in the New Testament the Old is explicitly quoted it may be assumed that the readers knew it and that it carried authority in their eyes. Yet when the OT is quoted it is not always done so explicitly. If the quotation is reasonably long and drawn from a well known passage (e.g. Eph. 5.21; 6.2, 3) it may be assumed that at least some of the readers will realise from where it comes and recognize its authority. Shorter quotations and allusions need to be looked at differently. They may simply be incorporated into the course of an argument (1.22; 2.17; 5.25; 5.26; 6.14; 6.15) and may not even have been used consciously but have come naturally to the pen of the writer because he has been grounded in the OT and thinks in its terms. Many of these will have been recognized by, at any rate, some of his readers; even if they did not recognise them they may still have been impressed by them and regarded these words as authoritative because their words were 'biblical' words. We may compare the way in which older people respond to the language of the King James Version of the Bible. The words carry an aura when used, even though not in a quotation, and affect their hearers disposing them to accept whatever argument is being advanced through their use. Liturgical and credal words can have the same effect. We have also to recognize that the OT when quoted is often varied from the original. This may consist in no more than a change in person or number or in the tense of a verb. Sometimes the variations are much greater and when we are unable to account for them we suppose the writer is using a text unknown to us. This may be what has happened in Eph. 4.8. It is also often true that it is difficult to determine the OT passage an author has in view, and if it is difficult to do this when we have the text of the OT how much more difficult will it be to detect liturgical material whose text we do not have or only possess in variant form in another New Testament writing. For instance it becomes practically impossible to determine if a line in the original has been omitted by the NT author in using it.

One of the best discussions of a liturgical or credal passage has been given us by the one to whom this volume is dedicated. In his *Carmen Christi*[1] Dr Martin carefully unearthed the original text of Phil. 2.6-11 before its incorporation into the letter, examined the additions Paul made in quoting it and offered reasons for the alterations. In respect of the addition about the cross he writes 'For the Philippians at least, the addition of θανάτου δὲ σταυροῦ would emphasize the abject degradation of Christ's lowly obedience, and drive home the lesson that His identification with men reached the lowest rung of the ladder'. And again, 'Paul thus directs the drift of the hymn's soteriological teaching—in its original form, somewhat vague and amorphous—into channels which are known to us from the

[1]Ralph P. Martin, *Carmen Christi. Philippians ii.5-11 in Recent Interpretation and in the Setting of Early Christian Worship* (SNTSMS 4; Cambridge, 1967), p. 221. From the earliest days of his work Dr Martin has shown his interest in our area as seen in his *Worship in the Early Church* (first published in 1954).

Pauline literature'.[1] In respect of the addition (2.10) about the persons (things) in heaven and on earth and under the earth, he writes 'The Christ-hymn enables the Church to see beyond the present in which the Head of the Church reigns invisibly and powerfully—but known only to faith—to that full proof of His reign in the heavenly sphere in which all the powers are veritably subject to Him and His dominion is manifestly confessed'.[2] Finally, in respect of the doxology to God the Father he writes,

> Yet, in both lines of thought which are interwoven in the hymn so that we should not be faced with the choice of either-or, the notion of a rivalry within the Godhead is scouted, and there is no thought that Christ is a usurper, nor any suggestion of a crude binitarianism. For the worship of the exalted Lord is 'to the glory of the Father'. The Biblical monotheism is safeguarded; and the purpose of the Father-God is seen to be honoured in the high place accorded to His Son.[3]

In effect Paul's additions have not altered the meaning of the hymn but sharpened its bite and brought it more fully into line with his own theology. Those who knew the hymn and heard the Pauline additions could not but be impressed by them and understand their significance. This is what happens when we ourselves use quotations; we often add little bits in order to bring out the significance of the whole for our argument.[4] Sometimes when we quote we do so simply to adorn what we are writing or to impress others with our literary knowledge. We can, I believe, acquit the author of Ephesians from making quotations with such ideas in mind. There are times also when we use quotations with the intention of refuting them; on these occasions we make our intention clear in the surrounding context and advance arguments explaining the errors in the quoted material. We have also to remember that sometimes when people quote they may in fact see a different meaning in what they quote from what the original author saw when he was writing. Can we detect anything similar to what happened in Phil. 2.6-11 in the way the author of Ephesians has used his credal and liturgical material? This material has normally been detected in 1.3-

---

[1] Martin, *Carmen Christi*, p. 226.
[2] Martin, *Carmen Christi*, p. 270.
[3] Martin, *Carmen Christi*, p. 283.
[4] This general point remains true even if Phil. 2:6-11 was written by Paul and therefore contains no alterations.

14; 1.20-23; 2.4-10; 2.14-18; 2.19-22; 4.4-6; 5.14.[1] We shall examine these in turn.

1.3-14

This was the first section of Ephesians to be suggested as based on a credal or liturgical *Vorlage*[2] and is also the most extensive.[3] Roughly speaking, those who have discussed it and detected in it almost always a liturgical *Vorlage* have tended either to see the passage as more or less identical with the *Vorlage*, possibly with a few variations, or to have sought within it a hymn which the author has considerably altered to suit his purposes. We consider first the former alternative. It is undoubtedly true that much of the language and style of the passage is elevated in tone and appropriate to a liturgy. But similar language and style are found in other parts of the letter.[4] Though 1.3-14 is an abnormally long and complicated sentence the letter contains other lengthy and complex sentences. The thought of the passage is not out of accord with what we find in the remainder of the letter; indeed some commentators believe that 1.3-14 was composed in order to introduce the main ideas of the letter. There are however other issues which are important here. An author might be expected to quote from a liturgy if this was known to his readers for it would then have more effect on them. If Ephesians had been written to one community which the author knew we could well imagine him using material known to that community so that his points would come across more easily. But Ephesians is a general letter written to a number of communities. Would all of these have been using the same liturgy? Was

---

[1]This is the list given by H. Merkel, 'Der Epheserbrief in der neueren exegetischen Diskussion', *ANRW* II.25.4, pp. 3222ff.

[2]T. Innitzer, 'Der Hymnus in Eph 1,3-14', *ZTK* 28 (1904), pp. 612-21.

[3]An almost complete list of those who have discussed the possibility of a *Vorlage* here is given in Merkel, 'Der Epheserbrief in der neueren exegetischen Diskussion', pp. 3224-7. To these we may add J.C. Kirby, *Ephesians: Baptism and Pentecost* (London, 1968), pp. 103-10, 126-38; R.C. Bankhead, *Liturgical Formulas in the New Testament* (Clinton, S. Carolina, 1971), pp. 91-101; K. Usami, *Somatic Comprehension of Unity: The Church in Ephesus* (AnBib 101), pp. 80-91; J. Schattenham, *Studien zum neutestamentliche Prosahymnus* (Munich, 1965), pp. 1-10; G. Castellino, 'La dossologia della lettera agli Efesini (1, 3-14)', *Salesianum*, 8 (1946), pp. 147-67.

[4]E.g. N.A. Dahl, 'Addresse und Proömium des Epheserbriefes', *TZ* 7 (1951), pp. 241-64; C. Maurer, 'Der Hymnus von Epheser I als Schlüssel zum ganzen Briefe', *EvT* 11 (1951/2), pp. 151-72.

the liturgy as settled in form and wording as this towards the end of the first century even in as limited an area as Asia Minor, assuming Ephesians was directed to that area? Most of those who regard 1.3-14 as derived from a liturgy suppose that it was part of a baptismal liturgy. In the *Didache* prayers are given in relation to the eucharist but not for the celebration of a baptism, though baptism is discussed. Even in the case of the eucharist prophets are left free to use their own prayers. Baptism may have been a much more unorganized service than it became latter. Paul does not appear to have thought it important that he should baptise his converts (1 Cor. 1.13-16). We do not know who did baptise. There was probably then at this time no regular order of service and no baptismal liturgy. It may however be said that the author was using the language of the liturgy of his own community. Yet this does not overcome the difficulty of the similarity of the language and style of 1.3-14 with that of the remainder of the letter. We might get round this by saying that the author of the letter had himself composed his community's liturgy. He would then be the author of the passage and there would be no *Vorlage*.

The liturgical language of vv. 3-14 may be accounted for in quite another way. Much of the language of Ephesians reflects that of Colossians, but if we did not possess Colossians we would never have been able to argue that the author of Ephesians was indebted to another letter and still less able to reconstruct Colossians from Ephesians. The author of Ephesians combines material from different sections of Colossians, sometimes in the process imparting fresh meaning to a word or phrase, but he does not take a section of Colossians and interlace it with his own comments. This provides a useful clue to the way his mind works, though perhaps more applicable to some of the later passages to be discussed. What it means is that when he writes 1.3-14 he may reflect the language of a liturgy without it ever being possible for us to reconstruct that liturgy.

The second of our possibilities, that the author of the letter utilised an existing piece of tradition which he considerably reworked, has led to a number of attempts to recover the original. Almost all of these attempts have sought an underlying hymn. This has led to the elimination from the existing text of words, clauses and even whole verses in order to create a poetic form. Those who have approached the problem in this way have also had to take into account the thought of the passage in comparison with that of the rest of the letter and so have sought in the passages they have retained as deriving from the *Vorlage* theological views at variance with those in the letter and therefore sentiments for which the author of the letter could not have been responsible. Thus Fischer[1] omits from his reconstruction vv. 8b-11 because these verses allot to Christ a central and cosmic position whereas the beginning and end of the passage deal with the redemption of believers. Yet when Fischer comes to reconstruct the hymn underlying 2.14-18 he supposes the author of Ephesians added clauses emphasising the redemption of believers and obscuring the cosmic position of Christ. It would be possible to take up and discuss here the many other attempts to discern an underlying hymn but this article would then become a book. All it is possible to do is to raise the general question as to the purpose of the use here of an underlying hymn. If the hymn is known to the readers then clarificatory amendments as Martin has shown in the case of Phil. 2.6-11 will serve to bring home to them points which the author wishes them to see as important. Large additions which alter the thought will hardly do this and in the course of them the readers may well forget that the hymn is being quoted and so lose the thread of the argument.

1.20-23

It is relatively easy to extract from these verses four lines which could have formed the core of a credal or liturgical statement:

> 20a [who] raised Christ from the dead
> 20b and set him at his right hand in the heavenlies
> 22a and put all things under his feet
> 22b and made him head over all things.

Sanders[2] argues that these lines have hymnic traits. Deichgräber[3] also settles on them but points out that they may be only a portion of a longer hymn which dealt with the pre-existence of Christ, his incarnation, sufferings and death in common with what seems to be a general pattern in early hymns about Christ. Other interpreters add to

[1]K.M. Fischer, *Tendenz und Absicht des Epheserbriefes* (FRLANT 111; Göttingen, 1973), pp. 111-18.
[2]J.T. Sanders, 'Hymnic Elements in Ephesians 1-3', *ZNW* 56 (1965), pp. 214-32.
[3]R. Deichgräber, *Gotteshymnus und Christushymnus in der frühen Christenheit* (Göttingen, 1967), pp. 161-65.

the four lines given above varying portions of what remains. Schille[1] is alone in rejecting part of this suggested hymn preferring instead a structure consisting of 20a, 20b, 21a, 22a. All are agreed that v. 21b with its 'not only' 'but also' is in a wholly other style and must be regarded as an addition of the author who wishes to make sure that the list of 21a may not be incomplete. All also agree that the reference to the church in 22b comes from the author. Fischer[2] adds 21a to the four lines. Those who do not add it would regard it as the author's interpretation of 'the heavenlies'; the latter phrase, ἐν τοῖς ἐπουρανίοις, is one of his favourite expressions (1.3, 29; 2.6; 3.10; 6.12) and this ought to lead to its elimination from the core in 20b; if so v. 21 would be automatically eliminated as its expansion. Ernst[3] would appear to wish to add the whole of v. 23 with the cosmos understood as the body of Christ. Although other commentators do not agree with Ernst in accepting v. 23 or part of it as belonging to the *Vorlage* they are in agreement that the hymn originally referred to the cosmos as the body of Christ and that the author of Ephesians adapted it to his own ecclesiological purposes. We shall return to this supposed adaptation of the hymn but before doing so we note that there is no citation formula introducing the hymn and that the hymn would have followed more easily without the first words of v. 20; instead of the personal pronoun of 20a there could then have been the name 'Christ'. Many commentators have noted that 1.20-23 has affinities with 1 Cor. 15.20ff.; most of the statements of the alleged hymn are in fact recognized christological statements which the author of Ephesians could have drawn on on his own. He did not then need to go to a hymn to obtain them. But the principal difficulty in accepting a hymn here must lie in the changed meaning which it has received on being incorporated into Ephesians. If we assume that his readers knew the original hymn or creed they must have been confused by his change in its meaning. If they did not know it, it was pointless to quote it without drawing attention to the fact that it was a citation (at 5.14 the author tells us he is quoting a hymn). It is also important to ask if the writer disagreed with the cosmic meaning of the original hymn; elsewhere he shows that he has an interest in the cosmic significance of his faith (cf 1.10; 2.7; 3.10, and 4.6 if the

[1]G. Schille, *Frühchristliche Hymnen* (Berlin, 1963), p. 103 n. 4.

[2]Fischer, *Tendenz und Absicht des Epheserbriefes*, pp. 118-20.

[3]J. Ernst, *Pleroma und Pleroma Christi* (Regensburg, 1970), pp. 106f.

forms of πᾶς in 4.6 are understood as neuter and not masculine). If then the author of Ephesians took up an original piece of tradition which referred to the cosmos and inserted the reference to the church, he was modifying it in an entirely different way from the modifications made in the Philippian hymn. We conclude that there is no deliberate and extensive quotation of a section of traditional material in 1.20-23.

2.4-10

Most of this is couched in the first person plural but vv. 5b, 8 are in the second plural, and v. 9 in the third singular; it is generally agreed that this verse should be eliminated from any hymn, creed or liturgy found in the remainder of the passage. Sanders[1] attempts to give the passage hymnic structure but the lines he suggests are of unequal length and have no rhythmic structure.[2] It is probably then better to regard it with Fischer[3] as part of a prose liturgy, and Stuhlmacher[4] suggests (Schille had already proposed regarding it as an initiatory hymn[5]) that it represents what those who were being baptised said (the sections in the first plural) while the sections in the second person are addressed to them by those who are already Christians. Here we need to remember that Ephesians is not directed to a particular community but is a general letter. We have already raised the question whether there was an accepted baptismal liturgy at this time so that the reference to baptism would have been recognised in a number of diverse communities. Moreover the author of the letter writes as if he has not visited the communities to which he is writing (1.15) and so may well not have known their form of liturgy. But could he not have been using the baptismal liturgy of his own community? Some of the language is similar to what he himself uses (e.g. 'the heavenlies', the use of a verb and its cognate noun in v. 4[6]). However if we are to attribute the liturgy to the composition of the letter's author it is easier to think of him as composing it to fit its context, and therefore as not

[1] J.T. Sanders, 'Hymnic Elements in Ephesians', *ZNW* 56 (1965), pp. 214-32.
[2] So Fischer, *Tendenz und Absicht des Epheserbriefes*, p. 121.
[3] Fischer, *Tendenz und Absicht des Epheserbriefes*, pp. 121-31.
[4] P. Stuhlmacher, *Gottes Gerechtigkeit bei Paulus* (FRLANT 87; Göttingen, 1965), pp. 216f.
[5] Schille, *Frühchristliche Hymnen*, pp. 53-60.
[6] Cf. E. Percy, *Die Probleme der Kolosser- und Epheserbriefe* (Lund, 1946), p. 32.

part of a liturgy.[1] The reference to the mercy of God in v. 4 follows on the discussion of human sin in vv.1-3 and the first words of v. 5 repeat part of v.1. The placing of the resurrection of Christians in the past (v. 6) has been already said in Col. 2.12; 3.1 and our author draws heavily on the language and ideas of Colossians (note how the words of Col. 2.13f have been used in our passage).[2] Another factor confirming the view that the author of Ephesians wrote our passage is the way in which it picks up the ideas of 1.20-23 relating to resurrection and heavenly session and applies them to believers. We conclude that our author wrote this passage though he was of course heavily dependent on expressions and thought current in the early church.

2.14-18

More discussion has taken place over a possible *Vorlage* to this passage than over any other in Ephesians. It is cast in the first person plural whereas both 2.11-13 and 2.19-22 are in the second person. The subject of 2.11-13 is resumed in 2.19-22 with words that are common. Haupt[3] therefore suggested that 2.14-18 is parenthetical to the main thrust of 2.11-22. Accepting this many from Schlier[4] and Schille[5] onwards have sought to unearth in it a hymn. The argument for the existence of a *Vorlage* has been supported by the number of words and concepts not found elsewhere in Ephesians and by features common to hymnic material, e.g. participles, relative clauses, *parallelismus membrorum*. The passage also appears to have an implicit ambiguity in that the author seems unable to decide whether his main emphasis lies on reconciliation between God and humanity or between two human groups. It also sets out Christ as the subject of the action of what happens whereas elsewhere God is regarded as initiating redemption. Taking these features as clues assisting decision as to what belonged to or did not belong to the original *Vorlage* a considerable number of attempts have been made to recreate it, none of which agree in detail.

---

[1]Cf. A. Lindemann, *Die Aufhebung der Zeit* (Gütersloh, 1975), pp. 116f.

[2]Cf. U. Luz, 'Rechtfertigung bei den Paulusschülern' in *Rechtfertigung*, ed. J. Friedrich, W. Pohlmann, E. Stuhlmacher (FS E. Käsemann; Tübingen, 1976), pp. 365-83.

[3]E. Haupt, *Die Gedankenschaftsbriefe* (KEK 7th edn; Göttingen, 1902).

[4]H. Schlier, *Der Brief an die Epheser* (Düsseldorf, 7th edn, 1971; 1st edn, 1957).

[5]Schille, *Frühchristliche Hymnen*, pp. 24-31.

Limitations of space prevent a full listing and examination of of all the attempts and we shall only look at two representative samples. These two unlike many others succeed in producing a good line structure. Before examining them there are several general observations to make. There is no agreement on the precise passage in which we should look for the *Vorlage*. Although the initial examination of the passage suggested that all of vv. 14-18 should form the basis more recent work has limited consideration to either vv. 14-17 or even to vv. 14-16. This means that the change of person and the parenthetical nature of vv. 14-18 which were the initiating cause for the search for a *Vorlage* are no longer relevant; they seem indeed to have been forgotten by those who choose one of the smaller sections on which to base their solution; they do not even seem to see the need to explain why the author continued v. 18 or vv. 17f. in the style of the *Vorlage* and did not revert to the earlier style of vv. 11-13 until v. 19. Again while attention has been drawn to the *hapax legomena* some of these are often omitted from the proposed reconstructions; the number of *hapax legomena* is in fact not statistically significant: 10 in a passage of 80 words where the average would suggest 7. The ambiguity in relation to reconciliation which runs through vv. 14-18 is not unique to it; in particular it is present in v. 13 where the Gentiles are said to have been made near without it being specified whether they have been made near to God or to the Jews. This ambivalence may be deliberate on the part of the author who sees the two as related and who thus allows the two aspects of reconciliation to penetrate what he writes next.

The first example is that of Gnilka:[1]

Αὐτός ἐστιν εἰρήνη ἡμῶν
ὁ ποιήσας τὰ ἀμφότερα ἕν
καὶ τὸ μεσότοιχον λύσας
τὴν ἔχθραν ἐν τῇ σαρκὶ καταργήσας
ἵνα κτίσῃ ἐν αὐτῷ καινὸν ἄνθρωπον
ποιῶν εἰρήνην
ἀποκτείνας τὴν ἔχθραν ἐν αὐτῳ
καὶ ἐλθὼν εὐηγγελίσατο εἰρήνην
[τοῖς μακρὰν καὶ τοῖς ἐγγύς]

[1] J. Gnilka, *Der Epheserbrief* (Freiburg: Herder, 1971), p. 149.

The essential thing to note here is that Gnilka has preserved the consistency of his *Vorlage* by excluding from it those elements in vv. 14-18 which imply that human beings are reconciled to one another. The only reconciliation is that between God and the human sphere, and this reconciliation is only implicit, for Gnilka makes the writer of Ephesians responsible for the introduction of the term. Christ has broken down the wall separating heaven and earth, and this apparently by his incarnation as indicated by the reference to 'flesh'. Leaving aside all questions as to the origin of the term 'middle wall' and assuming as is highly probable that the author has used this hymn because the hymn was known to his readers has he not introduced hopeless confusion into it by his references to the law, to the body which is the church, and to the cross so that the latter now governs the meaning of 'flesh'? The new man which in the hymn was the cosmos as *makroanthropos* has now become the corporate Christ. If the author of Ephesians was attempting to correct what he took to be bad theology in the *Vorlage* were there not easier ways to go about this? He could have stated the bad theology and controverted it. Without such a deliberate argument would his readers have been able to realise what he was about? If, to take the less probable position, the hymn was not known to the readers it is difficult to see why he should express himself through its use when he had to alter it so much.

The second example is that of Wilhelmi:[1]

I Αὐτὸς ἐστιν ἡ εἰρήνη
ὁ ποιήσας τὰ ἀμφότερα ἓν
καὶ
II τὸ μεσότοιχον τοῦ φραγμοῦ λύσας
τὸν νόμον τῶν ἐντολῶν καταργήσας
ἵνα
A τοὺς δύο κτίσῃ εἰς ἕνα καινὸν ἄνθρωπον
ποιῶν εἰρήνην
καὶ
B ἀποκαταλλάξῃ τοὺς ἀμφοτέρους ἐν ἑνὶ σώματι
ἀποκτείνας τὴν ἔχθραν.

Of all the suggested underlying hymns this is probably the best so far as rhythmical balance goes. Wilhelmi has taken considerable care to ensure that the lines are of similar length and that there is a proper

[1]G. Wilhelmi, 'Der Versöhner-Hymnen in Eph 2,14ff', *ZNW* 78 (1987), pp. 145-52.

parallelismus membrorum. The only feature breaking a proper hymnic structure is the ἵνα separating the two strophe. In the hymn God is the acting subject throughout. In I-II the reference is cosmic with the wall that between heaven and earth; in A-B it is human. The differences between the two strophe are considerable and Wilhelmi speculates that they may have had different origins. Two however of the original clues to the existence of a *Vorlage*, the change of person from second to first at v. 14, and the reverse at v. 19, and the mixture of heaven/earth and human/human reconciliation no longer operate so strongly to support the existence of the *Vorlage*. The first has simply disappeared; the second is still present, though in a less confusing way. But the major change when the hymn is used in Ephesians is the appearance of Christ and not God as the subject of the action. Some of the other changes, e.g. the reference to the cross, might be regarded as clarificatory but they are so extensive that it may be reasonably asked whether the readers of Ephesians, supposing they knew the hymn, would ever have recognized that the author was using it? If, however, the readers were not acquainted with the hymn some of these difficulties disappear since the author might be regarded as simply using it as a framework on which to hang his own thoughts. But then the whole point of the search for underlying traditions seems to disappear. Finally it should be noted that both the attempts of Gnilka and Wilhelmi and indeed of many others imply that the author of Ephesians used an interlacing technique in altering the *Vorlage* which we have seen was contrary to the manner in which he used material from Colossians.[1]

---

[1]Other attempts at formulating a *Vorlage* to this passage are discussed in J.T. Sanders, 'Hymnic Elements in Ephesians', and *The New Testament Christological Hymns* (Cambridge, 1971), pp. 14f., 88-92; Deichgräber, *Gotteshymnus und Christushymnus in der frühen Christenheit*, pp. 165-67; E. Testa, 'Gesù pacificatore universale. Inno liturgico della Chiesa Madre (Col. 1,15-20 + Ef. 2,14-16)', *SBFLA* 19 (1969), pp. 5-64; J. Gnilka, 'Christus unser Friede—ein Friedens-Erlöserlied in Eph 2,14-17', *Die Zeit Jesu* (FS H. Schlier; Freiburg, 1970), pp. 190-207; K. Wengst, *Formeln und Lieder des Urchristentums* (Gütersloh, 1972), pp. 181-86; Fischer, *Tendenz und Absicht des Epheserbriefes*, pp. 131-37; P. Stuhlmacher, '"Er ist unser Friede" (Eph 2,14). Zur Exegese und Bedeutung von Eph 2,14-18', *Neues Testament und Kirche* (FS R. Schnackenburg; Freiburg, 1974), pp. 337-58; C. Bürger, *Schöpfung und Versöhnung: Studien zum liturgischen Gut in Kolosser- und Epheserbrief* (Neukirchen-Vluyn, 1975), pp. 117-39, 144-57; Lindemann, *Die Aufhebung der Zeit*, pp. 156-58; W. Rader, *The Church and Racial Hostility. A History of Interpretation of Eph. 2:11-22* (Tübingen, 1978), pp. 196-201; H. Merklein, 'Zur Tradition und Komposition von Eph 2,14-18', *BZ* 17 (1973), pp. 79-102; and the commentaries ad loc. R.P. Martin, *Reconciliation: A Study of Paul's Theology* (London, 1981), pp. 167-76, assumes a much longer underlying piece of tradition running from v. 12 to v. 19, the core being vv. 14-16,

2.19-22

W. Nauck[1] has argued that these verses are drawn from a baptismal hymn and points to parallels with 1 Pet. 2.4ff. which he also regards as such a hymn. This view of 1 Pet. 2.4ff. has been disputed by the majority of recent commentators.[2] Nauck makes no emendations to the text of 2.19-22 and the text as it stands lacks many hymnic characteristics.[3] Moreover it is fully in the author's style. We may dismiss it from our discussion.

4.4-6

This section is not listed as possible liturgical material in Merkel's survey. Many recent commentators however find traditional material within it. Mussner[4] in the introduction to his commentary lists 4.5f. Almost all recent writers see v. 6 as deriving ultimately from Stoic formulae but reflecting passages like 1 Cor. 8.6; Rom. 11.36. They also see v. 5 as carefully constructed (note the appearance of the three genders of εἷς) and coming either from a baptismal liturgy or baptismal instruction. They are not clear whether the writer of Ephesians brought these two verses together or if they previously existed as a unit. Verse 4a, 'one body and one Spirit' is regarded as containing traditional material (the two phrases appear in close proximity in 2.16, 18). The stumbling block to taking v. 4 in its entirety as traditional is its final clause. This is written in the author's normal style (in particular he is fond of καθώς clauses, 1.4; 3.3; 4.4, 17, 21, 32; 5.2, 3, 25, 29) and is completely different from the other brief phrases all of which begin with 'one'. If the whole were pre-existing tradition it seems to some very peculiar that it should begin with a reference to the church and not to God or Christ, but this strangeness may arise only from the way in which we have become accustomed to

---

which 'was a hellenistic hymn of cosmic transformation' (p. 171); his reconstruction does not seem to escape the objections we have raised to the attempts of Gnilka and Wilhelmi.

1 'Eph. 2,19-22 - ein Taufleid?', *EvT* 13 (1953), pp. 362-71.

2 E.g., L. Goppelt, *Der erste Petrusbrief* (Göttingen, 1978), pp. 139f.

3 For detailed criticisms see Bankhead, *Liturgical Formulas in the New Testament*, pp. 107f.; H. Merklein, *Das kirchliche Amt nach dem Epheserbrief* (Munich, 1973), pp. 119f. The revised structure suggested by G. Klinzing, *Die Umdeutung des Kultus in der Qumrangemeinde und im Neuen Testament* (Göttingen, 1971), p. 190 n. 61, does not overcome most of these criticisms.

4 F. Mussner, *Der Brief an die Epheser* (GTB 509; Gütersloh, 1982), p. 19.

the traditional but later creeds. The order, 'Church, Christ, God', may be the order of importance in the mind of the author of Ephesians as fitting his theology[1] and so have been created by him. When we look at vv. 4-6 there is a quite remarkable change in style at the beginning of v. 4, broken only by v. 4b. At v. 7 we return to the author's normal argumentative style. So far as I can trace only F.F. Bruce looks on vv. 4-6 as a pre-existing unit: 'This section [vv. 4-6] has the nature of an early Christian *credo*'.[2] It is worth exploring this further. We do not need to look for any modification of a *Vorlage* in vv. 5, 6. If v. 4b is in the author's style then part of it may need to be eliminated to reach the original. This is easily done and we end with a verse containing three units each commencing with 'one' in harmony with the following verse; this enables us to conjecture a pre-existing unit:

> One body, one Spirit, one hope,
> one Lord, one faith, one baptism,
> one God and Father of all,
> who is over all and through all and in all.

This unit has a total of seven (a sacred number) units each introduced by 'one'; in the final unit (v. 6) containing 'all' (in fact there are three 'threes'). Its emphasis on 'one' suits the author's purpose which at this point is to stress the unity of the church before going on to concentrate on the variety within it (4.7-16). But he needs to link this to his ongoing discussion. This began at 4.1 with an emphasis on the call (note the verb and its cognate noun) which Christians have received. In 1.18 the author has already linked hope and calling; it is therefore natural for him to do so again; so he writes v. 4b tying in the tradition to his major purpose, and because v. 4b is now much longer he modifies the first half of it by introducing καί between its two units. Thus what we have here is the kind of modification which we might expect from someone who is using a piece of existing material and needs to relate it to his general argument.

---

[1]So K. Wengst, *Formeln und Lieder des Urchristentums*, p. 141f.

[2]F.F. Bruce, *The Epistles to the Colossians, to Philemon, and to the Ephesians* (NICNT; Grand Rapids, 1984), p. 335.

5.14

At only two points in his letter does the author of Ephesians say that he is quoting, 4.8 and 5.14, using on both occasions the same introductory formula, 'therefore it (he) says'. In 4.8 he cites the OT. Many attempts[1] have therefore been made to trace the quotation in 5.14 to the same source but all have proved unsuccessful and today it is generally agreed that a Christian hymn, or a portion of one, is being used, though it must be realised that since we do not know how our author defined Scripture he may have thought he was quoting it here; in any case it is certain that he was quoting. No one, so far as I know, has suggested any amendments to the existing text, though it may be that there was another strophe in the hymn; the strophe with which Clement of Alexandria continues it in *Protrepticus* 9.84.2 and 1 Tim. 3.16 have both been suggested. It has also been suggested that it may have had a different meaning in its original usage from its meaning in Ephesians.[2] There is no need then to look for an underlying *Vorlage* and speculate how and why our author may have changed it. We need to be careful here and not draw a wrong deduction from the fact that our author states he is quoting at this point but does not say so in relation to the other passages which have been suspected as quotations. We cannot automatically conclude that he is not quoting at those points, for he quotes the OT at points other than 4.8 but does not use an introductory formula. However the quotation he uses in 4.8 is not the normal biblical text and he may have used the introductory formula so that his readers would know that he was quoting something which was authoritative. The same may be true at 5.14. The hymn, perhaps one spoken by a Christian prophet inspired by the Holy Spirit (cf. 5.19), may not have been known to many or even all his readers (remember this is a general letter) and so he gives it authority by his introductory formula.

---

[1] See the commentaries.

[2] B. Noack, 'Das Zitat im Ephes. 5,14', *ST* 5 (1951), pp. 52-64, believes it had an originally apocalyptic intention.

3.5; 5.25-27

In addition to the passages enumerated by Merkel, M. Barth[1] suggests two other possibilities: 3.5; 5.25-27. In the case of 3.5 he points to the parallelism of its two halves and to non-Pauline terms ('sons of men', 'holy apostles and prophets'). This latter argument is of course only valid if Paul is the author of Ephesians. As to the former it is true that there was a tradition about a commission to go to the Gentiles given to the Twelve or a similar group (Mt. 28.16-20; Lk. 24.47-9; Jn 20.2lb; Acts 1.8). It is expressed in different terms in each of these references and it is impossible to derive a common *Vorlage* from them.[2] If one could be deduced it would only cover 3.5b, which itself is in a different form from any of those mentioned. It is therefore easier to assume that the author of Ephesians knew the tradition, reformulated it in his own words and added v. 5a, and created the parallelism (he has many such passages containing parallels). In the case of 5.25-27 Barth sees a hymn which the author of Ephesians quotes without modification. However when Barth sets it out he does so in English translation and the lines he suggests in English do not correspond to possible lines in the Greek (to get his English lines he alters the order of the Greek words!). He is however probably correct in seeing 5.25b, 'he loved the church and gave himself for her', as a brief credal form. We find equivalents in 5.2, 'he loved us . . .', with a brief expansion suiting the context and in Gal 2.20 where it is in the first person singular which again suits the context. When we examine the supposed hymn in 5.25-27 we see that it itself is an expansion of this brief creed adapted to fit the marriage context.

Before leaving the subject we should note that Kirby[3] understands the whole letter to be based on a liturgical text which the author transformed into a letter by the addition of 1.1-2; 1.14-22; 3.1-13 and a number of smaller additions in the paraenetic section 4.1ff. This text was used in a renewal of the covenant service at Pentecost and was related to baptism. His argument depends in large part on the liturgical fragments which others have detected and which we have discussed. If these are not so easily detected as he assumes his thesis

[1] M. Barth, *Ephesians* (AB; New York, 1974) I, pp. 331f.; II, pp. 621ff.

[2] See E. Best, 'The Revelation to Evangelize the Gentiles', *JTS* 35 (1984), pp. 1-30.

[3] Kirby, *Ephesians: Baptism and Pentecost*, *passim* and especially p. 132.

becomes difficult. It also has its own difficulties: why was the liturgy turned into a letter? who would have recognized the underlying liturgy so that it would have had authority for them?

Finally, a brief look at Col. 1.15-20 may be interesting, since like Phil. 2.6-11 it is generally assumed to have been a pre-existing hymn. As with the latter various suggestions have been made in relation to modifications the author of Colossians may have made to his *Vorlage;* most of these are expansions, e.g. v. 20b, but one, the addition of the reference to the body in v. 18 is said to alter the meaning so that while 'body' in the original referred to the cosmos it now refers to the church. Is it likely that this simple addition would have been sufficient to change the meaning in a way easily appreciated by the readers, whom it is to be supposed knew the hymn with the original reference? Surely the author would have needed to make much clearer his new understanding of the hymn and have shown in some way that the original was incorrect? There are two other possibilities: the explicit reference to the church may always have been there in which case there is no problem; alternatively the hymn lacking the explicit word 'church' may always have been intended to refer at this point to the church and the author, having found out that some of the community to which he was writing were misunderstanding it as a reference to the cosmos, has inserted the reference to the church to remove that misunderstanding.

Aspects of Worship in the Book of Revelation

Donald Guthrie

Introduction

Worship is an important theme in the New Testament, but nowhere does it come into such sharp focus as in the book of Revelation. Yet due allowance must be made for the high element of symbolism which runs throughout this book. The fact is the worship scenes which intersperse the judgment scenes are set in a heavenly sphere and the question at once arises as to the relationship between these scenes and the regular worship within the Christian church. Were the heavenly descriptions patterned to any extent on the actual liturgical procedures of the local churches with which the writer was associated? Or were the liturgical passages of the book of Revelation intended as suggestions which the local communities might follow in the development of their forms of worship? These questions have been widely debated and it is not our present purpose to discuss them. Yet it is of some importance for us to note the various views on whether actual procedures have been transposed to heavenly scenes or vice versa. Since the whole book purports to be a revelation and since it is difficult to trace most of the material to any specific literary source or sources, it would be reasonable to regard the worship passages themselves as having a revelatory and therefore exemplary character. In this case these passages would be of great importance in bringing out patterns of worship which are eminently worth examining as pointing to principles which have a universal application.

The worship passages provide indications under two aspects—the content of worship and the attitude of the worshippers. Our concern will be with both of these aspects and our aim will be to consider the cumulative effect of the sequence of passages culminating in worship in the New Jerusalem. But first some comment needs to be made on the significance of the worship passages within the book as a whole. Their occurrence is somewhat surprising in a book that concentrates so on judgment scenes, and must be intended to prepare the way for them. The writer is concerned that the reader should have a right view of God before predictions of his judgment are made. There is no doubt that since the worship passages present a high view of God, a study of them will not only lead to a higher view of worship, but also will help to put the justice of God in a right perspective.

The major worship passages are closely bound up with the series of hymns which run through this book. Although our study will not be confined to the hymns, it will be necessary first to note the various studies which have concentrated attention on these hymns, since their interpretation will affect the part they play in the worship scenes. One theory is that much of the material in the hymns has been taken over from earlier Jewish or Jewish-Christian worship (so O'Rourke[1]). Similarly, others have claimed to find evidence of a mixture of Christian and early Hellenistic synagogue sources (so Macdonald[2] and Ralph Martin[3]). These theories are strong only if it is supposed that the hymns may legitimately be isolated from the structure of the book as a whole. Otherwise the sense of unity throughout the book would militate against the attempt to isolate sources. As in our following discussion we shall take the view that the hymns are the work of the author himself, it will be seen that theories of sources are not as important as the consideration of what the writer intended to convey through the hymns in the worship passages.

Another theory is that some at least of the hymns belong to a eucharistic milieu. For this the main advocates are Luchli[4] and Cabaniss.[5] But both find it necessary to appeal to liturgies later than the book of Revelation, which considerably weakens their legitimacy. Moreover the hymns do not themselves reflect eucharistic language (so V. Taylor,[6] Moule[7]). Rather more significance may be attached to

---

[1]J. O'Rourke, 'The Hymns of the Apocalypse', *CBQ* 30 (1968), pp. 399-409.

[2]A.B. Macdonald, *Christian Worship in the Primitive Church* (Edinburgh, 1934).

[3]R.P. Martin, *Worship in the Early Church* (London: Marshall, Morgan & Scott, 1964).

[4]S. Lauchli, 'Eine Gottesdienststruktur in der Johannesbarung', *TZ* 16 (1960), pp. 359-78.

[5]A. Cabaniss, 'A note on the Liturgy of the Apocalypse', *Int* 7 (1953), pp. 74-86.

[6]V. Taylor, *The Atonement in the New Testament* (London: Epworth, 1954), pp. 34-43.

[7]C.F.D. Moule, *Worship in the New Testament* (London, 1961).

Prigent's[1] theory that at least in chapters 4 and 5 there is an adapted Jewish synagogue liturgy. Since the two chapters in question form a major part of any discussion of worship in this book, it would be of great relevance if Prigent's theory could be proved, but this is debatable (so Carnegie[2]). It is difficult to maintain this theory throughout all the hymns in Revelation. Another who sees liturgical overtones is Piper,[3] whose view is that in Revelation we are dealing with a very early liturgy. This theory supposes that Revelation is primarily a liturgical book; but as this is a dubious assumption, it is better to suppose that what liturgical elements may be present are there to set the apocalyptic elements in perspective rather than vice versa (so Thompson[4]). No more convincing is the view that the worship sections in Revelation are influenced by some kind of Temple liturgy (Carrington[5]), because the sections as a whole do not fit into such a pattern without forcing.

Another suggestion is that a Tabernacles motif underlies the Revelation passages. Comblin[6] has concentrated on the New Jerusalem visions, but sees some connection with the earlier worship passages. Similarly McKelvey[7] sees the New Jerusalem sections as forming a climax to the earlier worship passages under the Tabernacles motif. But while there is undoubtedly a connection between the worship passages and the New Jerusalem, the Tabernacles motif is more difficult to establish. The view that in this book we see evidences of a pascal liturgy is worth mentioning,[8] although it falls down on the dubious procedure of attempting to fit the sequences in the book of Revelation into a much later liturgical pattern.

A quite different type of theory is that which sees the hymns as part of a dramatic procedure after the manner of Greek tragedy, in which a chorus was used to comment on the actions of the actors (so Brewer[9] and Bowman[10]). This is a suggestive theory, since the hymns

---

[1]P. Prigent, *Apocalypse et Liturgie* (Neuchâtel, 1964).

[2]D.R. Carnegie, 'The Hymns in Revelation: Their Origin and Function', unpublished CNAA thesis, 1978.

[3]O. Piper, 'The Apocalypse of John and the Liturgy of the Ancient Church', *Church History* 20 (1951), pp. 10-22.

[4]L. Thompson, 'Cult and Eschatology in the Apocalypse of John', *JR* 49 (1969), pp. 330-50.

[5]P. Carrington, *The Meaning of Revelation* (London: SPCK, 1931).

[6]J. Comblin, 'La liturgie de la Nouvelle Jerusalem', *ETL* 29 (1953), pp. 5-40.

[7]R.J. McKelvey, *The New Temple: The Church in the New Testament* (Oxford, 1969).

[8]M.H. Shepherd, *The Pascal Liturgy and the Apocalypse* (London: Lutterworth, 1960).

[9]R.R. Brewer, 'The Influence of Greek Drama on the Apocalypse', *ATR* 18 (1936), pp. 74-92.

undoubtedly throw light on the action within the judgment visions. But the drama theory diminishes the sense of heavenly worship in the passages concerned and is not convincing as an account of the structure of the book.

We are bound therefore to conclude that the only satisfactory explanation of the worship passages is that they form an integral part of the structure of the whole book and that they are the contribution of the author. In order fully to appreciate them we need to examine the worship elements as a direct communication of an exemplary character to the readers. Without these passages, the message of the book would be forbidding indeed, one of unrelieved judgment. But in the light of the worship passages we are enabled to view the theme of judgment in an entirely different light, i.e. from the point of view of the one seated on the throne.

The Worship Scenes

It will be our contention in this study that the main focus in this book is on worship rather than judgment. The judgment sequences are in every case prepared for by some scene of worship, which suggests that a proper understanding of the function of the worship passages is essential for a right appreciation of the judgment themes. While the latter will necessarily have to be excluded from detailed comment, it is important to establish at the outset that the concentration on heavenly worship is not peripheral for a right understanding of the book as a whole. Our intention will be to note the various worship passages with a view to summarising those features which have relevance for modern worship patterns. Our contention will be that the worship scenes are intentionally of a heavenly kind to provide a pattern and maybe a corrective for current patterns of earthly worship.

Worship in Revelation 1

Although the major focus in this chapter is on the vision in verses 9 to 20, the three stages which lead to this are significant for our purpose. The prologue (vv. 1-3) makes clear that the writing claims to be a revelation from God. There is an aura of authority about what is about to be written. As a revelation it is therefore immeasurably

[10] J.W. Bowman, 'The Revelation to John: Its Dramatic Structure and Message', *Int* 9 (1955), pp. 436-53.

superior to whatever man has been accustomed to and this has a bearing on the worship sequences. The greeting (vv. 4-5) serves to underline this fact with the enigmatic introduction of God as 'him who is, and who was, and who is to come', linked with the mysterious reference to the sevenfold Spirit and the threefold description of Jesus Christ. This is preparatory to the introduction of an unexpected doxology (vv. 5-8). In no more effective way could John prepare his readers for the extraordinary vision which causes him to be overwhelmed in a dramatic way. The whole book begins with the writer himself in an attitude of awesome worship.

First we must note the setting of the vision. The surroundings were not particularly conducive. John's exile on the isle of Patmos was nevertheless transformed by his being 'in the Spirit',[1] suggesting that the spiritual dimension in worship was infinitely more important than the physical surroundings. The fact that John notes that it was the Lord's day may indicate that it was his usual practice to regard that day as a worship day and it is perhaps not surprising that he was in the right mind to receive the remarkable vision. Nonetheless, the loud trumpet was required to draw his attention to the significance of the occasion. It could scarcely be ignored. It is also worth noting that the vision is set within the compass of the seven churches. Clearly the revelation in the vision, exalted as it was, was intended to be of significance in the ongoing work and witness of the churches. However much the ambience was a heavenly one, it had a direct relevance to the earthly scene. This underlines the view that the heavenly worship scenes had an exemplary purpose.

We need not discuss all the details of the vision but there are important features which throw considerable light on the theme of worship in this book. The fact that the one who is revealing himself stands among the candlesticks at once anchors the vision as relevant to the present experience of the churches.[2] Also the fact that he is described as one like a son of man may be an allusion to the name Jesus so often used of himself in the gospels, or at least may be intended to link up with his humanity. The amazing character of the vision, however, clearly owes most to the resurrected Lord. It was aimed to

---

[1]P. Prigent (*L'Apocalypse de Saint Jean, Labor et Fides* [Geneva, 1988], p. 24) considers this expression approaches an experience of ecstasy, but it need not be so restricted.

[2]The risen Christ is no absentee, but a present reality (cf. G.B. Caird, *The Revelation of Saint John the Divine* [London: A. and C. Black, 1966], p. 25).

inspire, not only the writer, but also the readers in the seven churches.[1] The vision itself portrays Christ as dignified, with his full length robe and snow white hair, but also as majestic with his terrifying eyes, his brilliant face and his two-edged sword. The purpose was not to overwhelm, although it had that effect, but to reassure.

To what extent can modern worship learn anything from John's experience? Perhaps it is all too seldom that such an overwhelming view of God introduces us to the subsequent acts of worship. Clearly there is no room here for an over-familiar attitude towards the worship of God. John's prostration on the other hand is gently corrected with a touch of the right hand.[2] Nevertheless, a due sense of awe might lead our modern worshippers to a better appreciation of the true nature of Christ, similar to that found in verse 18. We may perhaps summarize the lessons in worship from chapter 1 under three points: (1) We must appreciate the greatness and uniqueness of Jesus Christ; (2) We must develop a humble attitude before him; (3) We must seek to experience the tender touch. No approach to worship which does not encourage these aspects conforms to this biblical pattern.

Worship in Revelation 4 and 5

In linking these two chapters rather than in treating them separately, we are aiming to view them as presenting a complete, although heavenly, service of worship. Our first concern must be the setting. Since this scene is the prelude to the first series of judgments, it forms an important part of the structure of the whole book. It provides the right perspective on judgment, i.e. when it is viewed through worship. There is a curious merging of the earthly with the heavenly here as John, representative of the earthly, gazes into the open door[3] of heaven. There is a sense of anticipation that is indispensable to true worship. This is emphasized by the repetition of the trumpet call already seen in chapter 1, which again introduces a heavenly scene.

---

[1] As Caird (*Revelation of Saint John the Divine*, p. 25) says, 'This is not photographic art. His (the author's) aim is to set the echoes of memory and association ringing'. This is clearly an important element in worship.

[2] G.R. Beasley-Murray, *The Book of Revelation* (London: Oliphants, 1974), p. 67, thinks that there is a close parallel here to Dan. 10.7ff.

[3] The door in heaven is thought by some to reflect the Hebrew concept of a solid firmament, but others think it may rather reflect the structure of the Temple with its different compartments (cf. J.M. Ford, *Revelation* [AB 38; New York: Doubleday], p. 7). Of far greater significance is the view that the door indicates access to the highest revelation of God (cf. P. Prigent, p. 72).

Here again John is said to be 'in the Spirit', strongly reminding us of the indispensability of the Spirit not only in the act of worship, but more importantly in the appreciation of heavenly worship.

It is extraordinary that in focusing on the object of worship the writer avoids any direct description of God. He is content with simply referring to the one on the throne. To those familiar with Old Testament imagery the description is abundantly adequate (cf. Isa. 6; Ezek. 1). The succinct expression succeeds in providing an aura of mystery inducive of reverence.[1] The following metaphors of rainbow and precious stones add to the mystery and warn against a too prosaic conception of God. Whatever the precise interpretation of the imagery, the sense of awe is unmistakable. The lightening flashes and thunder-claps linked immediately with sight of a sea as calm as glass present a merging of majesty with serenity.[2] The surrounding thrones and white clad elders add a further sense of dignity to the whole scene. In no more dramatic way could the readers be reminded of the greatness of the God whom the heavenly beings are worshipping. No lesser approach to God is acceptable.

There has been much discussion over the identity of the twenty four elders and we cannot here engage in that debate. But for our present purpose we shall assume that since they appear in a heavenly scene they must therefore be regarded as heavenly beings, although they may be representative of earthly people or communities. What is more important than their identity is their function within this heavenly worship service. They are participating worshippers and as such it is possible for us to identify with them. But it is significant that they are not the only participants, for in fact the worship is begun by the four living creatures.

These four creatures are by their description clearly intended to be representative of the created order.[3] Of particular interest is the fact that man is mentioned third in the midst of other creatures. Yet the symbolic nature of the creatures is evident from the six wings and the

---

[1]Caird cogently remarks that the writer allows his readers to look on the Eternal Light through the mirror of the worshipping host of heaven (*Revelation of Saint John the Divine*, p. 63).

[2]I.T. Beckwith, *The Apocalypse of John* (London: Macmillan, 1919; reprint ed., Grand Rapids: Baker, 1967), p. 500, considers the sea to refer to the splendour of the throne room pavement, but even so it presents a remarkable contrast to the storm raging in the background.

[3]This is a more likely interpretation than that which sees the creatures as identified within the signs of the Zodiac. The view adopted in this essay is not only of ancient tradition but is supported by many modern commentators (cf. Beasley-Murray, p. 117).

all-seeing eyes. It is perplexing at first sight to find such creatures in a heavenly worship scene, but since they perform an important function in initiating the worship their significance cannot be overemphasized. They provide the essential link between the earthly and the heavenly in this worship scene. Although there are clear parallels with Isaiah 6 in the recitation of the Trisagion, the form of wording here is stamped with its own peculiarity, particularly in the description of God in a way similar to Rev. 1.4, 8. The focus on the holiness of God has a direct bearing on the theme of this whole book, for the judgments of God must be seen to proceed from his holiness. The significance of this for our modern worship would be to raise the sense of awe in the presence of God to such a degree that the worshippers are bound to confess their own unholiness. Whatever forms our worship take, those that make no provision for an appreciation at the outset of a due sense of the utter purity of God must be considered deficient. Not only is the theme of holiness paramount, but the creatures ascribe honour and glory and thanks to him on the throne. The whole proceedings are God-centred.

The elders are of special interest not only for their anthems but also for their actions. There is particular dignity in their well orchestrated prostrations and the corporate act of laying their crowns before the throne. Since this is repeated in 5.14 at the close of the worship service, it must be intended to illustrate the appropriate attitude for worshippers of God to adopt. All authority is vested in God himself and this must be acknowledged. The obeisance is suggestive of an attitude of true humility before Almighty God. Even if the prostration is not necessarily to be repeated in the earthly counterpart, something approximating to it must be considered appropriate. This would rule out any rushing into divine worship without due regard for the solemnity of the occasion.

The elders' anthems are worth noting as a possible pattern for earthly worship procedures. The song in chapter 4 differs in theme from that in chapter 5, suggesting a progressive sequence. In 4.11 the themes are the worthiness of God and his creative will. There is here a firm conviction about the creative activity of God and an assured belief that he is sovereign in his creation. That this is the basis on which the following judgment scenes proceed again shows the contribution that this worship scene makes to the structure of the book as a whole. The focus here is upon God himself as contrasted with the focus on Christ in the song of Rev. 5.9, 10. This is clearly intentional, since the latter follows what might be described as a dramatic interlude in which there is a revelation of Christ. If our earthly procedures are to be in any way influenced by this heavenly pattern, worship must be governed by a God-centred and not a man-centred approach. There would not appear to be here much room for any warming-up procedures based on drumming up a sense of spiritual euphoria. In treating chapter 5 as a continuation of the same service as chapter 4, we are obliged to regard verses 1-7 as in some way a part of the worship. The idea of a dramatic interlude during which there is a revelation of Christ has much to commend it. The observer, John, narrates what he saw and it takes a symbolic form. The scroll written on both sides with its seven seals is best taken to refer to the various visions which follow in the book. In other words, it can be understood correctly only with reference to its place in the whole structure of the book. This seems better than interpreting it as the Old Testament as some have done. The search for a worthy person to open the scroll is a dramatic representation of the uniqueness of Christ since he only is worthy to perform the task. What is of particular interest in this scene is the fact that John himself somehow becomes involved in it. The dialogue between the seer and the elders brings home the close connection between this scene and human experience. Clearly there is no intention that heavenly worship should bypass human needs. Indeed John's tears and the concern of the elders to comfort at once makes the whole scene intensely relevant.

The revelation of the character of Christ in the double figure of a Lion-lamb is significant in view of the dominance of the Lamb in the remainder of the book. It is as if the writer (and the reader) must appreciate that even if the stronger lion-symbol is perfectly applicable, yet the chosen symbol is nevertheless that of the Lamb, not only because of its softer nature but because of its sacrificial significance. It at once introduces a paradox encased in a mystery. How can judgement be carried out by a Lamb? There is always an element of paradox in all true worship. If there is no sense of mystery the level of worship is not right. If all is plain to grasp, the revelation has failed to inculcate a due sense of worship. The description of the Lamb is intended to be mysterious for its evident wound and its seven horns and eyes cry out for interpretation. The wound is intelligible against the background of the sacrificial Lamb, but the horns seem out of keeping with it. No observer can avoid grasping at the mystery. The horns of strength conflict with the appearance of being slain. Although it becomes intelligible in the light of the risen Christ, it is nonetheless wrapped up in a challenging symbolic form. The whole dramatic interlude was not designed to appeal to human logic. It was rather an attempt to describe the indescribable, always an element in all true worship.

We may regard the second song of the elders as a natural sequence from the drama just enacted. The concerted obeisance of the living creatures and the elders is a prelude to this second song of adoration. This is a similar display of dignified humility to that which preceded the first song. We are not allowed to forget the need for such acknowledgement of the greatness of worship. Additional features in this part are the harps and the bowls of incense, symbolic of praises and prayers. The theme of this second song is the redemptive act of Christ. This linking of creation and redemption in the elders' songs is important because it focuses on the acts of God in Christ.

The service finishes with a great crescendo. Not only is an immense heavenly chorus brought in to sing the praises of the Lamb, but after the manner of an antiphonal chorus, all creatures in earth and heaven are brought in to echo the same theme. To cap it all the four creatures repeat their Amen.

To what extent may we apply any such patterns to our own worship? Reflection on this heavenly scene leaves us with a deep impression that the highest activity of the heavenly hosts is to praise God and the Lamb. There is an entire absence of any human experiential strains. Man only comes into it as the object of the sacrificial act of God. There is no room for introspection here—only pure adoration. It is surely exemplary! It forms a yardstick for our modern styles of worship. Do they enhance the saving work of Christ? Do they lead to acts of dignified humiliation? Do they help the worshipper to lose himself in the great crescendo of praise to God?

The Saints at Worship

We turn next to the worship section in 7.9-15. The description of the congregation precisely echoes the description of the objects of the redemptive work of Christ celebrated in 5.9. These redeemed people are now before the throne and in front of the Lamb. The fact that they wear white robes and hold palm branches is again symbolic. The white robes speak of cleansing from sin through Christ as verse 14 makes clear. The palm branches are a token of honour to the King. These people acknowledge their indebtedness to Christ for salvation, and the whole angelic chorus worship God as they repeat the worthiness of God. The same concentration on God is found here as in the former scene. Another interlude follows with one of the elders entering into a dialogue with John, during which some indication of the status of those who have passed through tribulation on earth but are now in heaven is given. Again the thought centres on the Lamb, but in no overawing manner. Indeed the tender imagery of a shepherd is introduced and the touching picture of a God who actually wipes away tears. This scene therefore contains a significant blend of the glory and tenderness of God, ever an important feature in true Christian worship.

Another Song of the Twenty-four Elders

The elders are still in an attitude of worship in 11.15-17, once again prostrating themselves before the throne as if nothing else would be appropriate. The occasion was the sounding of the seventh trumpet and the announcement of the divine kingdom. There was therefore a sense of awe about the occasion and this called forth a song in which there was a mixture of thanksgiving and judgment. The prevailing theme is that of wrath, reminding the readers that God is a just God, a theme which is reiterated in the final worship scene in 19.1-10. Throughout these worship sections the reader is not allowed to forget that no worship is possible divorced from a high view of God, which must include a due sense of his justice. This has a relevance for modern worship whenever it is sentimentalized by an over-emphasis on the love of God at the expense of his holiness. It may seem surprising that the balance in Revelation worship scenes is on the latter rather than the former, although against the background of judgment scenes it is quite intelligible. It is noticeable in this scene that it concludes with a reference to the temple and to the ark, reminiscent of the holy of holies in the Old Testament. It is also significant that there is a repetition of the storm imagery here to impress the reader with the power of God. Again the inculcation of awe is a major feature of the worship.

The 144,000

Another worship passage, 14.1-5, differs from those just mentioned in relating a worship scene but giving little detail. What is noticeable is the symbolic number of the congregation, the thunderous sound of the worship, the accompaniment of harps and the restriction of the worshippers to the redeemed. There is some echo here from the elders' song in chapter 5 which focuses on the redeeming activity of the Lamb. The centrality of the Lamb is the most significant feature for our present purpose. Although the new song is undefined there can be little doubt that its theme is a celebration of the saving action of the Lamb. Again there is a linkage with the earlier worship scene in chapter 7 where the same symbolic number 144,000 is found.

The Song of Moses and the Lamb

In 15.2-4, where this song is placed, the setting is more specifically of judgment, for the seven angels wait with the seven plagues. The worship scene is therefore a prelude to the final events of judgment. There is some tie-up with chapter 4 in that again we meet with a sea of glass, although this time the mixture with fire reminds us that all is not serenity.[1] The worshippers are those who have been victorious over the beast. They have had experience of the delivering power of God. They are given harps to aid their worship. This song is therefore different from the earlier ones in that the worshippers, although now in heaven, were formerly on earth. The song is clearly influenced by the song of Moses in Exodus 15. There is a parallel sense of victory and a similar high view of God and his accomplishments. The themes are the marvellous works of God, his justice, his holiness, his kingship and his worthiness to receive worship. We find strong resemblances here with the earlier theme songs of the elders. Once again the scene concludes with a clear Old Testament allusion, a reference to the tabernacle and the idea of the temple being filled with smoke, reminiscent once again of Isaiah 6. There is a solemnity here in the fact that this worship scene is a prelude to the most devastating display of God's wrath. It is intended to be reassuring, but the sense of awe and righteous wrath of God is unmistakeable.

---

[1]It is possible that the fire imagery here may be an echo of the fire imagery in Ezekiel 1 (cf. J.M. Ford, p. 253), although it is more likely to be a symbol of wrath (cf. Beasley-Murray, p. 235). Indeed Beasley-Murray sees the fiery aspect as indicating the overthrow of the Beast and its allies, parallel to the destruction of Pharaoh and his armies in the Red Sea.

The Hallelujah Chorus

The scene in 19.1-10 marks a fitting climax to the visions of judgment and serves to lead into the appearance of the New Jerusalem with its setting of perfect worship, which is so natural that no temple is needed. Following the vivid dirge over the fall of Babylon, it is time for rejoicing and this is centred in tumultuous worship in heaven. This worship scene is significant for its spontaneous outburst of praise in celebration of the victory of God over evil. Even if there is a strong eschatological emphasis here, we may enquire whether there are lessons to be learnt in patterns of worship for our present age.

There are four Hallelujahs. The first celebrates the fact that salvation and victory belong to God. It is entirely God centred. It again affirms that his judgments are just and true. The second Hallelujah is a responsive exclamation to affirm the truth of the first Hallelujah and stressing the finality of the overthrow of evil. These two were uttered by a great heavenly multitude, and it is twice stressed that the words were shouted.[1] The whole is set in a festal mood. The third Hallelujah came from the four living creatures and the twenty- four elders, who again do obeisance before the throne. The Hallelujah and the Amen are intended to endorse the affirmations of the multitude. After a mysterious single voice, the great multitude joins in a concluding Hallelujah which glorifies the reign of Almighty God and announces the wedding of the Lamb. In the structure of the book this clearly leads into a highly significant theme in which the tribulations of the church of God are now over and the bliss of union with the Lamb in the New Jerusalem begins. Although the future aspect of this scene is obvious, the sentiments expressed are not irrelevant for our present age. The church of God has every right to look forward to the consummation of the plan of God and there is a sense in which we may already join in this Hallelujah chorus since the final victory of the Lamb in this book is never in doubt. It is fitting that in this present age we should acknowledge the victory of the Lamb.

It is worth noting that at the end of this scene the writer himself falls down to worship. But he misjudges the object of worship and selects the angel. The rebuke he receives is perhaps a reminder to all his readers that they must as a matter of urgency ensure that honour is

[1] Many commentators consider these utterances were made by angels, but Prigent (p. 278) relates them to Christians, while Caird restricts them to martyrs.

given only to God. Throughout these worship scenes in this book there is the impression that God alone must be worshipped, that he must be worshipped in a dignified manner, that he expects the response of a spontaneous outburst of praise, and he expects worship to be whole-hearted. There is some warrant for the use of liturgical responses like Amen and Hallelujah, and perhaps support for some kind of antiphonal responses. But the overwhelming impression is of unrestrained acknowledgement of the greatness of God and his worthiness to be worshipped.

ASPECTS OF EARLY CHRISTIAN AND JEWISH WORSHIP: PLINY AND THE *KERYGMA PETROU*

Graham N. Stanton

In my view none of Ralph Martin's many distinguished contributions to New Testament scholarship surpasses his fine doctoral dissertation published in the SNTS Monograph series in 1967 as *Carmen Christi. Philippians ii. 5-11 in Recent Interpretation and in the Setting of Early Christian Worship*. In the opening pages he discusses briefly the comments on early Christian worship which Pliny, Governor of Pontus and Bithynia, passed on to the Roman Emperor Trajan in AD 111-12. He then examines other references to early Christian worship from this period before embarking on his detailed and meticulous study of Phil. 2.6-11.

I am convinced that this method is sound: it is often helpful in studies of earliest Christianity to work back from later, clearer evidence to the more problematic evidence of the New Testament writings. In this paper I shall also start with Pliny's comments on early Christian worship before turning to the *Kerygma Petrou*, which was written at about the same time as Pliny's letter to Trajan.[1] Pliny wrote as an astute 'outsider' who would have been aware of many of the differences between pagan, Jewish and Christian worship. The fragmentary *Kerygma Petrou*, written from the perspective of a Christian 'insider', underlines the differences explicitly.

I hope to show that while less astute pagan observers than Pliny would have been struck by the many *similarities* between Jewish and Christian worship, both Jewish and Christian 'insiders' would have been well aware of striking *differences*. Taken together, these writings confirm that early in the second century Christian worship dif-

[1] Since the fragments on early Christian worship in the *Kerygma Petrou* do not refer to the use of hymns, they are not discussed in Ralph Martin's *Carmen Christi*.

fered in several fundamental respects from synagogue worship. I do not doubt for a moment the enormous influence of Temple and synagogue worship on the development of Christian worship, but there were important differences, some of the roots of which are very deep.[1]

Pliny

In his letter to Trajan Pliny refers to some former Christians who had abandoned their faith; they were now worshipping Trajan's statue and the images of the gods, and were prepared to curse Christ.

> They asserted that this had been the sum total of their guilt or error, namely that on a fixed day (*stato die*) it was their custom to meet before dawn, to sing a hymn by turns (i.e. antiphonally) to Christ as to a god (*carmenque Christo quasi deo dicere secum invicem*), and to bind themselves by oath, not to some crime, but not to commit theft or banditry or adultery, not to betray a trust, not to refuse a deposit if requested. After doing this they were in the habit of parting and coming together again for a meal, but food common and harmless; they had stopped doing this after my edict, by which according to your instructions I had banned clubs.[2]

This is the first report on early Christian worship which we have from an 'outsider'. Before discussing five points which are of particular interest, I shall comment on its social and religious setting. The Graeco-Roman religious context does not need extended discussion here, but since this passage is not normally considered in the context of contemporary Judaism, I must first show why it is plausible to read Pliny's comments from this perspective.

Pliny must have had dealings with Jews during his prominent legal and political career in Rome before his appointment to Bithynia and Pontus in AD 109 or 110. His uncle and adoptive father, Pliny the Elder, included a number of factual references to Jews in his *Natural*

---

[1]For a useful discussion of recent scholarship on both Jewish and Christian worship, see Paul Bradshaw, *The Search for the Origins of Christian Worship* (London: SPCK, 1992), especially pp. 1-55. Bradshaw does not discuss either Pliny's comments or the *Kerygma Petrou.*

[2]I have quoted Molly Whittaker's translation, *Jews and Christians: Graeco-Roman Views* (Cambridge 1984), p. 151. However I have translated the crucial phrase *Christo quasi deo* as 'to Christ as to a god' rather than 'to Christ as God'. See A.N. Sherwin-White, *The Letters of Pliny: a Historical and Social Commentary* (Oxford: Clarendon, 1966). Sherwin-White notes (p. 702) that on the whole students of the development of early Christian liturgy have not made effective use of this passage.

History, a work which Pliny knew and greatly admired (see *Letters* III.5). Pliny's friend, close associate and correspondent Tacitus comments extensively (and at times inaccurately and adversely) on the origin, laws, rites, and history of the Jews (*History* V.1-13).[1] Although Pliny does not mention Judaism or Jews in any of his letters to Trajan, it is highly likely that he would have known about the presence of strong Jewish communities in Bithynia and Pontus.

Perhaps as many as a million Jews lived in Asia Minor at the time Pliny wrote.[2] We now have evidence of over fifty Jewish communities in the region.[3] About sixty or seventy years before Pliny wrote to Trajan, Philo noted that there were Jewish 'colonies' (ἀποικίαι) in 'most of Asia, right up to Bithynia and the corners of Pontus' (*Leg.* 281-2).

Some thirty years before Pliny wrote to Trajan about troublesome Christians, Luke had referred to the presence of Jews from Pontus in Jerusalem on the day of Pentecost (Acts 2.9), and had mentioned that in Corinth Paul met Aquila, a Jew from Pontus (Acts 18.2). An even more influential Aquila came from Pontus in Pliny's day: Aquila the Jewish proselyte who translated the Hebrew Scriptures into Greek.[4] Several important Jewish inscriptions have been found in Bithynia.[5]

Further indirect evidence for the presence of Jewish communities in Bithynia and Pontus comes from the northern coast of the Black Sea. Jewish communities there were probably established as offshoots of Jewish communities in Bithynia and Pontus on the southern coasts of the Black Sea.[6] A number of Jewish inscriptions have been found in and near Panticapaeum, one of which is dated 377 of the Bosporan era, i.e. AD 81. Another particularly important inscription (probably

---

[1]Ronald Syme suggests that Tacitus' proconsulate of Asia may have been concurrent with part of Pliny's tenure in Bithynia, and his experiences comparable. *Tacitus* (Oxford: Clarendon, 1958), I, p. 81; see also II, pp. 466-9 and Appendix 23, 'Tacitus' Proconsulate of Asia', pp. 664-5.

[2]This is P. van der Horst's estimate, 'Juden und Christen in Aphrodisias', in *Juden und Christen in der Antike* (Kampen: Kok, 1990), p.126. Van der Horst argues that in Aphrodisias (and perhaps elsewhere nearby) the Jewish community may have been so strong that Christianity failed to take root in the pre-Constantinian period.

[3]See P. Trebilco, *Jewish Communities in Asia Minor* (Cambridge: CUP, 1991), p. 11.

[4]See E. Schürer, *The History of the Jewish People in the Age of Jesus Christ*, Vol. III.1 (Rev. ed.; ed. G. Vermes et al.; Edinburgh: T&T Clark, 1986), §33A, pp. 493-8.

[5]See E. Schürer, *The History of the Jewish People*, Vol. III.1, §31, p. 36.

[6]Philo does not mention Jewish communities on the northern coast of the Black Sea, but they were probably established there soon after his day.

first century AD) almost certainly refers to a synagogue of 'Jews and God-worshippers'.[1]

Evidence from the provinces to the south of Bithynia and Pontus, especially Phrygia and Caria, is much more extensive. Recent archaeological discoveries confirm the accuracy of literary references to thriving Jewish communities.[2]

In short, in Pliny's time as governor in Bithynia and Pontus, Christians and Jews are likely to have lived and worshipped cheek by jowl as minority communities in a dominant pagan environment. Almost without exception, wherever Christianity flourished in the early second century there were also thriving Jewish communities. There is increasing evidence that they were frequently rivals. Both were seeking to attract God worshippers; 'Judaism and Christianity were waging a war over the pagan soul'.[3]

Many pagan observers at the beginning of the second century must have noted that in contrast with their own diverse patterns of religious practise, in several important respects Christian and Jewish worship was similar. (a) Some pagan religion was annual (e.g. *Saturnalia*), some was seasonal (e.g. harvest festivals), some was daily (e.g. offerings to the *lares et penates* at household shrines), some was irregular (e.g. oracular consultations), but there were no regular *weekly* observances. On the other hand, for both Jews and Christians worship on a fixed day each week was central. (b) Jews and Christians used the same Scriptures in weekly worship, and even shared some of the same methods of interpretation. (c) There were no 'sermons' in any of the diverse forms of pagan worship. In both Jewish and Christian worship, however, expositions of readings from authoritative writings were prominent. (d) Temples, sacrifices, and statues were of the very essence of pagan religion. All were conspicuous by their absence from Jewish and Christian worship in Asia Minor.[4] Jews and Christians alike spurned the local cults. With their monotheistic worship and

---

[1]See P. Trebilco, *Jewish Communities*, pp. 155-6; J. Reynolds and R. Tannenbaum, *Jews and Godfearers at Aphrodisias* (Cambridge: Cambridge Philological Society, 1987), pp. 48-66.

[2]In addition to the books cited in the previous note, see E. Schürer, *The History of the Jewish People*, Vol. III.1, §31, pp. 1-176.

[3]P.W. van der Horst, *Ancient Jewish Epitaphs. An Introductory Survey of a Millenium of Jewish Funerary Epigraphy (300BCE - 700CE)* (Kampen: Kok, 1991), pp. 135-6.

[4]Tacitus, *Histories* V. 5.4, notes that the Jews 'allow no statues in their cities, much less in their temples. This compliment is not accorded to kings nor honour to the Emperor.'

high ethical standards, Jews and Christians could easily have been confused by fellow inhabitants of many city states in Asia Minor.

In spite of these obvious similarities, more perceptive observers such as Pliny would surely have been struck by the differences between Jews and Christians in their patterns and forms of worship. In the paragraphs which follow I shall discuss Pliny's brief comments to Trajan on early Christian worship from this perspective. At the outset, however, a note of caution. Pliny does not give a full account of early Christian worship. He tells Trajan only as much as he needs to. His primary concern is to stress that while on the one hand the disloyalty of Christians to the emperor called for drastic measures, on the other their high ethical standards confirmed that they were not common criminals but adherents of a 'degrading superstition'.

1. *Worship on a Fixed Day.*

Pliny's phrase '*stato die*', 'on a fixed day', confirms that he is aware that Christians do not worship on the same fixed day of the week as Jews. Early in the second century most Romans in public life were well aware of the Jewish Sabbath.[1] For example, Pliny's friend Tacitus (*History* IV.11-18) knew about the Jewish Sabbath, as did Pliny's uncle and adoptive father Pliny the Elder (*Natural History* 31.24).[2] If Christians in Bithynia and Pontus in Pliny's day worshipped on the Jewish Sabbath, he would not have used the phrase '*stato die*'.

By the early second century Sunday worship seems to have been the norm for most Christians. Writing about the same time as Pliny, Ignatius of Antioch refers to Christians 'who no longer keep Sabbath, but live in accordance with the Lord's day. . .' (*Magnesians* 9.1).[3] From the context it is possible that Ignatius does know of some Christians who were advocating Sabbath observance.

Why did Christians abandon Sabbath observance and worship on a new day? In comments which follow the passage just quoted, Ignatius

[1]For Graeco-Roman comments on the Jewish Sabbath, see *Greek and Latin Authors on Jews and Judaism*, ed. M. Stern (3 vols.; Jerusalem: Israeli Academy of Sciences and Humanities, 1974-80); M. Whittaker, *Jews and Christians: Graeco-Roman Views*, pp. 63-73.

[2]In this brief note Pliny the Elder states, but without comment, that 'In Judaea there is a stream which dries up every Sabbath'.

[3]The exact date of the epistles of Ignatius cannot be established. A date between AD 100 and 118 is now generally accepted. See W.R. Schoedel, *Ignatius of Antioch* (Philadelphia: Fortress, 1985), p. 5.

explicitly links Sunday worship with the Lord's resurrection. The *Epistle of Barnabas*, written perhaps a decade after Ignatius wrote to the Magnesians, makes the same link. In Chapter 15 Barnabas uses a string of OT passages to attack Sabbath observance. At the culmination of his argument he quotes Isa. 1.13 and then writes,

> Do you see what God means (in Scripture)? It is not your present Sabbaths that are acceptable, but the Sabbath which I have made, in the which, when I have set all things at rest, I will make the beginning of the eighth day which is the beginning of another world. Wherefore we keep the eighth day for rejoicing, in the which also Jesus rose from the dead, and having been manifested ascended into the heavens. (15.8-9).

A generation later in his *Dialogue with Trypho* Justin developed still further an 'eighth day' theology as part of his rejection of Sabbath observance, and his defence of Christian worship on Sunday. The 'eighth day' is the first day of the new week, on which Christ rose. (See especially *Dialogue* 41.4; also 24.1; 138.1).

In Ignatius, Barnabas, and Justin there is a similar pattern of argument. All three writers reject Sabbath observance and underpin Christian Sunday worship by stressing that Sunday is the Lord's day, the day of resurrection. Differentiation from Judaism and 'resurrection day' theology go hand in hand.

Which came first? The traditional answer stresses that Christian convictions about the resurrection of Jesus were decisive in the shift from Sabbath to Sunday. The historical evidence, however, is not quite so straight forward. For the followers of Jesus in the immediate post-Easter period, proclamation of the gospel to Gentiles and worship on a new day would have been equally dramatic departures from established practice. Whereas in some New Testament traditions proclamation of the gospel to *all nations* is linked inextricably to the resurrection of Christ (Mt. 28.18; Lk. 24.47; cf. Rom. 1.3-4, 16; Gal. 1.12-16), traditions about the resurrection do not contain even a hint that henceforth followers of Jesus were to worship on a new day. In my judgement 1 Cor. 16.2; Acts 20.7; Rev. 1.10; *Didache* 14.1 all refer to Sunday worship, but in none of these passages is choice of a new day for worship explicitly legitimated by reference to the resurrection.

The evidence for the origin of Sunday as the Christian day for worship is meagre, and some of it is very difficult to interpret. Even though we cannot trace the earlier roots of their defence of Sunday worship, theological convictions about the resurrection of Jesus were probably influential long before Ignatius, Barnabas and Justin wrote in the second century. Social factors almost certainly played a role: in order to differentiate themselves sharply from local Jewish synagogues, Christians chose a new day on which to worship. The proportion of theological and social factors probably varied from place to place, and time to time.[1]

2. *Exclusive Worship of Christ.*

Pliny knows that Christian worship of Christ differs from pagan observance of the cults of local gods. He informs Trajan that some former Christians had confirmed their apostasy by 'worshipping both your statue and the images of the gods and cursing Christ'. If worship of Christ could simply have been added on to observance of local cults, there would not have been a problem. It was the unyielding insistence of Christians on *exclusive* worship of Christ which was perceived to be politically subversive, for it carried as a corollary disrespect for the official cults of the state gods and of the Emperor himself.

If, as I have argued, Pliny knew a good deal about Jews and their distinctive patterns of worship, he must have been aware that in spite of similarities, Christian worship was quite distinctive in one crucial respect: it was focussed on Christ. Pliny surely shared his good friend Tacitus's knowledge that Christ had been executed in the fairly recent past by the procurator Pontius Pilate (*Annals* 15.44.2f.).

3. *Hymn Singing.*

Pliny's comment that Christians sang a hymn antiphonally to Christ is equally intriguing. Hymn singing and the use of musical instruments were prominent in many forms of pagan worship, so 'singing a hymn' in the context of worship would not have seemed unusual to Pliny.[2] If

---

[1]The standard discussion of the origin of Sunday remains W. Rordorf, *Sunday* (ET; London: SCM, 1968). In his *From Sabbath to Sunday* (Rome: Gregorian University Press, 1977), S. Bacchiocchi claims that the need for Gentile Christians to differentiate themselves from Judaism was an important factor in the early Christian choice of Sunday for worship. Although he overstates his case, this general point is well made. However, his claim that the adoption of Sunday as a new day of worship first took place in Rome early in the second century (and hence has no support in the NT writings) is not convincing.

[2]On pagan hymns, see, for example, Robin Lane Fox, *Pagans and Christians in the Mediterranean World from the Second Century AD to the Conversion of Constantine* (London : Penguin, 1988), pp. 114-16.

Pliny was well informed about synagogue worship, would Christian use of hymns have been seen as a similarity or a difference?

It is not as easy to answer this question as we might suppose. Prayers, and readings and exposition of Torah and the prophets were undoubtedly at the heart of synagogue worship, but the use of hymns in the first and second centuries AD is not well attested. It is often claimed that unlike Temple worship in Jerusalem, music was not used in synagogues until Byzantine times.[1]

Although both Philo and Qumran seem to provide contrary evidence, on closer inspection that evidence is not directly relevant. Philo's comments on the 'charismatic' worship of the Therapeutae are striking. The President 'expounds the sacred scriptures' and then 'sings a hymn composed as an address to God, either a new one of his own composition or an old one by poets of an earlier day. . .' Hymn singing, often antiphonal, by choirs which include men and women then follows (*Vit. Cont.* 78-89). Eusebius was so impressed by similarities with early Christian worship that he believed that Philo was referring to the first generation of St Mark's Christian converts in Alexandria (*Hist. Ecc.* ii.17)![2]

Philo, however, is *not* describing a gathering on the Sabbath for worship. The references to hymns in worship summarised in the previous paragraph form part of Philo's description of a special festival occasion, probably Pentecost. Philo does refer briefly to the Therapeutae's composition of hymns and psalms for use in solitary daily spiritual exercises (*Vit. Cont.* 29), but in his comments on their Sabbath assemblies he does not say anything about the use of music (30-9).

The Qumran Thanksgiving Hymns (1QH) were probably intended for private use, or for use in the liturgical services of the Qumran community. G. Vermes speculates that they may have been used during the feast of the renewal of the covenant on the Feast of Weeks (Pentecost) and draws a parallel with the Therapeutae, the Egyptian 'contemplative Essenes'.[3] Be that as it may, there is no evidence in the

---

[1]See I. Elbogen, *Der jüdische Gottesdienst* (1931; 3rd ed. Hildesheim: Georg Olms), p. 502. Cf. Paul Bradshaw, *The Search for the Origins of Christian Worship*, p. 23: 'There is . . . an almost total lack of documentary evidence for the inclusion of psalms in synagogue worship.'

[2]This view has been revived without success in modern times. See F.H. Colson's discussion in his introduction to *De Vita Contemplativa* in Vol. IX of the Loeb edition of Philo's writings (Cambridge, Mass.: Harvard, 1941), pp 103-111.

[3]*The Dead Sea Scrolls: Qumran in Perspective* (London : Collins, 1977), p. 57 and p. 178.

Qumran writings which suggests that the Thanksgiving Hymns were used in a Sabbath liturgy.

Philo and the Qumran writings, then, do not refer to the use of music in synagogue worship on the Sabbath. However, two recently published inscriptions offer important fresh evidence. An epitaph from a Jewish catacomb in Rome reads, 'Here lies Gaianos, secretary, psalm-singer (ψαλμωδός), lover of the Law. May his sleep be in peace.'[1] The term ψαλμωδός refers to his formal role as a cantor in synagogue worship. The inscription is difficult to date, but others from the same catacomb come from the third or fourth century AD.

The now justly famous third century inscription from Aphrodisias records a charitable donation to a synagogue community by Jews (including a few proselytes) and 'God-worshippers'.[2] On face *a*, line 15 refers to Benjamin, a psalm-singer (ψαλμο[λόγος?]). The editors conclude their careful discussion by suggesting that

> it looks as though ψαλμο[λόγος?] here makes it even more probable that psalm-singing (in Greek, no doubt) was common in synagogue services in the western diaspora by the third century, and that it involved a choir, or at least individual singers, rather than general congregational singing alone.

These two inscriptions are much later than Pliny's day, but they suggest that early in the second century Christian use of psalms and hymns in regular weekly worship *may* well have had some precedent in synagogue worship.[3] The references in 1 Cor. 14.15, 26; Col. 3.16; Eph. 5.19 to the singing of psalms, hymns, and spiritual songs suggest that they were prominent, perhaps even central, in early Christian worship. Two of these passages link worship and Christian experience of the in-dwelling Christ (Col. 3.15) or the Spirit (Eph. 5.18). Clearly this is a distinctive feature of early Christian worship and experience. From the evidence which has come down to us (and fresh discoveries may well modify the picture unexpectedly), psalms and hymns seem to have been more prominent in Christian worship than in the synagogue liturgy, but we cannot say more than that.

---

[1]For the full Greek text and discussion see G.H.R. Horsley, *New Documents Illustrating Early Christianity* (Macquarie University, 1981), I, pp. 115-6.

[2]For the text and full discussion see Reynolds and Tannenbaum, *Jews and Godfearers at Aphrodisias*.

[3]Reynolds and Tannenbaum, p. 46, refer to 3 Macc. 6.32, 35; 7.13, 16 as a probable indication from the first century BC or first century AD that Jewish congregational worship (at least in Alexandria) included the singing of psalms and hymns.

Pliny's reference to a *carmen* in Christian worship probably points to a characteristic emphasis of Christian worship in comparison with synagogue worship, rather than to a unique feature.

4. *The Oath.*

Pliny's reference to the oath (*sacramentum* in Pliny can only mean an oath) taken by Christians in the context of worship has been much discussed. Christians bound themselves by oath 'not to commit theft or banditry or adultery, not to betray a trust, not to refuse a trust of a deposit if requested'. Since the last two items are not part of the Decalogue, this should probably be taken as a general list of Christian (and Jewish) ethical teaching rather than as a reference to the use of the Decalogue in Christian worship.[1]

Jewish and Christian use of the Decalogue is fascinating. In synagogue worship recitation of the Decalogue before the *shema* is attested from about 150 BC in the Nash papyrus. In the middle of the second century (most clearly in *Ptolemy's Letter to Flora*) Christians began to single out the Decalogue as that part of the Law which should be kept by Christians who had abandoned its 'ritual' aspects. The Decalogue was later dropped in synagogue worship. Why? A rabbinic tradition (*j. Ber.* 21a; *b. Ber.* 12a) says that its use was discontinued because of the 'insinuations of the sectarians'. This may well be a rare case of early Christian practice influencing the development of Jewish liturgy: the rabbinic tradition may be a reaction to the priority and centrality given by Christians to the Decalogue at the expense of the rest of Torah.[2]

5. *Parting and Coming Together Again for a Meal.*

Unfortunately Pliny's comment on a second meeting for a meal is too enigmatic to enable us to make meaningful comparisons with contemporary pagan and Jewish worship.[3] Pliny notes that at the end of the meeting before dawn, Christians 'were in the habit of parting and coming together again for a meal, but food common and harmless; they had stopped doing this after my edict, by which according to

---

[1]See A.N. Sherwin-White, *The Letters of Pliny*, pp. 706-7, for a discussion of suggestions that *sacramentum* is a reference to baptism and/or the eucharist.

[2]See further, E. Lerle, 'Liturgische Reformen des Synagogengottesdienstes als Antwort auf die judenchristliche Mission des ersten Jahrhunderts', *NovT* 10 (1968) pp. 31-42, esp. 34-5.

[3]E. Schürer, *The History of the Jewish People*, Vol. III. 1, pp. 144-5, notes that just as with the pagan cult-associations, 'festival meals' were arranged by Jewish communities, even in the diaspora.

your (Trajan's) instructions I had banned clubs'. We do not know at what time of the day the second meal took place. Was it a simple communal meal, the Agape perhaps? Or was it a eucharist? The phrase 'common and harmless food' (*cibum promiscuum et innoxium*) could refer to either.

There is a further puzzle. Who was prepared to abandon the second meeting following Pliny's edict banning clubs? The Latin is unclear at this point. If Pliny intended to indicate that the apostates stopped attending a second meeting, then it may well have been a eucharist. But if he is referring to the whole Christian community, then it is unlikely that they would have been willing to agree to stop meeting for a eucharistic meal.

The 'Kerygma Petrou'

I now turn to comments from an 'insider' which were written at about the same time as the 'outsider' Pliny's report on the nature of early Christian worship. In nine passages in his writings Clement of Alexandria quotes from or refers to the *Kerygma Petrou*. Clement has a high regard for this work, which he assumes was composed by Peter. Since it was used by the Valentinian Gnostic Heracleon in the middle of the second century, and by the apologist Aristides who wrote during the reign of Hadrian, it was almost certainly written at about the same time as Pliny wrote to Trajan, or only shortly afterwards.[1]

By far the longest quotation concerns early Christian worship. Clement quotes (and comments briefly on) four paragraphs which

---

[1]For a fuller discussion of the date of the *Kerygma Petrou*, see W. Schneemelcher in *New Testament Apocrypha* II, ed. E. Hennecke (ET; London: Lutterworth, 1965), pp. 94-8. (The section on the *Kerygma Petrou* in the fifth German edition of *Neutestamentliche Apokryphen* II, ed. W. Schneemelcher [Tübingen: Mohr, 1989], contains only a few changes from the English translation of the fourth German edition). See also R.M. Grant, *Greek Apologists of the Second Century* (London: SCM, 1988), pp. 34-43. Grant accepts that Aristides probably depends on the *Kerygma Petrou*. The literary relationship seems to me to be so close as to leave little doubt. Chapter 14 of the Syriac version of Aristides seems to be an abbreviation of the *Kerygma Petrou*; the reference to the shining of the moon (discussed below) has been omitted, no doubt because its significance was no longer appreciated. For an English translation of both the Greek and Syriac versions of Aristides, see the Additional Volume of the Ante-Nicene Christian Library, ed. A. Menzies (Edinburgh: T&T Clark, 1897). For an introduction, critical edition of the text, and commentary, see J. Geffcken, *Zwei griechische Apologeten* (Leipzig and Berlin: B.G. Teubner, 1907), especially pp. 82-3 on ch. 14.

clearly originally belonged together in the *Kerygma Petrou.* The extract opens with a statement about the one God 'who created the beginning of all things and who has the power to set an end'. It is followed by an exhortation 'not to worship this God in the manner of the Greeks' and standard Christian polemic against idols and animal sacrifices. The two paragraphs which follow are of particular interest:

> Neither worship (σέβεσθε) God in the manner of the Jews; for they also, who think that they alone know God, do not understand, serving (λατρεύοντες) angels and archangels, the month and the moon. And when the moon does not shine, they do not celebrate the so-called first Sabbath, also they do not celebrate the new moon or the feast of unleavened bread or the feast (of Tabernacles) or the great day (of atonement)...
>
> Worship (σέβεσθε) God through Christ in a new way. For we have found in the Scriptures, how the Lord says: 'Behold, I make with you a new covenant, not as I made (one) with your Fathers in Mount Horeb'. A new one has he made with us. For what has reference to the Greeks and Jews is old. But we are Christians, who as a third race (τρίτῳ γένει) worship him in a new way.[1]

Although Pliny does not relate early Christian worship directly to pagan or to Jewish worship, in my comments above I have tried to show that his report to Trajan can be considered from this perspective. The *Kerygma Petrou* provides strong support, for it differentiates sharply Christian worship from the worship of the (pagan) Greeks on the one hand, and from the Jews on the other. The fragment quoted above is our earliest explicit evidence for Christian self-identification as a *tertium genus*, a 'third people' over against both the Graeco-Roman world and Judaism;[2] the roots of this view are found in several New Testament writings.[3]

There is fierce polemic against the 'old' Jewish way of worshipping God by 'serving' angels and archangels, and the month and the

---

[1] I have quoted (with modifications) George Ogg's translation in *New Testament Apocrypha* II, pp. 99-100 (as cited in the previous note). (Ogg translates both σέβεσθε and λατρεύοντες by 'worship', thus missing the point to which I shall drawn attention below). I have quoted the Greek text from E. Klostermann's critical edition, *Apocrypha* I (Kleine Texte 3; Bonn: Marcus und E. Weber's Verlag, 1908), pp. 13-15.

[2] See also Aristides, *Apology* (Syriac) Ch. 14; *The Epistle to Diognetus* chs. 1 and 2; Justin, *Dialogue with Trypho* 10; Origen, *Contra Celsum*, I.26.

[3] See especially 1 Cor. 1.22-4; 10.32; 1 Pet. 2.19f.; Mt. 21.43 and 24.9. On Matthew, see G.N. Stanton, *A Gospel for a New People: Studies in Matthew* (Edinburgh: T&T Clark, 1992), pp. 160-1 and 378-80.

moon. By switching from σέβεσθε to λατρεύοντες, the author makes a careful distinction between true worship of God and what he takes to be mere cultic observances. Since, as we shall see in a moment, the polemic against Jewish celebration of the (first) Sabbath, new moon, and festivals is quite specific and can be correlated with Jewish evidence, it is probable that the author intends to describe a current Jewish angel cultus. Whether he has understood and interpreted it correctly is another matter.[1]

The reference in the *Kerygma Petrou* to the shining of the moon as a pre-requisite for the celebration of the 'first Sabbath', the new moon, and the three great annual festivals is elucidated by the Mishnaic tractate, *Rosh ha-Shanah* 1.1–3.1. At the time the *Kerygma Petrou* was written, and probably until the first half of the fourth century AD, the duration of each month (and hence the date of the festivals) was not fixed in advance; it had to be determined by observation of the new moon's appearance by trustworthy witnesses. If the sky was covered by clouds, then the new moon could not be hallowed.[2] Following formal declaration of observation of the new moon, messengers were sent to the diaspora. According to rabbinic traditions which are difficult to date, if the messengers did not reach the diaspora in time for Passover, Tabernacles or the Day of Atonement, an additional festival day could be observed in order to provide for doubts.[3]

The author of the *Kerygma Petrou* would not have bothered to comment in detail and to pour scorn on these practices unless he and his readers knew about them at first hand. We do in fact have evidence which confirms that it was the general practice in synagogues of the diaspora to celebrate new moons and the annual festivals, as well as the Sabbath.[4] And we also know from first century writings, as

---

[1]For a fuller discussion and a rather different view, see L. Hurtado, *One God, One Lord: Early Christian Devotion and Ancient Jewish Monotheism* (London: SCM, 1988), pp. 33-4.

[2]See the full discussion in E. Schürer, *The History of the Jewish People*, Vol. I, Appendix III, pp. 587-601; *The Jewish People in the First Century* (Compendium Rerum Iudaicarum ad Novum Testamentum), Vol. II, ed. S. Safrai and M. Stern (Assen/Amsterdam: Van Gorcum, 1976), pp. 834-64, esp. pp. 848-9.

[3]See *The History of the Jewish People*, II, p. 852.

[4]See H. Hegermann, 'The Diaspora in the Hellenistic Age', in *The Cambridge History of Judaism* (Cambridge: CUP, 1989), II, p. 153; E. Schürer, *The History of the Jewish People*, I, p. 144-5. See, for example, Josephus, *Antiquities*, xiv. 213-16 (Delos); xiv. 241 (Laodicea); xiv. 256-8 (Halicarnassus). For inscriptions from Rome, see H.J. Leon, *The Jews of Ancient Rome* (Philadelphia: Jewish Publication Society of America, 1960), p. 196.

well as from the *Kerygma Petrou* early in the second century, that many Christians rejected completely these Jewish religious observances.

Gal. 4.9 confirms that in Paul's day some Galatian Christians were adopting the Jewish calendar. Since the verb παρατηρέω which Paul uses to refer to observance of 'days and months and seasons and years' is not used in the LXX or the New Testament to refer to *religious* observance, commentators have long been puzzled. But perhaps παρατηρέω can be given its more usual sense, 'watch' or 'observe' (literally). The *Kerygma Petrou* may help us to appreciate Paul's polemic: perhaps he is ridiculing Jewish religious observances which all depend (ultimately) on literal observance of the arrival of the new moon.

Rom. 14.5 is also to be read in the light of the Jewish religious calendar. Some Christians in Rome (perhaps a Jewish Christian congregation) stress the importance of meticulous observance of 'days', i.e. Sabbaths and feast days; other Christians (perhaps another congregation) judge all days to be alike.[1] Col. 2.16 is more specific: observance of festivals, new moons, and Sabbaths are linked (and rejected), as in the *Kerygma Petrou.*

Since there is no trace of direct dependence of the *Kerygma Petrou* on Gal. 4.9, Rom. 14.5, or Col. 2.16, we have important evidence that in the middle of the first century and early in the second century Christians took pains to distance themselves from Jewish religious observances. In all four cases local rivalry between Jews and Christians may well be in the background. Since observance of the Sabbath, new moons, and annual festivals are linked already and criticised fiercely in Isa. 1.13-14, this line of Christian anti-Jewish polemic is a development of earlier 'inner Jewish' polemic.[2]

Conclusions

The *Kerygma Petrou* stresses that on the basis of the new covenant Christians worship God through Christ in a new way. Unfortunately we are not told what forms that new way of worship took, though it

---

[1] See especially F.B. Watson, *Paul, Judaism and the Gentiles: A Sociological Approach* (Cambridge: CUP, 1986), pp. 84-8.

[2] For positive references which link observance of the Sabbath, of the new moon, and of the annual festivals, see Judith 8.6 and 1 Macc. 10.34.

certainly did not include celebration of the Sabbath, new moons, or the Jewish festivals.

Although early Christian worship was deeply indebted to Jewish worship, much was simply abandoned. Why were only two of the Jewish festivals (Passover and Pentecost) taken over and adapted by Christians? In modern times many Christians have rediscovered the value of linking worship to the rhythms of the seasons. In the first and second centuries, however, Christians were more coy about adapting the religious festivals of their rivals. The only two which were 'Christianised' could be associated readily with the 'story' of Jesus Christ. Since the others could not, they were abandoned.

The 'outsider' Pliny's report to Trajan and the 'insider' who wrote the *Kerygma Petrou* both remind us that early Christian worship quickly became quite distinctive. Christians met on a new day and sang hymns to Christ 'as to a god'; the new way of Christian worship was *through Jesus Christ.* Both writings confirm that it was convictions about Christ which lay at the heart of early Christian patterns of worship which were quite unlike pagan religious practices, and, in spite of some similarities, very different from synagogue worship.

PART II

THEOLOGY

RIGHTEOUSNESS IN MATTHEW'S THEOLOGY

Donald A. Hagner

Although the Gospel of Matthew has in recent years become the focus of much academic study, as the appearance of a number of monographs and new commentaries testifies, on several central issues scholars have been unable to come to a common mind. This appears to be the case with the understanding of righteousness (δικαιοσύνη) in Matthew, even if a particular view may presently seem to be emerging as the majority opinion (viz., that the word consistently refers to the performance of righteous deeds in obedience to God).[1] A closely related question concerns the role of grace (if any) over against the obvious emphasis upon works in Matthew's perspective.

Matthew has commonly been seen as the antipode to Paul. Paul's doctrine of justification by faith apart from works of the law is usually regarded as diametrically opposed to Matthew's stress on a righteousness by works. An established principle of critical scholarship is that a document is to be understood on its own terms, within its own framework of thought. In accord with this, the cardinal error in dealing with such subjects as grace and righteousness in Matthew is to 'paulinize' Matthew, i.e., to read Matthew through the eyes of Paul. With the cry 'Let Matthew be Matthew!' no one, of course, should disagree. Yet it is a legitimate question whether some scholars have not overdrawn the differences between Matthew and Paul,[2] in fact by not listening carefully enough to either.

---

[1]Yet, reviewing the ongoing debate, W. Popkes can say 'Zumindest Stellen wie Mt 5,6 und 6,33 werden für die indikativische Interpretation reklamiert, sogar auf Kosten der Einheitlichkeit des matthäischen δικαιοσύνη-Verständnisses'. 'Die Gerechtigkeitstradition im Matthäus-Evangelium', *ZNW* 80 (1989), pp. 1-23 (2).

[2]For a recent attempt to correct the excessive polarization, see the excellent monograph of R. Mohrlang, *Matthew and Paul: A Comparison of Ethical Perspectives* (SNTSMS, 48; Cambridge: Cambridge University Press, 1984).

The present essay consists of three main parts, examining: (1) the tension between law and gospel in Matthew, (2) the place of grace in Matthew's theology, and (3) the specific occurrences of δικαιοσύνη in the Gospel.

The Law

It is hardly necessary to review in detail the conspicuous place given to the law in Matthew. Many know Matthew primarily through the Sermon on the Mount and its daunting description of righteousness. Near the beginning of the sermon, in 5.17-20, occurs a passage regarded by many as quintessentially Matthean. There Jesus speaks of not coming to abolish the law, and asserts that 'not one letter, not one stroke of a letter, will pass from the law', that even 'the least of these commandments' remains important, and that the righteousness of the disciples must exceed that of the scribes and Pharisees. This passage naturally requires interpretation,[1] but the importance it places upon faithfulness to the law is probably to be explained by the Jewish Christians for whom Matthew is writing. The sermon ends on a similarly strong note concerning obedience to the will of the Father (7.21) and the words of Jesus (7.24-27). We mention further only the importance of reward (μισθός) in the Gospel (e.g., 6.1ff.; 10.41f.) and such passages as 16.27, 'For the Son of Man is to come with his angels in the glory of his Father, and then he will repay everyone for what has been done' (cf. 25.31-46); 19.17, where Jesus says 'If you wish to enter into life, keep the commandments'; and the exceptionally important commission at the end of the Gospel to 'make disciples . . . teaching them to obey everything that I have commanded you' (28.19f.).

But if there is a particularly strong emphasis on *demand* in Matthew, there is also a strong emphasis—indeed, arguably a stronger emphasis—on *gift*. This is found in the 'gospel of the kingdom' (4.23; 9.35; 24.14), the dominant motif in Matthew of the arrival of the 'kingdom of heaven' (at the beginning of the ministry of Jesus, 4.17; and among many references, see esp. 10.7; 12.28 ['of God']; 19.14).

[1] A simple, straightforward reading of the passage is difficult to square with other material in the Gospel, e.g., the antitheses that immediately follow (especially the third, fifth and sixth), and Jesus' attitude towards the sabbath (12.1-14), the dietary law (15.1-20), and the Mosaic allowance of divorce (19.3-9).

The call to righteousness is made within the larger framework of the Gospel and its main theme, which is the announcement of the good news of the kingdom. The Sermon on the Mount itself must be understood within the framework of the whole Gospel and not in isolation.[1] Further to be noted is the fact that the Sermon is preceded by a statement of grace in the Beatitudes,[2] the first of which begins with the affirmation: 'Blessed are the poor in spirit, for theirs is the kingdom of heaven' (5.3; cf. the inclusio of 5.10). The kingdom is the gift of God, a matter of grace, not of human accomplishment.

Matthew, then, does not simply present a forceful restatement of the Torah. Nor is Jesus represented as the deliverer of a *nova lex* to be put in the place of the Mosaic law.[3] What Matthew is supremely concerned with is God's new act of grace in and through Jesus the eschatological Messiah,[4] whereby the hoped-for kingdom has begun to dawn. It is natural to ask, however, whether the priority and prominence of the gift of the kingdom in Matthew really have any functional significance in light of such strong statements concerning *demand* as those mentioned above. Is not Matthew's soteriology in the last analysis governed by the issue of obedience? Is not salvation finally determined by obeying the commandments of Torah as mediated by the teaching of Jesus?

To begin with, we should note that even in a writer such as Paul, whose commitment to the priority of grace is unquestionable, we encounter statements of uncompromising demand. A few of the more notorious ones may be found in Rom. 2.6-10, 'For he will repay according to each one's deeds . . . There will be anguish and distress

---

[1]'The SM is in the middle of a story about God's acted love, his gracious overture to his people through his Son, the Messiah Jesus. The story, read in its entirety, is about Jesus Christ, not just ethics; and it brings together gift and task, grace and law, benefit and demand'; W.D. Davies and D.C. Allison, Jr., 'Reflections on the Sermon on the Mount', *SJT* 44 (1991), pp. 283-309 (299).

[2]*Pace* U. Luz, *Matthew 1-7: A Commentary* (trans. W.C. Linss; Minneapolis: Augsburg, 1989), p. 215. Yet Luz regards the sermon as 'embedded in the history of God's action with Jesus', which is a matter of grace, and therefore concludes that its interpretation must 'proceed from Christology' (p. 215).

[3]Thus, rightly, both G. Bornkamm and G. Barth in Bornkamm, Barth, and Held, *Tradition and Interpretation in Matthew* (trans. P. Scott; Philadelphia: Westminster, 1963), pp. 35 (n. 2), 153ff. 'Nor can one speak of a *nova lex* in Matthew', notes Barth, in the sense 'that the Christian message has become a law . . . The law and the saving deeds of Christ in his death and resurrection do not fall apart, but are closely bound together by the concern of Matthew for the establishing of the judgment of God' (p. 159).

[4]Mohrlang concludes: 'the centre of Matthew's focus has shifted away from the law to Jesus himself'. *Matthew and Paul*, p. 25.

for everyone who does evil, the Jew first and also the Greek, but glory and honor and peace for everyone who does good, the Jew first and also the Greek,' and in Gal. 6.7f., 'Do not be deceived; God is not mocked, for you reap whatever you sow. If you sow to your own flesh, you will reap corruption from the flesh; but if you sow to the Spirit, you will reap eternal life from the Spirit' (cf. Gal. 5.19ff.). We may further note Paul's affirmative statements concerning the law itself. Thus in Rom. 3.31 he writes: 'Do we then overthrow the law by this faith? By no means! On the contrary, we uphold the law,' with which we may compare Rom. 7.12: 'So the law is holy, and the commandment is holy and just and good' and the quite remarkable statement in 1 Cor. 7.19: 'Circumcision is nothing, and uncircumcision is nothing; but obeying the commandments of God is everything' (NRSV; but the verbless clause ἀλλὰ τήρησις ἐντολῶν θεοῦ is probably more effectively translated: 'but what does matter is keeping the commandments of God').

It is of course not our intention in citing Paul to suggest that Matthew and Paul are saying the same thing, or to minimize the obvious differences between the two.[1] The point to be gained is that a strong commitment to the central importance of grace—even grace over against works (which of course we do not find in Matthew)—does not preclude very strong and positive statements about the law and the commandments, or the necessity of good works. Put differently: the stress on the law, the commandments and righteousness in Matthew is not necessarily incompatible with an emphasis on grace and even an appreciation of its priority. Matthew's distinctiveness in the NT canon is, in my opinion, primarily the result of his Jewish-Christian community and their needs. The evangelist has carefully searched the traditions available to him for anything that could be used to reinforce the conservatism of his community (e.g. 10.5f.; 15.24). For the same reason he refuses to take up certain elements of his major source (e.g., Mk 7.19c) and modifies others (cf. the whole of Mk 7.1-23 with Mt. 15.1-20). Matthew's Jewish-Christian community found itself somewhere between the non-Christian Jews on the one hand, and the Gentile Christian community on the other. The members of Matthew's community needed all that they could find to preserve some degree of credibility for their claims *vis-à-vis* the

---

[1]Mohrlang has, in my opinion, done a particularly fine job of capturing both the similarities and the clear differences between the two writers (*Matthew and Paul*, esp. pp. 42-47).

Jewish community which would almost certainly have continued to challenge their Christian faith.[1]

One of the most important items would have been the question of the ongoing faithfulness of the community to the Torah, which would in turn have raised the issue of Jesus' relation to the Torah. The evangelist takes material from the tradition concerning Jesus' attitude to the Torah and construes it in the most conservative way possible for the sake of his community. And yet he is unable to conceal altogether the radical aspects of Jesus and the Torah. For while Matthew looks for continuity with the old and will thus emphasize the law and the righteousness of obeying the commandments, he cannot suppress the inevitable newness that naturally accompanies the gospel of the kingdom and the presence of the Messiah who brings the kingdom.[2]

Grace

How much actual evidence, however, is there of an emphasis upon grace in the theology of Matthew? And where, if at all, does the evangelist articulate a doctrine of grace?

As we have indicated above, the main burden of Matthew's narrative—the message itself of the dawning of the kingdom in the ministry of Jesus—rests totally upon the grace of God. Since both the teaching and the healing ministry of Jesus are directly related to the reality of the gospel of the kingdom they can correctly be taken as manifestations of the grace of God. The motif of grace is conspicuously present (even if at times only implicitly) at a number of specific points. As examples we call attention to the following. A prominent theme in Matthew is the acceptance of the unworthy—in particular, the 'tax collectors and sinners' (cf. 9.10-13, and especially the final logion: 'For I have come to call not the righteous but sinners'; and 21.31f.). So striking was this attitude of Jesus that he became characterized as 'a glutton and a drunkard, a friend of tax collectors and sinners' (11.19). Consonant with this is the invitation of 'everyone'—'both good and

---

[1]See further, D.A. Hagner, 'The *Sitz im Leben* of the Gospel of Matthew', (SBLSP, 24; Atlanta: Scholars, 1985), pp. 243-269.

[2]For Matthew christology is of determinative importance. R. Banks has captured this well in his oft-quoted words: 'It therefore becomes apparent that it is not so much *Jesus*' stance towards the Law that he is concerned to depict: it is how the *Law* stands with regard to him, as the one who brings it to fulfilment and to whom all attention must now be directed'; *Jesus and the Law in the Synoptic Tradition* (SNTSMS, 28; Cambridge: Cambridge University Press, 1975), p. 226; cf. pp. 251f.

bad'—to the wedding feast, in the parable of 22.1-10, as well as the concern for the single straying sheep in 18.10-14 (even if Matthew has apparently altered this Q material by applying it to straying members of the Christian community).

The description of discipleship and greatness in terms of humble childlikeness (18.1-4; cf. 19.14) and service (20.26f.; 23.11f.), together with the repeated reference to the disciples as the μικροί, 'little ones' (10.42; 18.6, 10, 14), suggests total dependence on God and the gifts of God rather than on achievement which wins God's favor. So too the doctrine of election that emerges in a few passages (e.g., 11.27; 22.14) points in the same direction.

Although lacking some of the striking parables of grace contained in Luke (e.g., Lk. 15.8-10, 11-32; 18.9-14), Matthew does contain two unique parables related to this theme. The parable of the workers in the vineyard (20.1-16) tells of workers who came at the last hour being paid the same amount as those who had worked through the whole day, and concludes with the logion 'So the last will be first, and the first will be last'. The parable of the unforgiving servant (18.23-35) begins with the story of a servant being forgiven a debt so large as to be practically beyond imagination.

It is indeed the forgiveness of sins that constitutes the essence of grace. But that is precisely what the gospel, the story of Jesus, is all about. At the beginning of the narrative we are thus told 'he will save his people from their sins' (1.21). Centrally located in the Sermon on the Mount is the Lord's Prayer with its petition for the forgiveness of sins (6.12)[1] and, anticipating the parable of the unforgiving servant, the words 'For if you forgive others their trespasses, your heavenly Father will also forgive you; but if you do not forgive others, neither will your Father forgive your trespasses' (6.14f.). Several times in the narrative the forgiveness of sins is highlighted (e.g. 9.2, 6; 12.31). Of incomparable importance is the atoning death of Jesus: 'the Son of Man came not to be served but to serve, and to give his life a ransom for many' (20.28), with which we may compare 26.28: 'for this is my blood of the covenant, which is poured out for many for the forgiveness of sins'.[2] The conclusion of R. Mohrlang is correct: 'In effect,

---

[1]See P. Stuhlmacher, 'Jesu vollkommenes Gesetz der Freiheit. Zum Verständnis der Bergpredigt', *ZTK* 79 (1982), pp. 283-322 (311f.).

[2]In his denial of the importance of the forgiveness of sins as a part of Matthew's indicative (over against imperative), G. Strecker fails to mention the important passages 1.21; 20.28; and 26.28. *Der Weg der Gerechtigkeit: Untersuchung zur Theologie des Matthäus* (3rd edn; Göttingen:

grace is implicit in the *whole story* of Jesus told by the evangelist'.[1] To be sure, as Mohrlang points out, the 'underlying structure of grace' is 'presupposed' or 'taken for granted'. If this is the case, however, may we not conclude that Matthew's admittedly important imperative is built upon the indicative of God's grace? Although Mohrlang cautiously resists this conclusion, it could be argued that something as fundamental to the Gospel as this is, something that underlies the totality and is presupposed throughout (even in the passages of ethical demand), may be concluded to underlie and serve as the basis of the imperative.[2] According to G. Stanton, 'In the Sermon on the Mount and in the gospel as a whole, grace and demand are linked inextricably'.[3] Still, Matthew has not become Paul. He lacks altogether the vocabulary of grace (the frequent Pauline word χάρις does not occur once in Matthew) and does not explicitly connect grace and ethics as Paul so frequently does. Nevertheless, the difference between Matthew and Paul is not as great as has so often been thought.[4]

Righteousness

The foregoing discussion has attempted to show that the Gospel of Matthew, for all of its emphasis on the ethical imperative, gives far more place to the indicative, to gift and grace, than is often realized. In light of this, we propose to examine the correctness of the conclu-

---

Vandenhoeck & Ruprecht, 1971), pp. 148f. Cf. P. Stuhlmacher on the importance of forgiveness of sins for Matthew's community: 'Ihr Glaube ist deshalb bewusstes, tätiges Vertrauen auf Gottes Vergebung'; *Gerechtigkeit Gottes bei Paulus* (2nd edn; Göttingen: Vandenhoeck & Ruprecht, 1966), p. 191.

[1] *Matthew and Paul*, p. 80. On grace in Matthew, see R.T. France, *Matthew: Evangelist and Teacher* (Grand Rapids: Zondervan, 1989), pp. 268-70.

[2] Mohrlang points out that 'There is one point, however, at which Matthew's conception of God's grace clearly exceeds that of Paul; and that is in his understanding of Jesus' *teachings* as an expression of grace' (*Matthew and Paul*, p. 91). If this is correct, it may add support to the conclusion that the indicative is basic to the imperative for Matthew.

[3] 'The Origin and Purpose of Matthew's Sermon on the Mount', in G.F. Hawthorne and O. Betz (eds.), *Tradition and Interpretation in the New Testament*, Essays in Honor of E.E. Ellis (Grand Rapids: Eerdmans/Tübingen: J.C.B. Mohr, 1987), pp. 181-92 (190).

[4] For a helpful discussion on the issue of righteousness in Matthew and Paul, see H. Giesen, *Christliches Handeln: Eine redaktionskritische Untersuchung zum δικαιοσύνη-Begriff im Matthäus-Evangelium* (Europäische Hochschulschriften Reihe XXIII Bd. 181; Frankfurt am Main: Peter Lang, 1982), pp. 237-63. On the question of salvation by works in Matthew and Paul, see D. Marguerat, *Le Jugement dans l'Évangile de Matthieu* (Geneva: Labor et Fides, 1981), pp. 212-35.

sion that Matthew uses δικαιοσύνη to refer consistently and exclusively to the obedience of demand. Is it in principle an impossibility that the evangelist can on occasion have used the word in a quasi-Pauline sense, referring to the gracious activity of God? This of course can only be determined by a careful examination of the passages in question.

There is now evidence of a trend among leading Matthean scholars to take all seven occurrences of δικαιοσύνη as referring to the righteousness that corresponds to ethical demand. Although this view was taken already by G. Strecker,[1] D. Hill[2] and J. Dupont,[3] it has more recently received new life in part through the influential full-length monograph on the subject by B. Przybylski,[4] being accepted by R. Mohrlang[5] and now adopted in the two monumental commentaries currently being produced by U. Luz[6] and W.D. Davies-D.C. Allison.[7] At least two scholars (M.J. Fiedler[8] and H. Giesen[9]) have attempted, on the other hand, to defend just the opposite conclusion, i.e., that in all its occurrences in Matthew the word refers to the righteousness that is a gift dependent upon God's saving activity. In fact, however, the opposition is not always as absolute as this implies, since each side is occasionally willing to admit some truth on the other. Thus it can be admitted that underlying the demand is an element of presupposed gift, or that included in the gift is also an element of demand. The

---

[1]*Weg der Gerechtigkeit*, pp. 153-58, 179-81, 187. W. Trilling affirms Strecker's conclusion in his *Das Wahre Israel: Studien zur Theologie des Matthäus-Evangeliums* (SANT, 10; 3rd edn; München: Kösel, 1964), p. 184, n. 91.

[2]D. Hill, *Greek Words with Hebrew Meanings* (Cambridge: Cambridge University Press, 1967), p. 124-28; and *The Gospel of Matthew* (NCB; London: Marshall, Morgan & Scott, 1972).

[3]*Les Béatitudes*, vol 3, 'Les Évangelistes' (new edn; Paris: Gabalda, 1973), pp. 211-305.

[4]*Righteousness in Matthew and his World of Thought* (SNTSMS, 41; Cambridge: Cambridge University Press, 1980), p. 99.

[5]*Matthew and Paul*, p. 114. Mohrlang nevertheless adds that 'Behind the focus on demand and obedience . . . lie implicit elements of grace that, though rarely emphasised or drawn out, must not be overlooked' (p. 114).

[6]*Matthew 1-7*, pp. 177-79, 237f., 407.

[7]*The Gospel According to Saint Matthew* (ICC; Edinburgh: T. & T. Clark, 1988), I, p. 327, 'with the possible exception of 5.6'.

[8]*Der Begriff δικαιοσύνη im Matthäus-Evangelium, auf seine Grundlagen untersucht*, unpublished diss. theol. Halle, 1957. See his 'Gerechtigkeit im Matthäus-Evangelium', in *Theologische Versuche* 8 (1977), pp. 63-75; and also 'Δικαιοσύνη in der diaspora-jüdischen und intertestamentarischen Literatur', *JSJ* 1 (1970), pp. 120-43.

[9]*Christliches Handeln*, pp. 237-41. 6.1 appears to be an exception (p. 150), yet even here gift is the underlying reality that precedes the challenge to 'the new righteousness' (p. 165).

question concerns where the center of gravity lies, and on that point the difference in viewpoint remains clear.

In contrast to these viewpoints that stress Matthew's consistency in the use of the word δικαιοσύνη, a number of scholars conclude that sometimes the word is to be understood as gift and in other instances as demand. Here we may mention by way of example, P. Stuhlmacher,[1] J.A. Ziesler,[2] E. Schweizer,[3] J.P. Meier,[4] R.A. Guelich,[5] J. Reumann,[6] R.H. Gundry,[7] R.G. Bratcher,[8] and F.J. Matera.[9] Here again decisions are not always clear since sometimes

---

[1]*Gerechtigkeit Gottes bei Paulus* (2nd edn; Göttingen: Vandenhoeck & Ruprecht, 1966), pp. 188-91. Stuhlmacher finds gift in 5.6 and 6.33; demand in 3.15; and 5.10, 20.

[2]*The Meaning of Righteousness in Paul: A Linguistic and Theological Enquiry* (SNTSMS, 20; Cambridge: Cambridge University Press, 1972), pp. 130-36. For Ziesler all seven occurrences of the word refer to 'Christian behaviour' (p. 133; cf. p. 131 for 21.32), but since in 5.6 and 6.33 he also finds the gift of righteousness, we include him here rather than with those of the previous group, who see the word used consistently in Matthew.

[3]*The Good News According to Matthew* (trans. D.E. Green; Atlanta: John Knox, 1975), pp. 53-56. Gift: 5.6; 6.33; demand: 3.15; 5.20; 21.32; 'open': 5.10.

[4]*Law and History in Matthew's Gospel: A Redactional Study of Mt. 5:17-48* (AnBib 71; Rome: Biblical Institute Press, 1976), pp. 77-80. Gift: 3.15; 5.6; 6.33; demand: 5.10, 20; 6.1; 'both': 21.32.

[5]*The Sermon on the Mount: A Foundation for Understanding* (Waco, TX: Word, 1982), pp. 84-87. Guelich's excursus discusses only the five occurrences in the Sermon on the Mount. Gift: 5.6; 6.33; conduct: 5.10, 20; 6.1. Guelich concludes that righteousness in the sermon is, in addition to being ethical, soteriological and eschatological ('or, more accurately, christological'), p. 87.

[6]*Righteousness in the New Testament: 'Justification' in the United States Lutheran—Roman Catholic Dialogue*, with responses by J.A. Fitzmyer and J.D. Quinn (Philadelphia: Fortress/New York: Paulist, 1982), pp. 127-35. Gift: 5.6; 6.33; demand: 5.10, 20; 6.1. Reumann takes 3.15 and 21.32 as 'possibly' in the sense of salvation-history, or 'perhaps' as moral conduct. In his response to Reumann, Fitzmyer agrees that gift is to be found in 5.6 ('probably') and 6.33, and righteous conduct in 5.10, 20, and 6.1. He allows the possibility that 3.15 may refer to *Heilsgeschichte* (yet it 'does not transcend the ethical demand of the OT teaching', p. 218), but he takes 21.32 as John's preaching concerning righteous conduct (p. 219).

[7]*Matthew: A Commentary on His Literary and Theological Art* (Grand Rapids: Eerdmans, 1982). Righteous conduct on God's side: 5.6 and 6.33; the remaining passages refer to human conduct.

[8]'"Righteousness" in Matthew', *BT* 40 (1989), pp. 228-35. Bratcher's treatment is terse and his conclusions are not altogether clear to me. It is clear that he takes 3.15 and 21.32 in a salvation-historical sense. It also seems clear that he takes 5.10 and 6.1 as referring to demand, and 5.6 as God's vindication or deliverance, hence in the sense of gift (one would think). But then it is confusing to read that the meaning of 6.33 'is the same as that already established for 5.6 and 5.10' (p. 235). Bratcher takes 6.33 as meaning 'that we are to try to live our lives in conformity with the principles that inform the Kingdom', hence apparently in the sense of demand rather than gift. He regards 5.20 as referring to a righteousness different from that of the Law, but he does not specify whether it is to be understood in the sense of demand or gift.

[9]'The Ethics of the Kingdom in the Gospel of Matthew', *Listening* 24 (1989), pp. 241-50. God's salvation: 5.6; 6.33; demand: 5.10, 20; 6.1; 'difficult': 3.15; 21.32, adding that 'even when he accentuates one aspect, the other is near at hand' (p. 244). Matera's discussion is much truer to Matthew than that of F.H. Gorman, Jr., who gives law too central a role in Matthew and

both gift and demand are seen in the word, and sometimes a decision one way or other seems impossible. Often the issue seems to be whether the primary aspect in view is demand or gift.

1. *Observations*

We begin our examination of δικαιοσύνη in Matthew with a few preliminary observations. It is increasingly appreciated in our day that the meaning of any particular word is only to be determined by the sentence in which it occurs together with the immediate context. Obviously, furthermore, no author is obligated to use any word consistently in only one sense or with the same meaning. In the case of Paul, for example, δικαιοσύνη is clearly used in more than one meaning.[1] It is well known, of course, that the modified form δικαιοσύνη θεοῦ (e.g., Rom. 1.17; 3.5, 21f.; 10.3) refers not to God's abstract righteousness, but to the gracious, saving activity of God in faithfulness to covenant promises. The word δικαιοσύνη by itself can also refer to righteousness as gift, righteousness amounting to salvation (e.g., Rom. 4.5; 1 Cor. 1.30; 2 Cor. 3.9; Gal. 3.6). While in a number of occurrences the meaning of the word is debatable, Paul of course can also use the same word in a plainly ethical sense (e.g., Rom. 6.13, 16, 18ff.; 2 Cor. 6.14; 9.10).

It has been established that, far from being original with him, Paul's concept of righteousness as gift was already held by pre-Pauline Christianity[2] and ultimately depends on OT foundations.[3] This view of righteousness was furthermore hardly unknown in other strands of the early church, as can be shown from other writings of the NT.[4] Given all of this, the importance of the OT for Matthew,[5] and that

underestimates the discontinuity between the Hebrew scriptures and the Gospel of Matthew; 'When Law Becomes Gospel: Matthew's Transformed Torah', *Listening* 24 (1989), pp. 227-40.

[1]This has been established among others by Stuhlmacher, *Gerechtigkeit Gottes*; Ziesler, *Meaning of Righteousness*; and Reumann, *Righteousness*, pp. 41-123.

[2]Stuhlmacher, *Gerechtigkeit Gottes*, pp. 185-88; Reumann, *Righteousness*, pp. 27-40.

[3]Ziesler, *Meaning of Righteousness*, pp. 17-46; Reumann, *Righteousness*, pp. 12-22; Stuhlmacher, *Gerechtigkeit Gottes*, pp. 113-45, and for apocalyptic, pp. 145-75.

[4]Reumann, *Righteousness*, pp. 124-80.

[5]Przybylski draws a conclusion of determinative importance for his study when he regards the Dead Sea Scrolls and the Tannaitic literature as more important background for Matthew than the OT. But *is* it really clear, as Przybylski claims, that 'the influence of Old Testament thought upon the Matthean redaction is primarily of an indirect nature' (*Righteousness in Matthew*, p. 4) and that 'the Old Testament *per se* has only a very limited direct relevance as background literature for the Matthean concept of righteousness' (p. 8)? As I see it, the OT is far more important for understanding Matthew than are the Dead Sea Scrolls or the Tannaitic literature.

Matthew too, despite its distinctives, is to be understood as a part of early Christianity, it would seem likely a priori that the author of Matthew could have used δικαιοσύνη in a similar way. But did he?

δικαιοσύνη occurs in Matthew seven times—more than in any other writing of the NT except for Romans and 2 Corinthians. All these occurrences are unique to Matthew. In two instances (3.15; 6.1) the passages are peculiar to Matthew; the remaining instances involve redactional insertions (cf. especially 5.6 and 6.33). If other NT writings reflect a diversity of meaning for the word depending on context, why should not Matthew?[1] Yet in what we have already noted as an apparently growing trend, a number of important Matthean scholars insist that Matthew uses δικαιοσύνη consistently to refer to required ethical conduct.

2. *The Sermon on the Mount*

We must first point out that in some instances it can hardly be disputed that δικαιοσύνη is used in an ethical sense, i.e., referring to the conduct required of would-be disciples. Five of the seven occurrences of the word are in the Sermon on the Mount, which might in itself incline us a priori to expect that the word will be used primarily, if not exclusively, to refer to ethical conduct. Most clear are 5.20, 'For I tell you, unless your righteousness exceeds that of the scribes and Pharisees, you will never enter the kingdom of heaven',[2] and 6.1, 'Beware of practicing your piety [δικαιοσύνην] before others in order to be seen by them; for then you have no reward from your Father in heaven'. There is little reason to doubt that the ethical conduct of the disciples is in view in these passages.[3]

[1] 'Since a "monochromatic" use of δικαιοσύνη exists neither in the OT nor in Paul, we may be justly skeptical as we come to the claim that Mt always uses the word in the one and the same sense'. Meier, *Law and History*, p. 77.

[2] But to the extent that what is in view is not an outdoing of the Pharisees at their own kind of righteousness but a distinctive and new righteousness related to the coming of the kingdom, there is 'the sense of gift as well as demand' in the passage. See Reumann, ***Righteousness***, p. 129. This conclusion is strengthened if 5.6 is taken as referring to God's activity rather than the ethical righteousness of disciples. Przybylski, while admitting that 'a qualitative distinction is inherent in 5:20', focuses on a quantitative distinction from the righteousness of the Pharisees and denies that there is an aspect of gift here; ***Righteousness in Matthew***, p. 85.

[3] Przybylski points out, following Strecker and Fiedler, that 5.20 and 6.1 involve more redaction than simply the insertion of the word δικαιοσύνη and thus 'may best reflect the meaning which Matthew, as the final redactor, attached to this term' (***Righteousness in Matthew***, p. 79). Such an approach presupposes (1) that the evangelist had no sources for 5.20 or 6.1; (2) that Matthew's use

In the other instances, however, a meaning other than the ethical seems quite plausible. We begin with the δικαιοσύνη of 5.6, that of the fourth Beatitude, 'Blessed are those who hunger and thirst for righteousness, for they will be filled'. Although the word here has most often been taken in the ethical sense—i.e. as referring to the hunger for personal righteousness—this view is neither necessary nor is it the most natural meaning for the word in its context. The Beatitudes are addressed to the oppressed and the downtrodden. While they have a present dimension (note the present tense of ἐστιν, 'theirs *is* the kingdom of heaven' in vv. 3 and 10), they are also decidedly eschatological in tone (note the future tenses and the eschatological expectation of vv. 4-9),[1] involving as they do the fulfillment of OT prophecy (e.g., Isa. 61.2; Pss. 37.11; 34.3). It is most natural given this context to take the hunger referred to as the desire not for the realization of a personal ethical righteousness, but for the justice that will come with the salvation of the eschatological era.[2]

The righteousness in view in this case would involve the salvific activity of God wherein the suffering and the oppressed will be lifted up. The Hebrew word צדק(ה) has a variety of meanings in the OT depending on the context. This, of course, is also true of its LXX counterpart δικαιοσύνη. Among the most important of these meanings is found in the reference to the eschatological salvation and vindication brought to the people of God. This sense of the word as the saving righteousness of God is particularly prominent in the prophets. This can be seen in passages such as Mic. 6.5 (NRSV: 'the saving acts of the LORD'), 7.9 ('his vindication'), and the question of Mal. 2.17, 'Where is the God of justice?' The word has this sense very frequently in Second Isaiah (e.g., 46.13, 'salvation').[3] In the

of the word in these passages is determinative for its use in other passages; and (3) that Matthew uses the word only in one sense.

[1]The future-oriented Beatitudes all imply the realization of salvation (*pace* Przybylski, *Righteousness in Matthew*, p. 97).

[2]So too Reumann, *Righteousness*, p. 128; Meier, *Law and History*, p. 77; Stuhlmacher, *Gerechtigkeit Gottes*, p. 190; P. Bonnard, *L'Évangile selon Saint Matthieu* (2nd edn; Neuchâtel: Delachaux et Niestlé, 1970), p. 57; L. Goppelt, *TDNT*, VI, p. 18. C.H. Dodd, *The Bible and the Greeks* (London, 1935), p. 55; cf. T.W. Manson, *The Sayings of Jesus* (London: SCM, 1949), p. 47f. Ziesler finds a double meaning: 'we have here a righteousness which is at once a demand on men, and a gift promised to them' (*Meaning of Righteousness*, p. 133). Bratcher proposes the translation '. . . whose greatest desire is that God's purpose prevail'; '"Righteousness" in Matthew', p. 234.

[3]On this see G. von Rad, *Old Testament Theology* (D.M.G. Stalker, trans.; New York: Harper & Row, 1962) I, p. 372, who refers to Deutero-Isaiah as presenting the climax of understanding

LXX of 51.5 we have an especially good example: ἐγγίζει ταχὺ ἡ δικαιοσύνη μου, καὶ ἐξελεύσεται ὡς φῶς τὸ σωτήριόν μου, 'My righteousness [NRSV translates the Hebrew, "deliverance"] quickly draws nigh, and my salvation will go forth as light' (cf. the last clauses of vv. 6 and 8, where again σωτήριον and δικαιοσύνη are paralleled (cf. 61.11; 62.1f.). In 59.9 δικαιοσύνη is paralleled with κρίσις, 'judgment'. And in 63.1 we encounter the combination δικαιοσύνην καὶ κρίσιν σωτηρίου, 'righteousness and saving judgment'.

It is impossible to believe that the author of Matthew was unfamiliar with this meaning of δικαιοσύνη and could not have used it in this way.[1] As we have seen, this interpretation fits well with the immediate context provided by the other eschatologically oriented Beatitudes. It is furthermore in line with what was apparently in Q, the source used by Matthew, as reflected in Lk. 6.21: 'Blessed are you who are hungry now, for you will be filled'. Rather than totally altering the meaning of this Beatitude by turning it into a desire for ethical righteousness which will be fulfilled in the eschaton (but Matthew calls for that kind of righteousness in *this* life!), Matthew has simply expanded it to a more inclusive desire for righteousness in the sense of eschatological justice, which will of course involve the filling of the hungry. Further to be noted is that the verb χορτασθήσονται fits this sense of δικαιοσύνη much better than it does the notion of ethical righteousness.

If there is no reason to deny that Matthew could have used the word in this sense, and every reason to conclude that such an interpretation suits the context best, I see no need to insist that Matthew here, and everywhere, used δικαιοσύνη only in the sense of ethical righteousness.[2]

---

righteousness in this sense. In note 7 on the same page, von Rad gives a number of references where the plural צדקות יהוה refers to Yahweh's saving acts in history. For 'righteousness' with the same meaning in the Psalms, see H.-J. Kraus, *Theology of the Psalms* (K. Crim, trans.; Minneapolis: Augsburg, 1986), pp. 42f.

[1]Schweizer writes concerning the word in 5.6 that Matthew 'could hardly forget that the real fulfillment of righteousness will be God's eschatological act'; *Matthew*, pp. 91f. Cf. Reumann, *Righteousness*, p. 128.

[2]Strecker recognizes the appropriateness of the above argument concerning 5.6, but concludes that since this is the only place such an understanding is found (but this we challenge), the word δικαιοσύνη should be understood here too as human righteousness; *Weg der Gerechtigkeit*, p. 156.

The word δικαιοσύνη occurs again in the eighth Beatitude (5.10): 'Blessed are those who are persecuted for righteousness' sake, for theirs is the kingdom of heaven'. Here it is probably to be taken in the sense of ethical righteousness, and seems to have been understood that way in 1 Pet. 3.14, which is almost certainly a reflection of the same logion as contained in the oral tradition. What is striking about this Beatitude is that it is followed immediately by another Beatitude (5.11), now in the second person ('Blessed are you'), which also refers to suffering persecution—in this instance, however, not for righteousness' sake, but ἕνεκεν ἐμοῦ, 'for my sake'. This suggests that the righteousness in view in 5.10 can hardly be thought of apart from Jesus and the work he has come to do. The one who exhibits the righteousness of the kingdom is identified with Jesus, the eschatological Messiah who brings the kingdom. The idea of ethical righteousness as gift, as well as demand, can obviously be inferred from the juxtaposition of these statements. It is no important obstacle to our interpretation of 5.6 that the evangelist uses δικαιοσύνη there to refer to eschatological salvation/justice and here uses the same word in the sense of ethical righteousness.

The fifth and last occurrence of δικαιοσύνη in the Sermon on the Mount is found in 6.33: 'But strive first for the kingdom of God and his righteousness, and all these things will be given to you as well'. Here the meaning of the word seems more ambiguous. This is the one time in Matthew that we encounter reference to God's (αὐτοῦ, 'his') righteousness. As we have seen above, however, God's righteousness in the OT refers not abstractly to God's ethical character, but to his saving activity that brings about eschatological deliverance.[1] The expression is thus virtually the equivalent of the preceding phrase, 'the kingdom of God', and could be considered as epexegetical of it. Here the point is not that we should seek to be as righteous as God is, and that once we are, God will add the things we need, but that we should make God's kingdom and the righteousness that comes with it our priority. When the kingdom becomes the controlling factor in the disci-

[1]To be sure, as Strecker points out (*Weg der Gerechtigkeit*, p. 155), the phrase δικαιοσύνη θεοῦ refers in Jas 1.20 to the righteousness of human deeds (the righteousness approved by God). This does not, however, determine the interpretation of Matthew's language in the present passage, nor does it justify Strecker's conclusion that for Matthew, 'Gottes Gerechtigkeit und menschliche Gerechtigkeit schliessen sich nicht aus, sondern sind identisch' (p. 155). Cf. Stuhlmacher's conclusion that this verse refers to God's own righteousness (*Rechtswalten*); *Gerechtigkeit Gottes*, pp. 189f.

ple's life, there will be no room for anxiety, least of all concerning the mundane needs of life.

Since it is true, however, that the disciple who makes the kingdom a priority will also, in Matthew's view, pursue righteousness as a way of life, it is difficult to exclude altogether the possibility of a reference to ethical righteousness in this passage.[1] If there is such a reference here, then 'his righteousness' must be understood as ethical righteousness as defined by God, that is, the unique righteousness defined by Jesus in the Sermon on the Mount and differentiated from that of the scribes and Pharisees (5.20). But, for Matthew, as we have seen, this righteousness must be associated with the dawning of the kingdom in the ministry of Jesus. The demand is conditioned by the gift upon which it depends.[2]

3. *John the Baptist and Jesus*

The two references to δικαιοσύνη outside the Sermon on the Mount both have to do with the John the Baptist. Is this because John was a preacher of ethical righteousness or possibly for some other reason? The first of these references is in 3.15, after John refuses to baptize Jesus and argues that it is he who needs to be baptized by Jesus: 'But Jesus answered him, "Let it be so now; for thus it is fitting for us to fulfil all righteousness"'. The common view that righteousness here is to be understood in an ethical sense[3] does not seem satisfactory for the following reasons. First and foremost, there is no command in the OT regarding baptism. In what sense then is the deed to be thought of

[1]Ziesler also sees a double sense to δικαιοσύνη in this passage (*Meaning of Righteousness*, p. 143). Meier regards δικαιοσύνη in this verse as clearly the gift of God's salvation (he compares the verse to 21.43, where both gift and demand are juxtaposed); *Law and History*, p. 78. Cf. G. Barth, *Tradition and Interpretation*, p. 140.

[2]G. Schrenk writes of 6.33: 'Righteousness is here closely linked with God and His kingdom, again as a pure gift from God, like everything connected with the kingdom'. *TDNT*, II, p. 199. It is not clear to me, however, how Schrenk reconciles this statement with that on the preceding page that the understanding of δικαιοσύνη as the right conduct of human beings 'is the consistent usage in Matthew'.

[3]O. Eissfeldt provides a brief, but useful survey of opinions on this verse, dividing them into those which find 'special theological content' in δικαιοσύνη and those that regard it as referring to moral obligation. 'Πληρῶσαι πᾶσαν δικαιοσύνην in Matthäus 3.15', *ZNW* 61 (1970), pp. 209-15. Eissfeldt opts for the latter, arguing that here Jesus submits himself to the ordinary duty of human beings as he does in the example of the temple tax (17.24-27) and the emperor's coin (22.15-22).

as the 'fulfilling' of ethical righteousness?[1] Considered from an ethical standpoint, moreover, the baptism is a sign of repentance. How then is the baptism of one who, as the Son of God, had no need of repentance, to be considered a righteous deed? Second, what is the meaning of '*all* righteousness (πᾶσαν δικαιοσύνην)' in this interpretation? Can the baptism somehow be thought of as itself constituting the whole of righteousness or is it the last of a host of commandments now regarded as obeyed? Third, in what sense is John involved (note: 'for us', ἡμῖν) in the fulfilling of all righteousness? If the ethical righteousness of Jesus is in view, would we not expect the singular 'for me' (ἐμοί)?

With these difficulties in mind, let us turn to another possible understanding of this passage. If we think of δικαιοσύνη here as righteousness in the sense of God's salvific activity, then John and Jesus may together be understood as fulfilling the salvific plan of God in the inauguration of Jesus' ministry,[2] the culmination of which will be his redemptive death on the cross. If in fact the baptism of Jesus already involves an anticipation of his death, as the logion from heaven with its allusion to the Isaianic Servant suggests (3.17),[3] then the crucial stage of salvation history has been reached, worthy of the words 'fulfill' and '*all* righteousness'. The importance of the role of John as the messianic forerunner, preparing the way for the realization of eschatological salvation, is found just here in the baptism of Jesus (hence 'for us', i.e., John and Jesus),[4] in the process of which the Holy Spirit falls upon Jesus to equip him for the accomplishing of his

---

[1]Strecker recognizes the problem, but concludes nevertheless that the baptism of Jesus 'gehört zur Verwirklichung der geforderten Frömmigkeit und wird als Teil der δικαιοσύνη auch selbst zu einer Rechtsordnung'; *Weg der Gerechtigkeit*, p. 180.

[2]Meier argues in favor of this *heilsgeschichtliche* sense; *Law and History*, p. 79f. Cf. F.D. Coggin, 'Note on St Matthew 3.15', *ExpTim* 60 (1948-49), p. 258: 'Only by His very literal standing-in with His people will they see the saving activity of God completely brought about'. Similarly, H. Ljungman, *Das Gesetz Erfüllen: Matth. 5,17ff. und 3,15 untersucht* (LUA, N.F. Avd. 1, Bd 50, Nr 6; Lund: Gleerup, 1954), pp. 97-126. Note too Bratcher's translation: 'This is what we must do to make it possible for God's purpose to prevail'; '"Righteousness" in Matthew', p. 234.

[3]This view may be accepted even if O. Cullmann's argument about the baptism itself as a prefiguration of the cross is rejected; *Baptism in the New Testament* (ET; London: SCM, 1950). Cf. G. Bornkamm: 'by baptism Jesus enters on the way of the Passion and resurrection', cited favorably by G. Barth, *Tradition and Interpretation*, p. 140.

[4]Some commentators see a reference to the church in the plural pronoun 'us'. It is far from certain, however, that Matthew sets forth the baptism of Jesus, with its several unique aspects, as the model or precursor of the disciples' baptism. More appropriate is Meier's conclusion: 'It is a question of both John and Jesus playing their appointed roles at this moment of fulfillment'; *Law and History*, p. 70.

mission. In the light of what now is to occur as the culminating fulfillment of God's saving purposes, 'it is fitting (πρέπον ἐστίν)', i.e., it is in accord with God's saving will, that the baptism take place.

If we are right in our argument that Matthew need not be required to use the word 'righteousness' in only one sense, and that we have in 5:6 (and possibly in 6:33) an example of the use of the word to refer to the righteousness of God in his saving activity rather than to the ethical righteousness of the disciple, then the above argument has more reason to be taken seriously. It is at least as plausible as the commonly accepted interpretation and it avoids at least some of the difficulties of that interpretation.

The final occurrence of δικαιοσύνη in Matthew is in the reference to John the Baptist in 21.32: 'For John came to you in the way of righteousness and you did not believe him, but the tax collectors and the prostitutes believed him; and even after you saw it, you did not change your minds and believe him'. The expression 'in the way of righteousness (ἐν ὁδῷ δικαιοσύνης)' can of course be taken as referring to ethical righteousness.[1] Indeed, the same expression is found in 2 Pet. 2.21, where it clearly means righteous conduct. The phrase occurs also in the LXX, where it regularly means practiced righteousness (e.g. Prov. 21.16, 21; but more frequently in the plural ['ways' or 'paths of righteousness']: 8.20; 12.28; 16.17, 31; and 17.23).

Again, however, it may be asked whether Matthew may have understood righteousness here in the sense of God's righteousness, so that the phrase could possibly refer to the way of God's salvation (note the phrase 'going into the kingdom of heaven'). Something of a counterpart may be found in the phrase 'the way of God' in 22.16. The emphasis in the immediate context is not upon the practice of righteousness, but upon the receiving of the gospel; not upon doing, but upon believing (cf. οὐκ ἐπιστεύσατε αὐτῷ, 'you did not believe him', and ἐπίστευσαν αὐτῷ, 'they believed him'; 21:32). A major point here, of course, is that it is the unrighteous—'the tax collectors and the prostitutes'—who believe. The implicit appeal to the chief priests and Pharisees in this passage is not that they should do a better job at being righteous, but that they too should believe in, and accept

---

[1]So Strecker, who takes the phrase as referring to John as the upholder of the eschatological demand concerning righteousness; *Weg der Gerechtigkeit*, p. 187.

the gift of, the dawning of the kingdom of God now inaugurated by Jesus, of whom and of which John was the forerunner.

We may further note that Matthew, unlike Luke (cf. Lk. 3.10-14), does not stress John as a teacher of righteousness.[1] If our conclusion concerning the meaning of δικαιοσύνη in 3.15 is at all justifiable, then John's role as one involved in the fulfillment of salvation-history may also be reflected in the statement that he came 'in the way of righteousness'.[2] John was the one who had been called to prepare 'the way of the Lord'(3.3).

Conclusion

It is not the concern of this essay to detract from the importance of Matthew's regard for ethical righteousness. The prominence of the first major discourse and the longest of the five, the Sermon on the Mount, leaves no doubt about how important the practice of righteousness is for the evangelist and his community.[3] This is almost certainly to be attributed to the Jewish background of these Christians. We hope only to have put the obvious emphasis on ethical righteousness in proper perspective by seeing the larger framework of grace present in the Gospel. This new framework of grace makes possible a new fullness in the meaning of the word 'righteousness'.[4]

Jesus' exposition of the righteousness of the Torah in chs. 5-7, we have argued, can only be rightly understood when it is seen within the

[1]It has to be admitted, however, that as a preacher of repentance he was necessarily concerned with righteousness (this can be seen in his reference to the importance of bearing fruit in 3.8, 10).

[2]Thus also Reumann: '"The way of righteousness" is thus the course of *Heilsgeschichte* culminating in the Baptist and Jesus as salvation.' This does not, he adds, exclude the moral imperative; *Righteousness*, p. 133. A. Sand also accepts the salvation-historical meaning of the phrase; *Das Gesetz und die Propheten: Untersuchungen zur Theologie des Evangeliums nach Matthäus* (BU, 11; Regensburg: Friedrich Pustet, 1974), pp. 199ff.

[3]Ironically, after attempting to demonstrate that in all seven instances Matthew understands δικαιοσύνη in the sense of ethical righteousness, Przybylski concludes that the word is not of crucial importance to Matthew (*Righteousness in Matthew*, p. 115), being 'essentially a Jewish concept' (p. 123). More important for Matthew's disciples, according to Przybylski, is 'the will of God' as distinct from 'doing righteousness' (p. 115). This distinction is not well-founded, in my opinion, and fails to do justice to the importance of righteousness precisely for Matthew's Jewish-Christian community. Righteousness for Matthew *is* the doing of the will of the Father. So too, R.T. France, *Matthew: Evangelist and Teacher* (Grand Rapids: Zondervan, 1989), p. 267. Cf. Giesen, *Christliches Handeln*, p. 234.

[4]See the excellent essay by P. Stuhlmacher, 'The New Righteousness in the Proclamation of Jesus', in *Reconciliation, Law, and Righteousness: Essays in Biblical Theology* (Philadelphia: Fortress, 1986), pp. 30-49.

context of the proclamation of the kingdom—i.e., in the context of grace. Matthew's Gospel after all remains gospel: the good news that God sovereignly inaugurates the kingdom in and through the ministry of Jesus, apart from the achievement of righteousness on the part of his people. The call to righteousness in Matthew is thus, as in Paul's writings, properly understood as response to the grace of God. Prior to the demand is the gift.

To this extent, at least, Matthew's perspective may be said to resemble that of Paul. It is not therefore necessary to castigate as a paulinizing of Matthew the consideration of the possibility that Matthew on occasion used the word δικαιοσύνη in what is usually regarded as 'the Pauline sense'. But why should Paul alone have been able to understand the word in this sense? If Matthew understood the story of Jesus as the story of the grace of God in bringing salvation to his people, and if Matthew was familiar with the use of the word 'righteousness' (in either Hebrew or Greek form, or both) in the OT, to designate God's saving activity—which we believe can hardly be doubted—then it seems unnecessary and improper to limit his use of the word to the designation of ethical righteousness. That he does use the word to refer to the latter is unquestionable. But there is no need to force a preconception concerning Matthew's understanding of righteousness onto all the texts where the word occurs. In several passages, as we have tried to show, the more convincing conclusion is that Matthew uses the word 'righteousness' in the positive sense of the salvation brought by God, and hence with the idea of gift, rather than demand, primarily in view.[1] The difference between Matthew and Paul remains, although it is not an absolute one. This difference, and a host of others between the two authors, is to be explained—indeed, it is to be expected—by the fact that Matthew writes to Jewish Christians and Paul to Gentile Christians. Both writers know of gift and demand; Paul emphasizes the former, Matthew the latter.

It is for me both a privilege and a joy to write this essay for a volume honoring Professor Ralph P. Martin. I first met Ralph twenty-five years ago, when as a new post-graduate student at the University of

[1]K. Kertelge is correct when he concludes that righteousness for Matthew is on the one hand 'an expression of the salvation of God', and on the other, 'God's demand to mankind'. 'This double-sidedness characterizes Matthew's use of the concept of δικαιοσύνη in contrast to Paul's use'; *EDNT* (eds H. Balz and G. Schneider; Grand Rapids: Eerdmans, 1990), I, p. 329.

Manchester I sat in his scintillating lectures. For more than half the time since then I was privileged to work with him as his junior colleague in NT at Fuller Theological Seminary. He has always been for me a model NT scholar, whose excellence in the careful study of the scriptures and commitment to the upbuilding of the church have continually served as an inspiration. I join with many other grateful students, colleagues and friends in congratulating him on this occasion.

THE UNJUST STEWARD: A NEW TWIST?

Colin Brown

In honoring my friend and colleague at Fuller Theological Seminary, Ralph P. Martin, I would like to take a fresh look at a topic which some eighty years ago Adolf Rücker described as 'the problem child of parable exegesis',[1] the parable of the unjust steward (Lk. 16.1-13). My aim is not to reduplicate the recent able surveys that have tracked the numerous lines of interpretation.[2] Rather, by drawing on some notable attempts at explication, I wish to explore a new twist which might make better sense of the parable in the context of Luke's Gospel and in the mission of Jesus.

On the face of it the steward looks like a junk-bond artist who not only saves his skin by defrauding his master, but wins praise for doing so. It is not surprising that some interpreters have pronounced his actions fraudulent, though this has not prevented them from trying to

---

1 Adolf Rücker, *Über das Gleichnis vom ungerechten Verwalter* (Freiburg i.B.: Herder'sche Buchhandlung, 1912), p. 1.

2 The interpretation which I present here has grown out of many years of thinking about the parable, and testing my ideas with friends, colleagues, and even in the pulpit. I am grateful for the opportunity of presenting a draft summary at the Annual Meeting of the Society of Biblical Literature, Pacific Coast Region, at the Hebrew Union College, Los Angeles, on March 22, 1991. I particularly appreciate the input and encouragement of colleagues.

For surveys of interpretations see Herbert Preisker, 'Lukas 16,1-17', *Theologische Literaturzeitung* 74/2 (1949), pp. 85-902; M. Krämer, *Das Rätsel der Parabel vom Ungerechten Verwalter, Lukas 16,1-13. Auslegungsgeschichte—Umfang—Sinn. Eine Diskussion der Probleme und Lösungsvorschläge der Verwaltungsparabel von den Vätern bis Heute* (Biblioteca di Scienze Religiose 5; Zürich: PAS-Verlag, 1972); Warren S. Kissinger, *The Parables of Jesus: A History of Interpretation and Bibliography* (ATLA Bibliography Series 4; Metuchen, NJ and London: Scarecrow and The American Theological Library Association, 1979), pp. 398-408 et passim; Dennis J. Ireland, 'A History of Recent Interpretation of the Parable of the Unjust Steward (Luke 16.1-13)', *WTJ* 51 (1989), pp. 293-318. The latter is based on a doctoral dissertation, 'Stewardship and the Kingdom of God: An Exegetical and Contextual Study of the Parable of the Unjust Steward in Luke 16.1-13', Westminster Theological Seminary, 1989.

salvage a positive moral.[1] Within the options proferred, various subcategories of interpretation have been identified: monetary versus non-monetary, eschatological versus non-eschatological, negative example versus positive example, ironical versus non-ironical, stress on charity versus stress on socio-economic background.[2] Curiously enough, the core of the parable—the first eight verses, though not the appended sayings—is widely regarded as authentic. The Jesus Seminar has identified it as one of only five parables preserving Jesus' actual words.[3] Presumably in the minds of the scholars who voted for it, it met the criteria of being pithy, memorable, distinctive, having an edge, reversing roles, and frustrating ordinary, everyday expectations.[4] In short, it is surprising and shocking. But to say this does not carry us very far in determining its meaning and place in Jesus' teaching. In trying to get beyond this impasse I shall focus first on

---

[1] Joachim Jeremias sees the original parable as a story about 'a criminal who, threatened with exposure, adopts unscrupulous but resolute measures to ensure his future security . . . . The clever, resolute behaviour of the man when threatened by catastrophe should be an example to Jesus' hearers' (*The Parables of Jesus* [rev. ed.; London: S.C.M., 1963], p. 46). Jeremias sees the appended sayings as the church's extended application of the original meaning.

John Dominic Crossan focuses attention on the elegantly structured mini-drama in three scenes, each of which is an internal diptych (*In Parables: The Challenge of the Historical Jesus* [New York: Harper & Row, 1973], p.110). Crossan observes that the steward has created 'a sort of Robin Hood image out of his inefficiency . . . . The cleverness of the steward consisted not only in solving his problem but in solving it by means of the very reason (low profits) that had created it in the first place. In the light of all this the parable ends quite adequately at 16.7. The rest, including 16.8a, is commentary'. See also Crossan, 'Parable and Example in the Teaching of Jesus', *NTS* 18 (1971-1972), pp. 285-307.

Kenneth E. Bailey takes the point of the parable to mean that human beings should learn to stake everything on God's generosity (*Poet and Peasant: A Literary-Cultural Approach to the Parables in Luke* [Grand Rapids: Eerdmans, 1976], pp. 86-118).

Commenting on v. 8 which he sees as Jesus' verdict on the steward, J. Ramsey Michaels observes: 'Jesus does not approve of the steward's ethics but rather, his activism. Facing a crisis, the steward had assessed the alternatives and without looking back, acted quickly and decisively in his own interests. Those who would respond to God's forgiveness can do no less' (*Servant and Son: Jesus in Parable and Gospel* [Atlanta: John Knox Press, 1981], p. 224).

[2] For these categories see the work of D.J. Ireland, above.

[3] *The Parables of Jesus, Red Letter Edition: A Report of the Jesus Seminar*, ed. Robert W. Funk, Bernard Brandon Scott, James R. Butts (Sonoma, CA: Polebridge, 1988), p. 32.

[4] Robert W. Funk, 'Criteria for Determining the Authentic Sayings of Jesus', *The Fourth R* 3/6 (1990), pp. 8-10. On the voting see Robert W. Funk, 'Poll on the Parables', *Foundations and Facets Forum* 2/1 (1986), pp. 54-80. Evidently of the 29 scholars who voted, 15 voted red (authentic primary data for determining who Jesus was), 10 pink (authentic with reservations or modifications), 2 gray (not primary data but possibly of use), and 2 black (not primary data, and belonging to later tradition).

four novel interpretations, and then attempt to show how they might lead to a new twist in the story.[1]

Four Novel Interpretations

1. *J.D.M. Derrett*

The most ingenious modern interpretation is that of J.D.M. Derrett who sees the parable as a commentary on dubious Jewish commercial practices.[2] The steward is an agent (שָׁלִיחַ) who finds himself ensnared in usury which was forbidden by the law of God.[3] Derrett detects usury from the size of the debts and the amounts remitted: 100 measures of oil (v. 6) reduced to 50, 100 measures of wheat reduced to 80 (v. 7). Drawing on post-Biblical Jewish practices and more recent examples from India, Derrett deduces a rate of interest plus insurance of between 20% and 25%.[4] In order to evade the sin and scandal of usury, the figures are stated as loans on commodities by means of the rabbinic legal device of judging loans to be non-usurious, if the borrower already possessed some of the commodity, however little. What was forbidden by the law of God was thus permitted by the law of man.

---

[1]Notwithstanding Dennis J. Ireland's recent attempt to vindicate the traditional understanding of the parable as a summons to fundamental evaluation of possessions in the light of the kingdom which will lead the wise disciple to use his possessions in the service of the needy (see above), I believe that there is more to the parable than he recognizes. The same applies to John S. Kloppenborg's contention: 'The genius of the parable consists in bringing about narrative closure, but only at the expense of fracturing the cultural codes and expectations of the listener. It celebrates the master's "conversion" from the myopia of his society's system of ascribed honour. The listener is induced—if only momentarily—to doubt the absoluteness of this pivotal value, not by a polemical broadside but by pure narrative surprise' (*Bib* 70 [1989], pp. [474-95] 492-93).

[2]'Fresh Light on St Luke xvi.1. The Parable of the Unjust Steward', *NTS* 7 (1960-61), pp. 198-219; reprinted in J. Duncan M. Derrett, *Law in the New Testament* (London: Darton, Longman & Todd, 1970), pp. 48-88. References are to the latter. See also Derrett, '"Take thy Bond . . . and Write Fifty" (Luke XVI.6): The Nature of the Bond,' *JTS* (NS 23, 1972), pp. 438-40. Other interpreters who have taken a similar view include M.D. Gibson, P. Gächter, G.B. Firth.

[3]'You shall not lend upon interest to your brother, interest on money, interest on victuals, interest on anything that is lent for interest. To a foreigner you may lend upon interest, but to your brother you shall not lend upon interest; that the LORD your God may bless you in all that you undertake in the land which you are entering to take possession of it' (Deut. 23.19-20). Other biblical and rabbinic references are given in Derrett, *Law*, pp. 56-62.

[4]Derrett, *Law*, pp. 65-72. In modern terms they amount to 800-900 gallons of oil and over 1000 bushels of wheat. The oil amounts to the yield of about 150 olive trees, and would be worth three years' wages of an average working man (James Breech, *The Silence of Jesus: The Authentic Voice of the Historical Man* [Philadelphia: Fortress, 1983], p. 107).

According to Derrett, it was the master who was truly at fault, though the steward was also implicated, because (in the words of the rabbinic dictum) 'a man's agent is like himself'.[1] However, the steward used the same authority which implicated him in his master's sin to extricate both himself and his master from the sin of usury. The master would have no alternative but to 'take credit for pious conduct which he had not in fact initiated'.[2] God's law thus prevailed over man's law. The steward becomes a model for winning the rewards of righteousness by his use of worldly goods.

Derrett's interpretation has won notable converts,[3] but his victory has not gone unchallenged. J.A. Fitzmyer[4] and C.F. Evans[5] are among those who think that Derrett's interpretation shifts the emphasis, so that the import of the parable is no longer recognizable. To Fitzmyer,

> The master's approval bears on the prudence of the manager who realized how best to use what material possessions were his to ensure his future security. The 'dishonest manager' thus becomes a model for Christian disciples, not because of his dishonesty (his initial mismanagement and squandering), but because of his prudence. Christian disciples are also faced with a crisis by the kingdom/judgment preaching of Jesus, and the prudent use of material possessions might be recommended in the light of that crisis.[6]

Evans thinks that Derrett's interpretation fails, because it depends on the covert fact of the usurious contracts, the capacity of the audience to recognize it, and the difficulties that Evans finds in relating the interpretation of the parable to the ensuing sayings.[7]

---

[1] *B.M.* 96a; *B.K.*113b; *Kid.* 41b-42a, 43a; *Nazir* 12b; *Ned.* 72a (Derrett, *Law*, p. 52).

[2] Derrett, *Law*, p. 72.

[3] Ireland names H. Zimmermann, A.C. Thiselton, L.L. Morris, E.E. Ellis, I.H. Marshall, S.J. Kistemaker, and notes that M.D. Goulder reached a similar conclusion in 'The Chiastic Structure of the Lucan Journey' (*SE* 2 [1964], pp. 198), though without reference to Derrett (*WJT* 51 [1989]. pp. 315, n. 91). G.B. Caird also followed Derrett (*Saint Luke* [Harmondsworth: Pelican; Philadelphia: Westminster, 1963], pp. 186-88).

[4] J.A. Fitzmyer, 'The Story of the Dishonest Manager (Luke 16.13)', *TS* 25 (1964), pp. 23-42; reprinted in *Essays on the Semitic Background of the New Testament* (London: Chapman, 1971; Missoula: Scholars, 1974), pp. 161-84; and *The Gospel According to Luke (X-XXIV)* (AB; Garden City, NY: Doubleday, 1985), pp. 1094-1104.

[5] C.F. Evans, *Saint Luke* (TPI New Testament Commentaries; London: S.C.M.; Philadelphia: Trinity Press International, 1990), pp. 594-604.

[6] Fitzmyer, *Luke (X-XXIV)*, p. 1098.

[7] Evans, *Saint Luke*, p. 597.

For myself, I have to confess that I do not find such objections insuperable, not least because I cannot let my modern ignorance of ancient life prejudge what is feasible and determine what any trader might have known in the first century BCE.[1] Nevertheless, I am left wondering why Jesus should have attacked usury in this roundabout way, if that was his main point. It might be replied that the parable depicts the kind of conversion illustrated in the previous parable—that of the prodigal son—and by the story of Zacchaeus. But both of these contain an explicit confession of wrongdoing and change of heart (Lk. 15.18, 21; 19.8). In the case of the unjust steward we hear only of his prudence through his management of debts.

2. *Ehrhard Kamlah*

Almost contemporary with Derrett's proposal was Ehrhard Kamlah's alternative interpretation.[2] Kamlah detached the parable from the appended sayings which (he thought) merely obscured its original meaning and purpose.[3] Like other synoptic parables, it was designed to address a shared situation and provoke a reaction. It belongs to a series of parables found in Matthew and Luke which address the servant theme.[4] The focal point of all servant parables is the verdict of the Lord on the activity of the servants.[5] In some of them attention is fixed on the servant being placed in a position of authority. In others the theme is the attitude of the servants to the expected judgment of their lord. A further group deals with accusations. Though they share a common metaphor, each parable has a specific point.

Kamlah detected close connections between the role of the servant and that of the steward.[6] Moses was God's servant who is 'entrusted

---

[1]In his short note in *JTS* (NS 23, 1972), pp. 438-40, Derrett gives examples from the Hellenistic world which indicate that Luke's hearers would have at once understood what was going on.

[2]'Die Parabel vom ungerechten Verwalter (Luk. 16, 1ff.) im Rahmen der Knechtgleichnisse', in Otto Betz, Martin Hengel, and Peter Schmidt, eds., *Abraham unser Vater. Juden und Christen im Gespräch über die Bibel. Festschrift für Otto Michel zum 60. Geburtstag* (Arbeiten zur Geschichte des Spätjudentums und Urchristentums 5; Leiden-Köln: E.J. Brill, 1963), pp. 276-94.

[3]Kamlah, *Abraham unser Vater*, p. 281.

[4]Kamlah, *Abraham unser Vater*, pp. 284-86. They include the parables of the faithful and unfaithful servants (Mt. 24.45-51 = Lk. 12.42-46); the pounds (Mt. 25.14-30 = Lk. 19.12-27); the unmerciful servant (Mt. 18.23-24) and the unjust steward (Lk. 16.1-7) which stand in antithetical relationship; the unprofitable servant (Lk. 17.7-10); the exhortation to be ready servants in the eschatological discourse (Mk 13.34-37; Lk. 13.35-40, 47-48); and the laborers in the vineyard (Mt. 20.1-16).

[5]Kamlah, *Abraham unser Vater*, p. 286.

[6]Kamlah, *Abraham unser Vater*, pp. 287-289.

with all my house' (Num. 12.7).[1] Eliakim was given the key of David's house with authority to open and shut (Isa. 22.22). Kamlah linked the servant/steward theme to the woes pronounced on the scribes and Pharisees who shut the kingdom of heaven against men (Mt. 13.13). The metaphor of steward was taken over by early Christianity. Paul saw himself as a steward (οἰκονόμος) of the mysteries of God (1 Cor. 4.1). The term is used of a bishop (Tit. 1.7), and the recipients of gifts (1 Pet. 4.10).

According to Kamlah, the parable is about the proper behavior of the steward in relation to God and his fellow human beings. It is, in fact, the second parable in Luke to use the term οἰκονόνος. In Lk. 12.42 the Lord asks, 'Who then is the faithful and wise steward [ὁ πιστὸς οἰκονόνομος ὁ φρόνιμος], whom his master will set over his household to give them their portion of food in due time?' The reappearance of οἰκονόμος and the use of the adverb φρονίμως in Lk. 16.8 (also in connection with the Lord's praise of the steward) tie the two parables together. To Kamlah, both belong to the debate with the Pharisees about authority.[2] Both parables have to do with readiness for judgment. Lk. 16.1-7 is an exhortation to the Pharisees to lighten the burdens of others. Thus Jesus turns to the tax collectors and sinners against the scribes and Pharisees who lay heavy burdens on men's shoulders, but will not move them with their finger (Mt. 13.4), and who shut the kingdom against men and will not enter themselves (Mt. 13.13). Alongside Matthew's negative polemic, the parable of the steward presents 'the positive way which Jesus has walked with the outcasts, which he thus presents as the wise behavior of a "steward"'.[3] The way lies not in separation and observance of a

---

[1]The MT has עֶבֶד, but in rabbinic writings the term גִּזְבָּר is used, which S-B 2, p. 217 identifies with οἰκόνομος. The earliest instance of גִּזְבָּר is found in 2 (*Syriac Apocalpyse* of) *Bar*. 10.18 'You, priests, take the keys of the sanctuary, and cast them to the highest heaven, and give them to the Lord and say, "Guard your house yourself, because, behold, we have been found false stewards"'.

In addition, it may be noted that the term οἰκονόμος occurs in the LXX as a translation for עַל־הַבַּיִת in 3 Kgs 4.6; 4 Kgs 18.18, 37; 19.2; Isa. 36.3, 22; 37.2; in Esth. 1.8 for רַב בַּיִת; in Esth. 8.9 for פֶּחָה; and without exact Hebrew equivalent in 3 Kgs 4.6; 16.9; 18.3; 2 Chron. 29.6; 1 Esdr. 4.47, 49; 8.67; Isa. 36.11.

In a recent study Scott C. Layton identifies two types of steward in ancient Israel, the private steward and the royal steward in charge of a palace who was a government official ('The Steward in Ancient Israel: A Study of Hebrew [*'aser*] *'al-habbayit* on Its Near Eastern Setting', *JBL* 109 [1990], pp. 651-66). The steward in Isa. 22.15 was patterned after the administrative traditions of Canaanite city states.

[2]Kamlah, *Abraham unser Vater*, p. 292.

[3]Kamlah, *Abraham unser Vater*, p. 293.

multitude of purity ordinances, but in seeking acceptance among the master's debtors and reducing their burdens. The parable is thus a 'polemic against Pharisaic casuistry'.

3. *Stanley E. Porter*

Although several exegetes have detected irony in the parable, the most recent and the most thoroughgoing interpretation along these lines is that of Stanley E. Porter.[1]

> The master of the parable has discovered that his steward had already been associating with the sons of this age in his dishonest and probably wasteful behavior (he is 'praised' as τὸν οἰκονόμον τῆς ἀδικίας). The steward is then faced with a choice when he is dismissed from his position. He may choose to make the hard choice of doing honest work, or he may choose to sell out completely by ingratiating himself with the sons of this age so that they will receive him. He chooses the latter. It is this behaviour which the observant and insightful master ironically comments upon, in pointing out that the steward has not made a wise choice but a wrong choice. He is heading towards becoming a prodigal son, by setting as his goal becoming friends with the sons of this age. The commendatory statements of vv. 8ff. are clearly ironic. The steward, becoming like the prodigal son, is by his behavior attempting to make himself popular with the sons of this age, so that he may join their community. But he does not realise how fleeting are the values of this age. He is attempting to get inside the gates of the rich man's house, but he too will suffer the fate of Lazarus's rich man, if he is not reduced to the prodigal's condition sooner.[2]

Porter's interpretation is novel and audacious. But I wonder whether Porter is trying to have his cake and eat it, when he comes to v. 9, where (as he puts it) 'Jesus enters in his own words (καὶ ἐγω ὑμῖν λέγω) and applies the parable directly to his hearers'.[3] On the face of it v. 9 is a recommendation which endorses the action of the steward. 'And I tell you make friends for yourselves by means of

[1]Stanley E. Porter, 'The Parable of the Unjust Steward (Luke 16.1-13): Irony *is* the Key', in D.J.A. Clines, Stephen E. Fowl, and Stanley E. Porter, eds., *The Bible in Three Dimensions: Essays in Celebration of Forty Years of Biblical Studies in the University of Sheffield* (JSOTSup 87; Sheffield: JSOT, 1990), pp. 127-153. Virtually contemporary with Derrett and Kamlah, D.R. Fletcher had proposed an ironic solution in 'The Riddle of the Unjust Steward: Is Irony the Key?', *JBL* 82 (1963), p. 15-30. Other scholars who see irony or sarcasm in the parable include N. Levinson, P.G. Bretscher, G. Paul, G. Schwarz, E. Trueblood, J. Jónsson, and H. Clavier (see Porter, *The Bible in Three Dimensions*, pp. 127-28, n. 2).

[2]Porter, *The Bible in Three Dimensions*, p. 146.

[3]Porter, *The Bible in Three Dimensions*, p. 148.

unrighteous mammon, so that when it fails they may receive you into the eternal habitations [εἰς τὰς αἰωνίους σκηνάς, lit. "the eternal tents"]' (Lk. 16.9 RSV). Here apparently the irony falters, and is replaced by plain speech. For 'the eternal tents' are not the abode of the ironically portrayed worldly-wise debtors to whom the steward turned, as he plunged along his downward career. Rather, they represent 'the desired abode of the righteous, i.e. the kingdom, represented in its earthly sense as the banquet to which the prodigal is invited on his return and in its eschatological sense as the bosom of Abraham where Lazarus goes after his death'.[1] I certainly think that there is irony in the parable, but I am left wondering whether Porter's version of it fits the recommendation of v. 9.

4. *William Loader*

In diametric opposition to Porter (though he does not discuss him) stands William Loader. He too makes use of irony (albeit tacitly), but suggests that the parable should be interpreted christologically.[2] The bulk of Loader's discussion is devoted to comments on earlier interpretations. The predecessors who come closest to his own position are Kamlah and C. Paliard, whose approach was more allegorical and who read the parable in the light of a post-Easter perspective.[3]

To Loader, the context is the same as that of the three preceding parables. It is to be found in the statement of Lk. 15.1-2: 'Now the tax collectors and sinners were all drawing near to hear him. And the Pharisees and the scribes murmured, saying, "This man receives sinners and eats with them"'. The gist of Loader's position is stated in his conclusion:

> The parable of the unjust steward is an example of Jesus' use of a story to shock people and so break open their awareness for new insight. Accused of unauthorised and scandalous behaviour, in offering God's grace freely outside the prescribed pattern of the Law to sinners and no-goods, Jesus provokes his hearers with the story of a rogue who, despite

[1] Porter, *The Bible in Three Dimensions*, pp. 149-50.

[2] William Loader, 'Jesus and the Rogue in Luke 16,1-8A: The Parable of the Unjust Steward', *RB* 96 (1989), pp. 518-32.

[3] In Paliard's view the master represents the law, and the two different approaches of the master between vv. 2 and 8a represent the old and the new law. The parable foreshadows Christ's rejection, crucifixion, and subsequent resurrection. See C. Paliard, *Lire l'Écriture, écouter la Parole. La parabole de l'économe infidèle* (Lire la Bible 53; Paris, 1980), pp. 60-62, 133-34, cited by Loader, p. 529.

all, received his master's approbation. The thinly disguised allusions to forgiveness, through the familiar debt motif, and to authorization, in the position and activity of the steward, would not have been lost on the hearers faced with the controversies Jesus' ministry provoked. Jesus mounts no formal defense, but 'from below' tells a subversive story to topple the norms and expectations of his powerful critics. His is the roguery of divine grace which confounds the arithmetic of the righteous. Distilled in this parable is the essence of the gospel, coded for its contemporary context.[1]

In my judgment, the christological interpretation is essentially correct, though it does not preclude the insights of other interpretations. Loader has sketched an approach which for some time I had suspected to be the intended meaning. However, Loader's actual exposition occupies barely five pages, and he does not develop his view in any detail. In what follows I would like to examine how this new twist in the story might fit Luke's portrayal of Jesus.

The New Twist

1. *Luke's Portrayal of Jesus as a Steward*

Both Derrett and Kamlah make use of the 'agent' idea, though Derrett goes beyond Kamlah in identifying the οἰκονόμος as a שָׁלִיחַ. The question of the antiquity of the latter term has not gone unchallenged. It does not appear in the OT, and came to prominence only in the rabbinic period. However, there appears to be a growing consensus of scholars who trace the idea of the commissioned agent back through the NT to the OT, and who deem it legitimate to see the concept behind various relationships in the NT.[2] Recently Ben Witherington, III, has identified it as a key to understanding Jesus.

> A more adequate model for evaluating Jesus' self-image and explaining his sense of authority over both the law and Israel is that of the *shaliach*. Jesus saw himself as God's agent endowed with divine authority and sent on a divine mission to rescue Israel from impending disaster, while at the

---

[1]Loader, 'Jesus and the Rogue', p. 532.

[2] For a review of the debate and the literature examining the possible links between שָׁלִיחַ and ἀπόστολος see Francis H. Agnew, 'The Origin of the NT Apostle-Concept: A Review of Research', *JBL* 105 (1986), pp. 75-96. Agnew notes that the term שָׁלִיחַ is post-biblical, and recognizes that the institutionalized form of the office cannot have antedated the destruction of Jerusalem. Nevertheless, he sees the sending convention stretching back through the NT period into the OT.

> same time offering them one last chance to accept the rule of God and God's claim on their lives. On such a model we can see the reason that Jesus assumed his words were God's words for Israel, that his agenda was God's agenda for Israel, and that how one reacted to Jesus would determine one's final standing with God. But Jesus did not see himself as an agent of God, but as the *final* eschatological agent of God who brings in God's reign, and even casts fire upon the land if God's people do not respond properly to that inbreaking reign in the ministry of Jesus . . . . He did not conceive of himself merely in terms of a prophet or teacher. Rather, he saw himself as God's *Mashiah* and *Shaliach*, as the final Shepherd.[1]

To Witherington, texts like Mt. 10.40 and Lk. 10.16 indicate not only that Jesus was God's שָׁלִיחַ, but that the disciples were Jesus' שְׁלוּחִים.[2]

---

[1]Ben Witherington, III, *The Christology of Jesus* (Minneapolis: Fortress, 1990), pp. 142-43. Several scholars see the שָׁלִיחַ idea as a key to understanding the Fourth Gospel's account of Jesus. They include Peder Borgen, *Bread from Heaven: An exegetical Study of the Concept of Manna in the Gospel of John and the Writings of Philo* (NovTSup 10; Leiden: E.J. Brill, 1965), pp. 158-64; Borgen, 'God's Agent in the Fourth Gospel', in *Logos Was the True Light and Other Essays on the Gospel of John* (Relieff 9; Trondheim: Tapir, 1983), pp. 121-32; Jan A. Bühner, *Der Gesandte und sein Weg im 4. Evangelium. Die kultur- und religionsgeschichtlichen Grundlagen der johanneischen Sendungschristologie sowie ihre tradtionsgeschichtliche Entwicklung* (WUNT, 2; Reihe 2; Tübingen: J.C.B. Mohr [Paul Siebeck], 1977); and Howard Clark Kee, *What Can We Know about Jesus?* (Cambridge: Cambridge University Press, 1990), pp. 104-10. The idea is present in Jesus' statements about being sent to do the will of him who sent him (Jn 6.31-58; 13.16, cf. Mt. 10.24 and *Gen. R.* 78.1; 13.20, cf. Mt. 10.40).

The שָׁלִיחַ idea gives historical precision to the sociological analysis of Halvor Moxnes who depicts the social structure of Palestine in terms of patron-client relations ('Patron-Client Relations and the New Community in Luke-Acts', in Jerome Neyrey, ed., *The Social World of Luke-Acts: Models for Interpretation* [Peabody, MA: Hendrickson, 1991], pp. 241-68). Moxnes sees the steward in the parable as a broker between his master and his master's tenants (p. 253). 'The central theme of the Gospel is that God acts as a benefactor-patron through Jesus. Jesus is not a patron in his own right, distributing his own resources, but a broker who gives access to the benefactions of God. He mediates between the people of Israel and God . . . . And so his conflict with the old leadership of Israel becomes understandable, for it is a conflict over the right and power to give access to God' (p. 258).

[2]Witherington, *The Christology of Jesus*, p. 136. Witherington refers to *Berakoth* 5.5. The passage raises the intriguing question of errors on the part of the agent, and goes on to mention Hanina ben Dosa who is evidently thought of as an agent of God.

> If he that says the *Tefillah* falls into error it is a bad omen for him; and if he was an agent of the congregation it is a bad omen for them that appointed him, because a man's agent is like himself. They tell of R. Hanina b. Dosa that he used to pray over the sick and say, 'This one will live', or 'This one will die'. They said to him, 'How knowest thou?' He replied, 'If my prayer is fluent in my mouth I know that he is accepted; and if it is not I know that he is rejected' (cited from *The Mishnah*, tr. Herbert Danby [Oxford: Oxford University Press, 1933], p. 6).

For comparison of Jesus with Hanina ben Dosa and further literature see Colin Brown, 'Synoptic Miracle Stories: A Jewish Religious and Social Setting', *Foundations and Facets Forum* 2 (1986),

The agency of Jesus as God's Son is stated in Lk. 10.22: 'All things have been delivered to me by my Father; and no one knows who the Son is except the Father and who the Father is except the Son and any one to whom the Son chooses to reveal him' (RSV). Luke traces this authorization to Jesus' baptism and anointing by the Spirit (Lk. 3.21-22) which is further interpreted by Jesus' reading from the Isaiah scroll in the synagogue at Nazareth: 'The Spirit of the Lord is upon me, because he has anointed me to preach good news to the poor. He has sent me to proclaim release to the captives and recovering of sight to the blind, to set at liberty those who are oppressed, to proclaim the acceptable year of the Lord' (Lk. 4.18-19 RSV; cf. Isa. 61.1-2; 58.6).[1]

This theme is echoed in Jesus' reply to John the Baptist's question: 'Go and tell John what you have seen and heard: the blind receive their sight, the lame walk, lepers are cleansed, and the deaf hear, the dead are raised up, the poor have the good news preached to them. And blessed is he who takes no offence at me' (Lk. 7.22-23; cf. Mt. 11.5-6). The fact that John was languishing in prison poignantly raised the question of whether Jesus was indeed the one to come who would fulfil the mission of proclaiming release to the captives and setting at liberty those who are oppressed. As the Father's authorized agent, Jesus is entrusted with the mission that the Father has given him, and blessed are those who take no offence at him. In the light of John's subsequent execution it may be that some of John's disciples became disaffected with Jesus, and therefore could be counted among those who questioned his authority and were thus among those at which our parable is aimed.

In Luke's narrative it is the descent of the Spirit upon Jesus after his baptism which qualifies him for his mission as God's Son and agent to the afflicted and marginalized among God's people (Lk. 3.22; cf. 4.18-9; Isa. 61.1-2).[2] Leading up to this anointing, Luke notes the

---

pp. 55-76, especially 62-64. A major difference between Jesus and Hanina ben Dosa lay in the fact that, whereas Jesus' actions repeatedly brought him into conflict with the authorities over infringement of the Law, Hanina avoided innovative practices and was perceived to remain within Jewish orthodoxy.

[1]See Luke T. Johnson, *The Literary Function of Possessions in Luke-Acts* (SBLDS 39; Missoula, Montana: Scholars, 1977), pp. 91-93, on the programmatic nature of this passage in the structure of Luke. Johnson does not, however, use the שָׁלִיחַ concept.

[2]Cf. James D.G. Dunn, *Jesus and the Spirit: A Study of the Religious and Charismatic Experience of Jesus and the First Christians as Reflected in the New Testament* (London: S.C.M., 1975), pp. 53-67. Klaus Berger sees the anointing by the Spirit as the bestowal of authority which gave Jesus

providential circumstances of Jesus' birth and childhood, the attendant prophecies and revelations, and his genealogical descent from Adam, the son of God (Lk. 3.38). Not only does Jesus fit the concept of God's agent. He also embodies the qualities of 'the faithful and wise steward, whom his master will set over his household, to give them the portion of their food at the proper time' (Lk. 12.42).

2. *The Repeated Charges and Insinuations of Misconduct*

Interwoven with the theme of God's anointed representative is the discordant theme of wrongdoing. Luke's narrative reads like a litany of charges of misconduct. Jesus' claim in the synagogue at Nazareth to fulfil the prophecy of Isaiah and his adverse comparison of Israelites with the widow of Zarephath and Naaman the Syrian lead to an attempt on his life (Lk. 4.22-29). The call of Levi and the subsequent great feast at his house prompts the question: 'Why do you eat and drink with tax collectors and sinners?' and the response: 'Those who are well have no need of a physician but those who are sick; I have not come to call the righteous, but sinners to repentance' (Lk. 5.30-32). The failure of Jesus' disciples to fast often and pray compares unfavorably with the disciples of John and of the Pharisees (Lk. 5.33-35). The disciples' act of plucking corn raises the question of whether Jesus sanctioned the profanation of the sabbath (Lk. 6.1-5). The healing on the sabbath of the man with the withered hand causes the Pharisees to be 'filled with fury' and discuss 'with one another what they might do to Jesus' (Lk. 6.11).

Doubtless such episodes contributed to the reputation that Jesus evidently had acquired of having a demon, and of being 'a glutton and a drunkard, a friend of tax collectors and sinners' (Lk. 7.34). In other words, he fulfilled the qualifications for being denounced as a 'rebellious son' who could be repudiated by his parents and stoned to death by the community (Deut. 21.18-21; cf. *Sanhedrin* 7.4).[1] Perhaps the fear of this unenviable reputation lay behind the call of Jesus' mother and brothers and Jesus' reply: 'My mother and my

---

an 'offensive holiness' which empowered him to make holy that which was otherwise unclean ('Jesus als Pharisäer und frühe Christen als Pharisäer', *NovT* 30 [1988], pp. 231-62). It was this that lay at the root of Jesus' conflict with the Pharisees.

[1]Brown, 'Synoptic Miracle Stories', p. 70; cf. H.H. Cohn, 'Rebellious Son', *EncJud* 13, pp. 1603-1605. The procedure for dealing with a 'rebellious son' is also set out in the Temple Scroll, 11QT 64. J.W. Bowker has argued that Jesus was eventually condemned as a 'rebellious elder' (*Jesus and the Pharisees* [Cambridge: Cambridge University Press, 1973], pp. 42-52).

brothers are those who hear the word of God and do it' (Lk. 8.21). Events come to a head with the Beelzebul charge (Lk. 11.14-23) which, if it had been made to stick, would have carried the death penalty.[1] By comparison the charge that Jesus failed to wash before dinner (Lk. 11.37) appears to be an anticlimax. Nevetheless, it expresses a fundamental difference over the subject of purity, and provokes a sharp denunciation of Pharisaic practice.

3. *Like the Steward Jesus Made a Point of Remitting Debts*

In the impoverished society in which Jesus lived debt was an omnipresent reality. Richard A. Horsley observes that,

> The principal mechanism through which the peasantry could be destroyed was indebtedness. Because of bad harvests or unusual demands for tributes, taxes, or tithes, already-marginal peasant families would fall into debt. Then failure to pay the debt would lead to one or more family members' becoming debt-slaves, and finally to loss of land. The greatest threat to peasants, and probably their greatest fear, was falling heavily and hopelessly into debt.[2]

In this social structure the self-perpetuating, ruling elite governed the peasantry through patronage, i.e., by means of interpersonal bonds between social unequals. The ruling Jewish families were themselves clients of Rome, and had a vested interest in preserving the *status quo*. In this situation the temple and its related personnel, and such parties as the Pharisees occupied a precarious place. They were caught between disdain of their pagan oppressors and the need to avoid losing what they had by disturbing their fragile balance of power.

In contrast with the plight of the peasantry who constituted the vast mass of the Jewish people, wealth means almost by definition ill-gotten gain, for wealth could only be amassed at the expense of the peasants, through fraud, tax collection, tithes, lending, foreclosing and

---

[1]Brown, 'Synoptic Miracle Stories', pp. 57-58, 65-67, 71-72; Brown, *Miracles and the Critical Mind* (Grand Rapids: Eerdmans, 1984), pp. 300-324. In my judgment the charge was bound up with the conviction that Jesus was the kind of false prophet described in Deut. 13, the Temple Scroll, 11QT 54, the Mishnah tractate *Sanhedrin* 7, and the *Babylonian Talmud* 43a, who performed signs and wonders in order to lead people astray.

[2]Richard A. Horsley, *Jesus and the Spiral of Violence: Popular Jewish Resistance in Roman Palestine* (San Francisco: Harper & Row, 1987), p. 246; cf. Gerd Theissen, *Sociology of Early Palestinian Christianity* (Philadelphia: Fortress, 1978), pp. 33-46; Douglas E. Oakman, *Jesus and the Economic Questions of His Day* (Studies in the Bible and Early Christianity 8; Lewiston/Queenston: Edwin Mellon, 1986), pp. 72-80; Oakman, 'The Countryside in Luke-Acts', in Jerome H. Neyrey, ed., *The Social World of Luke-Acts*, pp. 151-79.

calling in loans. 'Mammon' in the sayings of Lk. 16.9 and 13 is not simply 'money', but that in which one placed one's trust. Far from being a token of divine blessing and approval, wealth was an ever-present snare which embroiled people in its destructive, dynamic structures.[1] It deterred the rich young ruler from following Jesus (Lk. 18.18-23). It is easier for a camel to go through the eye of a needle than for a rich man to enter the kingdom (Lk. 18.25). Corresponding to the beatitudes pronounced over the poor, the hungry, the sorrowing, and the reviled (Lk. 6.20-22) are the woes pronounced over the rich, the full, the self-satisfied, and the well-thought-of (Lk. 6.24-26). Such woes find vivid expression in the parables of judgment featuring the rich fool who laid up treasure for himself but was not rich toward God (Lk. 12.16-21), and the rich man who feasted sumptuously every day while Lazarus suffered and starved (Lk. 16.19-31). By contrast the Jesus of Luke's Gospel recommended a lifestyle characterized, not by ascetic renunciation of all money or possessions, but by giving and lending without hope of return (Lk. 6.30, 34), and by using possessions to help those in need (Lk. 10.30-37).[2]

Closely entwined with the theme of wealth and sin is the theme of sin as a debt.[3] The language of release from debt occurs in Jesus' words to the paralytic, 'Man, your sins are forgiven you [ἄνθρωπε,

---

[1]Horsley, *Jesus and the Spiral of Violence*, p. 248; cf. Fitzmyer, *Luke (X-XXIV)*, p. 1109, where Fitzmyer links the term with the root אמן, to be firm, meaning '"that in which one puts trust," from which a semantic shift to "money, possessions" would not be difficult'.

[2]Cf. Martin Hengel, *Property and Riches in the Early Church: Aspects of a Social History of Early Christianity* (Philadelphia: Fortress, 1974), pp. 23-30; Sean Freyne, *Galilee, Jesus and the Gospels: Literary Approaches and Historical Investigations* (Philadelphia: Fortress, 1988), p. 95. The call for renunciation (Lk. 14.34) and Jesus' praise of the widow who put her whole living into the temple treasury (Lk. 21.1-4) must be seen alongside the parable of the pounds (Lk. 19.12-27). Both passages are variations on the theme of stewardship.

[3]'The remission of debts could become an image of divine grace (Matt. 18.23ff.). And the praise of the unjust steward, who takes it upon himself to reduce the amounts owed by his master's debtors, only makes sense if the remission of debt is seen from the start as something positive (Luke 16.1ff.)' (Gerd Theissen, *Sociology of Early Palestinian Christianity*, p. 42).

For sin as a debt in Luke see I. Howard Marshall, *The Gospel of Luke: A Commentary on the Greek Text* (Exeter/Grand Rapids: Paternoster/Eerdmans, 1978), pp. 213, 460-61; Oakman, *Jesus and the Economic Questions of His Day*, pp. 149-56. Matthew Black points out that it has long been recognized that the term underlying Luke's ἁμαρτίας (Lk. 11.4) and Matthew's ὀφειλήματα (Mt. 6.12) in the Lord's Prayer is the Aramaic חוֹבָא (*An Aramaic Approach to the Gospels and Acts* [3rd ed.; Oxford: Clarendon, 1967], p. 140). ὀφειλέτης in the phrase 'worse offenders' (Lk. 13.4 NRSV) is the equivalent of חַיָּבָא, debtor, sinner. Black sees the parable of the two debtors as a further instance of conceiving sin in terms of debt, and notes the view expressed in the Samaritan Liturgy: 'Whoever receiveth sinners, Condoneth their sin'.

ἀφέωνταί σοι αἱ ἁμαρτίαι σου]' (Lk. 5.20, cf. vv. 21, 23, 24). Elsewhere the idea of forgiving is explicitly connected with debts. The verb ὀφείλειν (= to owe, be indebted) which occurs twice in the parable of the unjust steward (Lk. 16.5, 7) also occurs in the parable of the two debtors (Lk. 7.41), where remission of unpayable debts is praised as a godly example. Debts which cannot be paid can only be forgiven or the debtor punished. The parable of the two debtors is located within the story of the woman who was a sinner which is climaxed by Jesus' declaration to those at table, 'Therefore I tell you, her sins, which are many, are forgiven [ἀφέωνται], for she loved much; but he who is forgiven [ἀφίεται] little, loves little' (Lk. 7.47). Jesus then tells the woman, 'Your sins are forgiven [ἀφέωνται σου αἱ ἁμαρτίαι]', which leads to the further question, 'Who is this, who even forgives sins [ὃς καὶ ἁμαρτίας ἀφίησιν]?' (Lk. 7.49). The verb ὀφείλειν also occurs in Luke's version of the Lord's Prayer: 'And forgive us our sins as we forgive everyone indebted to us [καὶ ἄφες ἡμιν τὰς ἁμαρτίας ἡμῶν, καὶ γὰρ αὐτοὶ ἀφὶομεν παντὶ ὀφείλοντι ἡμῖν]' (Lk. 11.4).

What exactly is going on here? In the Lord's Prayer it is evidently the Father who forgives, though it may be noted that Joachim Jeremias sees the petition for forgiveness as a sign of the messianic age.[1] So too, it is the Father who is asked to forgive in the cry from the cross (Lk. 23.34). A number of scholars have questioned whether Jesus ever actually forgave anyone. What he did was to *pronounce* forgiveness.[2] The use of the passive voice—the *theological passive*—in the pronouncement 'Your sins are forgiven you' is a device employed to avoid directly naming God as the subject of the action.[3]

[1]Jeremias takes the petition to say in effect: 'O Lord, we indeed belong to the age of the Messiah, to the age of forgiveness, and we are ready to pass on to others the forgiveness which we receive. Now grant us, dear Father, the gift of the age of salvation, thy forgiveness. We stretch out our hands, forgive us our debts—even now, even here, already today' (*The Prayers of Jesus* [SBT Second Series 6; London: S.C.M., 1967], pp. 103-104). While acknowledging the eschatological element in forgiveness, J.A.T. Robinson thinks that the eschatological dimension can be exaggerated. He holds that 'The prayer makes perfectly good sense as: Give us the freedom of the new world, release us from the burden of indebtedness, the chain of *karma*, so that forgiven we can forgive, reconciled we can reconcile, liberated we can liberate' (*Twelve More New Testament Studies* [London: S.C.M., 1984], p. 60).

[2]J. Duncan M. Derrett, 'Forgiveness in Luke-Acts', in *New Solutions of Old Conundrums: A Fresh Insight into Luke's Gospel* (Shipston-on-Sour: Peter I. Drinkwater, 1986), pp. 142-61; Robert A. Guelich, *Mark 1-8:26* (WBC 34A; Dallas: Word, 1989), pp. 87-94.

[3]Maximilian Zerwick, *Biblical Greek, Illustrated by Examples* (Scripta Pontificii Instituti Biblici 114; Rome: Pontifical Biblical Institute, 1963), #236, p. 76. Joachim Jeremias sees the use of the

Thus Jesus' authority on earth as Son of man to forgive sins (Lk. 5.24), which in Luke's report caused some to wonder who he was (Lk. 7.49) and others to deem his action blasphemous (Lk. 5.21),[1] may be construed in the light of what was said earlier about Jesus as the Father's שָׁלִיחַ. As God's anointed agent, he acted on the Father's behalf preaching 'good news to the poor', proclaiming 'release to the captives', and setting at liberty 'those who were oppressed' (cf. Lk. 4.18).[2]

All this stands in sharp contrast with Luke's depiction of the Pharisees and lawyers, and Jesus' clash with them over the nature of holiness. Jesus upbraids the Pharisees for cleansing the outside and failing to cleanse the inside. This can be done only by giving 'alms from within; and behold everything is clean for you' (Lk. 11.41). The Pharisees are so obsessed with tithing that they 'neglect justice and the love of God; these you ought to have done, without neglecting the others' (Lk. 11.42). They are 'like graves which are not seen, and men walk over them without knowing it' (Lk. 11.44). For these reasons Jesus pronounces woe upon them. He then turns to the lawyers: 'Woe to you lawyers also! for you load men with burdens hard to

---

'theological passive' as a characteristic of the *ipsissima vox Jesu* (*The Prayers of Jesus*, p. 115). Zerwick observes that in rabbinic literature this passive construction is rare, its place being taken more frequently by the indefinite plural, as in Lk. 16.9 'that they [i.e. God] may receive you into the eternal habitations' (#236, p. 76; cf. #2, pp. 1-2).

[1]There has been much discussion of whether the imputation of blasphemy reflects historical reality or later tradition. Fitzmyer notes that Jewish attitudes to blasphemy derive from Lev. 24.10-11, 14-16, 23, where abusive use of the divine name is punishable by death. In later rabbinical tradition, the person was not culpable unless he actually pronounced the divine name (*Sanhedrin* 7.5). However, Fitzmyer thinks that this tradition may represent the Pharisaic tendency to mitigate penal laws, especially those involving capital punishment. A wider use of the term, reflected in the NT, may belong to another Jewish tradition which linked blasphemy to implied attacks on God's saving power (2 Kgs. 19.4, 6, 22), his glory (Ezek. 35.12), or his people (2 Macc. 15.24). The charges against Jesus imply that he claimed to be equal with Yahweh. See J.A. Fitzmyer, *The Gospel According to Luke I-IX* (AB 28; Garden City: Doubleday, 1981), pp. 584-84; H.W. Beyer, *TDNT* I, pp. 621-25.

[2]Derrett observes: 'From the case of the Paralytic onwards . . . it is clear that the Son of Man's task was to terminate not sin, but, in a more practical sense, suffering due to sin. His coming puts an end to the divine vengeance *qua* the individual sufferer (e.g. Dt. 32.15-26 as illustrated at Mk 9.17-22)' (*New Resolutions of Old Conundrums*, p. 146).

Douglas E. Oakman develops Lk. 4.18-19 in another direction. Liberation and healing are a 'hallmark' of Luke's Jesus with the passage's recall of the Jubilee tradition of keeping the covenant community healthy through redistribution of land, the redemption of slaves, and the abolition of indebtedness (Lev. 25; Deut. 15. Isa. 61; cf. Jerome H. Neyrey, ed., *The Social World of Luke-Acts*, p. 169). Ultimately, it is bound up with the destruction of the temple and the abolition of the prevailing order. '[F]or Jesus, debt remission and temple destruction were bound up with an ideology of God's kingdom that envisioned the abolition of social stratification per se' (p. 176).

bear, and you do not touch the burdens with one of your fingers' (Lk. 11.46). Like their fathers, they are guilty of shedding the blood of those who are sent to them. 'Woe to you lawyers! For you have taken away the key of knowledge; you did not enter yourselves, and you hindered those who were entering' (Lk. 11.52).

Marcus J. Borg sees these pronouncements as part of a broader pattern of conflict. It was not that the Pharisees were insincere or perfunctory in their practice. What is at stake here are two conflicting forms of *orthopraxis*. For the Pharisees the dominant paradigm was holiness which called for meticulous observance of the law. For Jesus, on the other hand,

> To the extent that the imitation of God as holy led to this meticulous concern to the neglect of the weightier matters of Torah, holiness was inappropriate as the dominant model for Israel's self-understanding and understanding of God. Instead such emphasis was subordinated to a concern pointing to a different dominant paradigm designated by the terms justice, mercy and faithfulness. These, like holiness, were all characteristics of God and should on an *imitatio dei* model be characteristic of the community which would be faithful to Yahweh.[1]

4. *How Does all this Fit the Parable?*

In a broad sense the nation collectively and individually may be seen as stewards of the land and the life that God has given them. But the

---

[1]Marcus J. Borg, *Conflict, Holiness & Politics in the Teachings of Jesus* (Studies in the Bible and Early Christianity 5; New York and Toronto: Edwin Mellon, 1984), p. 102.

Klaus Berger likewise sees the essence of the conflict to lie in different conceptions of purity ('Jesus als Pharisäer und frühe Christen als Pharisäer', *NovT* 30 [1988], pp. 231-62). Jesus' association with sinners (Lk. 5.8, 30; 7.34, 37, 39; 15.1-2; 18.11-13; 19.7) and such actions as touching the bier carrying the widow of Nain's son, the woman with the issue of blood, and the presumed dead daughter of Jairus (Lk. 7.14; 8.40-56) broke with the Pharisaic understanding of holiness and purity laws. However, Berger sees the key to the conflict with the Pharisees to lie in 'the concept of offensive holiness/purity' which Jesus had in virtue of his anointing by the Spirit which enabled him to set aside impurity. According to Berger, Jesus confronted orthodox Pharisaism with a new form of Pharisaism, 'an eschatological-pneumatic Pharisaism, because Jesus is a Pharisee endowed with supreme authority' (p. 247, author's translation).

John H. Elliott sees the conflict in terms of a conflict between the social institutions of the temple and the household ('Temple versus Household in Luke-Acts: A Contrast in Social Institutions', in Neyrey, ed., *The Social World of Luke-Acts*, pp. 211-40). The contrasting conceptions of righteousness are starkly presented in the parable of the Pharisee and the tax collector praying in the temple (Lk. 18.9-14) with its implicit allusions to wealth and release from debt. Paradoxically, the wealthy tax collector is released from his debt. It is he who 'goes to his house justified' (v. 14) rather than the Pharisee who had practised self-denial and tithing. Elliott sees temple and household and their respective networks of relations as exemplifying contrasting styles of piety and behavior (pp. 213-15).

Pharisees, the lawyers, and Jesus himself may be seen as stewards in a special sense, since they were agents acting on behalf of God seeking to show the way in which the people should walk. All are accountable, but Jesus and his adversaries are deeply divided and mutual recriminations fly back and forth. Who is attacking whom in the parable, and what is its point?

In trying to answer this question, I begin by acknowledging that I follow Derrett in seeing usury as a significant factor. But in my reading of the parable, the usury can be detected on two levels. The crippling interest owed on two essential commodities—oil and wheat—is, as Derrett has shown, a reflection of oppressive social conditions which were in fact condemned by the law of God. The steward's action is praised by his Lord as restoring a situation sanctioned by God's law. Release from crushing debt makes life for the children of God once more livable. The parable is thus an indictment of usury, and of oppressive social conditions and structures.

However, the parable can be read on another level. Sin also brings crushing burdens. The teaching of the Pharisees and the lawyers serves only to compound the burdens of those caught up in it. Only the release proffered by the steward can help. However, the steward does not say that the debtors owe nothing at all. What he does is to cut away the usurious interest which God did not require anyway, and leave the debtors with the debt that they truly owed. This true debt is elsewhere correctly formulated by a lawyer in dialogue with Jesus as 'You shall love the Lord your God with all your heart, and with all your soul, and with all your mind; and your neighbor as yourself' (Lk. 10.27; cf. Deut. 6.4-5; Lev. 19.18). It is exemplified by the woman who is forgiven much, and who therefore loves much and may go in peace (Lk. 7.47-50), by the sinner Zacchaeus who promises to give half his goods to the poor and restore fourfold to anyone he has defrauded (Lk. 19.8), and by the widow who in the climactic event of Jesus' public ministry puts all her living into the treasury in God's house (Lk.21.4).

Kamlah is, therefore, right in seeing the parable as a critique of the Pharisees who compare unfavorably with the steward who mirrors the practice of Jesus.[1] The Pharisees place burdens on people in the pur-

---

1 This of course raises the question of the historical accuracy of Luke's portrayal. Sean Freyne observes: 'The gospel of Luke assumed that those who controlled the wealth, namely the Pharisees, were interested only in sharing with those from whom they could expect to receive in return, and if

suit of their understanding of holiness; Jesus releases the already overburdened. From here it is but a hair's breadth to the christological interpretation offered by Loader and myself.

Porter is right to suggest that irony is the key to understanding the parable. Ironically, Porter's view of the steward, his reprobate ways, and his impending fate coincides with my understanding of how the scribes and the Pharisees viewed Jesus! In their eyes Jesus was defrauding God of what was owed to him, and was thus plunging recklessly down the path to ruin.

Finally, I wish to reiterate my agreement with Loader, but point out some differences. Loader appears to me to be correct in saying that in Luke's structure, Lk. 15.1-2 provides the context not only for the three parables of chapter 15 (the lost sheep, the lost coin, and the prodigal son). It also provides the context for the parables in chapter 16 (the unjust steward, and the rich man and Lazarus). But it should be noted that, whereas the three parables about 'the lost' are addressed to the Pharisees and scribes who 'murmured, saying, "This man receives sinners and eats with them"' (Lk. 15.2), the parable of the unjust steward is addressed to the disciples, though it is overheard by the Pharisees (Lk. 16.1, 14). The parables of Lk. 15 are parables about God's outgoing love for the lost through Jesus. The parable of the unjust steward is a parable about the reaction of Pharisees and scribes to Jesus. It takes the indignant elder brother theme of the previous parable a step further and presents a criticism of the criticism.

The (rich) father of the previous parable turns up now as 'a rich man who had a steward' (v. 1). It should be noted that it is not the rich man who brings the charges. Rather, he listens to the charges of others, and as presumably they are attested by more than one witness, he lets the charges stand. In this respect he is no different than Jesus'

---

the historical Pharisees are to be identified with the townspeople, following Josephus, then there must be a general assumption of verisimilitude for the Lucan portrayal' (*Galilee, Jesus and the Gospels*, p. 161). Anthony J. Saldarini observes: 'From a sociological viewpoint, the Pharisees function as rich powerful patrons within the village society and as brokers for the peasants in their relations with the outside world. Luke's objection to them is that they do not care for the poor who depend on them and have a claim to their patronage, especially their generosity and reciprocal, just relations. Luke also complains that the poor, because they are judged to be unclean and outsiders to the social order, are deprived of justice. The Pharisees' use of purity regulations to maintain social order leads to unjust relationships. In response Luke defines true uncleanness as moral, not ritual, deficiency and thus opens Christianity's group boundaries to the outcasts, Gentiles and sinners' (*Pharisees, Scribes and Sadducees in Palestinian Society: A Sociological Approach* [Wilmington: Michael Glazier, 1988], p. 176).

Father who let the charges against Jesus stand later on (Lk. 22.71; 23.2, 14, 24). In view of the charges made against Jesus already, it is clear that he too cannot last long. The days of his stewardship are numbered. What can he do? As the steward soliloquizes, he reflects that he is not strong enough to dig, and he is ashamed to beg (v. 3). He would thus seem to discount the life-style of the Cynic beggar philosopher who disdained possessions and was content to be supported by begging.[1] Stewardship is Jesus' vocation, and he has no alternatives. The only thing he can do is turn to his master's debtors who are, in fact, those whom he has cared for all along.

The parable is thus a reaffirmation of Jesus' values, an ironic rejection oracle comparable with a passion prediction, and a policy statement. I differ from Loader over the purpose of the parable. The story is not simply that of a disarming rogue who confounds the righteous with his daring and blarney in order to shock people into new insight. To me, the parable presents the grim challenge of rejection and stark choices. It carries on the theme of the great banquet (Lk. 14.15-23), where all the invited are excluded in favor of the poor, maimed, blind, lame, and those to be found in the highways and hedges. It contains a rumbling echo of the complaint of the elder brother of the previous parable against the father's reception of the younger brother who has wasted his father's goods (Lk. 15.27-32; cf. 15.13). It is a forerunner of the parable of the vineyard (Lk. 20.9-19 par. Mt. 21.33-46; Mk 12.1-12), where the final agent sent by the owner is clearly identified as the owner's son. In this last parable the stakes have been raised to the limit. In the parable of the unjust steward things have not gone quite so far. The outcome remains open-ended with the Lord's praise balanced against his previous dismissal.

Strictly speaking, the steward is not purely and simply 'the unjust steward'; he is 'the steward of unrighteousness' (τὸν οἰκονόμον τῆς ἀδικίας). The term itself is capable of *double entendre*. Typically the genitive is understood as Semitic construction, reproducing a Hebrew genitive to denote an attribute or quality.[2] Thus translators

---

[1]*Pace* Burton L. Mack, *A Myth of Innocence: Mark and Christian Origins* (Philadelphia: Fortress, 1988), pp. 67-68.

[2]M. Zerwick, *Biblical Greek*, #40, pp. 14-15; F. Blass and A. Debrunner, *A Greek Grammar of the New Testament and Other Early Christian Literature*, ed. Robert W. Funk (Cambridge/Chicago: Cambridge University Press/Chicago University Press, 1961), #165, pp. 91-92. However, Blass-Debrunner suggest an alternative meaning: 'on account of the damage caused' (#176, p. 96, citing Sophie Antoniadis, *L'Évangile de Luc* [Paris, 1930], pp. 376ff.).

generally take it to be the equivalent of the adjective ἄδικος, e.g. 'dishonest manager' (RSV, NRSV, NIV). But 'manager' has a modern ring to it, and fails to preserve the ancient cultural associations of 'agent' or 'steward'. Moreover, adjectives like 'unjust', 'unrighteous' and 'dishonest' obscure the ironic subtlety of the parable and predetermine its meaning by assuming that the steward is guilty as charged. The Greek can mean both 'unrighteous steward' and 'steward of unrighteousness'.[1] The parable, in fact, challenges hearers to become involved and make their own decision. Is the steward guilty as charged and apparently as confirmed by his formal removal from office? Or is he the steward of unrighteousness, i.e. the agent charged with handling evil in an evil world, who in fact wins his master's praise for his sagacious actions?[2]

If the latter is the case, the statement καὶ ἐπῄνεσεν ὁ κύριος τὸν οἰκονόμον τῆς ἀδικίας ὅτι φρονίμως ἐποίησεν (v. 8) may be compared with the retort to the charge of being 'a glutton and a drunkard, a friend of tax collectors and sinners!': καὶ ἐδικαιώθη ἡ σοφία ἀπὸ πάντων τῶν τέκνων αὐτῆς (Luke 7.35). The parable may thus be analogous to other shocking comparisons in which Jesus figures: the thief coming at the unexpected hour (Lk.12.39-40 par. Mt. 24.43); Jesus as one who casts fire on the earth (Lk. 12.49), and who does not bring peace but a sword (Lk. 12.51 par. Mt. 10.34).[3] Moreover, my reading of the parable is not

---

[1]Drawing on Qumran literature, Hans Kosmala argues that such translations as 'unjust', 'dishonest', and 'fraudulent' are not only inadequate but wrong. The term describes neither his character nor his deed; it is 'an expression which assigns him to a certain group or category of people: he belongs to this world as opposed to the children of light'. He is 'a man who is completely bound up with this world in which ἀδικία is the ruling principle'. See Hans Kosmala, 'The Parable of the Unjust Steward in the Light of Qumran', *ASTI* 3 (1964), pp. 114-21. From Kosmala's position it appears to be only a small step to the one advocated above. Similar expressions are ὁ μαμωνᾶς τῆς ἀδικίας (Lk. 16.8, 9) and ὁ κριτὴς τῆς ἀδικίας (Lk. 18.6). But these terms are also susceptible of alternative translations.

[2]Recently C.S. Mann has proposed a modification of Kosmala's position, suggesting that ἀδικίας might be a textual error for ἁλικίας, 'experience', 'expertise' (*ExpTim* 102/8 [1991], pp. 234-235). Thus, the steward is commended for his mature judgment, and Christians are to learn to live so as to be accepted by those whom 'the children of light' (the Essenes) have seen fit to condemn to outer darkness. However, ἁλικία is a Doric form of ἡλικία and would be a *hapax legomenon* in NT Greek. In Luke ἡλικία has the sense of 'life span' (12.25) and 'stature' (19.3). Only in Lk. 2.52 could it mean 'years' or 'experience', though it could also mean 'stature'. Moreover, the proposal would not solve the apparently questionable action of the steward in what Mann takes to be a futures market gone wrong.

[3]I owe this point to Professor Robert H. Gundry, who also drew my attention to the question of how my interpretation fits Luke's strong emphasis on the innocence of Jesus. For other examples

incompatible with Luke's emphasis on the innocence of Jesus, which is stressed more strongly than in the Marcan parallels (Lk. 23.4, 13-17, 22, 25, 40-41, 47; Acts 2.22-23; 10.37-43). For the point of the parable is to challenge hearers to see through the charges levelled against Jesus, to acknowledge him, and to follow him in his way.

The original parable would thus seem to end with the master's praise in v. 8a. It fits the contention of Joachim Jeremias that

> All the Gospel parables are a defence of the Good News. The actual proclamation of the Good News to sinners took a different form: in the offer of forgiveness, in Jesus' invitation of the guilty to taste his hospitality, in his call to follow him. It was not to sinners that he addressed the Gospel parables, but to his critics: to those who rejected him because he gathered the despised around him.[1]

Insofar as Lk. 16.1 notes that the parable was addressed to the disciples, while implying that it was overheard by the Pharisees (Lk. 16.14), this contention needs only minor modification. The parable addresses *criticism* of Jesus rather than the critics directly. But as the parable was delivered in the public arena, the thrust of Jeremias's assertion remains intact.

But the parable is also a metaphor for hearers and readers of later generations as it reaches beyond its original historical, social context with the challenge of its riddle.[2] It raises questions about personal identity and survival, attitudes to wealth and possessions, integrity and service to God. What the parable raises enigmatically the appended sayings state categorically. The sayings which Luke attaches reach beyond the pre-Lukan parable, and provide guidance for the ongoing life of the church.[3] They maintain the irony and paradox with regard to both vocabulary and their recommended outlook on life, which turns worldly values upside down. They link the historical situation

---

of the shocking and comic in Luke see Joseph A. Grassi, *God Makes Me Laugh: A New Approach to Luke* (Wilmington: Michael Glazier, 1986). However, Grassi does not include the unjust steward.

[1]Jeremias, *The Parables of Jesus*, p. 145.

[2]On parable as metaphor see Robert W. Funk, *Language, Hermeneutic and Word of God: The Problem of Language in the New Testament and Contemporary Theology* (New York: Harper & Row, 1966), pp. 133-62.

[3]Luke T. Johnson sees possessions as a metaphor for human relations. He observes that the sayings appended to the parable are 'complex and even paradoxical. What emerges from them is the sense that the disposition of possessions, while in some way exterior to the self, less important than the self, even in some degree unworthy of the self, is nevertheless of critical importance for the disposition of the self' (*The Literary Function of Possessions in Luke-Acts*, p. 158).

addressed by the parable to the perennial questions of poverty and wealth, fidelity, and human relationships with God.

Lk. 16.8b stands as a rebuke of the holy separatism of 'the sons of light'. The steward and those who follow his example are 'sons of this age' (οἱ υἱοὶ τοῦ αἰῶνος τούτου). They are 'wiser' (φρονιμώτεροι) in dealing with their 'generation' (γενεὰν), the mass of sinful, marginalized humanity, than are 'the sons of light'. Both the terminology[1] and the contrasting attitudes to the marginalized reflect the piety embodied in the Qumran literature. The saying of v. 8b, like the preceding parable, repudiates the piety which distances itself from the marginalized, and seeks instead to make the care of the marginalized a major concern. This concern was characteristic of Jesus in contrast to the kind of piety which excluded the marginalized[2] lest they defile the camp[3] and the blemished lest they profane God's sanctuary.[4]

---

[1]Fitzmyer suggests that the expressions 'sons of this world' and 'children of light' are illuminated by the Qumran literature (*Luke [X-XXIV]*, p. 1108; idem, *Essays on the Semitic Background of the New Testament* [London: Geoffrey Chapman, 1971], pp. 208-11). οἱ υἱοὶ τοῦ αἰῶνος τούτου appears to reflect כל בני תבל 'all the children of the world' (CD 20.34), a designation for people outside the Qumran community. τοὺς υἱοὺς τοῦ φωτὸς reflects בני אור (1QS 1.9; 2.16; 3.13, 24, 25; 1QM 1.3, 9, 11, 13; 4QFlor 1-2 i 8-9; 4Q177 10-11.7; 12-13 i 7-11). 'Sons of light' was a favorite self-designation of the community. It was taken over by the church (1 Thess. 5.5; Eph. 5.8; Jn 12.36). Here, however, it appears to be used ironically of those opposed to Jesus and of those who do not follow him in his way.

[2]I am indebted to Professor Howard Clark Kee for drawing my attention to the contrast between Jesus' attitudes to holiness and the rejected and those described in the Temple Scroll. Jesus' concern with outcasts and the nature of holiness is antithetical to that described in the Temple Scroll. On this see Yigael Yadin, *The Temple Scroll: The Hidden Law of the Dead Sea Sect* (New York: Random House, 1985); Johann Maier, *The Temple Scroll: An Introduction, Translation and Commentary* (JSOTS 34, Sheffield: JSOT, 1985). Handwriting styles indicate that the scroll dates from around 100 BCE (Yadin, pp. 59-61) or prior to 125-100 BCE (Maier, pp. 1-2).

Yadin notes that 'The biblical "camp" was all-embracing. Thus, all the ordinances concerning cleanliness and uncleanness were operative not for the Temple alone but also for the city of the Temple. The city was to be holy and clean, not only in name but also in practice' (p. 171). Following to the letter injunctions like Isa. 52.1, Joel 3.17, Lev. 21.17-23, the Scroll bans entry to the city to all who were unclean, including the blind, lepers, the lame, and the blemished (Yadin, *The Temple Scroll*, pp. 170-177; 11QT 45, ET in Maier, pp. 40-41; G. Vermes, *The Dead Sea Scrolls in English* [3rd ed.; London: Penguin, 1987], pp. 143-44). Perversion of justice and corruption likewise caused exclusion. 'For bribery perverts justice, and falsifies the words of justice, and blinds the eyes of the wise, and causes great guilt, and pollutes the house with the guilt of sin. Justice, justice, you shall strive after, so that you may live and come to inherit the land which I give to you as an inheritance for all time. And the man who takes a bribe and perverts justice in judgment shall be killed, and you shall not be afraid of killing him' (11QT 51.13-18; Maier, p. 45; cf. Vermes, p. 147).

[3]Yigael Yadin traces the underlying thought of both normative Judaism, crystallized by the rabbis of the Mishnah, and also of the extremist views of the Qumran community to the command of Num.

The ensuing sayings develop the theme of stewardship in the service of God and the marginalized. Hearers are exhorted to make friends by use of the Mammon of unrighteousness, so that when it fails 'they' (i.e. God, if the indefinite plural is a circumlocution for the name of God, or the beneficiaries, or both) may receive you into 'the everlasting tents' (εἰς τὰς αἰωνίους σκηνάς) (v. 9). Fidelity in the use of the Mammon of unrighteousness is a test of fidelity with regard to 'true riches' (vv. 10-13). Finally, hearers are reminded that no house slave (οἰκέτης), i.e. disciple as contrasted with the steward (οἰκονόμος), can serve two masters: 'You cannot serve God and mammon' (v. 13). Mammon may be used, but not served. God alone is the one who is to be served.

Contrary to appearances, neither the steward nor Jesus is serving two masters. Both exercise their stewardship in the service of those in need and the One whose praise alone counts. Jesus' concern is not with the 'righteous' (cf. Lk. 5.32) but with the wicked, the marginalized, the outsiders, and the outcasts.[1] It is a concern which has been consistently demonstrated in Luke's account of Jesus. It was this concern which proved to be the real cause of offence for the religious establishment.[2] Perhaps the difference between Jesus' attitude now and what it was before lies in the fact that time is running out not only for Jesus the steward, but also for the scribes and Pharisees. Up till now he has consorted with them, but from now on (as in the three previous parables about 'the lost') Jesus' exclusive concern will be with 'the lost'. Jesus will exacerbate offence with his barbed parable of the Pharisee and the tax collector (Lk. 18.9-14), and by going to be a guest in the home of a man like Zacchaeus who is a sinner (Lk. 19.8).

5.2-3: 'Command the people of Israel that they put out of the camp every leper, and every one having a discharge, and every one that is unclean through contact with the dead; you shall put out both male and female, putting them outside the camp, that they may not defile the camp, in the midst of which I dwell' (*The Temple Scroll*, p. 170). According to Yadin, the difference between the rabbis and the Essenes lay in the more lenient interpretation of the rabbis who applied different purity laws to different 'camps' of the people, whereas the Essenes applied all the ordinances to the temple and the temple city.

[4]Yadin links the exclusion of the blemished from the temple city to the injunction of Lev. 21.17-23 and the saying of 2 Sam. 5.8 which was taken to mean that disability was divine punishment for the sinful and impure (*The Temple Scroll*, pp. 175-76).

[1]J. Ramsey Michaels links this attitude with Jesus' own experience. 'Like the robbery victim in the parable, he learned who his neighbor was—not the Pharisee but the prostitute. He learned to approve what his culture despised. The woman's actions demonstrated to him that God had touched her, and in obedience he declared her sins forgiven' (*Servant and Son*, p. 225).

[2]E.P. Sanders, *Jesus and Judaism* (London/Philadelphia: S.C.M./Fortress, 1985), pp. 174-77.

It is the sinner Zacchaeus who will vindicate the stewardship of Jesus by giving half his goods to the poor and restoring fourfold to those whom he has wronged. It is not to the Pharisees but to Zacchaeus that Jesus will turn and say (with studied allusion to himself)[1]: 'Today salvation has come to this house, since he also is a son of Abraham. For the Son of man came to seek and to save the lost' (Lk. 19.9).[2]

---

[1]There is a double allusion here. The first is an allusion to Jesus' name. Ἰησοῦς corresponds to the Hebrew יֵשׁוּעַ, the abbreviated form of יְהוֹשׁוּעַ, which means 'Yahweh saves' (cf. Mt. 1.21). Thus there is a pun on Jesus' name which at the same time heightens the significance of what is happening. God has touched Zacchaeus' life in the person of Jesus, who as his agent has brought salvation to his house.

The second allusion recalls our parable. In befriending Zacchaeus and being received into his house Jesus has acted out the recommendation of Lk. 16.9 with regard to being received by the beneficiaries of wise stewardship.

[2]Since the above study was set up in print Mary Ann Beavis has put forward a fresh interpretation ('Ancient Slavery as an Interpretive Context for the New Testament Servant Parables with Special Reference to the Unjust Steward [Luke 16.1-8]', *JBL* 111 [1992], pp. 37-54). She contends that the steward was really a slave, and that the parable should be seen in the context of classical slave stories offering social comment. The slave stories that she notes do indeed illustrate social comment. However, they do little to explain the parable in the specific context of the Jewish social and religious situation, or its place in Luke's Gospel and in the life and teaching of Jesus. Moreover, the thesis that the steward was a slave does not seem to fit the parable itself. For the punishment envisaged for the steward's alleged mismanagement is not a whipping, demotion, imprisonment, or forced labor in the quarries, but dismissal from office. It prompts the steward to review his options and ponder the possibilities for life after stewardship. Manumission was rarely a reward for faithful service; it is unthinkable as a punishment for unfaithful service.

'THE BODY OF CHRIST' IN PAUL

James D. G. Dunn

1. *Introduction*

'The body of Christ' is one of the most important and most fascinating of the concepts used by Paul. More than any other it provides a bridge between Paul's christology and his ecclesiology. That is its importance. But that same fact gives it a tantalising character: what does it actually say about the relation between Christ and the church? That is its fascination. The issue thus posed is one which has intrigued me for many years, but opportunity to pursue it was lacking. The occasion of Ralph Martin's Festschrift is the opportunity needed. It is a particular pleasure to offer this small token of friendship and respect to one who has worked so long and so fruitfully in areas of NT studies closely adjacent to my own areas of interest.[1]

'The body of Christ' is one of the few themes in Pauline thought which is represented with equal strength and vigour on both sides of the line dividing the major Pauline letters from the later Paulines (Colossians and Ephesians). But while the same phrase (the body of Christ) can be used to denote the complete spectrum, the emphases and ways in which the theme is developed are clearly different. The briefer references in Romans 12 are very close to the developed treatment in 1 Corinthians 12 for us to recognize without dispute that the line of thought is basically the same. So too the briefer references in Colossians 1 and 2 seem close enough to the fuller treatments of Ephesians 1 and 4 for us to recognize closely parallel lines of thought. But between the two sets of pairs (Romans/1 Corinthians and

---

[1]Of particular relevance among his many studies in the larger area are *The Family and the Fellowship* (Exeter: Paternoster, 1979), pp. 69-72, and *The Spirit and the Congregation: Studies in 1 Corinthians 12-15* (Grand Rapids: Eerdmans, 1984), pp. 21-30.

Colossians/Ephesians) there seems to be a major shift in perspective, highlighted especially by the contrast between 1 Cor. 10.16-17 and 11.24, on the one hand, and Eph. 1.22-23 on the other.

We proceed by asking three simple questions: What are the points of continuity between the several Pauline usages and what are the main differences? How have they arisen? And what continuing significance might they have for our understanding of Paul's ecclesiology in particular?

But first, it might be helpful to set out the chief references, limited as they are to the four Pauline letters. I set them out in what is generally agreed to be the most likely chronological order of the letters.

1 Cor. 10.16-17	The bread which we break, is it not participation in the *body* of Christ? Because there is one bread, we the many are one *body*, for we all share in the one bread.
11.24, 27, 29	This is my *body* which is for you . . . . . . is answerable for the *body* and blood of the Lord. . . . not discerning the *body*.
12.12-13	Just as the *body* is one and has many members and all the members of the *body*, though many are one *body*, so also is the Christ. For in one Spirit we were all baptized into one *body* . . .
12.14-27	For the *body* does not have one member but many . . . There are many parts, but one *body*. . . . You are Christ's *body* and individually members.
Rom. 12.4-5	Just as in one *body* we have many members, and all the members do not have the same function, so we all are one *body* in Christ, and individually members of one another.
Col. 1.18, 24	He is the head of the *body*, the church . . . . . . his *body*, the church.
2.19	. . . the head, from whom the whole *body*, nourished and held together through its joints and ligaments, grows with the growth which is of God.
3.15	. . . you were called in one *body*.

Eph. 1.22-23	(God) has given him as head over all things to the church, which is his *body*, the fulness of him who fills all in all.
2.15-16	. . . in order that he might create the two in him into one new man, making peace, and might reconcile us both in one *body* for God through the cross . . .
4.4	There is one *body* and one Spirit . . .
4.12, 15-16	. . . for the building up of the *body* of Christ . . . . . . we may grow up in every way into him, who is the head, Christ, from whom the whole *body*, joined and held together through every joint which gives supply, according to the activity appropriate to each individual part, makes the growth of the *body* to build itself up in love.
5.23, 30	The Christ is also head of the church, he himself saviour of the *body*. . . . . . . we are members of his *body*.

2. *Continuity and Differences*

There are two very striking features common to all four letters.

2.1 *One Body.*

The first is the consistent and repeated emphasis on 'oneness'. The single most common phrase in the above passages is 'one body' (1 Cor. 10.17; 12.12-13, 20; Rom. 12.4-5; Col. 3.15; Eph. 2.16; 4.4). We may make an immediate deduction: *the fact that the physical 'body' provided a model for organic unity was a major factor in the attractiveness and usefulness of the theme to Paul.*

The continuity of the motif, however, masks a number of differences within the theme. In 1 Cor. 10 the oneness of the body is correlated with the oneness of the eucharistic bread; in some sense the oneness of the community of believers is a 'product' of the oneness of the loaf shared; or, to be more in tune with the emphasis of the passage, the oneness of the congregation focuses on and hangs upon their common *participation* in the bread (and wine) which is Christ's body (and blood).[1] In 1 Cor. 12, however, the oneness is a product of the one Spirit; or, again more precisely, of their common participation in the one Spirit. Only as manifestations of 'the same Spirit' (1 Cor. 12.4, 8-9, 11), of the 'one Spirit' (1 Cor. 12.9, 13 twice), are the charismata to be valued.[2] In the former, we may speak legitimately of '*the eucharistic body*'. In the latter, we may speak equally legitimately of '*the charismatic body*'. Paul does not provide any more indication of how they should be correlated in an overall ecclesiology. We should perhaps content ourselves with noting that they must have been correlated in Paul's thought; he can put them side by side without any sense of them rubbing against each other. But there is nothing in the immediate context to indicate whether one was primary in relation to the other.

In Rom. 12 the thought is essentially the same as in 1 Cor. 12: the body as a charismatic body; individuals as members of the body and thus having a 'function' (charism) within it; the diversity of members and of charisms as integral to and constitutive of the oneness of the body. It is important to note that the double reference to the 'one body' comes as part of a warning against pride and presumption regarding God's bestowal of grace (Rom. 12.3). In the absence of any reference or allusion to the Lord's supper, the inference is probably justified that of the two (eucharistic and charismatic unity), it is the latter which is more fundamental for Paul (cf. 8.9, 14).

In Colossians the motif of oneness is much diminished. It is absent from the early body references, and is picked up only in a passage containing many elements of established (Pauline) paraenesis (3.15). In contrast to the other treatments of the body of Christ in the Pauline letters, there was evidently less need to emphasize the motif. The fact that the appeal to the oneness of the body is nevertheless retained, however, shows how integral to the body theme was the thought of the oneness of the body.

The motif re-emerges with strength in Ephesians, particularly in chs. 2 and 4. In the former it is a quite new emphasis: the oneness is the oneness of Jew and Gentile in Christ; the crucified Christ as the point where the two become one. In the latter, despite the emphasis

---

[1]The thematic words are κοινωνία/κοινωνός = 'participation/partner' or 'sharing/sharer' (1 Cor. 10.16 twice, 18, 20) and μετέχειν, 'to share or participate in' (1 Cor. 10.17, 21, 30).

[2]It is the oneness of the Spirit which is the point of emphasis; the thought of one baptism as such is not to the fore.

on the oneness of the Spirit (4.4; as in 2.18), it is a more formally or credally conceived unity (4.4-6). And while the diversity of gifts (not 'charisms' here) is emphasized, there is little of the corresponding emphasis of 1 Cor. 12 and Rom. 12 that the *unity of the body* consists of and depends on the proper functioning of these gifts. The only unity mentioned is 'the unity of faith and the knowledge of the Son of God', and is presented as the goal of the gifts, the end-product of the maturing of the body (Eph. 4.13), rather than that (organic) unity which is constituent of the body as such. In Eph. 5, in a further variation, the clear implication is that the oneness of flesh of husband and wife is symbolical of the oneness of body between Christ and his church (5.29-32).

In summary, it is worth noting how many variations could be played on the theme of the body of Christ in terms of its oneness. At different times we read of a eucharistic unity, a charismatic unity, a unity of Jew and Gentile, a unity of faith, and a unity like that between husband and wife—all as manifestations of the oneness of the body. How do these hang together? Can we speak of any single integrating theme? Are they simply accidental expressions of a common perception regarding the organic oneness of a *body*, providing an occasion for fitting exhortation? Or is the motif of the oneness of the body *of Christ* itself the more fundamental feature of which the above mentioned are simply illustrations or expressions? These are questions which we will have to bear in mind as we proceed.

2.2 *The body of Christ.*

The second striking feature common to all four letters is the fact that the body in view is always 'the body of Christ' or the body (of believers) defined by its relation to Christ (1 Cor. 10.16; 11.24, 27; 12.12; Rom. 12.5; Col. 1.18, 24; Eph. 1.22; 4.12; 5.30). Although not all of the above body passages contain explicit references to Christ, it is sufficiently clear that *the Christ-relatedness of the body is constitutive of the whole theme*. That is to say, the Pauline use of the body imagery is determined not simply by the value of the imagery for asserting and describing organic unity, but because it also describes the relation between Christ and the church.

Here too, however, the variations within the theme are noteworthy. In 1 Cor. 10-11 'the body of Christ' refers (primarily) to the eucharistic bread (10.16; 11.24, 27); but the assembled believers are also called 'one body' by virtue of their participation in that bread (10.17; 11.29?). Are they then also 'the body of Christ'? It is often assumed so, but Paul does not actually say so.[1] Several exegetical possibilities are clear. Is the effect of sharing the one loaf that believers become *one* body?—the body imagery derived from elsewhere, with the emphasis simply on the *oneness* produced by the shared act? Or does the act of sharing the one loaf constitute the participants as one *body*?—their body-ness the result of their embodying (by eating) the one loaf? Or does the act of sharing the body of Christ (bread) constitute them as the body of *Christ* (assembled congregation)? And what is the relation of Christ to his body thus described? Is he the bread and/or congregation in some literal sense?—his very existence bound up in these entities of time and space?[2] Or do they simply represent him, or serve as the focus of his significance and Spirit in a special but not exclusive way? We touch here, of course, on matters of ancient controversy. But in trying to study our theme with fresh eyes it is well to pose the range of alternatives as they must have appeared to more than a few of Paul's original readership.

In 1 Cor. 12 the position is further complicated. 'So also is the Christ' (12.12). Does Paul mean that Christ *is* a body, or is *like* a body, or that believers by their relation to Christ constitute a body, that is 'the body of Christ'? The first seems to be what Paul says. But in 12.27 he calls the Corinthian church 'Christ's body'; does he then mean that the Corinthians are part of Christ's very existence? On the other hand, the closely parallel passage in Rom. 12.4-5 seems to point to the last alternative—not 'Christ is a body', or even 'you are Christ's body', but 'we are one body *in Christ*'. The fact that Paul can express such closely parallel thoughts (1 Cor. 12.27/Rom. 12.5) with such variation strongly suggests that the point being made is not one of dogmatic precision, but one of metaphorical imprecision, calculated more to stir the heart than to instruct the mind.

The jump to Colossians and Ephesians contains a shift of some significance. The exortation of Col. 3:15 has the same metaphorical imprecision as Rom. 12.5; and in Col. 1.18 and 24 'the church' is explicitly identified with Christ's body.[3] When compared with the

---

[1]See e.g. discussion in C.K. Barrett, *1 Corinthians* (London: Black, 1968), pp. 273-5; G.D. Fee, *1 Corinthians* (NICNT; Grand Rapids: Eerdmans, 1987), pp. 563-4.

[2]See J.A.T. Robinson, *The Body* (London: SCM, 1952), p. 58; S. Kim, *The Origin of Paul's Gospel* (WUNT 24; Tübingen: Mohr-Siebeck, 1981), p. 253.

[3]That there was an earlier form of the hymn in which Christ was depicted as 'the head of the body

earlier Pauline references, a fair implication would seem to be that opportunity has been taken to clarify the relation between Christ and the church: simply to call Christ a body and to identify the church with this body may well have caused some confusion. A neat solution is to call Christ the *head* of this body, particularly since both the word itself ('head') and the corresponding physiology (2.19) naturally combine to give the one so described a leading and dominant role over the rest of the body.[1] It should be noted, however, that so to distinguish the head within the body imagery as a whole runs somewhat counter to the oneness motif, particularly in its earlier form emphasizing mutual interdependence of all members of the body and warning against thought of undue pre-eminence on the part of any member (Rom. 12.3; 1 Cor. 12.14-26). This suggests in turn that the head-body distinction did not belong to the original Christianization of the body theme but is an adaption of it.

With Ephesians we hear the same melody as in Colossians only with richer harmonies. The church is indeed Christ's body; but now it is clear that the church is the church *universal*, whereas in the earlier Paulines the thought was consistently of the local congregation(s) of a city or region.[2] Moreover, the cosmic role for this Christ, which was only briefly alluded to in Col. 1.18-20, is now expressed with an amazing and breath-taking breadth of vision—the church itself as 'the fulness of him who fills all in all' (Eph. 1.22-23). Something of the old tension re-emerges in 2.15-16: is Christ the 'new man', the 'one body', or are Jew and Gentile the new man 'in him', reconciled in/by the one body of Christ crucified? Similarly in 4.12-16 there is some tension between the thought of the body of Christ, of Christ as the measure and stature of mature manhood, and the talk of growing up into Christ. What holds the whole together, however, is the motif of Christ's headship (Eph. 1.22; 4.15; 5.23): it fittingly describes the relation between the exalted Christ and the new order of things

---

(that is, of the cosmos)' is regularly assumed; cf. e.g. the discussion in E. Lohse, *Kolosser und Philemon* (KEK; Göttingen: Vandenhoek & Ruprecht, 1968), pp. 79-80, 93-96 and P.T. O'Brien, *Colossians, Philemon* (WBC 44; Waco: Word, 1982), pp. 48-52. Either way, however, the point for us is the identification of the church as Christ's body in the present form of the text.

[1] See e.g. H. Schlier, 'κεφαλή', *TDNT*, III, p. 674; E. Schweizer, 'σῶμα', *TDNT*, VII, p. 1036.

[2] That the Ephesians references (1.22; 2.10, 21; 5.23-25, 27, 29, 32) envisage 'the church' as a universal entity is generally recognized. For the earlier Pauline references see my *Jesus and the Spirit* (London: SCM, 1975), pp. 262-3 and n. 17.

(1.22);[1] in the elaboration of the thought expressed in Col. 2.19 it successfully combines the new emphasis on the mutual responsibility and interdependence of the body's members (4.15-16); and in 5.23-30 marriage provides a familiar symbol which includes thought both of the husband's headship and of the one-fleshness (body) of husband and wife. But again the inference lies close to hand that this emphasis on Christ's headship was not part of the original imagery but an adaption and development in the Christian use of it.

As with the oneness motif, so with the sustained talk of the body of Christ, we are left with the impression of a powerful theme which allowed both variation and development. Initially it was evidently unimportant that Christ should be clearly distinguished from the body which was the church: was Christ the body, or was the worshipping congregation one body in him? At this stage, we may summarize, the ecclesiology could be said to loom larger than the christology. Only with the later Paulines is there a coherent attempt made to clarify the relation of Christ to his body, the church, by designating him as the head of this body. Here christology begins to dominate ecclesiology. A striking consequence, however, is that the correlative picture of the church is one far removed from that of Romans and 1 Corinthians: the earlier dominated by concerns of personal relationships within particular congregations; the latter highly symbolical, an idealized depiction of cosmic proportions.

3. *How have such differences arisen?*

How may such differences be explained? The question is partly one about the origin of the theme itself, and partly one about the factors and influences which shaped its development.

3.1 *The origin of the theme.*

From where did Paul derive the theme of the body of Christ? The issue has been debated repeatedly and at great length during the pre-

---

[1]The dative τῇ ἐκκλησίᾳ is ambiguous. It could be taken in the sense 'for the church' and to indicate a degree of subordination of Christ to the church; cf. A.T. Lincoln, *Ephesians* (WBC 42; Dallas: Word, 1990)—'All the supremacy and power God has given to Christ he has given to be used on behalf of the Church' (p. 70). But the meaning is probably advanced better by the translation, 'gave to the church', with 'give' used in the sense, 'appointed' (BAGD, δίδωμι 5); the implication being that Christ exercises his lordship over all things *through* the church. At all events, the church can hardly be excluded from Christ's lordship over 'all things' (4.15; 5.23).

sent century, and we need not rehearse all the options and arguments. But some significant pointers emerge from the above review of the most relevant Pauline texts, and these do deserve some elaboration.

The first is the relation of the two motifs outlined above to each other. Despite the diversity within the motif of oneness, there is *a constant emphasis on the body as focus, expression, medium of oneness* as a way of dealing with differences—in social standing and related conduct (1 Cor. 10), in charisms (1 Cor. 12), in self-perception (Rom. 12), in relationships (Col. 3), between Jew and Gentile (Eph. 2), in expression of faith (Eph. 4), between husband and wife (Eph. 5). This constancy of emphasis stands in some contrast to the tensions within the other main motif, where the simply stated theme of 'the body of Christ' masks a range of questions about the relation of Christ to the church—Christ as the bread of the Lord's Supper (1 Cor. 10-11), or as the body which is the local church, or like a body (1 Cor. 12), or the church as a body in Christ (Rom. 12), or Christ as 'given to the church' and as the head of the church universal and cosmic (Col. and Eph.).

This observation suggests at once from where Paul derived the image of the church as body. Not directly from any Gnostic or proto-Gnostic concept of the cosmos as a body: quite apart from the issue of whether there was anything properly to be described as pre-Christian Gnosticism, the correlation between the body imagery and the cosmos appears only in the later Pauline letters; had that been the source of the imagery we would have expected more indication in the earlier letters.[1] Nor from any concept of Adam or Messiah as a corporate entity:[2] that explains neither the unresolved tensions within the body of Christ motif nor the constant emphasis on oneness in and through diversity. Nor from the revelatory words heard by Paul at his conversion/commissioning (according to Acts 9.4; 22.7; 26.14).[3] No trace of such a link is evident anywhere in Paul, either in the passages where he recalls his conversion/commissioning, or in the body of Christ passages. Nor simply from the eucharistic words:[4] this element is limited to only one of the four letters, and of itself hardly provides the flexibility which is such a feature of the Pauline treatment of the

---

[1]See e.g. Lincoln's concise discussion (*Ephesians*, pp. 68-69.).

[2]As in E. Best, *One Body in Christ* (London: SPCK, 1955) *passim*; Martin, *Spirit and Congregation*, p. 24.

[3]As by Robinson, *Body*, p. 58; Kim, *Origin of Paul's Gospel*, p. 253.

[4]Cf. L. Cerfaux, *The Church in the Theology of St. Paul* (New York: Herder, 1959), pp. 262-82.

relation between Christ and the church.

The answer is most likely to be found in the more widely attested use of the same theme to establish the same unity-despite-diversity principle. For the fact is that precisely the same body imagery was already quite commonly used in reference to the state, as a means of inculcating a due sense of mutual belonging and mutual responsibility of the different constituents within the state.[1] Since it is precisely this emphasis on mutual belonging and interdependence of different elements within the community of the church which is such a constant within the Pauline usage, it is much the most natural to assume that this same emphasis indicates the origin of the theme itself. *Paul reaches for the body imagery as a means to assert unity (oneness) in and through diversity because that was already the function of the imagery in common usage.*

To this we might add the observation that the actual experience of the early congregations seems to have been a major factor in determining the use of the theme. In the most sustained treatments of the body of Christ in the Pauline letters it is always the charismatic body which is in view;[2] the churches are one as sharing in the one Spirit and as diversely gifted by the one Spirit (Rom. 12; 1 Cor. 12; Eph. 4).[3] In the first two cases in particular, it is immediately clear why Paul drew on the theme of the 'one body': it was a way of holding the diversity of charismatic endowment within a unity of shared experience, mutual interdependence and common dedication; Eph. 4 seems to be a rather more formalized expression of a familiar and well established Pauline theme. Perhaps we may say then that it was such an experience of 'bodyness' which prompted Paul to draw the imagery into use in his own theology and paraenesis. That is to say, it may well have been the recognition that the same tensions which commonly afflict the state were present in his congregations, together with the conviction that the shared experience of the Spirit was the (only) basis of that unity of mutual recognition and interdependence which any state must aspire to, which attracted Paul to make such use of the body

---

[1] See references e.g. in H. Schlier, *Epheser* (Düsseldorf: Patmos, 1957), p. 91; Martin, *Spirit and Congregation*, pp. 22-23; Lincoln, *Ephesians*, p. 70.

[2] 'Only in the context of the effects and gifts of grace does the apostle utilize the ancient world's figure of the one body and the variety of its members'—G. Bornkamm, *Paul* (London: Hodder, 1971), p. 195.

[3] In Col. 3.15 the thought is still on the charismatic body, as the reference to 'spiritual songs' in particular (3.16) indicates.

imagery for his own congregations.

A crucial difference between Paul's usage and the wider usage of Greco-Roman world, of course, is Paul's understanding of the body-church as 'the body *of Christ*'. That, however, does nothing to alter the above conclusion; for it is precisely the relation between the two concepts (body/Christ) which causes the tension in the outworking of the theme. This feature again implies that the designation of the body-church as *Christ's* body is itself an adaption of the more fundamental imagery (body = state/community). No express reason is given as to why Paul should so adapt the wider model, but we may presume that one or more of several factors were influential.

For one thing, since Paul was adapting a more widely familiar imagery it would be necessary for him to mark out its distinctiveness from that other, wider usage. The most obvious differentiating feature was the relationship of the Christian community to Christ; it was precisely this relationship which constituted them as a community in distinction from other social, national, and religious groups in the cities of the Roman Empire. So they were 'one body in Christ' (Rom. 12.5). At the same time, the shared eucharistic bread, which provided another crucial focus of unity, equated Christ with the body (1 Cor. 10.16; 11.24). So Christ could be likened to a body. Moreover, the 'in Christ' language itself implied a conception of Christ as a 'corporate person'.[1] So the worshipping congregation, sharing in his Spirit, could be called his body. Presumably it was factors like these which made it obvious that the body imagery could be used for the Christian communities *only if it was related to Christ*. And presumably it was because these different convictions were not yet clearly coordinated that the relation between Christ and the body-church remained so ill-defined in the earlier Pauline letters.

In short, *the consistency of the oneness emphasis in the Pauline talk of the church-as-a-body strongly suggests that the theme entered Pauline theology as an adaption of the more familiar Greco-Roman presentation of the state-as-a-body*. Paul's designation of the body-church as 'the body of Christ' does not indicate the origin of the theme, but tells us rather how the theme was Christianized.

---

[1]See particularly C.F.D. Moule, *The Origin of Christology* (Cambridge University Press, 1977), ch. 2; cf. p. 154 n. 2 above.

3.2 *The Development of the Theme*
What then of the development of the theme in the Pauline corpus? Can we say anything about the influences which shaped the use of the theme through the Pauline letters? It is possible to detect three factors in particular.

a) *Stoic Thought.* The most striking development is from body of Christ = local congregation (1 Cor. 12.27) to body of Christ = universal church = fulness of him who fills everything in every way (Eph. 1.22-23). This development, remarkable though it may seem to the twentieth century reader, however, is much more understandable in terms of the conclusion just reached. For it was equally part of Stoic and the wider religious philosophy of the time to use the imagery of a body for the cosmos as for the state. For such thinkers, the rational being was as much part of the rational cosmos as he was of the ideally rational state. Fundamental to the Stoic conception of the wholeness and coherence of reality was the conviction that the cosmos was an organic unity, just like a body, of which each element in the universe was a part.[1]

Given then that Paul or the authors of the later Paulines were familiar with and dependent on the Stoic idea of the body-state, it would be natural for them to extend the imagery in the same way: the principle of coherence and unity by which Christ constitutes the Christian congregation is also the principle which gives coherence and unity to the whole cosmos. And since it is the church which is the current embodiment of that principle, the church itself has to be understood as a cosmic entity, 'the fulness of him who fills all in all' (Eph. 1.23).[2]

b) *The problem of Israel.* A second factor of significance is likely to have been Paul's wrestling with the problem of Israel, that is, the problem of how to correlate Jew and Gentile within the one community, while affirming that the blessings received therein are the blessings promised to Israel, still valid to Israel despite the large scale Jewish rejection of the gospel. This in fact provides the chief linking strand in the oneness motif between the early and later letters. Thus,

---

[1]See e.g. Schweizer, 'σῶμα', *TDNT*, VII, pp. 1029-30, 1037-39; Lohse, *Kolosser*, pp. 93-95.
[2]For the most recent and careful discussion of this difficult phrase see Lincoln, *Ephesians*, pp. 72-78.

while its first expression relates almost exclusively to the dangers of charismatic divisiveness in 1 Cor. 12, the re-working of the motif in Rom. 12 already reflects Paul's obsession with the problem of Israel. For in the latter, the warning against pride and presumption, which introduces the motif (Rom. 12.3), is precisely the same warning that Paul has pressed both upon Jews in relation to Gentiles (Rom. 2.1 - 3.31) and upon Gentiles in relation to Jews (Rom. 11.7-24).[1] The oneness of the body is precisely the oneness of the mixed Jew-and-Gentile churches in Rome (hence the climactic Rom. 15.7-12). The transition from this to Eph. 2.11-22 is not so great. For Eph. 2.11-22 is in fact the richest exposition of the earlier Pauline hope: that Gentiles will recognize that the relation with God into which they have been introduced is that first given to Israel; that the abolition of the cultic and legal barriers which previously divided Jew from Gentile now unites them in a new man who embodies a reconciliation which is the extension of Israel's privileges beyond the old boundaries and an embracing of Gentile as well as Jew within the same citizenship and household of God.[2]

That this Pauline concern for the problem of Israel is a factor in the development of the body theme is probably confirmed by the parallel between the end of Eph. 1 and the end of Eph. 2. In the former the church is equated with the cosmos, in adaptation of the Stoic imagery, if our suggestion is correct. In the latter the church is the household of God, 'a holy temple in the Lord', a transformation of the heritage of Israel (2.21). Presumably the correlation of the two implies that the latter imagery is equally as universal and cosmic as the former—a facet already implicit, we may note, in Rom. 11.12 and 15. The corollary would then be that Paul and/or his immediate heirs quickly came to see that the problem of Israel was part of a cosmic scenario and that it would only be resolved at that level.

c) *Christology*. The third factor is obviously Christology. For in both Colossians and Ephesians the cosmic dimensions of the body-church reflect also the cosmic significance of Christ (Col. 1.18-20; Eph. 1.20-23). Here again we need to take seriously the recognition

---

[1]J.D.G. Dunn, *Romans* (WBC 38; Dallas: Word, 1988), p. 720.

[2]Lincoln, *Ephesians*, pp. 163-65, overplays the degree of discontinuity between Israel of old and the 'new man', whose blessings after all are the blessings of Israel in their Christ focused fulfilment (2.19-22).

of the relative independence of the two elements of the theme: the body = community, and the body *of Christ*. That is to say, the emphasis on the cosmic significance of Christ is no more to be seen as a product of or derivative from the body conceived cosmically than the cosmic body-church is to be seen as derived from some pre-Christian primal man myth. Rather, it would seem fairly clear that the cosmic significance of Christ is an outworking of both *kyrios* Christology and Wisdom Christology. The former is most evident in Eph. 1.20-22, the latter in what is usually understood to be the other part of the Colossian hymn (Col. 1.15-17).[1]

Here then is another factor within Christian thought calling for expression in cosmic terms. If Christ is Lord of all, and somehow to be identified with divine Wisdom, hidden but pervasive throughout the cosmos, then that community which is related to him as his body must be conceived as somehow functioning cosmically too. It is true, of course, that to conceive of Christ in terms of Wisdom is in effect to identify him with the Stoic principle of divine rationality, likewise pervasive throughout the cosmos (Wisd. Sol. 1.7; 7.24), and thus to invite a Christ —> Wisdom —> cosmos —> body association of thought. But we know from such passages as 1 Cor. 16.22 and Rom. 10.9 on the one hand, and from 1 Cor. 8.6 and Heb. 1.2-3 on the other, that these Christological emphases were developed quite independently of the body theme. So at this point the emphases of Colossians and Ephesians are best seen as the product of a double trend towards affirming a cosmic significance for Christ and for the community which is conceived as his body. Most striking is the way this Christological emphasis transforms the Stoic cosmology still further, with the church seen as that which is (already) filled by Christ; the implication being that Christ's filling (or having already filled) the church is the beginning of Christ's filling everything in every way, that the church is the focus and medium of Christ's present role in the cosmos.[2]

On this schema, from where does the emphasis on Christ as 'head' of the body emerge? Not primarily from the factor we have designated 'the problem of Israel'; the Messiah as 'head' is not an element

---

[1] See my *Christology in the Making* (London: SCM, 1980, 2d ed. 1989), pp. 187-94. The theme of divine fulness/filling-full is also consistent with Jewish thought of Wisdom (Wisd. Sol. 7.24); see further E. Schweizer, *Colossians* (London: SPCK, 1976), pp. 77-79.

[2] See again Lincoln, *Ephesians*, pp. 72-78.

within Paul's treatment of this issue. Possibly from the third factor, *kyrios* and Wisdom Christology, since the *Lord*-ship of Christ is central in the former, and since Christ as Wisdom is πρωτότοκος; but while both of these emphases are consistent with the emphasis on Christ's headship, as Eph. 1.22 and Col. 1.18 and 2.10 confirm, it is only in these letters that this correlation is evident; which suggests that the correlation is itself a result of bringing the themes together rather than that the emphasis on Christ's headship of the body is a product of the Christology alone. Most likely the emphasis on Christ as head emerged, initially at least, from the first factor, since the Stoic concept of both state and cosmos as a body could include also thought of the ruler of the state or the divine principle of rationality in the cosmos (Zeus or the logos) as the head of the body.[1] Here, then, is a further indication that it was the broader Stoic idea which provided the basis for the Pauline working of the body theme, and that the definition of the body by relating it to Christ is part of the Christianizing of that theme, made possible in this case because Christ was already (independently) being conceived in terms (Lord, Wisdom) which made the identification of Christ as head of the body most natural.[2]

In short, several factors are evident in the influences which pushed Pauline theology of the body of Christ in the direction it took. Of these, *the fundamental community-as-body metaphor seems to have been provided by the wider religious philosophy of the time*, and its main development remains consistent with that original metaphor. But the distinctive features which mark out the Christian use of it are all the result of *adapting the metaphor to fit the more fundamental Christian and themselves developing convictions regarding Christ.*

4. *Conclusions*

As to the significance of these findings, we have room for only a few observations.

a) First, it is significant that the body imagery as used for the local congregations in Corinth and Rome was derived from the imagery of

---

[1]See again Schlier, 'κεφαλή', *TDNT*, III, p. 674; Schweizer, 'σῶμα', *TDNT*, VII, p. 1036; also Lincoln, *Ephesians*, p. 69.

[2]The situation addressed at Colossae could, of course, have been the catalyst in this development, as Lincoln, *Ephesians*, pp. 69-70 suggests.

the body for the state. To use just this metaphor for such, much smaller, ethnically diverse gatherings within the cities and old city states of the Roman Empire was a striking assertion of ecclesiological self-understanding. For it meant, in effect, that these small gatherings were being set forward as the equivalent to and substitute for the state. The sense of identity and belonging bound up with the state = body usage was being transposed to the setting of the church. Indeed, if we do not press the point too far, the sense that the church in this city or that region was the body to which believers belonged carried with it the implication that this belonging was more fundamental than any other citizenship, and perhaps also that the assembly gathered for worship should provide a model of community for the larger cities and states.

This sense of church as providing the social or corporate locus of identity helps explain the development of the theme in relation to the problem of Israel. Thus in Rom. 12 it is no accident that when Paul has completed in effect his re-definition of Israel in Rom. 9-11, he turns almost immediately to speak of the body of Christ (Rom. 12.3-8)—the implication being that the body of Christ is the Christian equivalent of ethnic or national Israel.[1] Hence too in Eph. 2.14-15 the identification of the body with the one new man who replaces the old opposition of Jew and Gentile. The body of Christ as part of the solution to the problem of Israel in terms of social and corporate identity, even if only as an eschatological hope, is an aspect of the whole theme which deserves further study.

The shift from church-body = local congregation to church-body = universal church in Ephesians need not imply any weakening of the first conclusion. On the contrary, it means that the church has to be seen as in some sense a para-cosmos, or rather as that which gives meaning to the cosmos, as that which most fully expresses the divine rationality within the cosmos. Indeed, if we take Eph. 1.22-23 seriously, it is only by filling the church that Christ is able, or chooses to exercise his role in filling the cosmos. Such a theological assertion puts an awesome responsibility on the church, by confirming, not least, the integration of the community of those being saved with the eschatological hope of a redeemed cosmos.

At all events, it is important theologically to recognize that for Christians the body can still provide an invaluable metaphor for the

[1] Dunn, *Romans*, pp. 705-706.

sense of oneness and mutual responsibility which must lie at the heart of any community if it is to thrive. Also that the church, whether local or universal, precisely by being designated the body of Christ, is probably being called upon to provide an alternative community and probably also to serve as a model of what true community should be.

b) The rationality and effectiveness of this alternative community or para-cosmos depends on its being seen as and on its functioning as the body *of Christ*. The imagery of community = body can be said to come from wider Greco-Roman usage, but not its rationale or character, beyond the common motif of oneness. The oneness of the church-body is not that of ethnic solidarity or social congeniality; it is the oneness of the shared experience of the Spirit of Christ. And the mutual responsibility of its members is not that of ethnic or civic obligation; it is the obligation to exercise the grace of Christ manifested in the charisms given to each. However the 'in Christ' is expressed in reference to the body, it is that shared identification with Christ which is what makes the Christian community a body, that is, the body of Christ. It has no coherence or rationale as community, as body, as church otherwise.

Though in some of the early formulations Christ seems to be absorbed into, or at least not distinguished from the community which functions as his body, in the later formulations Christ's headship over the body is explicit and stated repeatedly. Thus both the value of the metaphor is retained, and the otherness of Christ in relation to the community which is his body is reasserted. In this way Christ continues to give the church its identity without losing his identity within the church. So too the church can continue to function as a model for community and fulfilled cosmos, only insofar as it stands itself under the authority and judgment of Christ who is both Lord of the cosmos and the clearest expression of its created wisdom.

In short, 'the body of Christ' is a Pauline theme which provides a crucial key to Christian understanding of ecclesiology and Christology and of their mutual relationship. But its effectiveness depends on both elements receiving their due weight—the church both as the *body* of Christ, and as the body *of Christ*.

ABRAHAM GOES TO ROME: PAUL'S TREATMENT OF ABRAHAM IN ROMANS 4*

Andrew T. Lincoln

I. *Abraham Comes to Paul*

If one is inclined to talk of precursors of midrash in the new Testament, then it is widely held that Romans 4 provides one of the best examples.[1] Paul states his Scriptural text in v. 3—Gen. 15.6. He then expounds the significance of one of its major terms, ἐλογίσθη, in vv. 4-8, linking in Psa. 32.1. In vv. 9-21 he develops the meaning of another major term, ἐπίστευσεν, and this time weaves in material from Gen. 17 and 18 and from Gen. 15.5, the verse immediately preceding his text. Then in vv. 22-25 he returns to the wording of the original text in an explicit application to his audience. To label a passage as midrash, however, is not to explain its actual use of Scripture. The consensus view of Rom. 4 recognizes that its midrashic treatment of the Abraham story contains elements of typology and appropriates Abraham as a model for Paul's gospel of justification by faith. In this sense Abraham comes to Paul and comes to the aid of his exposition of his gospel. My main purpose is to suggest a further dimension to Paul's treatment of Abraham, but before doing so, I shall set out briefly the salient features of the conventional exegesis of the chapter, an exegesis which I might wish to qualify or elaborate but which I do not substantially dispute.

---

*This essay, exploring the relationship between tradition and pastoral context in Paul's ministry, is offered to Ralph Martin in gratitude for the benefits gained from his prolific scholarship and for the privilege of knowing him as a colleague and friend.

[1]Cf. e.g. J.D.G. Dunn, *Romans 1-8* (Dallas: Word, 1988), pp. 197-98; H. Moxnes, *Theology in Conflict* (Leiden: E.J. Brill, 1980), pp. 108-9; D.A. Koch, *Die Schrift als Zeuge des Evangeliums* (Tübingen: J.C.B. Mohr, 1986), pp. 224-6.

a) *Abraham's Justification Provides a Witness from the Law.*
On the consensus view, Paul's use of Abraham can be seen as enabling the apostle to respond to the objection of Jews and/or some Jewish Christians that his distinctive formulation of the gospel involves the abrogation or overthrow of the law (3.31a). In reply to such dialogue partners, Paul claims in 3.31b-4.8 that, far from abrogating the law, he upholds it and calls on Abraham as his witness. After all, Scripture, in a passage taken from the law—Gen. 15.6—says of the Jewish patriarch, 'Abraham believed God and it was reckoned to him as righteousness'. In contrast to the interpretations of Abraham elsewhere (e.g. 1 Macc. 2.52; Sir. 44.19-21; CD 3.2), which depicted Abraham as showing his faithfulness to the covenant by keeping the commandments and thus being reckoned righteous, Paul is able to seize on the fact that the text says nothing about Abraham's works, and therefore provides no grounds for boasting on the basis of performance (cf. also 3.27). It is only concerned with his faith. Faith is the means by which Abraham was reckoned as righteous. Paul has already declared in his thematic statement of 1.16, 17 that, in the gospel of which he is not ashamed, the righteousness of God is revealed through faith for faith; it involves faith from start to finish. And he has already given his Scriptural warrant from the prophets, from Hab. 2.4—'The one who through faith is righteous shall live'. Now his point is that this is exactly the way in which the law talks about Abraham—as the one who through faith is righteous. So Paul believes that his gospel does uphold the law. He appears to mean by this that it is in continuity with the law, since that law read in the light of his gospel supports the way of faith. As he has said just previously (3.21), in his gospel 'The righteousness of God has been manifested apart from law, although the law and the prophets bear witness to it'. There are further ways in which Paul appropriates Abraham for his gospel.

b) *Abraham's Justification was Prior to Circumcision.*
Through the exegetical device of *gezerah shawah*, linking two passages which contain the same term (here the verb λογίζεσθαι, 'to reckon'), Paul had drawn LXX Psa. 31.1, 2 into his midrash (vv. 6-8). He now goes on to claim in vv. 9-12 that the Psalm's pronouncement of blessing on the one to whom God reckons righteousness apart from works does not just apply to Jews, as his Jewish readers might well have supposed. Again it is the Abraham story that enables him to

make his point. This time he seizes on the fact that in the Genesis narrative the statement of Gen. 15.6 comes before the account of Abraham's circumcision in Gen. 17. So, lo and behold, the righteous-by-faith Abraham was uncircumcised! In the case of Abraham, his circumcision can be described, therefore, not in the traditional way as a sign and seal of the covenant but as a sign and seal of the righteousness he already had by faith. In fact, Paul argues, God's purpose in this sequence in the Abraham story was that Abraham's fatherhood should not be restricted to those who are circumcised or who become circumcised as proselytes but should embrace those, who like Abraham himself, are uncircumcised but have faith. He is to be seen as the father of both uncircumcised believers and circumcised believers, Gentile Christians and Jewish Christians (vv. 11, 12). The Abraham story, on Paul's reading, demonstrates that circumcision is irrelevant to a person's being reckoned righteous by God by means of faith.

c) *Abraham's Justification was Apart from Law.*

In Romans 2 Paul had argued that neither an appeal to the law nor an appeal to circumcision could offer any protection for Jews in the light of God's judgment. Reversing the order of topics, here in Romans 4 he uses Abraham to show that neither circumcision nor the law has any role in being reckoned righteous. He makes the latter point about the law in vv. 13-17a by reading the Abraham story in the light of his own contrast between promise and faith on the one hand and law and works on the other. What Abraham believed when he was reckoned righteous was God's promise that he would have innumerable descendants (cf. Gen. 15.5). So, Paul argues, building on his previous point, the promise did not come through the law; it was believed by Abraham before the law as anticipated in the requirement of circumcision was given. In fact, if there is to be any guarantee about inheriting the promise for Abraham and his descendants, the whole process has to depend on faith, because only in that way is the principle of grace rather than of law and performance (with their inevitable transgression and failure) brought fully into play. Faith in the promise creates certainty because in that way God and his faithfulness are allowed to be the ultimate guarantee. Paul can now restate his conclusion about Abraham's fatherhood from vv. 11, 12 in terms of law rather than circumcision. Abraham is 'the father of us all', believers who adhere to the law and those who simply share his faith without adhering to the law (v16b).

d) *Abraham's Faith was in the God who Gives Life to the Dead.*
In 4.17b-25 Paul points out that, in believing the promise that God would make him the father of many nations, Abraham had to believe in a God who raised the dead. With Gen. 17.15-21 and 18.9-15 in view, Paul can talk of Abraham displaying the strong faith that looked at the apparent impossibilities of his situation and yet still trusted completely in God to bring life (Isaac) out of death (his own body as good as dead—νενεκρωμένος—and the deadness—νέκρωσις—of Sarah's womb, cf. v 19).[1] This faith in the creator God and his life-giving power is what was reckoned to him as righteousness and is why Gen. 15.6 was written not only for Abraham but also for believers in the Christian gospel of the same God who raised Jesus from the dead. Abraham on this reading is clearly a 'proto-Christian', the type of Christian believers whose justification is through belief in Christ's resurrection, whereby Christ's vindication in the reversal of the verdict of condemnation also becomes theirs.

2. *Abraham Goes to Rome*

So far the consensus. But what I want to argue, and this has been virtually totally neglected,[2] is that Abraham not only comes to Paul, but also goes to Rome.

---

[1]In the case of Abraham his general advanced age and decrepitude appear to be in view rather than the more specific sexual connotations of the modern idiom of 'raising the dead'. What Paul would have said if anyone had been pedantic enough to quote Gen. 25.1-8 to him must remain interesting speculation (though cf. Dunn, *Romans*, p. 220).

[2]After completing the first draft of this essay I discovered that P. Minear, *The Obedience of Faith* (London: SCM, 1971), pp. 53-56, had anticipated me by pointing out some of the links between Rom. 4 and Rom. 14 and 15, though he interprets the data rather differently. Presumably his insight had been dismissed along with the dismissal of his idiosyncratic view of Romans as addressed to five different groups in Rome. Nevertheless, he rightly claims, 'there is an amazing degree of continuity between this picture of Abraham and the axioms of Paul's position in chs. 14 and 15' (p. 56). F. Watson, *Paul, Judaism and the Gentiles* (Cambridge: CUP, 1986) p. 139, also holds that Rom. 4 'is a far reaching reinterpretation of the figure of Abraham with important social implications, and not purely theoretical argument opposing salvation by one's own achievements with salvation by grace alone'. But he elaborates on this in terms of his own theory that 'Paul is seeking to persuade members of the Roman Jewish Christian congregation to separate themselves from the Jewish community and to recognize and unite with the Pauline Gentile Christian congregation' (pp. 141-

a) *The New Perspective on the Romans Debate as Presupposition.* The presupposition for this approach is the change of perspective in recent scholarship about the setting and purposes of Romans. The majority view is now that Romans, like Paul's other letters, is addressed primarily to the particular needs of its readers. The rhetorical situation reflected in the letter consists of Paul's attempt to exhort his primarily Gentile Christian audience to the obedience of faith. These Gentile Christians, however, face tensions with Jewish Christians, whom Paul evidently expects also to be among the recipients of his message (cf. e.g. 1.5-7; 14.1-5; 15.7; 15.14-16).[1] Most recent interpreters also bring much more clearly to the fore what can be discovered about the actual situation in Rome.[2] For the purposes of this essay the focus will be on the major problem, depicted in 14.1-15.13, between the self-styled 'strong in faith' and the 'weak in faith'. It is generally agreed that the former consisted predominantly of the Gentile Christian majority and the latter of the Jewish Christian minority. The Jewish Christians still saw the law as necessary for proper obedience to the will of God and their conscience required them to observe such regulations as *kashrut*, with its distinction between clean and unclean foods, and the keeping of sabbaths and other special days. Not surprisingly, they were suspicious of Paul's gospel and its adherents and the moral laxity they appeared to endorse. While the Jewish Christians majored on obedience, the Gentile Christians gloried in their faith, emphasizing the freedom it engendered. They considered the Jewish Christians to be weak in faith, because their faith did not allow them to accept all foods and treat all days the same. The real trouble consisted in the personal attitudes that accompanied the theological differences. As can be seen from the labelling in which they indulged as well as from Paul's exhortations, the 'strong' were despising and scorning the 'weak'. The 'weak', on the other hand, also felt morally superior and were

---

42). For criticisms of Watson's theory, see e.g. Dunn, *Romans*, p. lvii; N. Elliott, *The Rhetoric of Romans* (Sheffield: JSOT Press, 1990), p. 57.

[1] The thesis of Elliott, *Rhetoric*, is right in its emphasis on a primarily Gentile Christian audience, but neglects the Jewish Christian element, which he acknowledges to be there, and thus has to find strained explanations for those parts of the argument which seem clearly to have Jewish objections to Paul's gospel in view.

[2] Cf. e.g. Dunn, *Romans*, pp. xliv-lviii; A.J.M. Wedderburn, *The Reasons for Romans* (Edinburgh: T & T Clark, 1988); Elliott, *Rhetoric*, pp. 43-59.

condemning the 'strong'. Chapter 11 also provides evidence (cf. esp. vv. 20, 25) that the Gentile Christian majority's stress on faith had led them to an arrogant attitude toward Jewish unbelief. Paul appears to be correcting those who have interpreted his gospel to mean not only freedom from law but also the setting aside of any purposes of God for ethnic Israel.

In the new perspective on 'the Romans debate' a setting for the letter in the life of the writer is not neglected. Instead it becomes clear that the concerns of Paul in his situation dovetail neatly into those of his readers in Rome. Paul, the Jewish Christian who is apostle to the Gentiles, is about to set off from Corinth for Jerusalem with the collection, and the same issues that trouble believers in Rome—relations between Jewish Christians and Gentile Christians—trouble Paul on a larger scale, at the level of his whole Gentile mission. As he sets out his plans in 15.22-33, he reveals his anxiety about how the collection taken up from the churches of his Gentile mission and accompanied by delegates from those churches would be received by the Jewish Christian Jerusalem church (cf. especially 15.30, where he appeals to the Roman Christians to participate in his own struggle by praying 'that my service for Jerusalem may be acceptable to the saints'). Paul also believes himself to be at a crucial stage in his mission to the Gentiles (cf. 15.17-24). He has completed his mission in the eastern half of the empire and now feels free to look further west to Rome and beyond Spain, which represented the western extremity of his world. Only one thing stood between him and his mission in the West and that was the impending visit to Jerusalem with the collection. If the collection were to be accepted, it would signify the unity of the presently existing church and thus the successful wrapping-up of his mission in the East. Faced with this critical situation, the result of which will profoundly affect the outworking of his calling, Paul inevitably has to think yet again about the problem of unity between Jewish Christians and Gentile Christians and whether his gospel deserves the blame for the problem. He is therefore in a unique position to bring to bear the fruits of his reflection in a pastoral fashion on the similar problem of unity, which, he has been informed, is afflicting Roman believers.

Because the Roman Christians were not a church founded by Paul and because he needs their support for the completion of the western part of his world mission when he moves off to Spain, he does not address their main problem immediately and head-on. Instead he diplomatically elaborates on his distinctive gospel in such a way as to lay the foundation for his pastoral exhortation. He develops his argument with an eye on their situation throughout and with an awareness of both Jewish Christian suspicions and objections and Gentile Christian arrogance and misinterpretation. When he feels he can finally address the Roman Christians very boldly (cf. 15.15), it emerges that he clearly sides theologically with the strong in faith but has no time for their insensitivity towards the weak in faith. He wants mutual tolerance and lays out some principles on which this is to be developed. Above all, his goal is to unify the Gentile Christians and the Jewish Christians in the diverse housegroups in Rome so that they accept one another and 'with one voice glorify the God and Father of our Lord Jesus Christ' (15.6, 7).

Despite this new perspective, chapter 4 still tends to be read as a piece of general theologizing and as if it had very little to do with the situation to which Paul is addressing himself. Once the fuller picture of Paul's purposes in the letter is brought to bear, however, it generates a number of new insights into the force of his argument for his readers at this point.[1]

b) *Abraham as the Father of Us All.*

Clearly Paul's stress on Abraham being the father of both Jewish Christians and Gentile Christians (vv. 11b, 12) would have had force for his readers in Rome. Gentile Christians should see themselves as part of a larger family which can trace its ancestry back to Abraham. They cannot write off Israel's past as of no account. The blessings in which they participate are blessings promised to Abraham and his descendants. Their faith in Christ is faith in the one who has confirmed God's promises to the patriarchs, as Paul will remind them explicitly in 15.8. Jewish Christians in Rome should no longer consider Abraham as simply 'our forefather according to the flesh' (v. 1). If they were to go along with Paul's perspective, they would have to be willing to accept the Gentile believers there as equally children of Abraham solely on the basis of their faith.[2] Their faith in

[1]Moxnes, *Theology*, pp. 117-206, has shown that in all likelihood in 4.13-21 Paul makes use of a number of traditional motifs in the Jewish treatment of Abraham. Our focus is, however, on the force of Paul's distinctive formulation of these motifs for his Roman readers.

[2]Cf. Minear, *Obedience of Faith*, pp. 53, 55; Watson, *Paul*, p. 141, who expresses this somewhat differently.

Christ is faith in the one who became a servant to the circumcised not only to confirm the promises to the patriarchs but also 'in order that the Gentiles might glorify God for his mercy', as Paul puts it in 15.8, 9. Previously they would have perceived Abraham as the great dividing point in the history of humanity. Before Abraham there was the history of the nations, but with him began God's particularism in choosing out one nation. But now Paul has made Abraham the great rallying point for all who believe, whether Jews or Gentiles,[1] the symbol of unity for his Christian readers in Rome. Jewish Christians must see Abraham as 'the father of us all' (v. 16b). This would be quite different from what they were used to in their synagogues. There proselytes, who were regarded as Abraham's children by adoption, were not permitted to call him 'our father'. When in the liturgy Jews by birth called the patriarch 'our father', proselytes had to say 'your father'.[2] The clear implication of Paul's argument would be that, amongst the Christians in Rome, however, there should be no division between those of Jewish birth and those of Gentile birth. They are members of the same family, in which both groups can claim Abraham as their father.

c) *Justifying Faith as the Focus for Unity instead of Division.*

It is sharing Abraham's justifying faith that makes Jewish Christians and Gentile Christians equal members of the one family. 'That is why it depends on faith, in order that the promise may rest on grace and be guaranteed to *all* his descendants—not only to the adherents of the law [i.e. Jewish Christians who observe the law] but also to those who [simply] share the faith of Abraham [i.e. Gentile Christians], for he is the father of us all' (v. 16).[3] In the situation reflected in 14.1-15.13 justifying faith and its implications had become a divisive issue. The Roman believers were judging one another and forming parties according to their different interpretations of faith. The Gentile

---

[1]Cf. A. Nygren, *Commentary on Romans* (Philadelphia: Fortress, 1949), p. 175, who does not, however, apply this insight to the situation of the readers. J.P. Heil, *Paul's Letter to the Romans* (New York: Paulist, 1987), p. 47, does make the application.

[2]Cf. *m.Bikkurim* 1.4; also W.D. Davies, *The Gospel and the Land* (Berkeley: University of California Press, 1974), p.177.

[3]Cf. e.g. E. Käsemann, *Commentary on Romans* (London: SCM, 1980), p. 121; U. Wilckens, *Der Brief an die Römer* (Zürich: Benzinger, 1978), I, pp. 271-72; Watson, *Paul*, p. 141, who hold that the adherents of the law are Jewish Christians; *pace* e.g. Dunn, *Romans*, p. 216; Moxnes, *Theology*, pp. 112 n. 18, 250-51, who hold that they are Jews and that Paul is speaking from the perspective of the final eschatological salvation.

Christian majority viewed the differences in terms of the strength or weakness of justifying faith with their own brand naturally having a higher percentage proof of the genuine article. At one point in his exhortation Paul in fact has to tell his readers to stop advertising their faith because of the destructive consequences for community life of such a display. As he puts it in 14.22, 'The faith which you have, keep to yourself before God'. For Paul there could be different measures of faith (cf. 12.3), but not divisions because of faith.

It should not be surprising that, if Abraham is being presented as the exemplar of justification by *faith*, this might have a variety of implications for the issues of faith among the readers. The example of Abraham should have provided a further demonstration that it was precisely because justification was by faith rather than by some other means, such as law, that there could be unity. Paul had just previously, in 3.29, 30, reminded Jewish Christians of the first article of their faith from the *Shema*—God is one—in order to help them to recognize their unity with Gentile believers in salvation. Since there is only one God, Paul argues, this same God has to be the God of both Jews and Gentiles, and from the unity of his relation to all as the one God of all, Paul deduces a unity of principle in the way this God operates towards both groups. There are not two tracks for justification. No, the unity of God's relation to both is shown by his justifying the circumcised by faith and the uncircumcised through faith. So Paul's claim is that justification by faith is more appropriate to the universal monotheism of Judaism than is the law, because it places no limits on participation in a restored relationship with the one God. The Abraham story enables Paul to reinforce this point. Both groups are reckoned righteous before God on the same basis—faith. When he comes to make his explicit plea for unity in the paraenesis, Paul utilizes this fundamental conviction effectively.[1] He calls first on the strong to accept the weak and then on both groups to accept each other, and his warrant is that God and Christ have first accepted both (cf. 14.1, 3 and 15.7). The only appropriate behaviour for those who have been accepted solely on the basis of faith is to accept others whom God through Christ has justified by faith, whatever the differences in the expression of that faith.

---

[1] Cf. also Minear, *Obedience of Faith*, p. 55.

d) *Abraham as One Who is Strong in Faith.*

It is surely no accident, given what Paul knows about the situation of his readers, that, when he describes the quality of Abraham's faith in 4.19, 20, he does so in precisely the terms that are being used in the conflict in Rome. μὴ ἀσθενήσας τῇ πίστει . . . ἀλλ' ἐνεδυναμώθη τῇ πίστει, 'he did not weaken in faith . . . but he grew strong in faith'.[1] With reference to weakness, here the aorist participle of ἀσθενέω is used with the dative of πίστις, while in 14.1, 2 the present participle of the same verb is used as a substantive, again with the dative of πίστις. The phrase employed for the strong in 15.1—οἱ δυνατοί—involves a cognate adjective of the verb in 4.20 being used as a substantive.[2] In the paraenesis of 15.1 Paul does not hide his own position. He talks of 'we, the strong', and earlier has stressed his persuasion that nothing is unclean in itself (cf. 14.14, 20). So, in his depiction of Abraham, Paul signals clearly ahead of time where he stands theologically in the debate in Rome. Abraham does not merely exemplify the Pauline gospel as one who is righteous by faith, but he also joins the debate in Rome on the side of the strong in faith. Theologically, the strong have both the endorsement of Paul and the backing of Abraham.

Again Gentile Christians are obviously being encouraged to see Abraham as one with them. He is not simply the Jewish patriarch but a justified believer with whom they share their strong faith. Having a strong sense of their own solidarity with Abraham will prepare them to empathize both with Paul's lament for Israel, in which he anguishes over the fact that 'to them belong . . . the promises; to them belong the patriarchs, and of their race, according to the flesh, is the Christ' (9.4, 5), and with his assertion that ethnic Israel will not finally miss out on the salvation which Gentiles enjoy at present, because 'as regards election they are beloved for the sake of their forefathers' (11.28). They are to realize that their confident faith is in the same God as Abraham's, who will go back neither on his promises to them nor on his promises to Abraham.

What is likely to have been the effect of this move on the Jewish Christian minority? One suspects that some of them would have been none too pleased. It was bad enough that earlier in the argument they

[1] Cf. also Minear, *Obedience of Faith*, p. 54.

[2] δυνατός εἰμί is the functional equivalent of δύναμαι, 'be strong', while the passive of ἐνδυναμόω has the force of 'become strong'.

were being asked to give up their exclusive claim to be Abraham's descendants and to share him as father with Gentile Christians. But it would surely have added insult to injury for Paul now to depict Abraham as virtually defecting to the other side, as one of the strong.

So can this interpretation be right? What has happened to Paul the diplomat attempting to respond irenically to Jewish Christian suspicions and objections? Whatever his readers' response may have been, seen from Paul's point of view, this can still be considered part of his tactics of persuasion. He does in fact want all his readers to embrace his own position on the full implications of the gospel, however patient he is prepared to be for the sake of harmony amongst believers. He tolerates those who still feel the need to express their faith in the Messiah through the old identity markers, but ideally wants to see the sort of faith in what God has done in Christ that is complete and unqualified and is able to leave food laws and holy days behind. Sometimes, and understandably, his exhortation in chapters 14 and 15 to the strong to bear with the weak has been criticized for leaving the weak with a stranglehold on the strong. But this is to forget that accommodating the weak on the grounds of respecting their conscience is not the whole story in terms of Paul's long-term strategy. The responsibility of the strong towards the weak is expressed in very forceful terms in order to shake them out of arrogance, insensitivity and lack of love. Quarrelling, disputing and judging are to cease, but Paul has no intention that teaching and exhorting in the context of love and with the purpose of mutual edification and growth in faith should also cease (cf. 12.7, 8; 14.19). Indeed he presumably sees himself as supplying just such teaching (cf. 1.11, 12). So he has no desire that weak Jewish Christians should remain for ever with their particular measure of faith; he wants to move them on to maturity. He hopes they will already have been persuaded to think of Abraham as one who was justified by faith in the Pauline sense. He has also already implied in his language in 4.5 that Abraham was one of the Gentile ungodly who needed justification.[1] So why not go all the way in his retelling of Scripture? If Jewish Christians can be drawn into reading the Abraham story in Paul's way, they might just be coaxed into seeing not only the basic gospel message but all the issues differently. For on this reading to treat all food as clean and all days as holy need

[1]Cf. also Wilckens, *Der Brief an die Römer*, I, p. 263; B. Byrne, *Reckoning with Romans* (Wilmington, DE: Michael Glazier, 1986), pp. 96, 97; Watson, *Paul*, p. 139.

not be thought of as forsaking their election and becoming apostate but as emulating the strength of faith of father Abraham.

e) *The Qualities of Abraham's Strong Faith Required in Rome.*
Our reading of Paul's reading of the Abraham story appears to be confirmed when a number of other features of his depiction of Abraham are noted. Abraham is described as displaying the qualities of faith which Paul will later stress as essential in the situation in Rome. He does not doubt, but is fully convinced and gives glory to God (4.20, 21). Abraham did not doubt. The terminology employed in 4.20 is οὐ διεκρίθη and significantly the only other place in Paul's writings where the middle or passive διακρίνεσθαι, 'to doubt', is found is in Rom. 14.23, where doubt is one of the symptoms displayed by the weak in faith. If the weak go ahead and eat meat with doubts, because they are acting under the pressure of the convictions of others, they are condemned because they are not acting out of their own faith. Similarly, in 4.21 Abraham is said to have been fully convinced (πληροφορηθείς) and the only other place in Romans where the passive of πληροφορεῖν is employed in this way is in 14.5 (cf. Col. 4.12 for the only other occurrence in the NT). Whether Roman Christians hold that one day is more important than another or treat all days alike, what matters, claims Paul, is that they have Abraham's kind of faith that enables them to be fully convinced in their own minds. In addition, Abraham's was the kind of faith that gave glory to God (δοὺς δόξαν τῷ θεῷ—4.20). According to 15.9, the outcome of Gentile faith should be to glorify God for his mercy (δοξάσαι τὸν θεόν). A functionally equivalent expression in the paraenesis is in 14.6—'gives thanks to God' (εὐχαριστεῖ τῷ θεῷ). Again, whether a person eats or abstains, Paul is interested in whether the underlying attitude of faith has the quality of thankful dependence on God which does not draw attention to itself so much as gives God the glory which is his due (cf. also 1.21 where failure to display such qualities is seen as at the heart of Gentile sin). In 15.6, 7 also Paul reminds both weak in faith and strong in faith that what is of paramount importance is that their attitudes and actions result in God's glory (cf. δοξάζητε τὸν θεόν—v. 6; εἰς δόξαν τοῦ θεοῦ—v. 7). And Paul is convinced that what will bring glory to God from the existence of believers in Rome are unity and mutual acceptance. So when he addresses their problems directly, Paul in effect exhorts

the Roman believers to be like Abraham—not to doubt, to be fully convinced and to give glory to God.

Perhaps most important of all for the resolution of the divisions in Rome, Abraham as the one who is righteous by faith and who is strong in that faith also has hope through that faith.[1] According to 4.18 Abraham 'against hope, in hope believed'. It is with Abraham that Paul introduces for the first time in the letter the theme of hope that is to prove so significant in this argument. The main thrust of the immediately following section, 5.1-11, can be summed up in terms of Paul's assertion that eschatological life is already present in hope and this thought is developed in 8.18-39 with its note of confident assurance of full salvation and glory. The hope of glory in the midst of suffering is what characterizes the life of believers in the overlap of the ages. But it is in the paraenesis that Abraham's quality of hope is seen to be essential for the harmonious resolution of the divisions in Rome. As he completes his exhortation, Paul does so with the aid of Scripture citations, and this, he says, is in order that 'by the encouragement of the Scriptures we might have hope' (15.4). What is more, the last citation—from LXX Isa. 11.10—contains the notion of the risen root of Jesse as the hope of the Gentiles (15.12) and leads into the prayer wish which forms the climax of the whole paraenesis—'May the God of hope fill you with all joy and peace in believing, so that by the power of the Holy Spirit you may abound in hope' (15.13). As in the case of Abraham, hope is connected with believing. Paul holds that it is the kind of faith that is accompanied by hope that will enable the Roman Christians to overcome obstacles and move towards the realization of Paul's vision of harmony between Jewish and Gentile believers. It is not simply that as they join together in worship the social support necessary for hope will be engendered,[2] although that may well be the case. It is more that hope, confident assurance in the eventual fulfilment of God's promises for salvation, will provide the motivation for doing all that can be done to join together in the first place. It should not be forgotten that, when that final salvation is depicted at the end of Paul's discussion in chapters 9-11, it involves God having mercy upon all, both Jews and Gentiles (11.30-32). Just as Abraham's hope that he would be the

---

[1]Cf. Minear, *Obedience of Faith*, pp. 55-56 for a brief mention and different interpretation of this link.

[2]Cf. Watson, *Paul*, p. 139.

father of many nations impelled him to positive action in the present despite the obstacles, so abounding in the hope that Jew and Gentile are one and equal in eschatological salvation should impel Roman believers to accept one another and worship together in the present in unity and equality in Rome despite the difficulties and divisions.

3. *Abraham, Paul and Rome*

a) *Correlation of Three Levels.*
I have suggested that Paul's midrashic treatment of Abraham, like the letter as a whole, reflects a dual setting—the concerns of Paul about the formulation of his gospel in the context of his mission and the concerns of the Roman Christians with their specific problems. The Abraham story is made to speak again and to speak to both sets of concerns. Abraham comes to Paul and he goes to Rome. In the case of his journey to Rome, overtones which the original readers could well have grasped because of their obvious awareness of their own situation become available to the modern reader by reading chapter 4 in the light of the whole letter. Such a reading highlights Paul's interpretation of Scripture as tailor-made for his Roman readers.

Paul has produced this particular retelling of the Abraham story through making an imaginative correlation among the three ingredients of Scripture, his experience of and reflection on the Christian gospel, and his knowledge of the Christians in Rome. These three levels are interwoven in the midrash and Paul moves freely between them, only stopping to make explicit one feature of his correlation at the end (vv. 23, 24). Whether he respects the original sense of Scripture is beside the point. Sometimes his reading goes against the grain of the straightforward meaning; more often than not in this passage it is compatible with it. But it would not count as Old Testament exegesis by modern standards. What is more to the point is that, within the interpretative conventions of his time, in the meeting between the world of the text and Paul's world the semantic potential of the text can be exploited for his strategy of pastoral persuasion.

b) *Life from the Dead for Abraham, Paul and Rome.*
So far I have claimed that knowledge of Paul's gospel and particularly of the rhetorical situation of his audience sheds light on the shaping of the Abraham story in chapter 4. But might it not also be the case that

the textual interplay between the three levels can work in a different direction and that Paul's pattern of thinking in his retelling of the Abraham story sheds light on his thinking at the other two levels? It is fairly clear that for Paul the motifs of justification by faith, the fatherhood of Abraham, strong faith, and the cluster of other essential qualities of faith reverberate on all three levels. In the cases of strong faith and the qualities of full conviction, hope and glorifying God Paul simply moves between levels one (Abraham) and three (Rome) and so we have not spelled out their equivalents at the level of Paul's gospel. But this is easy to do. In Paul's rehearsal of his gospel strong justifying faith is the faith which knows itself to be no longer under law, to have died to the law (cf. 6.14; 7.1-6). His gospel of justifying faith produces full assurance and hope (5.1-11; 8.18-39) and has as its goal God's glory (cf. e.g. 5.11; 7.25; 11.33-36). But what about the major correlation that Paul makes between Abraham's belief in a God who gives life to the dead as the means of his being reckoned righteous and his Christian gospel of belief in the God who raised Jesus from the dead for justification? What we have seen about the links among the three levels suggests that it could be fruitful to take this further, even though Paul himself does not. What is readily apparent from Paul's pattern of thinking is that he holds that being restored to a right relationship with God is like Isaac being born despite Abraham being as good as dead and despite the death of Sarah's womb. It involves a radical intervention on God's part to rescue humanity from its situation of death and bring it into the realm of life.[1] And for Paul of course justification by faith and the enjoyment of eschatological life go hand in hand. 'The one who is righteous by faith shall live' (1.17) and the whole burden of 5.12 - 8.13 is that through sharing in the death and resurrection of Christ believers not only receive the free gift of righteousness but escape from death and reign in life. Paul's imaginative correlation between Abraham's faith and belief in the gospel proves illuminating for his further elaboration of his message.[2] It provokes us to ask whether it might also shed light on the situation in Rome. Is there any sense in which Paul's vision of unity coming out of division correlates with life coming out of death?

---

[1]Cf. also Moxnes, *Theology in Conflict*, pp. 275-76; D. Patte, *Paul's Faith and the Power of the Gospel* (Philadelphia: Fortress, 1983), pp. 214-22.

[2]Moxnes, *Theology in Conflict*, pp. 246-53, 278, has argued that Paul employs the designation of God as creator and lifegiver in defence of his general vision of a new community of faith which includes both Jews and non-Jews.

Once the question has been asked, the clues are there to be found. In the paraenesis of chapter 14 the death and resurrection of Christ to be lord is in fact used as an axiom of unity, since it makes both groups accountable to him and not to each other (vv. 7-9). In chapter 15 Paul's vision of unity involves Gentiles hoping in the risen root of Jesse (v. 12). But these are superficial links. What is more significant is the deeper pattern of thought that is at work. Paul leads into this section of paraenesis with a reminder that quarrelling and jealousy belong to the sphere of the flesh (13.13, 14), and, as the readers know by now, the sphere of the flesh is also that of death (cf. 7.5; 8.6, 13). On the other hand, the love (14.15), unity (15.5) and peace (14.17, 19; 15.13) Paul desires to see among believers in Rome all belong to the sphere of the Spirit (cf. 14.17; 15.13), and, as the readers know by now, the sphere of the Spirit is also that of life (cf. 7.6; 8.2-27). Indeed, 'to set the mind on the Spirit is life and peace' (8.6). What is more, in Paul's vision of eschatological unity, the salvation of both the Gentiles and Israel means 'life from the dead' in its fullest sense, the final resurrection (11.15). In the light of this pattern of thought, it becomes clear that, if the work of God among the Roman believers is not to be destroyed (14.20) and instead Gentiles and Jews are together with one voice to glorify the God and Father of our Lord Jesus Christ (15.6), they will need to live and act in the present out of their justifying faith and hope in the God who brings life out of death.

c) *Concluding Unscientific Postscript for the Weak and the Strong.*
For some, no doubt, this view of Paul's idiosyncratic use of Scripture may have reinforced questions about the implications of his creative freedom with the text. Indeed it may also have raised questions about my own creative freedom with Paul. How much have Paul's treatment of Abraham and my treatment of Paul to do with the original meanings and authors' intentions? Can I be sure that Paul's readers would have grasped all that I have found in the text? Does it matter? Do the readings contain valid insights anyway?

Just as Paul's reading of Abraham had force for both the weak and the strong in Rome, so this reading of Paul has force for both the weak and strong among his interpreters. I speak very boldly by way of reminder and not of course for disputes over opinions, but perhaps there are some among us who are weak and some who are strong. There are students of the New Testament who are suspicious of the libertine tendencies of reader-response, intertextuality and deconstruction, who cannot with a good conscience give up their reliance on the sufficiency of the historical-grammatical method and who may even believe that if Scripture does not have one determinate meaning then God cannot speak through it. These are those who claim that there is no difference between the original sense of Old Testament texts and Paul's use of them[1] or who attribute much of Paul's creative use of Scripture to revelation or merely cultural factors and hold that his approach can only be followed 'where . . . it treats the Old Testament in more literal fashion, following the course of what we speak of today as historico-grammatical exegesis'.[2] Our reading beckons them to leave behind any bondage to the historical-critical method. They may find that they are not giving up the authority of Scripture but joining the apostle Paul! To the strong, to those who glory in the fact that meaning occurs in their encounter with the text and who boast in the free play of textual associations, this reading is saying that Paul is one of them. Yet they too need to be cautioned not to despise the tradition, not to consign the discipline and stimulus of historical exegesis to a past that is no longer relevant. If the strong are claiming Paul as their father, they will not be tempted to think that Scripture loses its power in a total hermeneutical flux, that language is all there is, and that there is no possibility of a 'transcendental signified'. Abraham, Paul and Rome are the equivalents of Scripture, gospel and community. To follow in the footsteps of father Paul may be to exploit fully their own encounter with the text and to welcome a variety of other readings, and to do so in faithfulness to the God of Israel's Scripture and to the Christian gospel and in the service of a community of faith, love and justice.[3] But in any case, as father Paul might have said, 'One person esteems one method as more valid than another, while another person esteems all methods alike. Let every one be fully convinced in his or her own mind'.

---

[1]Cf. e.g. W.C. Kaiser. Jr., *The Uses of the Old Testament in the New* (Chicago: Moody, 1985).

[2]Cf. R.N. Longenecker, *Biblical Exegesis in the Apostolic Period* (Grand Rapids: Eerdmans, 1975), p. 219.

[3]For an excellent discussion of Paul's use of Scripture along these lines, see R.B. Hays, *Echoes of Scripture in the Letters of Paul* (New Haven: Yale University Press, 1989), esp. pp. 1-33; 154-92.

STOICISM, ΕΛΕΥΘΕΡΙΑ AND COMMUNITY AT CORINTH*

Terence Paige

What were the forces shaping the thoughts and actions of the church of God at Corinth, the forces which, in the relatively short time between Paul's founding the church and the writing of 1 Corinthians, led to the rise of behavior and teaching so at variance with what the apostle laid down? What I suggest here is that the influence of Stoicism or a Stoicizing source (perhaps with Cynic tendencies) may have been one very significant element affecting the Corinthian Christian leadership. The presence of Stoic thought would account for several problems at Corinth often attributed to Gnosticism[1] or Jewish Wisom Theology, especially the apparent pursuit of a spirituality that was elitist and devoid of a community-oriented dimension. Other items that could be explained on the basis of a Stoicizing influence include the characterization of the Corinthians as kings and as rich; the assertion of absolute freedom for the Christian who is σοφός, together with the creed 'πάντα μοι ἔξεστιν'; the Corinthian argument that an idol is 'nothing'; and the highly individualistic approach to moral problems (e.g. ch. 8; 6.12-20; 11.17-22). In addition to evidence of the Corinthian's language and behavior, Paul's own answers or correctives sometimes use Stoic-sounding language: the apostles as a 'spectacle' (4.9);[2] the argument from conscience (8.7); his defense of his actions at Corinth as one who is

---

*First delivered as a paper at the 1990 Tyndale New Testament Conference, Tyndale House, Cambridge. Its inclusion here is meant to celebrate Ralph Martin's long-standing interest in the Corinthian epistles, and his contributions to the study of them.

[1]Including here 'gnosis' and 'proto-Gnosticism'.

[2]J.N. Sevenster, *Paul and Seneca* (Leiden: Brill, 1961), pp. 115f., and G.D. Fee, *The First Epistle to the Corinthians* (NICNT [ns]; Grand Rapids: Eerdmans, 1987), pp. 174f. n. 50. Both point to the intent of Paul's expression as differing greatly from the sense found in Seneca of a proud display of the wise man's triumphant will before men and gods.

ἐλεύθερος (9.1, 19); his advice to Christians to live as though not married, not possessing, unattached to ephemeral things so that they may be ἀμέριμνος, 'without care' (7.29-32); the description of the purpose of Spirit-endowments as πρὸς τὸ συμφέρον, 'for the purpose of profit' (12.7);[1] the use of 'body' imagery (chap. 12); and the argument from 'nature' (φύσις, 11.14).[2]

The similarity of Paul's language in many places to that of the Stoa, especially Seneca's, has been observed for some time. Sevenster chronicles the debate concerning the relationship between Paul and Seneca, which has lasted over a hundred and thirty years.[3] The debate whether Paul borrows from Seneca or vice versa seems to have ended in a general acceptance of the view carefully argued first by Lightfoot and later by Sevenster, that the similarities of expression in the writings of Paul and Seneca most often turn out to be purely formal. Paul is neither a Stoic nor is he expressing Stoicizing thoughts when he uses body[4] imagery, speaks of an indwelling Spirit, commends the imitation of God, or decries the sinfulness of man—all of which may be found in Seneca. The fundamental conceptions of deity and of the relationship between man and God are very different between the two. Sevenster showed that there is no ground to believe that the two ever met, or that Seneca borrowed language from Paul (which is the other way to explain the similarities).[5]

The question I wish to raise is *not* whether or not *Paul* thought in Stoic manner; rather, could it be that he is writing to people who themselves use such language, think in a Stoicizing manner, or are impressed with Stoic ideas? Otherwise why does he so frequently use language that appears Stoic, though he operates with different assumptions? After all, the manner of Paul's expression is not shaped solely by his Jewish background and Christian confession, but surely to some extent by the needs of his audience as well? Do not their

---

[1]Diogenes Laertius (=D.L.) 7.93, 98f., 149. Compare Plutarch's attack on Stoic ἀπαθεία, of which he says ἔξω καὶ τοῦ δυνατοῦ καὶ τοῦ συμφέροντος οὖσαν (*Consolatio ad Apollonium* 102C): 'it is beyond what is possible and what is beneficial'.

[2]Discussions of many of these may be found in Conzelmann or Fee, *ad loc.*

[3]Sevenster, *Paul and Seneca*, esp. pp. 1-5; cf. also J.B. Lightfoot, 'St. Paul and Seneca', in *Dissertations on the Apostolic Age* (London: Macmillan and Co., 1892), pp. 249-322 (originally part of Lightfoot's commentary on Philippians, 1890).

[4]Though this is not to say he could not have adapted Stoic themes to suit his own purpose. See J.D.G. Dunn, 'The "Body of Christ" in Paul' in this volume.

[5]Sevenster, *Paul and Seneca*, pp. 6-25.

problems, vocabulary, and level of understanding influence the manner of the apostle's communication with them?

In order to better assess the viability of this proposal, I begin with a brief synopsis of Stoicism's influence in the era I BC — AD I, and then its view of the 'wise man' and its orientation in ethics.

Stoicism was a native Greek philosophy which had thrived for some three hundred fifty years prior to Paul's arrival in Greece. By the beginning of our era, Sandbach believes Stoicism to be 'without doubt the predominant philosophy among the Romans'.[1] Stoic philosophers befriended and were in turn patronized by Roman aristocrats and senators beginning in the second century BC.[2] Several emperors also maintained Stoic philosophers, notably Augustus and Nero.[3] One Stoic supported by Augustus was Athenodorus of Tarsus, from Paul's home town. He was in his later years entrusted with a mission to straighten out the constitution and leadership of Tarsus, where he became its chief citizen.[4] Several other Stoic teachers hailed from Tarsus as well. It is only reasonable to expect that Stoicism would be known to Paul, and would be a lively intellectual current in the Corinth of the first century: what better ground could there be for a Greek philosophy popular with Romans than a major city of Greece refounded by Rome? A Stoicizing influence could easily have entered the church via its members who had received some education in their youth. Christians coming from citizen families, and especially families of wealth or social status, would have become familiar with rhetoric and philosophy if they had attended tertiary education; and even if they only made it through secondary education, some philosophy had entered the syllabus of general education (ἐγκύκλιος παιδεία) by this time: and the Ephebic colleges also included a smattering of rhetoric and philosophy.[5] Such training was believed to

[1]Sevenster, *Paul and Seneca*, p.16.

[2]F.H. Sandbach, *The Stoics* (London: Chatto & Windus, 1975), pp. 16f., 142-44.

[3]Nero eventually forced Seneca to suicide and had other Stoics put to death, including a senator (Thrasea Paetus) and a governor of Asia Minor (Barea Soranus). These judgments, which did not occur until AD 65-66, were inspired by the assassination conspiracy and Nero's suspicious paranoia (Sandbach, *The Stoics*, p. 144). Hadrian, Antoninus Pius, and Marcus Aurelius also supported Stoics.

[4]Sandbach, *The Stoics*, p. 142f,; OCD s.v. 'Athenodorus' (of Tarsus); Pauly-Wissowa Suppl., V, p. 47ff.

[5]H.I. Marrou, *A History of Education in Antiquity* (trans. George Lamb; London: Sheed & Ward, 1956), pp. 108, 210-11; Stanley F. Bonner, *Education in Ancient Rome* (London: Methuen & Co., 1977), pp. 85-87, 110. Some of the wealthier families might hire a qualified private tutor to train their children at home. A famous example of this in pre-Roman Corinth was the household of

fit one for public service.[1] I use the term 'Stoicizing' influence, because I am not talking about people who are full-time philosophers or are necessarily acquainted with the system in great depth.[2]

For the Stoa there was a vast gulf between the 'wise man' (ὁ σοφός) and the common people (οἱ πολλοί). The σοφός (who is also described as σπουδαῖος, 'good', and φρόνιμος, 'wise/prudent') is one who has made the goal of his existence the 'life in accord with nature' (κατὰ φύσιν ζῆν). This is intended to aid the pursuit of virtue, which is the only absolute 'good' recognized by the Stoa.[3] Only virtue is necessary to be happy (εὐδαίμων) and wise; all else is ἀδιάφορον ('indifferent').

However, one could pursue a life according to nature and yet not have achieved virtue and not be a Stoic wise man. For the Stoa consider no degrees of virtue or progress. One who is 'making progress' is still drowning and not yet safely ashore, still committing 'sins' and far from virtue. Either one is *perfect*, a σοφός, or one is still φαῦλος, a scoundrel who is lost.[4] Attaining the status of a σοφός could be described as a kind of enlightenment that put one in a class above all others, with instinctive insight into the world. From Plutarch's sarcastic description of the Stoic wise man we can still see this ideal of the enlightened sage who stands above the rest of humanity in regard to virtue:

> Among the Stoics the man who is most vicious in the morning, if so it chance to be, is in the afternoon most virtuous. Having fallen asleep demented and stupid and unjust and licentious and even, by heaven, a slave and a drudge and a pauper, he gets up the very same day changed into a blessed and opulent *king*, sober and just and steadfast and undeluded by fancies. He has not sprouted a beard or the token of puberty in a body young and soft, but in a soul that is feeble and soft and unmanly and unstabel has got perfect intelligence, consummate prudence, a godlike

---

Xeniades, who purchased the Cynic philosopher Diogenes in a slave auction to become his sons' tutor (D.L. 6.30-31).

1R.L. Fox, *Pagans and Christians* (New York: Alfred Knopf, 1987), pp. 13-15, 18.

2So Rist remarks 'many Stoics had merely read their Stoicism or talked to Stoicizing individuals, and then claimed to be Stoics or desiderant Stoics' ('Are You a Stoic? The Case of Marcus Aurelius', in *Jewish and Christian Self-Definition*, vol. 3: *Self-Definition in the Greco-Roman World* [ed. Ben Meyer and E.P. Sanders; London: SCM, 1982], p. 23).

3Sandbach, *The Stoics*, pp. 53f.; Terence Irwin, *A History of Western Philosophy*, vol. 1: *Classical Thought* (Oxford: Oxford University Press, 1989), p. 174. The living of a life according to nature may even be said to be equivalent to living virtuously (D.L. 7.87).

4D.L. 7.120f.; Sandbach, *The Stoics*, p. 44; A.H. Armstrong, *An Introduction to Ancient Philosophy* (3d ed.; London: Methuen & Co., 1957; rpt. ed., 1968), p. 126.

> disposition, *knowledge* free from fancy, and an unalterable habitude and this not from any previous abatement of his depravity, but by having changed instantaneously from the most vicious of wild beasts into what may almost be called a kind of hero or spirit [δαίμων] or god. For, if one has got virtue from the Stoa, it is possible to say 'Ask, if there's aught you wish; *all will be yours* [πάντα σοι γενήσεται]'. It brings *wealth* [πλοῦτον], it comprises *kingship* [βασιλείαν], it gives luck, it makes men prosperous and *free from all other wants* and self-sufficient [αὐτάρκεις], though they have not a single drachma of their own.[1]

The italicized words parallel descriptions of the Corinthians (by themselves or by Paul) in 1 Corinthians which are usually thought to arise from an over-realized eschatology. So 1 Cor. 4.8, 'Already you are full, already you have become rich, without us you reign (as kings—ἐβασιλεύσατε) . . .' Yet the use of these terms could have arisen from a misplaced, Stoic-like ideal of themselves as wise. For according to the Stoa, only the wise man is truly happy, truly wealthy, truly fit to govern as king, truly free.[2] This is because he shares the world with the gods, and is enriched with the wisdom of the divine λόγος which governs nature.

Besides the ideal of an enlightened sage, the Stoic understanding of virtue is closely tied to *knowledge*. The key is to know what is 'according to nature' and then what is virtuous—which is akin to nature, since for the Stoic God is in nature everywhere. God has shaped nature and Destiny or Fate as well, therefore virtue is in accord with the divine reason or λόγος as expressed in the formation of the universe. In fact, according to I.G. Kidd, the true Stoic wise man at the pinacle of his moral progress leaves behind the study of ethics to concentrate on the *logos*-philosophy, since understanding the mind of Nature/God is the higher pursuit.[3] To achieve virtue, the student must begin his training by learning to *choose* rightly the things that are κατὰ φύσιν.[4] If one asks how the wise man is to know what is κατὰ φύσιν, the Stoa never give a clear answer. They seem to

---

[1]Plut., *Compendium argumenti Stoicos absurdiora poetis dicere* 1058B-C (H. Cherniss' translation in the Loeb edition of the *Moralia*, vol. 13.2, pp. 615, 617).

[2]Cf. also Plut., *De communibus notitiis* 1060B; 1062E; D.L. 7.122.

[3]I.G. Kidd, 'Stoic Intermediates and the End for Man', in *Problems in Stoicism* (ed. A.A. Long; London: Athlone Press, 1971), pp. 165-66.

[4]Compare Paul's argument to the Corinthians at 1 Cor. 11.14.

picture him as intuitively understanding both his own nature and that of the cosmos, and these are in harmony.[1]

This heavily rationalized view of virtue saw error or 'sin' accordingly as simply a bad judgment of the intellect, and denied the existence of any irrational forces in the soul.[2] The goal of the wise life then was aided by the extirpation of irrational 'passions', products of bad judgment of the mind. Those who were not wise were foolish, ruled by irrational passion, incapable of real friendship and therefore enemies of the wise.[3]

What most people held to be important and necessary for happiness the Stoics regarded as 'indifferent', dispensable. Such things included health, wealth, clothing, reputation, even death. Therefore, most people's pursuit of the normal things of life, and their sadness at the loss of such things, was treated by the Stoa as simply examples of irrational passion. These were things to be overcome, not something to sympathize with or to help along. Even the death of a spouse or children is classed as an 'indifferent', and to grieve over such things is irrational, the mark of one who does not yet think aright and is not perfect.[4] Such a philosophy could easily lead to a callous attitude towards one's fellow human beings.

The odd thing is that the Stoics did advocate involvement in political life.[5] And many Stoics are recorded in the Roman senate and high government offices from the late first century BC to the second century AD. Terence Irwin attempts to uphold the Stoic claim that they are truly unselfishly interested in others' welfare by their involvement in public life, yet in the end must concede 'Stoic ethics seems to be an

---

1 'It has been argued in the preceding pages that to live consistently with nature was an aim accepted by all Stoics, that this nature was universal nature, with which man's fully-developed nature must always coincide, and which in great part allowed him to have what suited his own individual nature' (Sandbach, *The Stoics*, p. 59). Kidd argues that in the first stage of progress toward becoming wise, the Stoic-in-training was thought to look toward harmony with his own (human) nature, eventually leading him into harmony with the universal nature and world-*logos* which shaped him (Kidd, 'Stoic Intermediates', pp. 165-67).

2 D.L. 7.111; Sandbach, *The Stoics*, p. 41f. Plato had postulated an irrational part of the soul that fought against the rational part, and was seated in a different locus from it. Posidonius was the only Stoic to admit such an irrational 'force' in the soul (which he held to be a unified whole, in Stoic fashion).

3 D.L. 7.32-33.

4 Irwin, *A History of Western Philosophy*, pp. 174-76.

5 Though none of the leaders of the school was in politics until after the time of Chrysippus in the mid II BC (cf. D.L. 7.121). When Chrysippus was asked why he did not enter politics, he replied 'Bad politics displeases the gods; good politics the citizens'.

unstable combination of self-sufficiency and concern for others'.[1] For the true Stoic sage neither wishes to nor can he extend any 'passionate sympathy' to others. Pity and compassion (ἐλεημοσύνη) are *vices*, not virtues.[2] They arise from a wrong judgment of things that are really indifferent.

Further, there is a strong drive in Stoicism, as noted by Irwin, to self-sufficiency. This they inherited from Cynicism, where the 'life according to nature' was usually interpreted to mean a way of life dependent on no one and nothing but the barest essentials, a kind of hyper-Socratic existence.[3] For Cynic and Stoic ethics, pursuit of virtue is a wrestling with oneself and the world; it is the individual seeking to embrace nature and his Fate, whatever is thrown at him. All that happens to one can be seen as opportunities for personal testing, advancement and victory over circumstances. You must test the appearances of things, says Epictetus, not accepting what they seem to be (good or evil), but judging them rationally in line with nature (φύσις; Epict. *Diss*. 3.12.14f.). Even the encounter with another human being is reduced to an opportunity to 'test the appearances of things', to exercise oneself in judgment and in passionlessness (Epict. *Diss*. 3.12.1-8, 10-12). It is not viewed as an opportunity to do good to the other, or to shun doing evil to the other. The only evil one can do is to oneself. The other is seen only in respect of the needs of oneself. There is no sense of community obligation, or of any community bond.

The Stoic can indeed say that Zeus is father of all, and this man is my brother[4]; but in reality it is only the σοφοί/σπουδαίοι who can have true community. Only the perfect can be true friends and share all things with the gods. They have nothing in common with the masses, who are base and do not know how to love (D.L. 7.124; 7.32-33). This limits 'community' to the perfect few, though even here one wonders what kind of mutual empathy and society could exist. The wise man, it is said, is able to be content alone and solitary, like Zeus at the end of the world. He needs no one but himself to speak to (Epict. *Diss*. 3.13.4, 6-8). The Stoic will neither give nor receive sympathy for any of the common pains and troubles of life.

---

[1] Irwin, *A History of Western Philosophy*, p. 182.

[2] D.L. 7.115 lists pity along with envy and strife as a sickness of the soul.

[3] Armstrong, *An Introduction to Ancient Philosophy*, p. 117 (Cynics); Epict., *Diss*. 3.13.

[4] Epictetus, *Diss*. 1.3; 1.9.6-7.

Now as with most philosophies, and especially one as rigorous as Stoicism, few practised what they preached. But where the Stoics, their pupils and admirers tended to lapse was not in the direction of more love of neighbor and good community feelings than they ought to have. Rather, they tended to begin justifying the pursuit of so-called 'indifferents' (ἀδιάφορα), which everyone else called 'goods', such as health and wealth. So Aristo from Chios, a pupil of Zeno's who was denounced by his master, argued that none of the 'morally indifferent' things had advantage in or of itself, and so the wise man ought to be free to do whatever he chooses, whatever seems good to him 'without pain, desire, or fear'.[1] Seneca, while praising the poor and simple life according to nature and the brotherhood of men, was amassing one of the greatest fortunes of the empire, with the aid of hosts of slaves, and had complicity in several political murders, including that of the emperor Nero's mother.[2] Epictetus complained that most who professed to be Stoics lived like Epicureans (*Diss.* 2.19).

As said earlier, a Stoicizing influence on prominent Corinthian Christians (and through them, on the whole church) may help to explain many things in the letter. Thus the Corinthians can claim to be satisfied, rich and kings—not because the kingdom has already arrived, but because by the Spirit they have moved from being base to being σοφοί and τελειοί. Compare D.L. 7.121-23:

> μόνον τ' [τὸν σοφόν] ἐλεύθερον, τοὺς δὲ φαύλους δούλους· εἶναι γὰρ τὴν ἐλευθερίαν ἐξουσίαν αὐτοπραγίας . . . οὐ μόνον δ' ἐλευθέρους εἶναι τοὺς σοφούς, ἀλλὰ καὶ βασιλέας . . . ἔτι καὶ ἀναμαρτήτους, τῷ ἀπεριπτώτους εἶναι ἁμαρτήματι.

> [The wise man] alone is free, while the common people[3] are slaves; for freedom is the power of independent action . . . and not only are the wise free, but also kings . . . and further, they are also sinless, not being liable to sin.

These Stoicizing-Christian Corinthians see themselves as wise ones who share all with God and have true insight (γνῶσις) into the universe. They know that an idol—that is, an image—is 'nothing' in the

[1] Cicero, *de fin.* 4.69, 43; Sandbach, *The Stoics*, pp. 38f.
[2] Sandbach, *The Stoics*, pp. 155f.; OCD s.v. 'Seneca'. Seneca's *De Beata Vita* contains some self-justification in its defense of the wise man's guilt-free enjoyment of wealth (25.1-2).
[3] Or perhaps 'bad people'.

cosmos, and that only one God exists (1 Cor. 8.4; 10.19). It is interesting to compare this argument with Zeno's prohibition of building temples in the ideal city of his *Republic*, because no work of human builders is worth much, and consequently not sacred.[1] A similar argument against the divinity of images or temple precincts, but now bolstered with a more pure monotheism, is used by the 'strong' at Corinth to justify their attendance at temple feasts or their partaking of food that had been dedicated to pagan gods (8.1-13; 10.14-24). The reaction of the 'weak' to this new development is regarded by the 'strong' solely as the problem of the weak. It is a matter of choice—of how one regards the appearances of things—and of having knowledge or insight into the true nature of the universe. One can only be offended and stumble if his/her thinking is amiss. After all, does not even the Apostle himself agree that it is wrong to think of images as having any power or sacrificial meat as having any significance (1 Cor. 10.19)? The problem, think the strong, surely lies in the sick passions and fears of the weak.

Some premises that Paul agrees with—and which he may have asserted himself in his preaching at Corinth[2]—were being made to serve a conclusion at variance with Paul's theology and, further, at odds with the new existence in Christ. For though the idol is 'nothing', yet to act in accord with those who serve idols is something. Though my conscience may not be harmed, yet to harm another's conscience, to act in a way that encourages another brother or sister to question his faith or return to idolatry is *not* an ἀδιάφορον, an indifferent thing. In Christ the existence of the other Christian is interlinked with my existence (1 Cor. 8.12; 12.27). Hence a choice which may be rationalized on one level may affect one's Christian existence at another level because the believer has a union with the risen Lord and with other believers through the Holy Spirit. This union might be expressed as the 'fellowship in [God's] Son Jesus Christ' (1 Cor. 1.9) or the 'fellowship of the Holy Spirit' (2 Cor. 13.13). 'It is', says Ralph Martin, 'the common life shared by all believers on the ground

---

[1] D.L. 7.33; Plutarch, *De Stoicorum repugnantiis* 1034B: 'it is a doctrine of Zeno's not to build temples of the gods, because a temple not worth much is also not sacred and no work of builders or mechanics is worth much'.

[2] For example, most commentators agree that the principle of individual freedom (9.1; 10.29, 31; cf. Gal. 2.4; 5.1, 13) originates with Paul, not the Corinthians.

that they all, by their calling as Christians, participate in Jesus Christ.'[1]

Just such a callousness of individuals toward others as we find at Corinth, such a disregard for the community dimension of their new existence, would likely be fostered by a Stoicizing influence, which would in fact exalt the individual σοφός at the expense of the community. And a Stoic could behave in this individualistic, community-destroying fashion at the same time that he believes he is pursuing a virtuous life according to nature and reason, asserting his divine right of freedom of choice (αὐτοπραγία). We could say Paul counters this by asserting that a Christian's 'interlinked-ness' with Christ limits independence of action for the true σοφός.[2]

Again in chapter 6 Paul warns that some actions corrupt the relationship we have with the indwelling Christ. So to be 'joined' to a prostitute, by an exegesis of Gen. 2.24, is said to form a union which is intolerable for a member of the body of Christ. Mental choice and attitude are not the only determining factors in one's existence. Neither can one dismiss what is done with the body as an ἀδιάφορον. Paul reminds them that there is a question of ownership in the new existence. They belong to God; the Spirit of God they have is resident within them, but is not subject to their autonomous control.

> Or don't you know that your body is the temple of the Holy Spirit within you, which you possess *from God*? And that *you do not belong to yourselves*? You were purchased with a price: therefore glorify God in your bodies (6.19-20).

πάντα μοι ἔξεστιν, the defense of those whom Paul is correcting (6.12), is not only to be understood as a gnostic proclamation; it expresses very well the prerogative of the Stoic wise man who is good and perfect:

---

[1]R.P. Martin, *The Family and the Fellowship: New Testament Images of the Church* (Exeter: Paternoster, 1979), p. 37; *idem*, *2 Corinthians* (WBC; Waco, TX: Word, 1986), pp. 254-55, 504-505; 'The Spirit in 2 Corinthians in Light of the "Fellowship of the Holy Spirit" in 2 Corinthians 13:14', in *Eschatology and the New Testament* (ed. W.H. Gloer; Peabody, Mass.: Hendrickson, 1988), pp. 113-28. See also A.R. George, *Communion with God in the New Testament* (London: Epworth, 1953); Jerome Murphy-O'Connor, 'Eucharist and Community in First Corinthians', *Worship* 50 (1976), pp. 370-85; and *idem*, 'Eucharist and Community in First Corinthians', *Worship* 51 (1977), pp. 56-69; esp. 50:383-85; Josef Hainz, *KOINONIA: 'Kirche' als Gemeinschaft bei Paulus* (Regensburg: F. Pustet, 1982).

[2]Cf. 1 Cor. 10.15, 'I speak as to φρονίμοις' in his warning against taking part in events at pagan temples. φρόνιμος is a synonymn for the σοφός in Stoic literature.

> οὐκοῦν οἱ φρόνιμοι ὅσα βούλονται πράττειν, ἔξεστιν αὐτοῖς· οἱ δὲ ἄφρονες ὅσα βούλονται οὐκ ἐξὸν ἐπιχειροῦσι πράττειν. ὥστε ἀνάγκη τοὺς μὲν φρονίμους ἐλευθέρους τε εἶναι καὶ ἐξεῖναι αὐτοῖς ποιεῖν ὡς ἐθέλουσι . . . (*SVF* III:356).[1]
>
> Therefore whatever the wise wish to do is permitted, but whatever the foolish wish to do, though it is not permitted, they attempt to do. So of necessity the wise are free and it is permitted them to do as they wish . . .

The wise man may do whatever he wishes, since he alone has right judgment. The case under consideration in 1 Cor. 6.12-20 need not be a libertine whose fleshly actions make no difference. It is not inconceivable that a Stoic could have regarded this sort of sexual immorality (as we call it) an ἀδιάφορον. Though it is true the Stoics generally held up marriage as a good thing,[2] Zeno had advocated a radical communism of women (as had Plato), and a rather free attitude towards sexual matters characterized the school.[3] But more significant is that the specific immorality mentioned in 1 Corinthians chapter 6 is concourse with a prostitute (not sexual immorality in general). And this was usually not held to be in the same class at all as an affair with a married woman.[4]

It is also interesting that Paul begins the defence of his conduct at Corinth in chapter nine with the words, 'Am I not free?' Freedom is one of the most cherished and exalted of attributes of the Stoic wise man: freedom from irrational passions; freedom to choose or reject

---

[1]From Dio Chrys. *Or.* XIV.17 (64.17 in von Arnim ed.); cf. Plut., *Stoic. absurd.* 1058B-C, above.

[2]So Antipater of Tarsus (*SVF* III:254f., ap. Stobaeus, *Florileg.* LXVII.25); cf. Sandbach, *The Stoics*, p. 118; Marcia L. Colish, *The Stoic Tradition From Antiquity to the Early Middle Ages*, vol. 1: *Stoicism in Classical Latin Literature* (Leiden: Brill, 1985), p. 41.

[3]Zeno had taken a radical view of marriage, advocating that the wise hold all women in common; however, his view was not maintained after Chrysippus (Sandbach, *The Stoics*, pp. 25f.; Colish, *The Stoic Tradition*, p. 38).

[4]Prostitution had been common in Greece for well over six centuries, Solon having introduced public brothels, and the Romans were relatively lenient on it as well (W. Krenkel, 'Prostitution', *Kleine Pauly* IV:1192-94). Though one would not usually bring a prostitute home, to frequent the brothels was regarded as a mere *peccadillo*. Antisthenes the Cynic is said to have commented, on seeing an adulterer fleeing the scene of his crime, 'ὦ δυστυχής, πηλίκον κίνδυνον ὀβολοῦ διαφυγεῖν ἴσχυες' (D.L. 6.4): 'Oh unfortunate man, what a great danger you could have escaped with the price of an obol'—referring to the price of a prostitue, whose company would not have brought down on the man's head a husband's wrath.' Compare Plutarch's advice to the newly married wife to look the other way if her husband should share his drunken debauchery with a girl servant or prostitute (ἑταῖρα); she should consider it a sign of his respect for her that he does not behave so indecently with his lawful wife (*Conj. praec.* XVI/140B).

those things which are in his power; freedom to live the life according to nature and to pursue virtue. But Paul overturns this self-centered perspective by his very life, which in its *imitatio Christi* makes a new definition of freedom: Ἐλεύθερος γὰρ ὢν ἐκ πάντων πᾶσιν ἐμαυτὸν ἐδούλωσα, ἵνα τοὺς πλείονας κερδήσω (9.19). Bultmann vividly describes the Pauline concept thus: 'This freedom arises from the very fact that *the believer*, as one "ransomed", *no longer belongs to himself* (1 Cor 6.19) . . . He recognizes himself to be the property of God (or of the Lord) and lives for Him'.[1] And in another place, 'this basic freedom may at any moment take on the form of *renunciation*—seemingly a renunciation of freedom itself, but in reality it is a paradoxical exercise of that very freedom'.[2] The reason self-renunciation may be the order of the moment, and the reason freedom is not an absolute principle for Paul is the coterminous theological principle of κοινωνία, the community or fellowship which Christians have with God, Christ, and the Holy Spirit on the one hand and with one another on the other hand. This is not the *koinonia* which the Stoic wise man has with God whereby all things belong to him, for it is not individualistically oriented. It signifies a mutual and interconnected existence which has a reality established by God, and which is affirmed emotively by believers.

The same idea is signified in chapter twelve by the expression 'body of Christ' (12.12f., 27). As the parts of a body fit together and serve each other, so the Christians who form Christ's body must be aware of their interdependence, and of their collective dependence on Christ (12.12-27).[3] Such intimate interlinking of individual lives and such a call for emotive union would be unthinkable for the Stoa (despite their affirmation of political life). We know that community was breaking down in this church, for one member could say of another, 'I have no need of you' (12.21)—and yet this apalling sentiment is exactly the sort of proud boast that the σοφός of the Stoa would make, that he needs nothing but himself and nature to be happy and virtuous.

However, the 'parts' of Christ's 'body' must be concerned for each other (12.25). Christians who are truly wise and perfect regulate

[1] R. Bultmann, *Theology of the New Testament* (trans. Kendrick Grobel; London: SCM, 1952), I, p. 331.
[2] Bultmann, *Theology of the New Testament*, I, p. 342.
[3] Cf. R.P. Martin, *The Spirit and the Congregation: Studies in 1 Corinthians 12-15* (Grand Rapids: Eerdmans, 1984), pp. 19-30.

their 'freedom' in the light of the *koinonia* of believers and the example of their Lord. 'Everything is permitted' can no longer be understood in Stoic fashion, because 'not everything builds up' (10.23). The salvation which is from the Crucified One brings forth the demand, 'let no one seek his own good, but the good of others' (10.24). This is consistent with the 'message of the cross' which is the foundation of the community's new existence in Christ (1.18). It is not that Paul is unconcerned for the fate of the individual; rather, his care for individuals is most intimately linked with their participation in the community and the expression of community life—or danger to that life—that their individual lives represent.

Although the problems at the community's celebration of Eucharist (11.17-22) are not directly related to problems of ἐλευθερία and γνῶσις, the attitudes displayed by the wealthier members are attitudes that could easily be furthered by Stoicizing teaching.[1] The Stoic's belief that any apparent evil may be 'overcome' by a proper judgment (in this case, that the lack of the poor is not really an evil and cannot affect their virtue), coupled with his firm belief in a divine Fate which has determined everything rationally, could easily support a lack of concern for the poor.

Given the popularity of Stoicism in the first century, the mixed Greek and Roman character of Corinth, the presence of Stoicizing terminology in 1 Corinthians and the evidence of Corinthian attitudes just discussed, it is not unreasonable to suppose that part of the problem at Corinth may well have been a Stoicizing (or Cynic- and Stoicizing) influence. Such an influence would not only explain the presence of Stoic-like terminology, but the development of an elite group of self-styled *sophoi* within the church who held a highly individualistic, self-centered ethics. This influence probably helped to foster a similarly self-centered spirituality. It advocated a concept of Christian 'freedom' which was at odds with community. This was

---

[1]These are also the members who could have afforded rhetorical and philosophical education in their youth. For recent analyses of 1 Corinthians pointing to evidence of sociological stratification and problems arising from the wealthier, more influential members at Corinth, see G. Theissen, *Studien zur Sociologie des Urchristentums* (WUNT, no. 9; Tübingen: J.C.B. Mohr, 1979) = ET *The Social Setting of Pauline Christianity* (trans. John Schütz; Philadelphia: Fortress, 1982); Abraham J. Malherbe, *Social Aspects of Early Christianity* (2d enlarged ed.; Philadelphia: Fortress, 1983), p. 30, 82-84; Wayne A. Meeks, *The First Urban Christians: The Social World of the Apostle Paul* (New Haven & London: Yale University Press, 1983), pp. 70-71, 118f.; Jerome Murphy-O'Connor, *St. Paul's Corinth: Texts and Archaeology* (Wilmington, Delaware: Michael Glazier, 1983), pp. 153-61.

leading to a breakdown of community, and Paul's answer was to display the fully dependent status of their existence in Christ. No one is autonomous (6.19-20; 12.12-27). And *koinonia*—with the Son Jesus Christ (1.9), with the Holy Spirit (2 Cor. 13.13; cf. 1 Cor. 3.16; 6.19), and with each other—has the status of a theological principle which also must co-determine ethics, spirituality, and worship.

The Parousia in the New Testament—and Today

I. Howard Marshall

Some years ago at an evangelistic rally in Aberdeen the audience's first introduction to the gospel was an invitation to sing a chorus whose burden was 'Soon, and very soon, we are going to see the King', or, put in theological jargon, 'the imminence of the parousia as a motive for response to the gospel'. I felt somewhat embarrassed on behalf of the non-Christians present who were being invited to join in this ditty with gusto and wondered what they made of it. The memory of that occasion has partly inspired the theme of this paper, namely the place of the second coming of Jesus in the New Testament and the place it should have in Christian theology and preaching today. My approach has a definitely pastoral concern, but this is entirely appropriate in a book of essays dedicated to one who has always seen his task as a scholar in terms of service to the gospel and the church.

The concept of the parousia proper is linked with a number of closely associated ideas and it is not easy to separate them from one another. I shall assume that the basic concept is the coming of the exalted Jesus from heaven to earth, and that it is associated with the final coming of the kingdom or rule of God, with the winding up of human history; the judgment of God and the inauguration of the new age. If one summed up our theme as the final event in which Jesus is involved, this would give a good broad definition, but the characteristic element is the thought of the coming or revelation of Jesus. The concept and the associated vocabulary are found in every main part of the NT to greater or less extent.[1] What I want to do here is simply to

[1]The word παρουσία, which means 'coming' or 'presence', occurs 24 times in the New Testament. There are 17 references to the coming of Jesus in the future (1 Thess. 2.19; 3.13; 4.15; 5.23; 2 Thess. 2.1, 8; 1 Cor. 15.23; Jas 5.7, 8; 2 Pet. 1.16; 3.4, 12; 1 Jn 2.28; the remaining

ask how the parousia functions in the thinking and teaching of the New Testament. I shall do so by looking at one or two representative writers to see what part the parousia plays in their thinking. I am going to look at one of the Gospels, then at the message of the early church in Acts, and then at one of Paul's letters.

The Teaching of Jesus in Mark

In the earliest Gospel, that of Mark, there are surprisingly only three passages specifically referring to the future 'coming' of Jesus (8.38; 13.26-36; 14.62). At the outset of the Gospel it is made clear that Jesus is the Son of God entrusted with a mission by God the Father. He preaches that the kingdom or rule of God has drawn near (Mk 1.15). Whether this verse means that the kingdom has already arrived or that it is to come in the near future, there is a future element elsewhere. It is clearest in 14.25 where Jesus looks forward to drinking the fruit of the vine new in the kingdom. In ch. 4 the parables show that the kingdom grows and develops, presumably over a period of time.

It is not really until ch. 8 that a future element comes strongly into the teaching of Jesus. He warns that people who lose their lives will save them, and people who want to save their lives will lose them. And then in v. 38 he utters a warning that if anybody is ashamed of him the Son of man will be ashamed of that person when he comes in the glory of his Father with the angels. Three comments may be made:

---

four occurrences are in Matthew (24.3, 27, 37, 39), but since the parallel verses in Luke which record the same teaching of Jesus do not contain the term, it is most likely that Matthew has followed the entirely proper procedure of using the word to explain what Jesus said in terms familiar to his readers). Other words used to refer to the same event include 'revelation' (ἀποκαλύψις; 1 Cor 1.7; 2 Thess. 1.7; 1 Pet 1.7, 13; 4.13.) and the verb 'to reveal' (Lk. 17.30; cf. 2 Thess. 2.3, 6, 8 of the rebel figure.); 'manifestation' (ἐπιφάνεια; 2 Thess. 2.8; 1 Tim. 6.14; 2 Tim. 4.1, 8; Tit. 2.13.) and the verb 'to come' (Mk 8.38; 13.26, 35f.; 14.62; cf. Mt. 10.23; 16.28 (diff. Mark); 24.42-46; 25.31 (cf. Lk. 12.36-45); Lk. 18.8; Jn 14.3; Acts 1.11; 1 Cor. 4.5; 11.26; 2 Thess. 1.10; Jude 14; Rev. 1.7; 3.11; 22.20; et al.). Other phrases have a similar reference. When Paul, for example, talks of waiting for God's Son from heaven (1 Thess. 1.10), it is clear what is in his mind (cf. also the verbs ἥκω, Heb. 10.37; and ὁράω, Heb. 9.28). References to the 'day of the Lord' also convey the same sense (Mk 13.32; the day of the Son of man, Lk. 17.24, which is explained by Matthew as his parousia; 1 Cor. 1.8; 5.5; 2 Cor. 1.14; Phil. 1.6, 10; 2.16; 1 Thess. 5.2, 4; 2 Thess. 1.10; 2.2; these are the clearest texts, but there are others where the same sense must be meant.). This complex terminology, which is found in every main part of the New Testament to greater or less extent, bears witness to the importance of our subject.

First, for Mark the Son of man is none other than Jesus. In the Gospels it is the parousia of the Son of man, who is Jesus, which is in mind.

Second, Jesus is destined to suffer and to rise from the dead; hence the rejection of Jesus is bound up with unwillingness to accept the crucified Saviour and to take up one's cross and follow him. It is those who refused to side with the Son of man in his suffering who will not share in his glory. The thrust of the saying is thus decidedly negative, although it also implies what is stated elsewhere in the Gospels, namely that if somebody is not ashamed of the Son of man, then the Son of man will not be ashamed of him (cf. Lk. 12.8).

Third, the reference to the coming of the Son of man fixes, as it were, the time and nature of the judgment. It takes place when the Son of man comes, a phrase that certainly reflects Daniel 7.13 (with 7.26). Moreover, the phrase establishes the glory and dominion of the Son of man. It may be that the immediately following scene, the transfiguration, is meant to give a foretaste of this heavenly glory, an anticipatory vision of what is to be.

The next reference to the parousia is in ch. 13, a section which is devoted to the prophecy of Jesus that the temple will be destroyed and to the questions of the disciples arising from this. The chapter paints a picture of future troubles, civil strife, persecution of Jesus' followers, a terrible tribulation in Judaea, the rise of deceivers, and then celestial signs. On top of all this the Son of man comes in clouds with great power and glory and gathers together his chosen people (Mk 13.26-27). Jesus emphasises both the certainty that this will happen and the uncertainty of when it will happen. The final message to the disciples is thus that they must be watchful and ready, lest the return of the master finds them asleep and failing to keep watch (13.35-36). The function of the parousia in this context is twofold. It comes as relief to those who are oppressed and longing for deliverance; the primary motif is promise. But there is also the element of warning—not to the godless, who do not figure in the picture, but to the disciples who may be caught unawares.

There is only one reference to the parousia left.[1] At his trial Jesus is asked if he is the Messiah, and he replies that his hearers will see the Son of man sitting on the right hand of Power and coming with the

---

[1] I exclude Mark 14.28 from consideration, although some scholars consider that it is a reference to a parousia in Galilee.

clouds of heaven (Mk 14.62). This verse links together OT prophecy about the Messiah (Psa. 110.1) and the Son of man (Dan. 7.13), and the order of events suggests that the heavenly session of Jesus followed by the parousia is meant. The latter is a visible event and the symbolism is that of triumph and vindication of the statement that Jesus is the Messiah.

If we try to sum up what is said in Mark about the parousia, the following elements seem to be constitutive:

a. The future activity of Jesus is carried out as the 'Son of man'.
b. This activity is based on OT prophecy.
c. The 'coming' in itself is a sign of divine vindication. It shows that in terms of prophecy Jesus is the Son of man.
d. He comes to gather the elect and rescue them from tribulation.
e. He is associated with judgment over those who were ashamed of Jesus.
f. His coming is unpredictable, and therefore people must be ready at any time for it. The implication is clearly that it could happen in the lifespan of his contemporaries, although this is not stated definitely.[1]

But we must also ask about the place of this motif in the Gospel as a whole.

a. It is not exactly the most central theme in the Gospel. Essentially there are only three passages which refer to the parousia, Mark 8.38; 14.62 and 13.24-36. The last of these is the only passage in Mark where the parousia becomes a theme in its own right. In ch. 8 the motif is used to back up teaching about the need for commitment to Jesus; in ch. 14 it is used to explicate Jesus' claim to Messiahship. Only ch. 13 takes up the theme at any length, and there it is part of a general discussion of future events in a context where the main emphasis is perhaps on the theme: 'Don't be led astray, and don't give up'.[2]

b. By contrast other motifs are more important in the Gospel. The kingdom of God is announced as the main theme of the proclamation of Jesus in 1.14-15. It is not too difficult to structure most, if not all, of the teaching of Jesus around this concept. The teaching about the parousia will fit into it without undue difficulty, in that it is associated with the vindication of God's Messiah as he is finally

---

1 A.L. Moore, *The Parousia in the New Testament* (Leiden: Brill, 1966).
2 T. Geddert, *Watchwords* (Sheffield: Sheffield Academic Press, 1990).

installed as ruler and judge. The connection is made in Dan. 7. Even so, it is remarkable that in none of the gospel sayings are the phrases 'Son of man' and 'kingdom of God' brought together. They function as two parallel but outwardly unconnected concepts that sum up the teaching of Jesus. Mark appears to make the kingdom a theme of the teaching of Jesus which, one might say, needs to be explained, but the Son of man is introduced almost casually, and it is what is said about him, rather than the figure itself, which is more important.

c. The teaching about the parousia must be seen in the context of other references to the Son of man in Mark. As is well known, the phrase is introduced without any emphasis or explanation in Mk 2.10 and 28 where it is associated with the present authority of Jesus to forgive sins and to exercise lordship over the sabbath. Then we have a series of sayings, Mk 8.31; 9.9, 12, 31; 10.33, 45; 14.21a, 21b, 41, all of which refer to the passion, resurrection, service and betrayal of the Son of man. In terms of sheer number of sayings there can be no doubt where the emphasis lies. It is the suffering, serving Figure who is central in this Gospel.

The effect of this survey is to show principally that the parousia is only one element in the total picture in Mark and that it is of less importance than the suffering of the Son of man. It functions as a hope to the followers of Jesus in distress, as a sanction warning the unfaithful, and as a symbol of the vindication and victory of Jesus. The details of the parousia are given with the utmost economy, and there is no indication that a more detailed knowledge would affect the behaviour of the disciples in any way. It is rather the way of the cross which provides the pattern for their living.[1]

The Preaching in Acts

If we turn to the account of the preaching and teaching of the early church in Acts we again find that the parousia occupies a subordinate position. The first reference is found in the story of the ascension of Jesus. Here two things are interesting.

---

[1] At the risk of being dogmatic, it can be said that the picture given in the other Synoptic Gospels is not essentially different. The same elements are present, and there are no significantly new ones. Similar teaching is presented from other sources, and a comparison of these is important for establishing the full extent and form of the teaching of Jesus.

The first is that the disciples ask the risen Jesus: 'Will you at this time restore the kingdom to Israel?' This question could well have arisen because the resurrection of Jesus was seen as the inauguration of the last days, and this is perhaps confirmed by the way in which Peter alters the wording of Joel 2.28 in Acts 2.17 to make it a prophecy of the coming of the Spirit in the last days. If so, the disciples are perhaps asking whether Dan. 7 is going to find its fulfilment with the saints of the Most High receiving the kingdom. If that was their expectation, Jesus' answer shows that the prophecy had to be reinterpreted. The time of that event is unknown, which is not to say that the hope has been abandoned. Instead the disciples are to bear witness to Jesus in the power of the Spirit right round the earth, and it may fairly be said that this is the way in which the kingdom is to come into being. Put otherwise, the ascended Lord will extend his reign through the witness of the disciples.

The second point is that the disciples are also promised that, as the Lord departed from them into heaven on a cloud, so he will come again in the same way; here the promise of Dan. 7.13 is clearly in mind, and it is this hope which undergirds the great commission given to the disciples. But the point is that the disciples must not stand gazing into heaven and longing for the Lord to return; they have a task to do for him. This emphasis fits in with the gospel teaching on being like servants who await the return of the master but who show their eagerness for his return precisely by doing their appointed duties properly and not by sitting waiting and speculating when he will come.

Thereafter, the parousia concept almost disappears from Acts. When the good news is preached, all the emphasis is on showing that Jesus is the Messiah promised in the OT and declaring that God has exalted the One who, according to his purpose, was put to death by wicked men to be a Saviour. It is as the risen and exalted Lord that he pours out the Spirit and offers salvation.

Twice, however, the gospel message is concluded with a reference to the fact that Jesus has been ordained to be the judge of all people both the living and the dead, and the resurrection is seen as the basis for this expectation (Acts 10.42; 17.31). Here a general resurrection of all people to judgment is presupposed, and the fact that Jesus has been resurrected and exalted is the basis for this statement. In any case, there is no reference to the parousia in the sense of a coming of Jesus as judge.

But there is a coming in the one remaining passage which we must examine. In Acts 3 the Jews are urged to repent so 'that times of refreshing may come from the presence of the Lord, and that he may send the Christ appointed for you, Jesus, whom heaven must receive until the time for establishing all that God spoke by the mouth of his holy prophets from of old' (Acts 3.19-21). The significance of this text may be that the repentance of the hearers will hasten on the process of the conversion of the nations which must precede the return of Jesus. He must remain in heaven until the time comes for the fulfilment of the prophecies relating to the End. They are urged to repent in order that they may enjoy these blessings, a promise which incidentally would not make much sense unless a fulfilment within their lifetime was a serious possibility. The difficulty would be eased if the 'times of refreshing' (a unique phrase) were to be taken as something present and preceding the sending of the Christ. More probably the reference is to the times of blessing which will come in the new era inaugurated by the return of Jesus; here interestingly instead of Jesus 'coming', which is the usual word, he is said to be 'sent' by the Father. It may be that behind this wording lies the prophecy that God would send Elijah at the end (Mal. 4.5), so that in this passage we would have Jesus likened both to Elijah and to Moses.

Looking at the material as a whole, we must say that the parousia is mentioned remarkably rarely in Acts. It may be that Luke assumes that his readers have already read his Gospel with its fuller references in the teaching of Jesus. But this is hardly a full explanation. Rather Luke shows that the early church was told to get on with the job of evangelism and not to spend its time waiting for the parousia, and in the apostolic preaching the parousia plays little role, all the accent falling on the cross and resurrection of Jesus. This is a surprising conclusion, since it is often thought that the early church was obsessed with the hope of the parousia. Indeed, some people have gone so far as to suggest that Luke has deliberately underplayed this element, and that what he says in Acts, especially in ch. 1, is meant to damp down any over-enthusiasm for the parousia in his own day.[1]

---

[1]E.g., R.P.C. Hanson, *The Acts* (Oxford: Oxford University Press, 1967), p. 58.

The First Epistle to the Thessalonians

For our test-probe into Paul's teaching we shall look at 1 Thessalonians. If we had chosen instead the letter to the Galatians, our task would have been rather easy. Here we have a substantial doctrinal letter by Paul which contains a mature statement of his doctrine of justification and the Holy Spirit and yet contains not one single reference to the parousia. Indeed, it scarcely refers to the future at all, except for a reference to the kind of people who because of their sins will not inherit the kingdom of God (Gal. 5.21), and a general warning that we shall reap what we sow, whether corruption or eternal life (Gal. 6.7-8).

However, to do justice to the parousia in Paul we must turn elsewhere. The prominence of the parousia in 1 Thessalonians can scarcely be exaggerated.

1. In 1 Thess. 1.9-10 Paul describes how the Thessalonians became Christians, and he says that they were converted to serve the living and true God, and to wait for his Son from heaven, whom he raised from the dead, Jesus who delivers us from the wrath to come. This suggests that the essence of conversion, or rather of the converted life, is that the Christian spends his time in serving God and does so in the joyful expectancy of the coming of Jesus from heaven. This is a hope that clearly makes sense only if there is a real possibility that the Lord will come in the lifetime of those who hold it. And to people in whose lifetime Jesus had risen from the dead the hope of his return must have seemed very real and strong. The emphasis at this point is wholly positive, and we may note that active service for God and eager expectation of his Son go together. We should note particularly that the language of early Christian preaching is probably reflected here.

2. In 2.19 it becomes clear that Paul himself shares this hope, and that it is closely related to his service for God. He looks forward to exulting at the parousia in the members of the church at Thessalonica, the fruits of his missionary labours. In language that could be misunderstood he speaks of being able to boast or glory in them; they will be like the crown awarded to a winner in the games, and he will be joyful like a successful athlete. If the members of the church had fallen away from their faith, then Paul would have no grounds of joy at the parousia, and so some of the incentive for his missionary work

came from the desire to have something to show at the parousia. This needs to be balanced by Paul's clear teaching elsewhere that nobody can boast of his achievements in the Lord's presence. But the point that concerns us here is that the return of the Lord is the time of judgment and approbation, and it is he who is the judge.

3. At the end of the next chapter, 3.13, Paul prays for his converts to be blameless at the parousia when Jesus comes with all his holy ones. It is not clear whether 'holy ones' here refers to Christian believers or saints who accompany Jesus into the presence of God or to the heavenly host of angels who attend both the Father and the Son, but the answer is not of great importance. The point is that Paul expects Christians to be free from blemish at the parousia. Again the parousia is the moment of examination and judgment, but Paul expects that his friends will successfully pass the test. Similar thoughts are expressed at the end of the letter in 5.23.

4. The fullest discussion of the parousia comes in 4.13-5.11. The following points emerge:

a. Paul's teaching is based on a word of the Lord, which I take to be a saying by the earthly Jesus.
b. Paul ties the parousia closely to the resurrection of believers, a factor which his readers seem to have forgotten, and insists that all believers will thus share in the great event.
c. The main point is that all believers are caught up to be with the Lord for ever. He comes for them, and future salvation is described simply as being with the Lord.
d. The parousia will come unexpectedly and thus as a surprise to unbelievers, taking them unawares. But not so for Christians. It will not surprise them, like an unexpected burglar who finds the way into the house left open, because they will be ready at any time, being always sober and watchful. Nevertheless, Christians need to be exhorted to be ready, lest they succumb to the temptation to sleep and misuse the present time like unbelievers.

From this survey it is clear that the parousia occupies a very prominent position in 1 Thessalonians, whereas the usual Pauline themes of the cross and resurrection of Jesus are much less prominent. Why is this so? (a) It is partly because of the problems faced by the readers. The lengthy discussion in 4.13-5.11 is clearly due to a problem which loomed large in their minds. (b) But the parousia must have been prominent in Paul's evangelism and teaching in order for it to have become a problem for them. This is clear from Paul's description of the nature of conversion. And the parousia is surely important for Paul himself in the letter. He did not need to introduce the theme in chs. 2, 3 and 5. It must have been an important doctrine for him, even if it was not equally prominent in all his writings.[1]

The Parousia in the New Testament

We can sum up the discussion so far as follows:

1. The hope of the coming of the Son of man is firmly attested in the teaching of Jesus as recorded in the Gospels.[2]

2. The basic character of the parousia as the coming of Jesus to gather together and save his people and to exercise judgment on those who have refused to accept him is taught in the Gospels. The parousia will come unexpectedly, and therefore the disciples are warned to be ready for it. Yet the parousia is not the most important element in the teaching of Jesus; it is part of his message, not the centre of it.

3. The preaching of the early church according to the record in Acts shows that the parousia was not the central element in the preaching and teaching of the early church. Contrary to a widespread impression the centre of the church's teaching was the death and resurrection of Jesus and his exaltation as Messiah and Lord. The parousia is the point of completion of his work, when what is incomplete will be brought to consummation.

4. The picture in Paul is a mixed one, with the parousia almost absent from some letters and rather more prominent in others.

5. However, in one epistle the parousia plays a much more central role, and it is clear that Paul must have laid some considerable emphasis on it. This is in 1 Thessalonians where the context may well

[1]Space forbids a consideration of the other Pauline letters, in which the parousia is much less prominent than in 1 Thessalonians.

[2]In this essay we are concerned simply with the place of the parousia in the NT writings, as we have them. We have, therefore, not tackled the controversial and difficult question of the authenticity of Gospel material as teaching of Jesus. At the very least, however, it could be argued that the hope goes back to the earliest stages of the church's traditions of what Jesus said, and it is to my mind impossible to conceive that this belief could have arisen if Jesus himself had not initiated it.

be that of persecution and the element of hope is the stronger.[1] This shows that the parousia was an important piece of Paul's teaching in relation to future hope and judgment, but it does not contain the centre of his message of grace.

The Parousia Today

In the contemporary world the parousia seems to have suffered one or other of two fates. On the one hand, there are the people who virtually exclude the parousia from their working theology and their preaching. Even though people are still concerned about the future of the planet on an ecological level, the whole concept of an end to human history, a cataclysmic interruption of the process of natural causes and effects, is regarded as absurd in a universe which is understood by means of modern science, and therefore the idea is either abandoned or reinterpreted in some kind of way.

A further reason for excluding the hope lies in the even more pressing urgency of the question already asked in the first century, 'Where is this "coming" he promised? Ever since our fathers died, everything goes on as it has since the beginning of creation' (2 Pet. 3.4). If we reply in terms of an apparent 'delay', the response is that there comes a point when the theory of delay must surely give place to the theory of cancellation or rather to the theory of the completely misunderstood promise. Upholders of the parousia are entertaining a false hope.

On the other hand, there are Christians who pin their hopes on the fulfilment of biblical prophecy and in particular on the literal return of Jesus to wind up history and bring salvation for his people. Sometimes, as we noted initially, this theme is used as a major one in evangelism, and people are encouraged to become Christians by appeal to the swiftness and suddenness of the Lord's appearing and the need to be ready lest it strike them like a thief in the night. Often an elaborate program is also drawn up on the basis of prophecy; it is very pessimistic about the dreadful times ahead which will be brought to an end by the parousia, and it is extremely detailed in its precise

[1] The same may be true of Philippians, where the parousia is also important; the centrality of the motif in 2 Thessalonians obviously arises from the need to take further the teaching of 1 Thessalonians and to clear up misunderstandings.

concern with the signs of the times and the actual course of events leading up to and continuing on from the parousia.

Where is the truth to be found? In what follows we shall explore the relevance of what we have seen about the place of the parousia in the NT for the church today. In so doing we must bear in mind that the NT teaching falls within the category of apocalyptic, and that therefore the language is to be interpreted in a poetic and symbolic manner and not literalistically.

Christ as the Centre of Christian Hope

There is a tendency in some Christian thinking today to assert the reality of resurrection from the dead and to deny or play down the parousia. It is the hope of continuing existence which seems most important to some people, and they think that they can hold on to the hope of eternal life without also believing in the parousia. This is the opposite mistake from that which seems to have been made in Thessalonica. There the Christians seem to have had a lively hope in the coming of Jesus for living Christians, but they were quite at a loss to know what would happen to those who had died, and Paul had to show them afresh that the parousia must be closely linked with the resurrection of the dead, so that the dead would not be at a disadvantage compared with the living. Furthermore, Paul had to cope with a similar problem at Corinth, where it seems that again some Christians did not believe in the resurrection but perhaps only in some kind of immortality of the soul or possibly in no sort of future at all for those who had died. In this situation Paul had to stress the fact of resurrection.

The mistake which people make nowadays is to think that they can have resurrection apart from the parousia. But a resurrection to a new life is pointless and empty if it is not a resurrection to new life with Jesus. In 1 Corinthians Paul emphasises that the resurrection hope stems from the fact of the resurrection of Jesus, and he explains that the resurrection is bound up with the parousia of Jesus (1 Cor. 15.23). It is when the second man comes from heaven that the resurrection takes place, and it is accompanied by the same imagery of the last trumpet as in 1 Thessalonians 4. Similarly, in 1 Thessalonians the resurrection is tied to the parousia; and it is this which makes it a resurrection worth experiencing. When the resurrection takes place, the factor that makes it Christian is the presence or coming of Jesus. The coming of Jesus also serves as the link between the living and the dead; he comes with the resurrected dead for the living believers. Thus Jesus is the centre of the Christian expectation.

This may be seen in another way. When Paul comforted the Thessalonians who were grieving over their dead like the others who had no hope, he did not console them by saying simply that the dead would be resurrected to be with them, but rather his point is that we shall be for ever with the Lord; it is the reuniting of God's people to be with the Lord which is what matters. So much is this the case that the New Testament scarcely says whether we shall even know our deceased relatives and friends at the parousia/resurrection, and all the emphasis is that we shall know and be with the Lord. One might be tempted to say that the Lord will so fill our attention that we shall not know or be bothered about other people, but that would be an ungrounded conclusion.

So the point is that the resurrection must be a uniting with Christ; it is he who is the centre and substance of the Christian hope. But is the concept of the parousia necessary to establish this? Is it not sufficient that the dead be raised with Christ to be with Christ for ever? This, however, would go against the biblical picture. The biblical picture is often assumed to be that resurrected believers go to heaven to be with the Lord. But this is not biblical teaching. In Revelation the future abode of believers is the new earth, which is a transformed earth, and therefore it is necessary that Christ comes from heaven to be with his people on earth. Moreover, when the New Testament speaks of a bodily resurrection, this implies that Christ too must appear in bodily form, and again this fits in with the picture of Christ coming rather than of a passive Christ who sits at the right hand of God and does nothing. The resurrection is an action of Christ, just as the incarnation was an action of Christ. People may say, if they will, that all this is symbolical language, but the point is that within the symbolical frame of reference it is an essential part of the symbolism. The picture presented is one of a Christ who is active and who is present with his people in a form that goes beyond the spiritual presence which we now experience.

The Cross and the Parousia

The most significant fact which has emerged from our survey is that the parousia is not mentioned anything like so often in the NT as the death and resurrection of Jesus. The implications of this point now need to be examined.

First of all, this suggests that we should preserve the same proportion in our preaching and teaching. The centre of gravity of the NT lies in the incarnation of Jesus, in his life, cross and resurrection. This complex event is the focus of our message. For we are saved not by the parousia of Jesus but by his cross. The grace of God has already appeared for the salvation of all mankind. That it was Christ crucified who was the centre of the apostolic message should scarcely need proof. To put it in extreme form: a Christian message which included only the death and resurrection of Jesus but excluded his parousia would still be recognisably and authentically Christian, even if it is incomplete, but a Christian message which included the parousia but excluded the death and resurrection of Jesus would have no possibility of being recognised as genuinely Christian. It is not the parousia which gives its authentic character to Christianity but the cross. This is of fundamental importance. The New Testament focuses on a kerygma which is concerned with what has already happened in the arena of historical fact.

Second, it follows that, if the parousia is, as we have seen, the event which puts Christ at the centre of our expectation, we must define it more precisely as the return of the One who was incarnate, crucified and resurrected. It is 'this same Jesus' (Acts 1.11; cf. Heb. 13.8) who will return. To put it otherwise, the parousia is the return of the One whom we know already, the One who is defined by the gospel story, and if the parousia is the coming of an unknown or fresh figure, then it is not the NT parousia. The Lamb in the Book of Revelation bears the marks of sacrifice; the risen Christ shows the wounds in his hands and his side. And it is the Jesus who was raised from the dead who returns. What the parousia affirms, then, is that the future is filled with the hope of the return of the One who died for our sins and was raised for our justification. That is the most important thing that can be said about the parousia. It is the triumph of the crucified and nothing else. We can never separate the parousia from the passion, the return from the resurrection, the second coming from the first. They are two parts of one great act

It certainly follows from this that the centre of evangelistic preaching must be the cross and resurrection. There is no other way to be faithful to the biblical emphasis than by doing this. We saw that this was the case in the Gospel of Mark, in Acts and in the summaries of the gospel in Paul. It is so self-evident that it should scarcely need to be said, and yet from time to time preachers may fail to give it is proper place.

The Relevance of the Parousia

What, then, is the significance and relevance of the parousia? What would be missing from the Christian message if the parousia is not placed alongside the death and resurrection of Jesus? In 1 Thessalonians Paul defined the Christian life in terms of waiting for the Lord and being ready for his coming. Even if the parousia was not the centre of Paul's message, it was nevertheless an essential part of his teaching for believers. It was a source of encouragement to them.

First, it meant the fulness of salvation. If salvation here and now meant fellowship with Jesus, then obviously it was incomplete and needed to be brought to perfection. This was the promise of the parousia: it would bring them to be with Jesus in the fullest sense.

Second, it meant the completion of God's purpose for the lives of his people. At the parousia they would be brought blameless and pure into the presence of Christ. Paul does not explain how this happens, but he appears to think of it as a work of God which would be effected by his Spirit and which would reach its conclusion when Jesus appeared. Consequently, the hope of the parousia was an incentive to believers to live lives of devoted service to God. There is a paradox here in that the same process can be regarded as one effected by the Spirit or by the grace of God and also as one in which believers cooperate with God. Thus Paul could look forward to having his crown at the parousia for faithful missionary service, and yet he could insist that it was not he who worked but the grace of God in him. Either way, the parousia becomes an encouragement to Christian sanctification and service.

Third, the parousia meant the end of opposition and tribulation. When we turn over into 2 Thessalonians we find that the believers were being persecuted, but Paul prophesied that their persecutors would suffer for their deeds at the revelation of Jesus as judge. He expands on this in ch. 2, speaking about the revelation of evil in the world which will be brought to an end by the appearing of Jesus. The point of this is not that Christians should gloat over their persecutors, an element which is absent from Paul's teaching. It is rather that believers can be assured that their cause will in the end be upheld by God and demonstrated to be right. It is the thought of vindication rather than of vengeance which is present. We can easily confuse the two, but we must avoid doing so, or else we fall into sub-Christian attitudes.

And, fourth, the parousia is an incentive to be continually on the alert, ready for the coming of Jesus and not growing weary in well-doing or falling asleep on the task. This should not happen to believers, Paul's teaching being that the day should not take the sons of light unawares.

These seem to me to be the four main points that Paul makes in this letter; a wider survey would not seriously affect the picture gained from this one letter. One or two further comments are needed.

First, there is the question whether the hope of the parousia affects the nature of our conduct. Here we need to distinguish between the nature of Christian behaviour and the motives for Christian behaviour. The nature of Christian behaviour comes from the revelation of God's requirements, his pattern of life for his people, and this is expressed for us in the teaching of Christ and the apostles that is preserved in Scripture. Ultimately it depends on the will and character of God himself who purposes that we should be like our heavenly Father and conformed to the image of his Son. The parousia does not add anything to this revelation, but it does supply a motive or incentive, for it expresses the fact of a future meeting with Jesus and raises the question whether we will be ready and fit to meet him. So the parousia becomes an incentive to holy living.

To talk like this of being ready to meet the Lord implies that the Lord is like an absent householder who may come back at any time and want to know how his servants have been behaving in his absence. But of course this is only part of the truth. The rest of the truth is that the Lord is with us here and now even though we cannot see him.

Paul spoke of having communion with him, and we believe in his presence with us by the Spirit. He is the person to whom we can pray. Therefore he is not completely absent, but he is in us and we in him. We are not hidden from him even now. The trouble is that we can sin and put up a barrier between ourselves and him, and then his coming may surprise us. Even though we know his spiritual presence, there is the added joy of his manifestation so that we see him and know that he is with us in a way which is not true at the moment. Thus the picture of Christ's coming in the future has to be balanced by the fact of his presence now, and we should not understand the parousia in such a way that we imply that Christ is not with us at present; note how the coming and the presence of Jesus are balanced in 1 Corinthians 1.7-9.

Second, there is the question of how far the parousia should be put before unbelievers as an incentive to conversion or as a warning against judgment. This is an aspect of the biblical message which is passed over by some and unduly emphasised by others. The New Testament certainly presents the reality of judgment and the wrath of God which will be revealed on the day of Christ, and this motif is found in association with the preaching of the gospel. I therefore believe that it is proper and necessary that unbelievers should be warned of the realities of the situation, and that the fact of the wrath of God revealed against sin should be clearly made known. But it must be put into perspective and related to the offer of the gospel. I believe that it must be related clearly to righteousness and to the victory of righteousness. It is evildoers who will be punished. And it must be clearly related to the gospel that God gave his Son to save us from wrath and judgment.

Conclusion

From all this I draw the conclusion that the parousia has an important place in our proclamation of the Christian message, but that it is not as central as the death and resurrection of Jesus. Its significance is that it puts Jesus at the centre of our Christian hope and that it affirms that the ultimate destiny of this world lies in the hands of the crucified and risen Christ who comes to reign. It is not a matter for speculation, but rather its imminence urges us to Christian action here and now and warns us to be ready at any time for the judgment of the world. Thus, in short, the parousia is an essential expression of Christian belief; it is what makes Christian hope truly Christian. Our hope is that the Christ who came and is with us will return so that we shall be with him for evermore.

PSEUDONYMITY AND CANONICITY OF NEW TESTAMENT DOCUMENTS*

E. Earle Ellis

Ancient pseudepigrapha, that is, documents written under a name other than the true author, are to be distinguished from writings later misattributed to a wrong name, such as the book of Hebrews in the New Testament, Ecclesiastes in the Old and probably the Wisdom of Solomon in the Apocrypha.[1] They should also be classified to distinguish fictional romances and student exercises written in the name of a famous man, which did not and did not intend to deceive, from pseudepigrapha that were fraudulent and deceptive, whether for religious,[2] financial,[3] political, personal[4] or other motives. Only the latter may rightly be termed forgeries for, in the words of J.D.

---

*For Professor R.P. Martin on the occasion of his retirement.

[1]M. Smith ('Pseudepigraphy in the Israelite Literary Tradition', *Pseudepigrapha I* [ed. K. von Fritz; Genève: O. Revedin, 1972], pp. 191-215) argues that Israelite literature, including Ecclesiastes and the Wisdom of Solomon (p. 210), was customarily anonymous and then misattributed. Only under Greek influence did Jewish pseudepigrapha appear, apparently as the product of related sectarian groups (p. 215). But see D.G. Meade, *Pseudonymity and Canon* (WUNT^2 39; Tübingen: Mohr, 1986), pp. 55-66.

[2]According to R.H. Charles (*Eschatology* [New York: Schocken, 1963; ^{2}1913], p. 204f.) the general view that inspiration had ceased (cf. BT *Sanhedrin* 11a; Josephus, *Against Apion* 2.38-42) required apocalyptic writers after 200 BC to write under the name of an ancient prophet or patriarch in order to get a hearing.

[3]The physician, Galen (+ c. AD 200), wrote the tract *On His Own Books* to counter the sale of forgeries of his writings (*Galeni scripta minora* 2 [Leipzig, 1891], pp. 91-124; cited in B.M. Metzger, 'Literary Forgeries and Canonical Psuedepigrapha', *JBL* 91 [1972], p. 6). The libraries at Alexandria and Pergamum paid well for famous authors, and forgery flourished. Cf. J.S. Candlish, 'On the Moral Character of Pseudonymous Books', *The Expositor: Fourth Series*, vol. IV (ed. W.R. Nicoll; 10 vols.; London: Hodder, 1890-94), p. 95 = GT: in N. Brox, ed., *Pseudepigraphie in der heidnischen und judisch-christlichen Antike* (Darmstadt: WBG, 1977), p. 11; J.A. Sint, *Pseudonymität im Altertum* (Innsbruck: Wagner, 1960), p. 116f.

[4]E.g. Pausanius, *Description of Greece*, 6, 18, 4f.: To foster hatred against his enemy, Theopompus, Anaximenes forged a treatise in his name.

Denniston, 'with a true forgery, the attribution must be made by the real author himself, and there must be intention to deceive'.[1] Such forgeries were produced in abundance by both pagan and Christian writers.[2] But are they to be found in our canonical New Testament?

I

The claim that pseudepigrapha are present in the New Testament began with the 'tendency' criticism of Edward Evanson two hundred years ago.[3] Forty years later, with a Hegelian twist, it was more successfully advocated by F.C. Baur, who considered the General Epistles and all but four of Paul's letter's to be pseudepigrapha.[4] With Adolf Hilgenfeld's increase of the genuine Pauline Epistles to seven,[5] the Baur School and its followers maintained a fairly fixed identification of New Testament pseudepigrapha. With few exceptions,[6] they are the root of all subsequent scholarship that assigned pseudepigraphal authorship to New Testament documents.

Although his chronology was telescoped, and his Hegelian dialectic sometimes dropped, by the turn of the twentieth century Baur's 'tendency' criticism and diachronic reconstruction achieved a broader acceptance and in the work, say, of Adolf Jülicher was the assumed

---

[1] J.D. Denniston, 'Forgeries, Literary I. Greek', *Oxford Classical Dictionary* (ed. N.G.L. Hammond; Oxford: Clarendon, [2]1970), p. 444.

[2] Cf. W. Speyer, *Die literarische Fälschung im heidnischen und christlichen Altertum* (München: Beck, 1971).

[3] E. Evanson, *The Dissonance of the Four Generally Received Evangelists* (Ipswich: G. Jermyn, 1792), pp. 255-89.

[4] Cf. F.C. Baur, 'Die Christuspartei . . .' (1831), 136-205f., reprinted in *Ausgewählte Werke*, vol. I (5 vols.; Stuttgart: F. Frommann, 1963-75), pp. 1-146; idem, *Paul*, vol. I (2 vols.; London: Williams, 1876 [1845]), pp. 248f. = GT: pp. 278f.: vol. II, pp. 106-111 = GT: pp. 116-122; idem, *The Church History of the First Three Centuries*, vol. I (2 vols.; London: Williams, 1878-79), pp. 122-131, 149f. = GT: pp. 116-24, 143. Cf. E.E. Ellis, 'Foreword' in H. Harris, *The Tübingen School* (Grand Rapids: Baker and Leicester: Apollos, [2]1990), xi-xv.

[5] A member of the Baur School, A. Hilgenfeld, *Historisch-kritische Einleitung in das Neue Testament* (Leipzig: Fues, 1875), pp. 246f., 330-334, added Philippians, 1 Thessalonians and Philemon to the 'genuine' Pauline corpus.

[6] Bruno Bauer and the Dutch School (e.g. A.D. Loman, W.C. van Manen), those A. Schweitzer calls the 'Ultra-Tübingen' critics, were apparently influenced (also) by Evanson, *The Dissonance of the Four Generally Received Evangelists*. Cf. A. Schweitzer, *Paul and his Interpreters* (London: Black, 1948 [1912]), pp. 117-150. Baur was the decisive figure although a few before him had rejected the genuineness of the Petrine and certain Pauline letters. Cf. W.G. Kümmel, *The New Testament: History of . . . its Problems* (Nashville: Abingdon, 1972), pp. 84ff. = GT: pp. 100-102; E.E. Ellis, 'Dating the New Testament', *NTS* 26 (1980), pp. 494f. = GT: *TZ* 42 (1986), pp. 419f.

starting point. That is, the Baur hypothesis became the Baur tradition.[1] This tradition has been predominant in German New Testament studies throughout much of the century[2] and has had a strong influence in America[3] and, after mid-century, in England.[4] Appropriately enough, it has received its most notable converts in recent decades from those who honor tradition, Conservative Evangelicals[5] and Roman Catholics,[6] perhaps with the thought that any wine of a 150-year vintage can't be all bad.

---

[1] A. Jülicher, *An Introduction to the New Testament* (London: Smith, [4]1904), pp. 16-30 = GT: pp. 12-20, who is congenial with Baur's approach, regards the Pastorals and most of the General Epistles as pseudepigraphic (pp. 174-255) but ascribes the rest of the Pauline corpus to the Apostle with the possible exception of Ephesians (pp. 142-47). W.G. Kümmel's (*Introduction to the New Testament*, [Nashville [17]1975]) revision of P. Feine-J. Behm's *Einleitung in das Neue Testament* (Leipzig 1965 [[9]1951]) reflects a similar shift and accommodation to the Baur tradition, as does J. Weiss' *The History of Primitive Christianity* (2 vols.; New York: Wilson-Erickson, 1937 [1917]) vis-à-vis his father, B. Weiss (*A Manual of Introduction to the New Testament* [2 vols.; London: Hodder, 1887]), who found no pseudepigrapha in the New Testament.

[2] Recently defended by G. Lüdemann, *Opposition to Paul in Jewish Christianity* (Philadelphia: Fortress, 1989).

[3] With reference to Ephesians, the Pastorals and the General Epistles, J. Moffatt, *An Introduction to the Literature of the New Testament* (Edinburgh: Clark, [3]1918), pp. 315-428; E.J. Goodspeed, *Introduction to the New Testament* (Chicago: University, 1937), pp. 222-39, 265-95, 327-55; with reference to Ephesians and the Pastorals, J. Knox, *Chapters in the Life of Paul* (Macon, GA: Mercer, [2]1987 [1950]), pp. 8f., 54; idem, *Marcion and the New Testament* (Chicago: University, 1942), pp. 58ff., 73-76.

[4] With the waning of the influence of 'the Cambridge Three': J.B. Lightfoot, B.F. Westcott, F.J.A. Hort. For a survey of recent studies, cf. T.D. Lea, 'Pseudonymity and the New Testament', *New Testament Criticism and Interpretation* (edd. D.A. Black and D.S. Dockery; Grand Rapids: Zondervan, 1991), pp. 549-53; Meade, *Pseudonymity and Canon*, pp. 1-16. See also D. Guthrie, 'Epistolary Pseudepigrapha', *New Testament Introduction* (Leicester: Apollos,[4]1990), pp. 1011-1028; Metzger, 'Literary Forgeries and Canonical Psuedepigrapha', pp. 3-24.

[5] I.e. who identify as pseudepigrapha a number of Pauline and/or Petrine letters. Cf. R.J. Bauckham, *Jude, 2 Peter* (Waco: Word, 1983), p. 148, passim; J.D.G. Dunn, *Unity and Diversity in the New Testament* (London: SCM, 1977), pp. 147, 346, passim; R.P. Martin, *New Testament Foundations* II (Grand Rapids: Eerdmans, [2]1983), pp. 232f., 305, passim; Meade, *Pseudonymity and Canon*, pp. 118, 186, 190, passim; Metzger, 'Literary Forgeries and Canonical Psuedepigraphy', p. 22; idem, *The New Testament* (Nashville: Abingdon, [14]1978), pp. 214, 258f.

[6] The Roman Catholic work, *The Jerome Biblical Commentary* (edd. R.E. Brown et al.; London: Chapman, 1970, [2]1990), identified only 2 Peter as a pseudepigraphon in the first edition. The revision (1990) followed Hilgenfeld's (*Historisch-kritische Einleitung in das Neue Testament*) list of Pauline/Petrine pseudepigrapha to the letter except for 1 Peter, where the patristic witnesses and Catholic tradition prevailed. A. Wikenhauser's *Introduction to the New Testament* (London, 1958) identified only 2 Peter as ungenuine (p. 515). Its revision by J. Schmid (1973) agreed with Hilgenfeld completely, with the possible exception of Colossians.

Critics of Baur's views, in earlier[1] and recent times,[2] raised two important queries: (1) Was his reconstruction historically based? (2) If it was, should the pseudepigraphal documents be retained within the New Testament canon? The present paper addresses the latter question.

Baur thought that for the 'pseudo-Pauline' letters one should not think of 'deception and intentional forgery' (*Fälschung*). However, he continued, 'if it be asserted that the matter is not intelligible except on this hypothesis [of forgery], that cannot be maintained as an argument (*wäre diess keine Einwendung*) against its possibility and likelihood'.[3] Elsewhere, he states that one could, if one must, give up the canonicity of 2 Peter, the Pastorals and 'other smaller letters of our canon', without giving rise to any danger for the historical foundation of Christianity.[4]

Most of Baur's adherents were not so easygoing on this matter. His colleague, F.H. Kern, took the Epistle of James to be forged in order to refute Pauline views but asserted that such an imposture would have been an acceptable and irreproachable practice of the time.[5] A. Jülicher contended that 'the ethical notion of literary property' is a modern conception and that for the early church forgery applied only to the heretical distortion of *religious* truth and not to false authorship as such.[6] Others echoed the same opinion[7] and/or

---

[1]E.g. J.B. Lightfoot, 'St. Paul and the Three', *Galatians* (London: Macmillan, [10]1892), pp. 292-374; idem, *Essays on . . . Supernatural Religion* (London: Macmillan, 1893), passim; (implicitly) T. Zahn, *Introduction to the New Testament* (3 vols.; Grand Rapids: Kregel, 1953 [1909]); A. Harnack, *Geschichte der altchristlichen Literatur* II. *Chronologie*, vol. I (2 vols.; Leipzig: Hinrichs, 1958 [1896]), viii: 'In the whole New Testament there is, strictly speaking, only one single writing that can be called pseudonymous: the Second Letter of Peter'. However, he thought that other writings, e.g. the Pastorals suffered later interpolations, a hypothesis that in the light of current textual and historical criticism is very improbable. Cf. E.E. Ellis, *The Making of the New Testament Documents* (forthcoming); K. Aland, 'Neutestamentliche Textkritik und Exegese', *Wissenchaft und Kirche* (ed. K. Aland; Bielefeld: Luther, 1989), p. 142.

[2]E.g. H. Harris, *Tübingen School;* E. Barnikol, *Ferdinand Christian Baur als rationalistisch-kirchlicher Theologe* (Berlin: Evangelische, 1970); W. Geiger, *Spekulation und Kritik: Die Geschichtstheologie Ferdinand Christian Baurs* (München: Kaiser, 1964).

[3]Baur, *Paul*, vol. II, p. 110f. = GT: p. 121.

[4]F.C. Baur, 'Abgenöthigte Erklärung', *TZT* 3 (1836), p. 208 = *Werke*, vol. III, p. 296.

[5]F.H. Kern, 'Der Charakter und Ursprung des Briefs Jakobi', *TZT* 2 (1835), p. 72, cited in A. Neander, *History of the Planting and Training of the Christian Church* (London, [3]1851), p. 360. He later affirmed that the author was James, the brother of Jesus: F.H. Kern, *Der Brief Jakobi* (Tübingen: Fues, 1838), pp. 70-73.

[6]Jülicher, *Introduction to the New Testament*, p. 52 = GT: pp. 38f. Cf. A.T. Lincoln, *Ephesians* (Dallas: Word, 1990), lxxi: 'The idea of "intellectual property" basic to . . . authorship . . . played little or no role in [antiquity]'. More accurately, 'in the Jewish-Hellenistic sphere as contrasted with

hypothesized Pauline[1] and Petrine[2] disciples who up-dated and published the apostles' teachings after their deaths. Kurt Aland argued that, since the authors were only instruments of the Holy Spirit, a particular pseudo-authorship was not all that significant.[3] Klaus Koch suggested that the heavenly Paul may have been viewed as speaking after his death through his disciple somewhat like God or the heavenly Jesus spoke through his prophets![4] On this approach, of course, one might justify the canonization of all 'orthodox' New Testament apocrypha. To counter this, James Dunn conjectured that there was a radical shift from first-century Jewish Christianity, which accepted pseudepigrapha as an innocent device like the Jews accepted, for example *1 Enoch* and *4 Ezra*, and second-century Gentile Christianity, which excluded such writings from the canon. Unfortunately, since the Jews also excluded *1 Enoch* and *4 Ezra* from their canon, it is difficult to see how Dunn's examples support his hypothesis.[5] In conclu-

---

the Greco-Roman world the consciousness of intellectual property and individual authorship was underdeveloped' (M. Hengel, 'Anonymitat, Pseudepigraphie und "literarische Falschung" in der judisch-hellenistischen Literatur', in von Fritz, *Pseudepigrapha* I, p. 283).

[7]E.g. W.H. Simcox, *The Writers of the New Testament* (London, [2]1902), p. 38: At that time it was 'as legitimate to compose a letter as to compose a speech in the name of a great man . . .'; F.W. Beare, *The First Epistle of Peter* (Oxford: Blackwell, [3]1970 (1947): To suggest that pseudepigrapha are fraudulent 'is a purely modern prejudice' (p. 48); C.L. Mitton, *The Epistle to the Ephesians* (Oxford 1951), p. 222: '[P]seudonymity is "the manner approved by ancient literature" [E.F. Scott] . . ., a judgement in which Moffatt entirely concurs . . .'. Cf. Moffatt, *Introduction*, pp. 40-44; E.F. Scott, *The Literature of the New Testament* (New York: Columbia, 1949 [1932]), pp. 179f.

[1]E.g. Lincoln, *Ephesians*, lxxii, who followed Meade, *Pseudonymity and Canon*, pp. 153-57, and Meade's teacher, Dunn, *Unity and Diversity*, pp. 344-59, who in turn followed German adherents of the Baur tradition. On the Catholic side cf. P. Trummer, *Die Paulustradition der Pastoralbriefe* (Frankfurt: Lang, 1978), p. 241: The [post-Pauline] Pastorals have been consciously constructed on the model of passages in the Pauline letters even though a literary dependence can be shown only in a few places.

[2]Cf. L. Goppelt, *Der erste Petrusbrief* (Göttingen: Vandenhoek, 1978), pp. 69f.

[3]K. Aland, 'The Problem of Anonymity and Pseudonymity in Christian Literature of the First Two Centuries', *The Authorship and Integrity of the New Testament* (edd. K. Aland et al.; London: SPCK, 1965), pp. 1-13, 7f.; critiqued by H.R. Balz, 'Anonymität und Pseudepigraphie im Urchristentum', *ZTK* 66 (1969), pp. 403-36, 419ff. Cf. A. Meyer, 'Religiöse Pseudepigraphie als ethisch-psychologisches Problem', *ZNW* 35 (1936), pp. 262-79 = Brox, ed., *Pseudepigraphie in der heidnischen und judisch-christlichen*, pp. 90-110: If a prophet can speak in the name of God, it is no great step further if one should feel justified to write in the name of a patriarch or of an apostle (p. 107).

[4]K. Koch, 'Pseudonymous Writing', *The Interpreter's Dictionary of the Bible: Supplementary Volume* (ed. K. Crim; Nashville: Abingdon, 1976), p. 713.

[5]J.D.G. Dunn, *The Living Word* (London: SCM, 1987), pp. 68, 83ff.: 'There was no intention to deceive [by the pseudepigrapher of the Pastorals and of 2 Peter] and almost certainly the final [*sic*] readers were not in fact deceived' (p. 84). Cf. B.S. Easton, *The Pastoral Epistles* (New York:

sion these writers, who are representative of a much larger group, offered no historical evidence for their assertions that New Testament pseudepigrapha were recognized as such and were regarded as innocent compositions, and it seems that most of them were chiefly concerned to defend, on Baurian assumptions, the traditional New Testament canon.

II

In pagan, Jewish and Christian circles of the Greco-Roman world the use of a false authorship for purposes of fraud and deception was widespread, as Wolfgang Speyer has demonstrated.[1] This fact presupposes a conception of intellectual property that could be violated. Already in 1891 James Candlish concluded that

> in the early Christian centuries, when any work was given out as of ancient or venerable authorship, it was either received as genuine . . . or rejected as an imposture . . . .
>
> There would seem to be no external evidence that pseudonymous works were in ancient times composed in perfect good faith . . . not intended to deceive anyone.[2]

Frederik Torm expressed himself similarly: 'The view that religious circles of Greco-Roman antiquity "understood pseudonymity as a literary form and straightaway recognized its rightness is a modern invention"'.[3]

The attitude of early Christian leaders toward pseudepigrapha, especially those in the name of an apostle, supports this view of the matter. It is illustrated by the responses of the Asian elders to the

---

Scribner, 1947), p. 19: '[The author] was in no sense a "forger" . . . . The first recipents knew perfectly well who wrote them . . .'. On the Jewish canon see E.E. Ellis, *The Old Testament in Early Christianity* (Tübingen: Mohr, 1991 = Grand Rapids: Baker, 1992), pp. 9, 17, 35, 38, passim.

1 Speyer, *Die literarische Fälschung im heidnischen und christlichen Altertum*, pp. 5-10, passim. Cf. also Metzger, 'Literary Forgeries and Canonical Psuedepigrapha', pp. 5-11.

2 Candlish, 'On the Moral Character of Pseudonymous Books', pp. 103, 262 = GT: pp. 20, 24. Jerome (*Letters* 120, 11) doubted on internal evidence that the same man could have written 1 and 2 Peter and decided that in 2 Peter the Apostle employed a disciple as secretary. So also, J. Calvin, *Hebrews, St. Peter* (Grand Rapids: Eerdmans, 1963 [1551]), p. 325 (Preface).

3 F. Torm, *Die Psychologie der Pseudonymität im Hinblick auf die Literatur des Urchristentums* (Gütersloh: Bertelsmann, 1932), p. 19 = Brox, ed., *Pseudepigraphie in der heidnischen und judisch-christlichen Antike*, p. 119.

Acts of Paul and of Serapion (+AD 211), bishop of Antioch, to the Gospel of Peter. Presumably, Serapion at first thought that the Gospel of Peter could be genuine but, noting heretical opinions in it, investigated further and concluded that it was not. In his counsel to the church of Rhossus in Cilicia he states the operative principle:

> For we, brothers, receive both Peter and the other apostles as Christ. But pseudepigrapha in their name we reject, as men of experience, knowing that we did not receive such [from the tradition].[1]

That is, the test for reading in church was apostolicity determined by received tradition. On examination the bishop discovered apparently that the Gospel of Peter was not a Petrine document heretically doctored, say, like Marcion's Romans, but a pseudepigraphon. As such he excluded it.

Asian elders deposed a colleague from office for authoring, out of 'love for Paul', an Acts of Paul that included an apostolic pseudepigraphon, *3 Corinthians*. They condemned the man for presuming to write in the name of an apostle and apparently not because, in his story, he allowed a woman to baptize converts. That was Tertullian's later complaint.[2]

Other apostolic pseudepigrapha that raised no doctrinal objections—for example the *Preaching of Peter* (c. AD 100-150), *Apocalypse of Peter*, *Epistle of the Apostles*, the *Correspondence of Paul and Seneca*[3] and probably the *Epistle to the Laodiceans*[4]—were nevertheless excluded from the church's canon. The exclusion of such

---

[1]*Apud* Eusebius, *Ecclesiastical History* 6, 12, 3; cf. 3, 25, 4-7. On doctored apostolic letters cf. E.F. Evans, *Tertullian Adversus Marcionem*, vol. II (2 vols.; Oxford: Clarendon, 1972), pp. 644ff. On the uncertainty about the Petrine writings in the late second century cf. The Muratorian Canon, which lacks 1 Peter and mentions the doubts of some either about 2 Peter or about another 'Apocalypse of Peter' (cf. D. Theron, *Evidence of Tradition* [Grand Rapids, 1958], p. 112).

[2]Tertullian, *On Baptism* 17.

[3]Cf. 'Kerygma Petrou', 'Paul and Seneca', 'Apocalypse of Peter', *New Testament Apocrypha*, vol. II (2 vols.; ed. W. Schneemelcher; London 1965), pp. 94-102, 133-41, 663-83. On the *Epistle of the Apostles* cf. B.M. Metzger, *The Canon of the New Testament* (New York: OUP, 1987), pp. 180ff.

[4]So, J.B. Lightfoot, *Colossians* (London, 1875), pp. 347f.; Schneemelcher, *New Testament Apocrypha*, vol. II, pp. 130f. Otherwise: A. Harnack, *Opuscula*, vol. II (2 vols.; Leipzig: Antiquariat DDR, 1980), pp. 644-54, who argues that the letter had Marcionite tendencies. Cf. *Muratorian Canon* in Theron, *Evidence of Tradition*, p. 112: 'forged according to the heresy of Marcion' (*fictae ad haeresem Marcionis*). But see B.F. Westcott, *The History of the Canon of the New Testament* (London, [5]1881), p. 218: 'bearing on the heresy of Marcion'.

documents presupposes, as H.R. Balz has argued,[1] that the 'apostles of Jesus Christ'[2] had a normative authority and that writings in their names were regarded as deceptive and fraudulent.

III

The unique authority of the apostles, however, was already present in the first-century church, and it underlies Paul's insistence on his own apostolic status. In 1 Cor. 9.1-3 he writes:

> Am I not free? Am I not an apostle?
> Have I not seen Jesus our Lord...
> If to others I am not an apostle, I am to you
> For in the Lord you are the seal of my apostleship
> This[3] is my answer (ἀπολογία)
> To those who are discerning (ἀνακρίνουσιν) me.

Paul here alludes to the task of the pneumatics to discern, i.e. to examine and give judgement on one another's revelations.[4] In effect he excludes the apostles from such judgements and thus places their gift above that of prophets, i.e. pneumatics.[5] In 2 Corinthians he contests the questioning of his apostleship and brands his opponents 'pseudo-apostles'.[6] Apparently for similar reasons, in Galatians he underscores his status as 'apostle through Jesus Christ' and his parity with the apostleship of Peter.[7] Such passages reveal the unique significance of apostolic status for the church of the fifties. 2 Thess. 2.2 also may refer to pseudo-writings in Paul's name that are to be rejected.[8] If so, it shows the authority that an apostle's name carried and the negative

---

[1]H.R. Balz, 'Anonymität und Pseudepigraphie im Urchristentum', *ZTK* 66 (1969), pp. 403-36, 420.

[2]On the distinction between 'apostles of Jesus Christ' and 'apostles of the churches' = missionaries cf. E.E. Ellis, *Pauline Theology: Ministry and Society* (Grand Rapids 1989), pp. 66, 89ff.

[3]Taking the αὕτη to refer, as always in classical Greek, to the preceding matter. Cf. Mt. 3.3; 27.58; Acts 8.26; 1 Cor. 6.4; Gal. 5.17; Phil. 1.22; M. Zerwick, *Biblical Greek* (Rome: Pontifical Institute, [5]1979), pp. 67f. (Section 213); A.T. Robertson, *A Grammar of the Greek New Testament* (London, 1914), pp. 697f.

[4]1 Cor. 2.14f.; cf. 6.5; 14.29 (διακρίνειν).

[5]1 Cor 4.3f., 9; 14.37f.: 'If anyone thinks that he is a prophet or a pneumatic let him acknowledge that what things I am writing to you are a command of the Lord'.

[6]2 Cor. 11.13; 12.11f.

[7]Gal. 1.1; cf. 1.12, 17; 2.8f.

[8]Cf. 2 Thess. 3.17; F.F. Bruce, *1 & 2 Thessalonians* (Waco: Word, 1982), p. 164.

judgement of apostolic pseudepigrapha at an early time, whether this is Paul's admonition or a pseudo-Paul's contrivance.

IV

Strictly speaking, the only New Testament writings that can be classified pseudepigrapha are Pauline and Petrine epistles.[1] Assuming such an origin, do certain of these documents, say, Ephesians, the Pastorals and 1-2 Peter, also fall under the verdict of fraud and imposture placed against (other) second-century apostolic pseudepigrapha?

To begin with, it should be noted that the early Christians knew how to transmit the teachings of an authority figure without engaging in pseudepigrapha. For example, Mark introduces his work as 'the beginning of the Gospel of Jesus Christ',[2] and an anonymous author begins his as 'The Teaching of the Twelve Apostles'.[3] Luke's Acts gives a third-person narration of apostolic teaching. They deceived no one. Also, unlike these writers, the pseudo-Pauline and pseudo-Petrine authors did not merely create a title but engaged in an elaborate and complex deception to transmit their own ideas under apostolic color.

In 2 Thessalonians (2.2f.) pseudo-Paul, like the author of the *Preaching of Peter* (*Epistula* 2.4; *Contestatio* 5.2), condemns other forgeries as he creates his own. In Ephesians he not only carefully imitates the introductions[4] and to some degree the conclusions[5] to the Apostle's letters but also fabricates situations in Paul's lifetime and possibly sets up the readers to anticipate another pseudo-Pauline letter:

> I, Paul, prisoner of Christ Jesus . . . (3.1).

---

[1]'Jude . . . brother of James' (Jude 1) and 'James . . . servant of the Lord Jesus Christ' (Jas. 1:1) are less precise and could refer to a number of individuals.

[2]For the possibility that 'gospel' (Mk 1.1) refers to Mark's book cf. R. Guelich, 'The Gospel Genre', *The Gospel and the Gospels* (Grand Rapids: Eerdmans, 1991), p. 197 = GT: p. 208. Tertullian (*Against Marcion* 4:5) says of the Gospels of Mark and of Luke: 'It is permissible for works that disciples [Mark, Luke] publish to be regarded as belonging to their masters [Peter, Paul]'. But this comment does not refer to pseudepigrapha, *pace* Lincoln (note 22), lxxii.

[3]J.P. Audet (*La Didachè: instructions des apôtres* [Paris: Gabalda, 1958], pp. 187-206) dates it to AD 50-70, others to the second century.

[4]Cf. Eph. 1.1 with 2 Cor. 1.1.

[5]Cf. Eph. 6.23f. with 1 Cor. 16.23f.; 2 Cor. 13.11, 14; Gal. 6.18. Cf. 2 Tim. 4.19-22 with 1 Cor. 16.19f.; Gal. 6.18.

> As I wrote you before in a brief letter, by which, when you read it, you will be able to know my understanding in the mystery of Christ (3.3f.).
>
> For [the gospel] I am an ambassador in chains (6.20).
>
> Tychicus . . . I have sent to you . . . that you may know our circumstances . . . (6.21f.).

Hypocritically, he condemns the very deceit he is engaged in: 'Putting away all falsehood, let each one speak truth with his neighbor' (4.25).

In the Pastorals the fraud is made even more explicit. In the words of R.P. Martin, 'a later writer employed Paul's name to give credibility and authority' to his own writing.[1] L.R. Donelson, who accepts the Baur tradition without question and without argument, expresses this view even more candidly:

> In the interest of deception [the author of the Pastorals] fabricated all the personal notes, all the . . . commonplaces in the letters . . . [He employs] any device that . . . might seem necessary to accomplish his deception.[2]

Pseudo-Paul chooses to address Timothy and Titus because they are known to be Paul's co-workers[3] and, to further the pretense, he integrates into the letters Pauline idiom, themes and traditions.[4] In 1 Timothy he writes:

> I commit this charge to you, Timothy my son (1.18).
>
> These things I write to you, hoping to come to you shortly (3.14).
>
> Until I come, give attention to the reading . . . (4.13).
>
> I desire that the younger [widows] marry . . . (5.14).
>
> I charge you before God . . . that you keep the command . . . (6.13f.).

He also censures lying even as he practices it:[5]

---

[1]R.P. Martin, '1, 2 Timothy and Titus', *Harper's Bible Commentary* (ed. J.L. Mays; San Francisco: Harper, 1988), p. 1237.

[2]L.R. Donelson, *Pseudepigraphy and Ethical Argument in the Pastoral Epistles* (Tübingen: Mohr, 1986), pp. 24, 55.

[3]Cf. Rom. 16.21; 1 Cor. 4.17; 16.10; 2 Cor. 1.1, 19 (Timothy); 2 Cor. 2.13; 8.23; 12.17f.; Gal. 2:1 (Titus).

[4]Cf. M. Wolter, *Die Pastoralbriefe als Paulustradition* (Göttingen: Vandenhoek, 1988); P. Trummer, *Die Paulustradition der Pastoralbriefe*.

[5]Cf. also 1 Tim. 1.9f.

> Some shall fall away . . . through the hypocrisy of lying words . . . (4.1f.).

In 2 Timothy the author enlarges the fictional references to Pauline situations which, even if they contain genuine fragments,[1] are utilized only to give a semblance of genuineness.[2]

> Stir up the charism from God that is in you through the laying on of my hands (1.6).
>
> All those in Asia deserted me . . . [But] Onesiphorus . . . when he was in Rome, sought me . . . (1.15ff.).
>
> '[You know] what happened to me in Antioch, Iconium, Lystra . . . (3.13).
>
> I am already being offered up, and the time of my departure has come (4.6).
>
> [Come] quickly, for Demas has deserted me . . . Crescens has gone to Gaul, Titus to Dalmatia. Luke alone is with me. [Bring] Mark . . . (4.9ff.).

The pseudepigraphers of 1-2 Peter are quite as brazen. In 1 Peter he writes with double-tongued artistry:

> Putting away . . . all guile and hypocrisy . . ., I beg [you to] . . . conduct yourselves well among the pagans in order that, seeing your good works, they may glorify God . . . (2.1, 11f.).
>
> I . . ., witness of the sufferings of Christ, exhort the elders among you (5.1).[3]
>
> I have written you briefly through Silvanus . . . Mark, my son, greets you (5.12).

In 2 Peter pseudo-Peter writes similarly:

---

[1]Especially 2 Tim. 4. So, P.N. Harrison, *The Problem of the Pastoral Epistles* (Oxford: OUP, 1921), pp. 115-27. But see J.N.D. Kelly, *The Pastoral Epistles* (London: Black, 1963), pp. 29f.: The fragments theory 'is a tissue of improbabilities'.

[2]Cf. also 2 Tim. 1.8, 11f., 13.

[3]*Pace* Kümmel, *Introduction to the New Testament*, p. 421, in 1 Pet. 5:1 the 'I' refers back to 'Peter Apostle of Jesus Christ' (1.1) and his eyewitness to Christ's sufferings. Peter is 'fellow-elder' but not 'fellow-witness' with his recipients.

> We [were] eyewitnesses of his majesty . . . And we heard this voice from heaven . . . when we were with him on the holy mountain (1.16ff.).
>
> The pseudo-teachers will go after you with forged (πλαστοῖς) words (2.3).[1]
>
> This is a second letter I am writing you . . . (3.1f.).
>
> Our beloved brother Paul . . . wrote you (3.15).

Given the unique authority of the apostle in the church, these letters display, if they are pseudepigrapha, clear and sufficient evidence of a deceptive intention.

V

While certain ancient writings were composed—as school exercises and otherwise—in the name and style of an ancient master with no intention to deceive,[2] apostolic pseudepigrapha are not analogous to them.[3] For they were produced in a community where the apostles' teaching had a unique 'Word of God' authority[4] and where its content and even the identity of true apostles were subject to continuing dispute.[5] In this context they inevitably involved a deceptive imposition of apostolic status on a non-apostolic writing. That they may have been written with good intentions or by 'disciples' is irrelevant. As James Packer has well said, 'Frauds are still fraudulent even when perpetrated from noble motives'.[6]

The role of the apostle in the earliest church, the evidence for literary fraud in Greco-Roman antiquity, and the New Testament letters

---

[1]Cf. H. Braun, πλαστός, *TDNT* VI (1968/1959), p. 262 = GT: p. 262f.

[2]For examples, cf. the articles on 'Letters, Greek', and 'Pseudepigraphic Literature' in Hammond *Oxford Classical Dictionary*, pp. 497, 743; Speyer (note 6), pp. 32-35. For a modern analogy cf. Robert Graves' *I, Claudius* (London, 1934).

[3]Even less analogous are rewritings of Scripture, say, the *Targum of Job* and the Temple Scroll at Qumran or the *Targums of Onkelos and Jonathan*. They reflect Jewish hermeneutical practices in which the Scriptures were contemporized and interpreted, and they were recited or read alongside their biblical *Vorlage*.

[4]1 Thess. 2.13; 1 Cor. 14.36f.; 1 Pet. 1.23ff. Cf. 2 Cor. 2.15ff.; Col. 1.25; 2 Thess. 2.15; Heb. 13.7; 2 Pet. 3.2; Jude 17; *1 Clem.* 42:1; Ign. *Rom.* 4:3.

[5]See 1 Cor. 9.1-3; 2 Cor. 11.13; 12.11f.; Gal. 1.1; cf. 1.12, 17; 2.8f. Cf. Rev. 2.2 Cf. E.E. Ellis, *Prophecy and Hermeneutic in Early Christianity* (Tübingen: Mohr, 1978), pp. 105-108, 230-35.

[6]J.I. Packer, *'Fundamentalism' and the Word of God* (London, 1958), p. 184.

themselves combine to show that apostolic pseudepigrapha were a tainted enterprise from the start. At no point in the church's early history could they avoid the odor of forgery. Only when the deception was successful were they accepted for reading in church, and when they were found out, they were excluded, for example 2 Peter, by the minority who regarded it as pseudonymous.

In the light of these factors scholars cannot have it both ways. They cannot identify apostolic letters as pseudepigrapha and at the same time declare them to be innocent products with a right to a place in the canon. Secular scholars for whom the canon is only an antiquarian curiosity will have little concern for what books are in and what are out. However, historians in the Baur tradition who, with the patristic and reformation church, recognize the canonical books as an inspired message from God and the basis for Christian doctrine,[1] are presented with a more serious problem. Clearly one may, as Baur suggested, drop and urge the church to drop forged letters from the canon. But one may not, I think, sidestep the question with talk about innocent apostolic pseudepigrapha.[2]

---

[1]This distinction is drawn between canonical and apocryphal writings, for example, by Origen (*Commentary in Matthew 28* [on Matthew 23:37-39]) and by Jerome (*Prologus in Liber Salomonis*, cited in B. Fischer, ed., *Biblia Sacra iuxta Vulgatam Versionem*, vol. II (2 vols.; Stuttgart: Bibelanstalt, 1969, p. 957). Cf. Ellis, *Prophecy and Hermeneutic in Early Christianity*, pp. 17, 32; Westcott, *The History of the Canon of the New Testament*, pp. 12f.

[2]It may be, of course, that the Baur tradition itself is an unhistorical reconstruction based on false assumptions of 19th century scholarship and that, as John Robinson and earlier Theodor Zahn have argued, there are no pseudepigrapha in the New Testament. But that is another topic. Cf. J.A.T. Robinson, *Redating the New Testament* (London: SCM, 1976); T. Zahn, *Introduction to the New Testament* (3 vols.; Minneapolis: Klock, 1977 [^{3}1909]); E.E. Ellis, 'Dating the New Testament', *NTS* 26 (1980), pp. 487-502; idem, *The Making of The New Testament Documents*.

INTERCESSION IN THE JOHANNINE COMMUNITY: 1 JOHN 5.16 IN THE CONTEXT OF THE GOSPEL AND EPISTLES OF JOHN

Marianne Meye Thompson

While 1 John has its share of enigmatic statements, few have fostered more ingenious interpretations than 5.16: 'If you see your brother or sister committing what is not a mortal sin, you will ask, and God will give life to such a one—to those whose sin is not mortal. There is sin that is mortal; I do not say that you should pray about that' (NRSV).[1] The chief problem typically cited here has been to determine what 'mortal sin' (or, 'sinning unto death') is.[2] Naturally, this also raises the question of what kind of sin is not mortal, that is, does not lead to death. The distinction between these two kinds of sin has occupied the attention of exegetes and theologians and has generally been taken as providing the interpretative key to this puzzling passage.

But a second problem—often upstaged by the first—is found in the statement, 'There is sin that is mortal; I do not say that you should pray about that' (5.16b), which appears almost as an afterthought. The difficulties raised by this verse are both pastoral and theological, for it appears to prohibit intercession with respect to 'sin that is mortal'. It is not easy to understand why one should be allowed to intercede with respect to some sins and not others, nor why one should be especially forbidden to do so the more serious the sin appears to be. Surely it is precisely in such cases that intercession ought to be made!

---

[1]For clarity we shall divide 1 John 5.16 into two main parts, 16a and 16b, which correspond to the sentence divisions in the NRSV. On the problems of translating 5.16a, see below.

[2]The range of interpretations is catalogued fully by R.E. Brown, *The Epistles of John* (AB; New York: Doubleday, 1982), pp. 613-19, and need not be rehearsed here. See also the lucid summary by D.M. Scholer, 'Sins Within and Sins Without: An Interpretation of 1 John 5:16-17', in *Current Issues in Biblical Interpretation* (ed. G.F. Hawthorne; Grand Rapids: Eerdmans, 1975), pp. 230-46.

Solutions to this puzzle are legion. Not all commentators take the verse as proscribing intercession in certain cases. As has often been pointed out, the author does not *explicitly* forbid intercession for those 'sinning unto death'.[1] In fact, some interpreters argue that the author does little more than cast a side-long glance at 'sin unto death'. Almost parenthetically, he states that such sin is not in the scope of his discussion at the moment. Accordingly, 5.16b ought to be translated, 'I am not now speaking about that (*sc.* the sin that leads to death)'.[2] In another vein, attempts have been made to find a significant difference in the meaning of αἰτεῖν and ἐρωτᾶν, as if one kind of petition (αἰτεῖν, 5.14-15) may be made but the other (ἐρωτᾶν, 5.16) may not.[3] Taking the distinction between αἰτεῖν and ἐρωτᾶν even further, P. Trudinger argued that the author of the epistle does not forbid *praying* for the sinner, but *asking questions* or debating about the sin unto death.[4]

Most proposed solutions tend to deny that intercession is in any way restricted and so try to mitigate the perceived offensiveness of the text.[5] But suspicion lingers that despite many attempts to ameliorate the author's words about intercession, their surface meaning is their real intent: to forbid intercessory prayer in certain circumstances. Not only is the traditional translation of 5.16b—such as that found in the NRSV (above)—the most natural way of rendering the Greek,[6] but it is quite logical to understand this part of the verse as prohibiting

---

[1]So A.E. Brooke, *A Critical and Exegetical Commentary on the Johannine Epistles* (ICC; Edinburgh: T.&T. Clark, 1912), p. 147; S. Cox, 'The Sin Unto Death', *The Expositor* 2:1 (1881), p. 417; I.Howard Marshall, *The Epistles of John* (NICNT; Grand Rapids: Eerdmans, 1978), p. 246 n. 19; Rudolf Schnackenburg, *Die Johannesbriefe* (HTKNT; Freiburg: Herder, 1963), p. 278; Scholer, 'Sins Within', pp. 242-43.

[2]Many interpreters take the περὶ ἐκείνης with λέγειν rather than with ἐρωτᾶν; so Scholer, 'Sins Within', pp. 242-43, and note 61; Schnackenburg, *Johannesbriefe*, p. 278; E.H. Sugden, 'Critical Note on 1 John v. 16', *The Expositor* 2:3 (1882) p. 159. Schnackenburg states that this reading makes better sense since one prays for the *sinner*, not the *sin*.

[3]See, e.g., B.F. Westcott, *The Epistles of John: The Greek Text with Notes* (London: Macmillan, 1883), p. 192; G. Stählin, *TDNT*, I, p. 193; H. Greeven, *TDNT*, II, p. 806.

[4]P. Trudinger, 'Concerning Sins, Mortal and Otherwise: A Note on 1 John 5, 16-17', *Bib* 52 (1971), pp. 541-42. See also Sugden, 'Critical Note', p. 159.

[5]S.M. Reynolds ['The Sin unto Death and Prayers for the Dead', *Reformation Review* 20 (1973), pp. 130-39] however, suggests that the epistle *does* forbid intercession—for the sin of the unrighteous dead.

[6]Scholer ('Sins Within', p. 243) argues that 5.16b should be translated 'I speak not concerning that ("sin unto death") in order that (ἵνα) anyone should pray (ἐρωτήσῃ) [about it]'. Brown (p. 612) points out one should then repeat the prepositional phrase with the second verb: 'so that one should pray [about that]'.

intercession in certain instances.[1] In fact, there is an important but implicit contrast between the two parts of this verse. In 5.16a the author refers to instances in which intercession is made, the request heard, and the one who is prayed for is given life.[2] But 5.16b implies that there are times when prayer would not be efficacious and the one prayed for would not be given life. In these instances, intercession ought not to be made.[3]

In this essay I would like to explore this understanding of 5.16—a reading generally perceived as offensive. To do so we will first of all survey the understanding of intercession implicit in John and 1 John. Here one finds that in interceding for the brother or sister who sins, Christians carry out a ministry that is modeled on the intercession of Jesus, who offered (and continues to offer) prayers for 'his own'—a significant qualifier. Following this survey, we will examine some remarkable passages in the Old Testament and in apocryphal and pseudepigraphical literature which suggest that the restriction of intercession was not unique to John or the Johannine community. On

---

1While it is true that the author's comment on intercession appears almost as a parenthesis or aside, the acknowledgment of that fact makes a statement only about the literary structure of the text. It says little about the relation or importance of that idea to the author's thought. I would, therefore, disagree with Scholer's comment that '1 John "plays down" the "sin unto death" by not speaking about it' ('Sins Within', p. 242). While it is true that the author does not here dwell on this 'sin unto death', the prohibition of intercession with respect to it has the effect of underscoring its magnitude.

2There is a difference of opinion in how to understand the subject of the verbs 'he will ask and he will give him life'. Specifically, is the subject of 'he will give him life' the same as the subject of 'he will ask'? That is, does the *petitioner* bestow life on the sinner? So R. Bultmann, *The Johannine Epistles* (Hermeneia; Philadelphia: Fortress, 1973), p. 87 n. 16; C.H. Dodd, *The Johannine Epistles* (MNTC; New York: Harper & Brothers, 1946), p. 135; C. Haas, M. DeJonge, J.L. Swellengrebel, *A Translator's Handbook on the Letters of John* (London: United Bible Societies, 1972), p. 127; J.R.W. Stott, *The Letters of John* (TNTC; England/Grand Rapids: Inter-Varsity/Eerdmans, 1988), p. 189; Georg Strecker, *Die Johannesbriefe* (KEK 14; Göttingen: Vandenhoeck & Ruprecht, 1989), p. 298 n. 23. Or is *God* the subject of 'he will give him life'? So NEB; RSV; NRSV; NIV; Brown, *Epistles*, pp. 611-12; F.F. Bruce, *The Epistles of John* (Grand Rapids: Eerdmans, 1970), p. 124; Marshall, *Epistles*, p. 246 n. 171; Schnackenburg, *Johannesbriefe*, p. 276; Scholer, 'Sins Within', pp. 239-40; and Stephen S. Smalley, *1, 2, 3 John* (WBC; Waco, Texas: Word, 1984), p. 300. In the Greek, it is most natural to assume that the same person is the subject of both verbs. Hence, it is the petitioner who gives the sinner life. However, most commentators who adopt this viewpoint also acknowledge that ultimately it is God who is the source and giver of life. This particular passage assigns a crucial mediating role to the petitioning Christian. By implication, there are situations in which the petitioner's prayers would not grant life to the sinner.

3For similar interpretations, see Brown, *Epistles*, p. 618; A.H. Dammers, 'Hard Sayings—II', *Theology* 66 (1973), pp. 370-72; A. Klöpper, 'Zur Lehre von der Sünde im 1. Johannesbrief, Erläuterung von 5,16 fin.', *ZWT* 43 (1900), pp. 585-602; Strecker, *Die Johannesbriefe*, p. 298.

the contrary, there is ample evidence for the view that intercession for forgiveness was at times prohibited, and that such prohibition was a sign of God's judgment upon unbelief and disobedience. By correlating the Johannine theology of intercession with passages in biblical and extra-canonical literature that reflect similar views, it becomes clear that where some have found offense or a puzzle, there is rather a testimony to the efficacy of Christian intercession and to the sufficiency of Christ's atoning work (1 Jn 1.9).

The Johannine View of Intercession

1. *The Prayers of Jesus*

At the outset it is instructive to note that there are relatively few narratives of Jesus at prayer in the Gospel of John.[1] At 6.11 we read that Jesus gave thanks (εὐχαριστήσας) for the bread. Beyond this brief note, however, there are only three other passages: Jesus' prayer prior to raising Lazarus (11.41-42); the Johannine version of the prayer in Gethsemane (12.27-28); and the high priestly prayer of John 17. In addition, the epistle speaks of the intercessory role that Jesus now exercises on behalf of penitent sinners.

John 11.41-42. John 11.41-42 refers to Jesus' thanksgiving that he has been heard by God. This is obviously a prayer,[2] but we do not have the content of the petition, nor is it specified in what request Jesus 'has been heard'.[3] The raising of Lazarus suggests that the petition concerns the accomplishment of the miracle. But the previous question to Martha 'Did I not tell you that if you would believe you would see the glory of God?' may suggest that Jesus prays for God to be glorified. Indeed, in the only other narratives in John which report Jesus' prayers, the specific petition is for the Father to glorify his own name

---

[1]Cf. the Synoptic references, Mt. 14.23, 19.13, 26.36-44, 27.46; Mk 1.35, 6.46, 14.32-39, 15.34; Lk. 3.21, 5.16, 6.12, 9.18, 28-29, 11.1, 22.41-45, 23.46.

[2]The elements that indicate this is a genuine prayer are (1) the lifting of the eyes to heaven; (2) the address to God as 'abba', characteristic of the prayers of Jesus recorded in the Synoptics and elsewhere in John; (3) the initial thanksgiving, typical of Jewish prayers of the time.

[3]Barrett (*The Gospel According to St. John* [2nd ed.; Philadelphia: Westminster, 1978], p. 402) suggests that no specific moment or prayer is in mind here; Jesus is always in constant communion with the Father. However, as Schnackenburg (*The Gospel according to St. John* [New York: Seabury, 1980], II, p. 339) notes, the confident expectation of an answer to Jesus' prayer presupposes that a request has been made.

(12.28; 17.1). Here it is through granting life to Lazarus through Jesus that God will bring glory to his name (11.4, 40; cf. 5.19-21).

That Jesus has been heard by God testifies that he is obedient to God, for 'God does not listen to sinners' (9.31).[1] Jesus himself does not need such affirmation, but the bystanders do (11.42).[2] They must come to understand that the raising of Lazarus is God's work in response to Jesus' prayer. It is not that Jesus entreats God to do something that God is otherwise ill-disposed to do. God hears Jesus at all times. God does what Jesus asks, because Jesus asks in accord with the will of God. The intimacy and union between the Father and the Son manifest themselves in Jesus' conviction that God hears him at all times, and in God's accomplishment of that which Jesus asks. In fact, the language of 'asking' and 'answering' is almost superfluous, for it suggests conversation between two persons, each trying to discern the mind of the other. But there is no such gap between Jesus and God. For even as God hears Jesus, Jesus also hears or understands God (cf. 5.37). This is graphically depicted in the following passage.

John 12.27-28.[3] Faced with imminent death, Jesus ponders his fate and prays, 'Father, glorify thy name'.[4] Jesus does not pray to escape

---

[1]For references to God as the God who hears prayer, see Prov. 15.8, 29; Sir. 21.5, 35.16-21; *m. Ber.* 4.4; 3 Macc. 2.10; *T. Jos.* 10.1-2; *T. Sim* 2.2; *T. Levi* 4.2; and the 15th Benediction of the *Shemoneh `Esreh* (Palestinian recension; see Emil Schürer, *The History of the Jewish people in the age of Jesus Christ* [rev. ed.; Edinburgh: T. & T. Clark, 1979], II, p. 460).

[2]Because of Jesus' statement 'I have said this on account of the people standing by', a number of commentators have viewed this prayer as highly artificial, more a display of Jesus' power or Johannine theology than an account of Jesus at prayer. Lindars (*John*, p. 401) suggests that this is actually a petition for the bystanders, specifically that they may have the perception to see in the miracle the glory of God. But Schnackenburg (*Gospel According to St. John*, 2:339) seems closer to the mark when he comments that the prayer is for the sake of the people so that they may come to understand the miracle as God's testimony to Jesus' mission and be exhorted to faith. Although the prayer is not simply a demonstration of that unity, the fact that the prayer is made and answered will serve to verify such unity for those who have ears to hear.

[3]The material in 12.27-28 reflects a knowledge of the tradition of Jesus' agony in Gethsemane such as is found in the Synoptics. Barrett (*Gospel according to John*, pp. 424-25) suggests a knowledge of Mark. Others prefer to see knowledge of a similar or related tradition. Jürgen Becker (*Das Evangelium nach Johannes* [ÖTKNT 4/2; Gütersloh: Gerd Mohn/Würzburg: Echter-Verlag, 1981], p. 387) suggests that the story is designed to offer an alternative to the traditional expectation that Jesus will pray for deliverance.

[4]The statements 'What shall I say to this? Father, save me from this hour?' can be punctuated in various ways. The second sentence, 'Father, save me from this hour' is not a true petition in the Johannine version, but rather a question, directed to the crowds. D.A. Carson (*The Gospel According to John* [Grand Rapids: Eerdmans, 1991], p. 440), however, argues that if this statement is read merely as a question it sounds 'faintly histrionic' and 'means that what is troubling Jesus . . .

death, but rather asks that even—or perhaps particularly—in the hour of death, God will be glorified.[1] Jesus receives an affirmative answer to his prayer when a voice from heaven answers: 'I have glorified it, and I will glorify it again'. It is the voice of God attesting the unity of the mission of Jesus and the Father.[2] Characteristic of John, God's voice is understood by Jesus, but not by the crowds. The voice that tells Jesus that God has heard him sounds to their ears merely like thunder.[3]

John 17. The prayer of Jesus in chapter 17 expounds at some length the theme of the other two prayers of Jesus in John, namely, the mutual glorification of the Father and Son (17.1). Speaking of his work in retrospect, Jesus asserts that he has glorified the Father (17.4). Through Jesus' death, resurrection, and ascension, the Father will now bring glory to Jesus (17.1, 5). But the bulk of the prayer focuses on the disciples. They have been called from the world, and Jesus prays that the Father will sanctify them, make them one, and keep them safe, that is, keep them from falling away or succumbing to temptation (17.9, 11-12, 15, 17, 19). Similarly, Jesus prays for subsequent generations of believers, that they might be one with prior generations of believers, as well as united with the Father and the Son.

In short, the prayer of Jesus in John 17 is a prayer for believers, that they might stand firm in their knowledge of the Son and the Father, and so continue to receive eternal life (17.3; cf. 20.30-31). This is precisely the prayer Jesus cannot and does not make for the world. To be sure, there is a witness to the world (17.18). But Jesus

---

is given no substance'. He asserts that 'Father, save me from this hour!' is a positive prayer which fully reveals Jesus' agony. Against Carson, the present passage has no concern with Jesus' psyche as he approached his death. Rather, it shows that Jesus was always obedient to God. And since, at this point, obedience entails death, Jesus will not pray for salvation from a fate from which human beings ordinarily shrink.

[1] As Carson (*John*, p. 440) aptly states, 'This is not some compromise petition'.

[2] This is not the *bath qol*, the mere echo of the divine voice, but God's own testimony to the Son; cf. 5.37, 44; 1 Jn 5.9-12.

[3] Barrett (*Gospel according to John*, p. 426) suggests that although the crowd did not understand what the voice said, the thunder itself may have been sufficient to indicate divine assurance. But it is possible that the Evangelist intends a double meaning here; cf. the OT passages which speak of God 'thundering' (1 Sam. 7.10; 12.18). The crowds hear the thunder, but it remains true that 'his voice you have never heard', because they do not believe the witness of the Father (5.37). Although they do not comprehend the voice, it comes for their sake, so that they might come to believe. Jesus, however, because he comes from God and remains in constant communion with God, does not need verification that God hears him.

intercedes only for believers, since the prayer which is made is for God's glory to be known in them, and for them to remain one with the Father and Son, and with each other. The world *qua* world cannot participate in such realities.

1 John 2.1. In 1 John 2.1, the word 'paraclete' is applied to Jesus. While many commentators (and translations) take this in a forensic sense—either that Jesus speaks in defense of believers or enters a plea and defends them in a court of law—it is also possible to understand paraclete primarily as an intercessor, especially in light of the description of him as 'righteous'.[1] Because Jesus is now with God (πρὸς τὸν πατέρα; 1 Jn 1.2; Jn 1.1), he has immediate and intimate communion with God. So he intercedes for Christians when they pray for forgiveness (1.9). There is no sense that Jesus tries to persuade God to do something that God is unwilling or reluctant to do. There exists such a unity of will between Jesus and the Father that what Jesus asks will be granted. And what is asked for in this instance is forgiveness of sins. Much like the prayer of John 17, Jesus intercedes for believers that they be held in eternal life.

Summary. It is characteristic of Johannine theology that Jesus has the confidence that his prayers are heard by God, and that this assurance is a token of and due to their constant and intimate communion. Specifically, Jesus functions as a righteous intercessor who prays for and mediates life from God to those who believe. Indeed, it is God's purpose to give life to the world (Jn 3.16), and as part of that purpose, Jesus intercedes for the perseverance and forgiveness of believers. Jesus' prayers do not merely petition God for the life of believers; they actually confer it. This indicates his perfect union with God and perfect understanding of God's will.

2. *The Prayers of Christians*

There is a striking parallel between what is said or assumed of Jesus' prayers and those of believers. They may have the same kind of confidence that Jesus had that their prayers are heard. Furthermore, they

---

[1] See Brown, *Epistles*, pp. 216-17, who discusses both options and concludes that both ideas are present in 1 John 2.1. The righteousness of Jesus referred to here qualifies him to be either an advocate or an intercessor. For the idea that the prayers of the righteous were particularly effective, see the material cited below in the synthesis section dealing with the OT, pseudepigraphal and rabbinic literature; and Jas 5.16.

are heard because of their relationship of belonging to God. And, finally, through its prayers the Christian community functions as Jesus' agent in bringing life to the world and so bringing glory to God. Besides 1 Jn 5.13-17, there are four passages in the Gospel and epistles which speak of prayer.

John 14.13-14. In these verses there is the promise that whatever Christians ask of Jesus will be done for them, for in the granting of these requests the Father glorifies the Son. The question that troubles many modern believers is the content of the 'whatever' (v. 13). While the promise that 'whatever you ask' will be given is qualified by the phrase 'in my name' in v. 13, v. 14 contains a more absolute form of the same promise: 'if you ask anything in my name, I will do it'.

The context of these verses helps to define the content of 'whatever'. In verse 12, Jesus is reported as saying that whoever believes in him will also do the works that he has done; indeed, believers shall do 'greater works'. We may note briefly several key points of this promise. First, the promise applies to believers in union with Jesus. Second, the Johannine term 'works' is not simply equivalent to signs, but is more encompassing. It includes all that Jesus says and does, and points particularly to the unity of Jesus' mission with God's activity in the world. The work of Jesus is the work of God. Third, the works are 'greater' not because they are more spectacular or because there are more of them, but because they reach further into the world. In short, verse 12 speaks of the mission that believers are to carry out in the world after Jesus' departure from them.

In the context of this mission comes the promise that 'whatever you ask in my name, I will do it, that the Father may be glorified in the Son'. The promise that prayer will be answered is connected to the previous statement not only grammatically (καί) but also in terms of its substance. The requests which will be heard are those in which the Father is glorified in the Son,[1] or (as the context suggests) requests that have to do with the continuation of Jesus' work, that is, the work of bringing life to the world. As Schnackenburg expresses it, these prayers have to do with the tasks of proclaiming the Gospel.[2] That

---

[1]R.E. Brown, *The Gospel According to John* (AB; Garden City: Doubleday & Co., 1970), II, p. 636.

[2]Rudolf Schnackenburg, *The Gospel According to St. John* (New York: Crossroad, 1982), III, p. 72.

prayer is made in Jesus' name, and that it is granted by him shows that Jesus 'continues to be active on behalf of the disciples'.[1] The granting of the disciples' requests shows the unity of the work of the disciples with Jesus' own work. So their work and mission receive divine affirmation, even as Jesus' mission was attested by the Father himself.

John 15:7, 16. The command 'ask whatever you will' appears twice in chapter 15 (15.7, 16). The granting of the requests of the disciples is assured, but we note that it is (a) contingent upon the relationship of the believer to God through Jesus (expressed in terms of 'abiding', 15.7; friendship, 15.15; choosing and sending, 15.16); (b) related to mission, described in these two verses as 'fruit-bearing' (15.8, 16); and (c) intended for the glory of God (15.8). That the disciples' requests are granted depends upon their continuing faithfulness to Jesus and so, in turn, testifies to their union with him. The requests mentioned are specifically petitions that have to do with the mission of the disciples.

John 16.23-24, 28. Like the assurances to the disciples in John 14 and 15, Jesus' words here promise that what they ask of the Father will be given to them; therefore, they are to ask so that they may receive (16.23). And they may pray confidently to the Father through 'Jesus' name' (v. 26), but they will not need his intercession on their behalf (16.26). That there is no need for an intercessor indicates the unity and love that the disciples share with the Father.

1 John 3.19-23. In this passage, the Elder assures his readers that 'we receive from [God] whatever we ask' (v. 22). That God grants their requests is evidence that they adhere to the truth (v. 19) and that they have kept the commandments of God to believe in Jesus and to love each other. Those who do what pleases God (v. 22) have confidence in God's presence. That is, they need not be afraid of judgment. They are the children of God, much beloved by God (3.1-2).

Synthesis. The parallels between Jesus' prayer and the prayers of believers are striking. Because of their relationship to God, they can approach God with confidence as they pray. Because their prayers

---

[1]Schnackenburg, *The Gospel According to St. John*, p. 72.

are heard, they can be assured that they belong to God. God 'does not listen to sinners' (Jn 9.31).[1]

And yet there are 'conditions' attached to the prayers of believers. Specifically, their prayers are answered when they pray 'in the name of Jesus' (Jn 14.13-14; 15.16; 16.23, 26), continue in fellowship with him (Jn 15.7), and do what is pleasing to God (1 Jn 3.22-23). These conditions are not understood as magical formulas or rituals which, if performed or repeated correctly, guarantee that God will accede to a certain request. Indeed, the idea of begging or manipulating God to agree with human requests is entirely foreign to these passages. Rather, these 'conditions' highlight the parallels to both Jesus' intercession and his relationship to God. The qualifiers associated with prayer are not prerequisites one must meet in order to insure that prayer will be answered. These conditions are ways of speaking of the Christian's commitment to God; the assurance of divine response a corollary.

On the model of Jesus, Christians are those with open and free access to God; they have kept God's commands, and so do what pleases God. Again, the emphasis falls on the mutuality of interaction and communication between the petitioner and God. As the narratives of Jesus' prayers underscore that he was always heard and that this indicated divine attestation to Jesus, so too the assurance to Christians that their prayers are heard similarly affirms their identity as the friends of Jesus and the children of God.[2]

The prayers that are heard are those which, like the prayers of Jesus, concern God's saving mission in the world. We noted that the Gospel recounts only a few instances of Jesus at prayer and that the content of these prayers tends to be rather fixed. Jesus prayed for restoration of life to Lazarus, for the glorification of the Father through his actions, for the safe-keeping of the disciples, and for the forgiveness of their sins. These all fit under the rubric of the life-giving work of the Son. Lazarus is raised, Christians are forgiven: in

---

[1]'Sinners' means those who do not heed and do the will of God. Those who are not sinners are not perfect or free from sin, but understand and commit themselves to carrying out God's will.

[2]Promises that one will receive what one asks for are found also in the Synoptics (Mt. 7.7-11 and Lk. 11.9-10). But here both the subject and object of the request are qualified. The one who 'asks', 'seeks' and 'knocks' is a child of the heavenly Father, as shown by the parable which follows these instructions. What is given are the blessings of the kingdom of God (in Lk. 11.13, the Holy Spirit). See further Robert A. Guelich, *The Sermon on the Mount: A Foundation for Understanding* (Waco, Texas: Word, 1982), pp. 377-79.

both cases, Jesus brings life. Through the prayers of Jesus the life-giving mission of the Son is carried out. These prayers manifest the unity of the Son with the Father as well as the identity of their work.

Jesus' intercessory prayers are thus a paradigm for Christian intercession. The promises that 'whatever you ask will be given' are found consistently in contexts that have to do with the identity and mission of the Christian community. The promise of receiving what one asks is granted to the community *qua* community, and the requests that are so granted are those in response to intercessory prayers through which the life-giving mission of the Son is carried out.

Through intercession, then, the community becomes an agent of mediating life and forgiveness.[1] To this role it was expressly commissioned by the risen Jesus: 'And he breathed on them and said to them, "Receive the Holy Spirit. If you forgive the sins of any, they are forgiven; if you retain the sins of any, they are retained"' (Jn 20.22-23).[2] *How* the community carries out this commission is a subject of considerable discussion and debate, for the Gospel does not explicitly say. Given the parallel between Jesus' sending and that of the disciples (Jn 20.21), it is possible that the tasks of forgiving and retaining sin are to be correlated specifically with proclamation.[3] Those who respond with repentance and belief are forgiven; those who reject the Gospel are not. This two-fold nature of the work of the community is grounded in the work of Jesus himself. Although

[1]Leon Morris (*The Gospel according to John* [NICNT; Grand Rapids: Eerdmans, 1971], pp. 848-50) correctly insists that the commission is given not to individuals, or to individuals who spoke for the church (such as an ordained ministry), but to the church as a whole.

[2]The literature on this passage is extensive. See Brown *[Gospel*, pp. 1041-43] who notes in passing a possible connection between the disciples' authority to forgive sins and intercession. See also D.E. Aune, *The Cultic Setting of Realized Eschatology in Early Christianity* (NovTSup 28; Leiden: E. J. Brill, 1972), pp. 82-83; Gary M. Burge, *The Anointed Community: The Holy Spirit in the Johannine Tradition* (Grand Rapids: Eerdmans, 1987), p. 120. It is worth noting that in Mt. 18.18 the saying about loosing and binding is followed immediately by the assurance that 'if two of you agree on earth about anything they ask, it will be done for them by my Father in heaven' (18.18-19). Thus Matthew also links assurance in answering prayer with the mission of the disciples.

[3]The Protestant reformers, for example, disputed the Roman Catholic interpretation that John 20.21-23 validated the sacrament of penance. Instead, sins are forgiven and retained through the preaching of the gospel, as well as in the sacraments. So Luther, WA 21.262-63, 30^{II}.503; Zwingli, *Commentary on True and False Religion* (Durham: Labyrinth Press, 1981), pp. 172-74; Calvin, *The Gospel According to St. John* (Grand Rapids: Eerdmans, 1959, 1961), *ad loc.* For modern commentators who hold this view, see Carson, *John*, pp. 655-56; G. Beasley-Murray, *John* (WBC; Waco, Texas: Word, 1987), pp. 383-84; and F.F. Bruce, *The Gospel of John* (Grand Rapids: Eerdmans, 1982), p. 382.

Jesus' mission mediates eternal life, there is another side to it, for those who do not believe already stand under God's judgment precisely because of their unbelief (3.16-21; 9.39-41).

But it is also possible that the tasks of forgiving and retaining sin are to be correlated with intercession. That is, whereas the Christian community through its intercession served an intermediary role in conferring life upon penitent believers, so in its abstention from intercession it functioned to retain sins. This is not to say that forgiving and retaining sins occur only through intercessory prayer, but rather that even as the community mediates forgiveness and judgment, as did Jesus, so it at times mediates these things through intercession, as did Jesus. Those who do not believe in Jesus as the Son of God and repent their unbelief—in short, 'the world', as opposed to 'his own'—are not properly recipients of the intercessory prayer of Jesus or the community. That intercession is not made for them is a sign of God's judgment upon them for their unbelief. They do not stand within the community of those who can confidently trust that God hears their prayers, particularly when they intercede for each other for the forgiveness of sins.

To be sure, this is not explicitly stated in the commission to the disciples (Jn 20.22-23). They are not forbidden to intercede for unrepentant sinners. Indeed, they are not commanded even to intercede for each other. But if intercession were a way in which forgiveness and judgment is effected or pronounced, then such an understanding would also make sense of 1 John 5.16. Then the statement, 'I do not say that you should pray about that', could be understood not as an explicit but an implicit prohibition, based on the community's shared understanding of Jesus' work which leads to life for those who believe and to judgment for those who do not.[1] Is this sheer conjecture? Actually, no. The idea that intercession may at times be forbidden would not be new to John, for it is already found in various prophetic books of the Old Testament and in Jewish literature preceding and contemporaneous with the New Testament. John's realized eschatology merely sharpens the picture. We turn, then, to an examination of some material which suggests the currency of the idea that God's

---

[1]The passive voice used in 20.23 as well as the suggestion that the proper context for this activity is intercessory *prayer* point clearly to God as the source of forgiveness. The community proclaims and mediates this forgiveness, which comes from God through Christ, the 'lamb of God who takes away the sin of the world'.

judgment upon sinners manifests itself in the ineffectiveness or even prohibition of intercession for the forgiveness of sins—material which may well explain John's own use.

The Prohibition of Intercession

There are several provocative texts in the OT, as well as in the Apocrypha and Pseudepigrapha, where intercession is prohibited because of excessive sin or lack of repentance on the part of the people, or because the day of judgment has finally arrived. There are also times when intercession does not avail. The following is only a sampling of these texts.

In 1 Samuel 7.3-9, Samuel appears as intercessor. But he intercedes only after 'Israel put away the Baals and the Ashtaroth, and they served the Lord only' (v. 4). After they had repented, they gathered to confess their sin (v. 6) and they urged Samuel, 'Do not cease to cry to the Lord our God for us' (v. 8). In fact, continual intercession is Samuel's duty (1 Sam. 12.23), but even as he intercedes he warns the people to fear the Lord and serve him with all their heart, for if they act wickedly, they shall be swept away (1 Sam. 12.20-25). Even so, there are instances in which intercession is not effective. Eli laments that if one sins against the Lord, 'Who can intercede for him?' (1 Sam. 2.25).

Jeremiah also alludes to the futility of intercession in certain instances. Some passages go beyond such skepticism to an explicit prohibition against interceding for the wrong-doer. Jeremiah is commanded 'do not pray for this people . . . and do not intercede with me, for I do not hear you . . .' because 'they pour out drink offerings to other gods' (Jer. 7.16-18). This prohibition appears again (11.14; 14.11; 15.11). Intercession is denied because the people 'have gone after other gods' (11.10); they have broken the covenant (11.10); their 'gods have become as many as their cities' (11.13); and they have set up 'altars to burn incense to Baal' (11.13). Consequently, no prayer or ritual act will avert punishment (14.11) nor would the intercession of even Moses or Samuel (Jer. 15.1).

Job 42.8 illustrates the effectiveness of the intercession of a righteous person for one who has done wrong (cf. Ezek. 14.14, 20). Job's friends are to offer sacrifice and also to ask Job to pray for them so that God 'will not deal with [them] according to [their] folly'.

Testimony is borne to Job's reputation as an intercessor when, in another context, it is said that even Noah, Daniel, and Job could not intercede to save the land which God had determined to destroy; they would save only 'their own lives by their righteousness' (Ezek. 14.12-20). Even the most righteous of intercessors cannot atone for the sins of the faithless.

The themes of the intercession of the righteous and the prohibition of intercession as God's judgment appear in several pseudepigraphical works.[1] Thus in *2 Apoc. Bar.* 85.1, the prayers of the righteous are heard and sin is forgiven: 'Further, know that our fathers in former times and former generations had helpers, righteous prophets and holy men. But we were also in our country, and they helped us when we sinned, and they intervened for us with him who has created us since they trusted in their works. And the Mighty One heard them and purged us from our sins'.

Again in *1 Enoch* 39.5, the righteous intercede and offer petitions and prayers on behalf of the children of the people. Their prayers are heard and are made effective because of 'the blood of the righteous' (*1 En.* 47; 104.2). Not only are these prayers offered *by* the righteous, they are also offered *for* the righteous, that is, those whose allegiance is to God and his covenant. But no intercessor is found for the wicked. Neither is there any comfort in prayer for sinners nor any assurance that their prayers for themselves or for their children will be heard. That is their judgment (14.7; cf. 84.6). In *1 Enoch* 13-14, Enoch writes down the prayers of the watchers because their prayers 'will not be heard throughout all the days of eternity; and judgment is passed upon you' (14.4). Indeed, the prayers of the righteous seem to bring that judgment upon the wicked (*1 En.* 97.3, 5): 'What do you intend to do, you sinners, whither will you flee on that day of judgment, when you hear the sound of the prayer of the righteous ones? . . . In those days, the prayers of the righteous ones shall reach unto the Lord; but for all of you, your days shall arrive.' At the time of judgment, no one will arise to intercede for the sinners (cf. 89.57).

In the third vision (6.35-9.36) of the book of *4 Ezra*, Ezra makes inquiry concerning the fate of the righteous and the wicked. He is particularly concerned whether the righteous will be able to intercede on the day of judgment. The answer comes that 'no one shall pray for

[1] All translations of pseudepigraphical works are taken from *The Old Testament Pseudepigrapha*, ed. James H. Charlesworth (2 vols.; Garden City, New York: Doubleday & Co., 1983).

another on that day' (7.105); the righteous will not be able to intercede for the ungodly or to entreat the Most High for them (7.102). This is a difficult and troubling word, and Ezra puzzles about the famous intercessors of old (Abraham, Moses, Joshua, Samuel, David, Solomon, Elijah, and Hezekiah): if these righteous individuals prayed for the ungodly in this world, why will they be unable to do so at the judgment (vv. 106-111)? Again, the angel's answer seems harsh: the fate of the unrighteous and wicked has already been sealed. 'At the end of the age no one will be able to have mercy on him who has been condemned in the judgment, or to harm him who is victorious' (v. 115). When Ezra realizes the fate which awaits the sinner, he implores God's mercy and forgiveness, since all have committed iniquity (7.126, 139; 8.35). His special plea, however, is for the forgiveness of the sins of the righteous, for those who have served God in truth (8.26), who have kept the covenant (8.27), and who feared God (8.29). God tells Ezra that all were given free choice (7.129; 8.56), but the wicked chose death, were contemptuous of God's law and even said in their hearts 'there is no God—though knowing full well that they must die' and, he implies, receive punishment in the after life (7.129-131; 138-139; 8.56-58). In short, though all are sinful, the righteous are those who humble themselves and acknowledge God (8.48). Their sins are forgiven, and there is 'joy in heaven' over their salvation (8.38-39); 'there shall not be grief at [the] damnation [of the wicked], so much as joy over those to whom salvation is assured' (7.131).

In *Jubilees* Moses appears again as the intercessor for the people, pleading with God that they be preserved from error so that they might not be destroyed (cf. *Ass. Mos.* 11.17-19). God responds to the prayer of Moses by sketching the future of the people: once they confess their sin and that of their forebears, they will repent, return to God, and follow him and his commandments forever (1.19-25). Another intercessor of old, Noah, appears not only to intercede for the righteous (10.4), but also to pray for the judgment and doom of the ungodly (10.5-6). Still a third intercessor, Abraham, prays that Jacob may be cleansed from sin and forgiven his inadvertent transgressions (22.14; cf. 22.23). However, there are also mentioned in *Jubilees* sins for which there is no atonement (e.g., Sabbath breaking, 2.27; cf. 30.10; 33.13, 16). The penalty for committing a 'mortal sin' is that God 'will hide his face from you and deliver you into the power of your sin' (21.22).[1] The punishment also involves being cast out from the people of God.

Although the *Psalms of Solomon* have no passages explicitly about intercession, several passages reflect ideas similar to those illustrated above. More than once it is affirmed that the Lord hears the prayers of the poor or righteous (5.2, 5, 12; 7.7; 15.1; 16.1-15). Like the passages cited from *1 Enoch* and *4 Ezra*, the *Psalms of Solomon* also distinguish the sins of the righteous—those within the covenant community—and the sins of the wicked (or sinners; cf. 17.5, 'because of our sins, sinners rose up against us'). The righteous are to be careful to guard their ways and to confess and atone for even unintentional sins, but they can be sure that God forgives the repentant (3.7-12; 9.6-7; 13.7-10). Although God may also chastise the righteous (13.7-12; 16.1-15; 18.4), that discipline is not the same as the judgment of sinners, for the righteous are not destroyed (13.7-12). God's mercy is upon the righteous; his wrath will come to rest on hardened sinners (2.31, 34; 5.9-11; 7.4-10; 9.6-11; 15.12; 18.1-4). Therefore the Psalmist is sure that the righteous shall live (14.3) or inherit life (14.10; 2.31; 3.12).

A few passages from Sirach may also be cited here. Those who repent and turn from their sins experience the greatness of the Lord's mercy and forgiveness, but even prayer and the humility of fasting do not avail for the person who sins and 'goes again and does the same things' (34.27; 17.24-26, 29). There is such a thing as being overly confident of the efficacy of atonement (5.4-7). Those who are truly repentant, however, rely on prayer as the vehicle for atonement (21.1, 5; 28.2; cf. 28.4; 34.27) and can be sure that their prayers are heard and that God will vindicate them (21.5; 35.17-18; 51.8-12).

Finally we may cite some pertinent material from Qumran.[2] Here again one finds the assumption that while God hears the prayers of the faithful it is a judgment on the wicked that they are not heard. This sentiment is worded particularly harshly at 1QS 2.9, where one finds the prayer (curse) that not only may God not hear the prayer of the 'men of the lot of Satan' but, even more, that rather than offering

1 The phrase 'sin unto death' appears also in 26.34 and 33.18, but apparently refers to a sin which merits capital punishment. See also *T. Iss.* 7.1, where 'sin unto death' includes—but is probably not limited to—adultery, lust, drunkenness, covetousness, and deceitfulness. Contrasting virtues are concern for the poor, integrity, truthfulness, and love for God and fellow human beings.

2 Translations are taken from G. Vermes, *The Dead Sea Scrolls in English* (2nd ed.; New York: Penguin, 1968).

pardon he may 'raise His angry face towards [them] for vengeance!' At first glance this appears to conflict with the more tolerant statement, 'For judgment of all the living is with God and it is He who will render to man his reward'. However, that same passage continues: 'I will not grapple with the men of perdition until the Day of Revenge, but my wrath shall not turn from the men of falsehood and I will not rejoice until judgment is made. I will bear no rancour against them that turn from transgression, but will have no pity on all who depart from the Way. I will offer no comfort to the smitten until their way becomes perfect; I will not keep Satan within my heart' (1QS 10.19-21).

Synthesis

In these passages, the intercessory prayer of the righteous person secures forgiveness of sin and often preserves the life of the sinner.[1] It can even be said that such intercession makes atonement. The intercessory prayers of those steadfastly faithful to God (Abraham, Noah, Enoch, Moses), were thought to be especially effective in entreating forgiveness. But in all cases it is assumed that the sinner has confessed and repented of his or her transgression.[2] There are regular assurances that such prayers are heard and that the sinner is forgiven. And, as a result, the penitent is said to receive life on this earth or in the hereafter.

But forgiveness always presupposes the repentance of the guilty party; for subsequent or continued sin or lack of repentance, God no longer holds back punishment. Moreover, in some instances of deliberate and continued sinning, intercession is expressly forbidden. In these cases it is clear that the very prohibition of intercessory prayer for the sinner is a part of God's judgment. Even the intercession of the most righteous does not atone for the unrepentant: either it is simply not offered (on the assumption that repentance is the necessary condition for receiving forgiveness) or it is explicitly forbidden. One also finds (e.g. at Qumran) the prayer that God may *not* forgive the wicked. That intercession does not avail is a sign of God's judgment. This is particularly clear in cases where it is forbidden, such as in

[1] There are of course other references to intercession and intercessors. Jacob's prayer saves the life of Reuben (*T. Reub.* 1.7; 4.4-6) and Gad (*T. Gad* 5.9-11). On angelic intercession, see Dan. 10.13, 21; 12.1; Tob. 12.12, 15; 2 Esdr. 4.1.; *T. Levi* 3.5-6; 5.6; *T. Dan* 6.1-2; *1 En.* 20.5, 89.76, 90.14.

[2] For prayers of confession and intercession, see 1 Kgs 8.33-34; Dan. 9.1-19; Bar. 1.10-3.8; *T. Sim.* 2.13; *m. Yoma* 3.8, 4.2, 6.2.

Jeremiah and *4 Ezra*, and in the repeated assertions that while God hears the poor, the humble, or the righteous (i.e. the penitent), he does not hear the wicked so as to forgive them.

The Interpretation of 1 John 5.16

How, then, does this material in John, in the OT, and in Jewish literature shed light on the interpretation of 1 John 5.16? In short, the ample evidence for the view that the righteous may not petition God for the forgiveness of the sins of the wicked and that the interdiction of such intercession manifests God's judgment offers a cogent conceptual framework in which a literal reading of 1 John 5.16b makes sense. Here, too, intercession for the forgiveness of sinners is understood to be ineffective and implicitly forbidden. A brother or sister in the community may pray for another. But intercession is not effective when undertaken outside the community of the faithful, when either the petitioner or the sinner who is prayed for cannot properly be called a 'brother' or 'sister'. This assertion needs to be unpacked.

We note, first, the definition of 'brother' or 'sister'. A 'brother' or fellow believer is characterized, among other things, by the acknowledgment of Jesus Christ come in the flesh (4.2) and by confession of sin (1.8-9).[1] Those who do not make these acknowledgments are not born of God, and hence not true brothers and sisters to those who are truly the children of God. In the historical context, the author has in view the secessionists from the Johannine community (see 1 Jn 2.18-19), who apparently withdrew because of differences with respect to spirituality and Christology. One of the charges the Elder implicitly makes against them is that they do not acknowledge their sin, and so seem to deny their need for an intercessor with the Father (1.6-2.2). Those who do not confess their sin do not receive God's forgiveness, and those who do not acknowledge Jesus Christ

---

[1] Bultmann [*Johannine Epistles*, p. 28] takes ἀδελφός as referring not to a fellow believer but to 'one's fellowman, the neighbor'. But few other commentators agree. Those who are 'brothers' and 'sisters' to each other are so because they are 'children of God', and the child of God is one who professes faith in Christ. See the discussion in Brown, *Epistles*, pp. 269-73. That the righteous are characterized by confession of sin is common in the Psalms and Proverbs, and is characteristic of the ethical tradition known as the doctrine of the ways. Cf. Ps. 32.1-5, 10-11; *T. Ash.* 1.6, 'if the soul wants to follow the good way, all of its deeds are done in righteousness and every sin is immediately repented'.

come in the flesh cannot appeal to him as an intercessor with the Father (2.1). Because they have rejected God's provision of forgiveness, intercession would serve no purpose.

This leads us directly to the thesis advanced by a number of scholars that the distinction between 'sin unto death' and 'sin that does not lead to death' is not so much a distinction between kinds of *sins* as it is a distinction between kinds of *sinners*.[1] Simply put, those who 'sin unto death' are not believers, while those whose 'sin is not unto death' are. While 1 John 5.16a states that it is a 'brother' or 'sister' committing the sin which does *not* lead to death, the verse does not say that it is a *brother*, that is, a fellow Christian, committing the sin which leads to death. Moreover, in the context of 1 John this seems impossible. For if 'sin unto death' is sin that leads to death and already provides evidence that one is even now in the realm of death, then a child of God cannot and does not 'sin unto death'. The child of God has been transferred from the realm of death and darkness to the realm of life and light (1 Jn 3.14). When the author notes that 'all wrongdoing is sin' (5.17), it is almost as if he were anticipating the question why those who have life nevertheless need intercession. Sin must still be confessed and forgiven. And where sin is acknowledged and confessed, it is also forgiven, and so does not lead to its natural end, to death. The intercessory prayers of Jesus and the community reaffirm to believers who sin that they do indeed have life.[2]

This leads us then to investigate the contention that intercession is not effective when the *petitioner* is not a brother or sister within the community.[3] Those within the community of the faithful have the

---

[1]Brown, *Epistles*, 617-18; R. Alan Culpepper, *1 John, 2 John, 3 John* (Knox Preaching Guides; Atlanta: Knox, 1985), p. 111; J.L. Houlden, *The Johannine Epistles* (HNTC; New York: Harper & Row, 1973), pp. 133-35; Robert Kysar, *I, II, III John* (Augsburg Commentary on the New Testament; Minneapolis: Augsburg Publishing House, 1986), pp. 114-15; Wolfgang Nauck, *Die Tradition und Charakter des ersten Johannesbriefes: Zugleich ein Beitrag zur Taufe im Urchristentum und in der alten Kirche* (WUNT 3; Tübingen: J.C.B. Mohr [Paul Siebeck] 1957), pp. 144-46; Scholer, 'Sins Within', p. 238. This interpretation also provides a solution to the problematic texts in 1 John which speak both of the sinfulness (1.6-2.2) and sinlessness (3.4-10; 5.18) of the children of God. See especially Scholer, 'Sins Within', the material cited in this article from *1 Enoch*, 4 Ezra, *Psalms of Solomon*, and the previous note.

[2]So Schnackenburg, *Die Johannesbriefe*, p. 276; Scholer, 'Sins Within', p. 240; and R. Seeberg, 'Die Sünden und Sündenvergebung nach dem ersten Briefe des Johannes', *Das Erbe Martin Luthers und die gegenwärtige theologische Forschung*, Festschrift für D. Ludwig Ihmels, ed. by R. Jelke (Leipzig, 1928), p. 27.

[3]On this point, see Scholer, 'Sins Within', p. 239; Nauck, *Charakter und Tradition*, pp. 145-46; and Strecker, *Die Johannesbriefe*, pp. 297-98.

confidence that 'if we ask anything according to [God's] will, he hears us'.[1] Just as Jesus was confident that God heard him always (Jn 11.42), so too faithful believers have the conviction that they are heard by God. Their relationship with God is such that they can be assured of God's faithful granting of their petitions.

The next question arises from the statement 'we have obtained the requests made of him'. What are the requests? What is asked for? According to the text, 'he will ask and he will give him life'. It seems logical to assume, then, that the petitioner asks for just that: that the sinner be given life.[2] Here we are reminded of John 17, where Jesus prayed that his followers be kept safe from the evil one (cf. 1 Jn 5.18). It is truly the will of God to give life to those who trust in the name of the Son of God (5.13), as well as to preserve them in life (5.18). The reminder that there is an effective intercessor, Jesus Christ the Righteous (2.1), and that the community of believers may likewise intercede for the sinner (5.16), serves to assure the believer of God's intent.

But even the faithful petitioner may not ask for forgiveness and life for those who do not believe in the name of the Son of God (5.13)—at least, not so long as they remain unrepentant and outside the fold of faith.[3] The author does not comment on any schismatics who returned to the fold, nor does he deny the possibility of their return.[4] Presumably if they did come back, confessed their sin, and trusted in the name of the son of God, they would be forgiven (1 Jn 1.9). It is just these 'conditions' which are assumed to exist in cases where intercession does avail.[5] By contrast, where there is no con-

---

[1]In this instance, the masculine pronoun probably refers to God, not to the Son of God named in v. 13.

[2]However, it would not be very different if we understood the petitioner to ask for forgiveness, for to receive forgiveness is to have life with God.

[3]See *m. Yom.* 8.9 which states that the Day of Atonement is ineffectual for deliberate and repeated sins.

[4]So also Schnackenburg, *Die Johannesbriefe*, p. 278; Scholer, 'Sins Within', p. 243. Strecker [*Die Johannesbriefe*, p. 298] overstates the case when he asserts that 'sin unto death' divides one from Christian fellowship, puts one under the final judgment of God, and prohibits return to the community.

[5]This may strike one as an odd proviso. But one notes the agony of a Jeremiah or the author(s) of *1 Enoch* when faced with the prospect of judgment upon the unrepentant sinners in their midst. We may speculate that in the Johannine community, where there must have been relatives and friends of the faithful among the secessionists, there would be the temptation to hope that God would suspend the rules and revoke judgment. The 'prohibition' against intercession in 5.16b reminds the readers of 1 John that there is forgiveness through Jesus, the Son of God—and only through Jesus. See also Klöpper, 'Lehre von der Sünde', esp. pp. 590-91.

fession of sin and no faith in Christ, one cannot presume upon the mercy of God for forgiveness. No one may intercede for life in these circumstances. For God's judgment falls on those who do not believe in the Son of God. Intercession must always be made in the light of God's saving activity in Jesus Christ.

In conclusion, 1 John 5.16 speaks of the role of the community in mediating God's forgiveness to each other. In this function it does not usurp the role of Christ as intercessor, but carries on the 'greater work' that he delegated to them, the work of carrying the message of forgiveness and salvation throughout the world. It may, then, seem strange that 1 John 5.16b acknowledges the role of the community in mediating judgment as well. But Christians offer a false hope when they offer forgiveness apart from Christ or apart from the repentance of the sinner. 1 John 5.16b does not deny the possibility of repentance nor forbid carrying the message of forgiveness to the sinner. Indeed, its denial of the efficacy of intercession for those who do not repent comes as a word of exhortation to both the Christian community and the unbeliever. But the promise that the community holds out is that 'If we confess our sins, God is faithful and just to forgive us our sins, and to cleanse us from all unrighteousness' (1 Jn 1.9).

Part III

Ministry

FAITH: THE ESSENTIAL INGREDIENT OF EFFECTIVE CHRISTIAN MINISTRY

Gerald F. Hawthorne

It is for me both a great pleasure and a distinct privilege to participate in a Festschrift honoring Professor Ralph P. Martin, a beloved man, who has devoted his life to the ministry of the church through his faith in God, his love and care for his family, his parish work, his writings, his teaching and his pastoral concern for his many students. I gladly salute this one whose very life incarnates the concept of ministry in and to the church.

In thinking now about the ministry of the early church it strikes me that one often overlooked and infrequently mentioned but nonetheless important ingredient is faith. Perhaps it is *the* essential ingredient that goes into making Christian ministry what it indeed is—a creative, many faceted, humble and devoted service offered to God for others, for the welfare of others (cf. Mt. 25.44). Notice that in 1 Thessalonians 1.3, where the triad, faith, hope and love, the quintessence of Christianity, is formulated for the first time (cf. also 1 Cor. 13.13; Col. 1.4-5), it is 'faith' that Paul places first in his description of the ministry that was being carried on by believers in Thessalonica. He wrote: 'We always give thanks to God for all of you . . . remembering . . . your *work of faith* (τοῦ ἔργου τῆς πίστεως), your labor of love and steadfastness in hope'. By the words, 'your work of faith', the apostle was not saying that he was thanking God because the Thessalonian Christians were working *at* their faith in order to promote its growth (although certainly he would have been filled with gratitude for that). Rather, Paul was saying that his thankfulness for them upon every remembrance of them was because their work, that is to say, their service, their ministry, in whatever form it took (cf. 1 Pet. 4.10), grew out of, sprang from, originated in their faith. What was it then that motivated them to do the work they did? What was it that put what they did in proper perspective? What gave meaning to their efforts? What made their ministry effective? Paul's answer is, 'faith'! Faith, even before love (although not without love), was for him the dynamism, the power, the creative force behind Christian service. He wrote again, 'The only thing that counts is faith working (πίστις . . . ἐργούμενη)' (Gal. 5.6). One might say, therefore, that the very nature of faith is productiveness, creativeness, generative power, and that its effect will be action, performance, creation, accomplishment. Thus any ministry or service, in the Christian understanding of 'ministry', can only truly be done through faith (πίστις).

And by faith as the fundamental, essential requirement for an effective Christian ministry I have in mind faith in God (cf. Mk 11.22).[1] But I do not mean a mere impersonal or intellectual acceptance of some doctrinal statement about God, but rather a personal experience of the living God (cf. Rom. 4.16-21), of the God who has completely and fully revealed himself in Jesus Christ (cf. Heb. 1.1-2; Acts 9.1-9). I mean by faith an existential assurance, a resolute confidence—the highest kind of knowledge—that this God exists and that he acts in history, in our histories (Heb. 11.6). I mean by faith a complete and loyal trust in God that carries the whole person with it and determines that person's character and action. I mean by faith that which gives eyes to the soul (cf. Heb. 11), so that the person of faith has the ability to see beyond the limiting barriers of matter and sense, and to penetrate the secret of spiritual reality, to see beyond human predicaments to God, and the goodness and wisdom and power of God, to see beyond the problems to the possibilities that God presents, to see beyond natural limitations to the limitlessness of the omnipotence of God, and to believe God for the solutions to life's problems, for making the possible a reality, for bursting the boundaries of human constrictions. Thus faith that is prerequisite for any

---

[1]This phrase, 'have faith in God', which is found nowhere else, is, according to C.S. Mann, 'grammatically barely defensible. Generally we have faith 'toward God' (Greek *pros ton theon*)—1 Thess 1.8—or 'in God' (Greek *epi theou*)—Heb 6.1—or a variant of 'in God' (*eis ton theon*)—John 14.1'. See C.S. Mann, *Mark* (AB; New York, 1986), p. 453. But Mann seems to have overlooked several places where the objective genitive— 'in something/as the object of something', occurs after πίστις (cf. Acts 3.16; Col. 2.12; 2 Thess. 2.13; and see also such texts as Rom. 3.22, 26; Gal. 2.16; Eph. 3.12; Phil. 1.27, 3.9 and Rev. 14.12).

effective ministry is that which knows God, 'sees' God, trusts God and sets no limits to the power of God.[1]

In order to illustrate what has been stated and to attempt to remove it from the realm of the theoretical, I turn now to a brief study of the life and ministry of Jesus, the supreme model for all the various kinds of ministry that later would be carried out in his name. And because of the limitations of space, I shall confine myself to only a single incident from among the many incidents of Jesus' ministry that could be used to illustrate the claim that faith in God is essential for effective service for God.

One must not, however, think that it is unreasonable to take Jesus as our model. Although it is possible, and necessary, to assert with the writers of the New Testament that Jesus was divine, the Logos, the Son of God, God even, yet it is equally possible, and necessary, for us to assert what these same writers imply in their letters—that in the mystery of the incarnation, God the Son chose to encapsulate his divinity *totally* within the confines of humanity, that he chose to make all his attributes of divinity latent, potential within these human confines (cf. Phil. 2.6-11), so that as a consequence he faced life *precisely* like any other human person faces life: limited physically and mentally, dependent on others, subject to all sorts of temptations (even to the temptation to doubt?), unshielded from weakness and weariness, susceptible to frustrations and vexations, vulnerable to death.[2] Hence,

---

[1] 'Faith is the assertion of a possibility against all probabilities, in spite of any contrary indication provided by our experience of life or the realities of the world, and in constant battle against temptation (Mk 9.23). What is it that differentiates this faith from mere illusion, which breaks down upon the hard rock of reality? It is not a faith which reaches vaguely into the void, but one that firmly trusts [God]. Such a faith has nothing else than [God] in the middle of a world which scoffs at all our hopes and fears. It fastens on to [God] with all the strength at its command, and if the demonic power of the storm becomes overpowering, then the last resources of [our] nature give vent to the cry, "Lord, I believe; help thou mine unbelief". . . .' E. Stauffer, *New Testament Theology* (New York, 1955), pp. 168-69. See also G.E. Ladd, *A Theology of the New Testament* (Grand Rapids, 1974), p. 270; R. Bultmann, *Theology of the New Testament* (New York, 1951), I, pp. 314-24; Idem, 'πιστεύω, κ.τ.λ.', *TDNT*, VI, pp. 203-28; H.M. Shires, 'Faith', in *Dictionary of the Bible* (ed. J. Hastings; rev. ed. F.C. Grant and H.H. Rowley; New York, 1963), pp. 288-90; O. Michel, 'Faith', *NIDNTT*, II, pp. 599-605.

[2] See B. Hebblethwaite, *The Incarnation* (Cambridge, 1987), pp. 1-10, 21-26; A. Farrer, 'Very God and Very Man', in C. Conti (ed.), *Interpretation and Belief* (London, 1976); P.T. Forsyth, *The Person and Place of Jesus Christ* (London, 1909); H.R. Mackintosh, *The Doctrine of the Person of Jesus Christ* (Edinburgh, 1912); O.C. Quick, *Christian Beliefs and Modern Questions* (London, 1923), pp. 53-74; idem, *Doctrines of the Creed* (London, 1938), pp. 146-83. I also have written about this elsewhere in far greater detail than can be presented here: see, G.F. Hawthorne, *The*

Jesus is indeed one of us. He stands alongside us, on a plane with us, to show us the way to go, the way to live, the way in which to carry out that particular ministry God has given us in order that we might carry it through to completion.

It is not necessary here to go into detail concerning proofs for the genuineness of Jesus' humanity, but for the study at hand it will be useful to point out that one of these proofs is the fact that Jesus was a person of faith.[1] He, like us, was dependent upon God his Father for the success of his ministry. He trusted God unwaveringly, even though very likely he (as we) at times was assailed by temptations to doubt God. The New Testament will not allow this fact that Jesus was a person of faith to pass unnoticed. For example, one of the New Testament writers readily describes Jesus as 'the pioneer and perfector of our faith' (Heb. 12.2), the person of faith *par excellence*. 'This', writes Philip Hughes, 'seems to be the primary sense of the Greek original [in Heb. 12.2] . . . [Jesus'] whole earthly life is the very embodiment of trust in God (Heb. 2.13). It is marked from start to finish by total dependence on the Father and complete attunement to his will (10.7-10) . . . In looking to Jesus, then, we are looking to him who is the supreme exponent of faith, the one who, beyond all others, not only set out on the course of faith but also pursued it without wavering to the end'.[2]

Having made these remarks about ministry, faith and the person of Jesus, I wish now to show how these all converge in a single narrative from the life of Jesus to support the thesis that faith is fundamental, absolutely essential, for an effective Christian ministry.[3] The narrative is the story of the 'Epileptic Boy' (Mk 9.14-29, Mt. 17.14-10; Lk. 9.37-43a). It is told most fully and graphically by Mark in his inimitable story-telling fashion, distilled into its essentials by Matthew and Luke, and placed by each of the synoptic writers immediately after the transfiguration of Jesus. Its *dramatis personae* include Jesus, his disciples, a crowd of people, some scribes and the tragic figures of an

---

Presence and the Power: The Significance of the Holy Spirit in the Life and Ministry of Jesus (Dallas, 1991).

[1]R. Butterworth, 'Bishop Robinson and Christology', *RelS* 11 (1975), pp. 81-82, was quick to point this out in his reaction to J.A.T. Robinson's *The Human Face of God* (London, 1973).

[2]P.E. Hughes, *A Commentary on the Epistle to the Hebrews* (Grand Rapids, 1977), pp. 522-23.

[3]The idea for this thesis I owe to Ralph Martin himself, who first set my mind to work by a casual remark he penned in a personal note dated 22 April, 1991, and subsequently by his all too brief but quite to the point comments to be found in his important little book, *Mark* (J.H. Hayes, ed.; Knox Preaching Guides; Atlanta, 1981), pp. 56-57—a gift from him.

unidentified man and his son. Both father and son are in torment; the father because of the illness of his son, and the son because he is tortured by a destructive spirit that renders him unable to speak, that seizes him and dashes him down and causes him to foam and grind his teeth, that convulses him and mauls him and tries to cast him into fire and water. Jesus learns all this from the father who is on his knees before him (Matthew), begging him to look with favor on this his only child (Luke). Jesus learns some additional disturbing news from the father as well. He learns that this suffering boy was brought to his disciples while he was not present with them, in order that they might exorcise the spirit and heal him, but that they could not do so! Yet these were the disciples to whom Jesus himself had given authority over unclean spirits, to cast them out, and authority to cure every disease and every sickness (Mt. 10.1). In spite of the fact that Jesus had bestowed such authority upon them, they could not give relief to this child. Whatever detail one or another of the synoptic writers may have left out in the telling of the story, this is one particularly painful detail that none of them felt could appropriately be omitted from the narrative. Each has the courage to state the impotence of the disciples in the face of this extraordinarily difficult situation. None of them refrains from showing up the disciples' inability to carry out their ministry of healing when they encountered this battered child and its father who had begged them to heal him. Why did they fail? Why were they impotent? Why were they unable to effect the cure?

The answer lies in the immediate response of Jesus spoken to his disciples[1] in words that seem to carry overtones of disappointment,

---

[1]Since neither Matthew nor Luke provide any direct object for the participle ἀποκριθείς ('answered'), and Mark provides only the ambiguous pronoun αὐτοῖς ('them'), many commentators are hesitant to be as precise as I in assigning Jesus' rebuke solely to the disciples. See H. Anderson, *The Gospel of Mark* (NCB; Grand Rapids, 1976), p. 230; E.P. Gould, *A Critical and Exegetical Commentary on the Gospel According to St. Mark* (ICC; Edinburgh, 1896), p. 168; Mann, *Mark*, p. 370, C.F.D. Moule, *The Gospel According to Mark* (Cambridge, 1965); A.E.J. Rawlinson, *St. Mark* (London, 1925), p. 124; H.B. Swete, *The Gospel According to St. Mark* (Grand Rapids, 1956 repr.), p. 198; V. Taylor, *The Gospel According to St. Mark* (London, 1957), p. 398. And yet the context seems to demand that Jesus' words be directed towards his disciples—the crowd has long since been forgotten, the father cannot be censured for having no faith, since he brought his child here for help, and it is the disciples, those people who had been with Jesus, endowed by him with gifts of healing, taught by him to trust God, who had failed. This was not the first time that lack of faith on their part and the perversity of their hearts had been the objects of rebuke by Jesus (cf. Mk 4.40; 8.17-18). Cf. also C.E.B. Cranfield, *The Gospel According to Saint Mark* (Cambridge, 1972), p. 301 and W.L. Lane, *The Gospel According to Mark* (Grand Rapids, 1974), p. 332.

weariness, frustration, and anger: 'You faithless [ἄπιστος] generation, how much longer must I be among you? How much longer must I put up with you?' (NRSV). With these stabbing remarks Jesus seems to be saying to his disciples, 'You people have no faith! You have failed to take God into the equation. You have focused on the problem and have been daunted by its severity. You have lost sight of the possibilities that are open to you because of the limitless power of God. You are people who have allowed your thinking and acting to be twisted, distorted, turned in the wrong direction (διεστραμμένη)[1] by the human predicament and not by the divine potential. What more can I do ? What more can I say? I have not long to be with you, to teach you, to show you, to make it clear to you that faith, faith in God, is the key to an effective ministry'—I seem to hear all of this in these few pain-filled words of a disappointed Jesus recorded in each of the synoptic gospels.

The narrative then proceeds, hurriedly and immediately in Matthew and Luke, much less so in Mark, to show that Jesus *was able* to cast out the demon, the unclean spirit, and to cure the lad (Mt. 17.18; Lk. 9.42; Mk 9.25-27)—to do precisely what the disciples could not do. Why was it possible for Jesus to do this and the disciples not? Because one was divine and the other human? Because Jesus was God and the disciples were men? I hardly think that this is the answer, for the inference ready to be drawn from these gospel accounts is that Jesus succeeded where his disciples failed, because he had faith and they did not. In essence the evangelists say that the disciples saw the chronic (ἐκ παιδιόθεν) condition of a severely damaged and perhaps grossly disfigured boy, and their faith failed them. The language of the gospel writers leaves it open to us to suspect that they may have never even tried to cure this patient. They had had a good deal of experience in exorcisms, but they may have felt at once that this case was beyond them, and they may have failed to make the necessary effort.[2] They could not heal the boy because they did not believe. But Jesus, on the other hand, believed that God would cure the child through him (cf Acts 2.22). He saw that same seemingly hopeless case of a nearly destroyed human person, but he looked

---

[1]To Mark's ἄπιστος ('faithless'), Matthew and Luke, and W, P^{45} in Mark, add the adjectival participle διεστραμμένη ('perverse, distorted, twisted,wrong-headed'), possibly borrowed from Deut. 32.5.

[2]T.H. Robinson, *The Gospel of Matthew* (London, 1928), p. 148.

beyond that tragic situation to God, and by faith in God he was made keenly aware of the immenseness of the divine power that was readily available to him through the Holy Spirit by which he could heal. He was thus able to effectively fulfill his ministry because of his faith. The disciples were unable to do so because of their lack of faith.

Matthew draws this conclusion at the very end of his story about the sick child (17.19-20). He tells us that the disciples came to Jesus when they were alone, away from the crowd and away from the boy and his father, and asked him, 'Why could we not cast [the demon] out?' Jesus' answer was simple, and it underscores our thesis—'[You could not carry out the ministry of exorcism and healing that was entrusted to you] because you have so little faith (ὀλιγοπιστίαν ὑμῶν)',[1] i.e. because you have so little faith in God that it amounts to no faith at all (ἀπιστίαν).[2] In effect he was saying that when confronted with this particularly vicious species of demon, their assurance, their trust, their confidence in God and in the superior power of God to any and every destructive force that exists in the world, had vanished. At the same time, when Jesus answered this question that the disciples asked about the ineffectiveness of their ministry in terms of faith—'*your* so little faith, *your* lack of faith'—he was also forcefully, yet gently and humbly, stating, paradoxically by not putting his statement into words, what is nevertheless clearly implied in his apocopated response, that his ministry, on the other hand, was effective because of *his* faith, *his* confidence and trust in the God of the impossible.

Mark draws the same conclusion, but does it differently from Matthew. He does not make the point of the disciples' lack of faith, and of Jesus' faith quite as clearly as Matthew at the end of his story

---

1 'Ολιγοπιστίαν was perhaps chosen to soften the severity of Jesus' rebuke, even though its choice tended to create a paradox by the words that follow which teach that faith, even a little faith, can achieve the impossible.

2 Some scribes apparently understood what Jesus had to say to his disciples in precisely this way—ὀλιγοπιστίαν in the sense of 'no faith', for ἀπιστίαν actually appears in the MSS tradition (C D L W, the Majority Text as well as several ancient versions). The adjective ὀλιγόπιστος is decidedly a Matthean word, used by Matthew 4 of the 5 times it appears in the NT (6.30; 8.26; 14.31; 16.8), and each time it is used it seems to imply, not that the ones so addressed had a little faith, but that they had none at all. And as T.H. Robinson says, 'faith is always of the same quality and efficiency. The point is that if the disciples had had any at all, even the smallest quantity, they would be superior to all ordinary limitations and conditions' (*Matthew*, p. 148).

(although it is certainly implicit there as well).[1] Rather, he makes this point earlier on in his amplified version of the cure. There, according to Mark, when the evil spirit that possessed the boy saw Jesus it immediately convulsed him, throwing him to the ground and causing him to roll about foaming at the mouth. Then after what seemed like endless delay during which Jesus asked diagnostic questions, the desperate father, unable to contain himself any longer, cried out, addressing himself directly to Jesus and to no one else, with these pathetic words: 'If *you* [*you*, not your disciples] are able (δύνῃ) to do anything, please help us! Please have pity on us!' (9.22). Jesus seems quite startled or surprised by the way this plea for help is worded, for his response to it is not an immediate act of healing, but an instantaneous reply in words of instruction that burst from him in an extremely compressed form, one that has given trouble both to ancient copyists[2] and to interpreters of the text. His reply has been variously interpreted in the translations, 'If thou canst believe, all things are possible to him that believeth' (KJV); 'Yes . . . if *you* can! Everything is possible for the person who has faith' (GNB); '"If You can!" All things are possible to him who believes' (NASB); '"If you can"? . . . Everything is possible for him who believes' (NIV); 'If you are able!—All things can be done for the one who believes' (NRSV).

One of these, the Authorized Version, based on an inferior textual reading (εἰ δύνῃ [δύνασαι] πιστεῦσαι, πάντα δυνατὰ τῷ πιστεύοντι) shifts the subject of the verb, 'can/are able', from Jesus to the father, as though by his reply Jesus was putting the blame on the father for the continued illness of his son—as though Jesus were saying, 'It is not a question of whether or not I can do anything, but a question of whether or not you can believe'. And the other versions cited above still have the potential of leaving the English reader with the same wrong impression as that most clearly articulated by the

[1] At the end of this pericope in Mark, where the disciples question Jesus as to why they were unable to cast out the demon, his reply to them was that it was because of their lack of prayer (9.28-29). If this was the original answer of Jesus to their question, and Matthew changed it to read, 'because of your so little faith', Matthew nevertheless did not distort the meaning of Jesus, but simply clarified it. For to attempt to exorcise spirits of such malignity, had they tried to do so, without prayer, was to rely on whatever quasi-magical powers they thought that they themselves possessed, and not on God, and the power of God. Prayer is the expression of faith considered as dependence on the divine power and confidence in that power. (See, Gould, *Mark* , p. 171).

[2] τὸ εἰ δύνασαι πιστεῦσαι is read by A Ψ and the Majority Text; εἰ δύνῃ (–νασαι) πιστεῦσαι is read by D K Θ; εἰ δύνῃ is read by P[45] W; τὸ εἰ δύνῃ, πάντα δυνατὰ τῷ πιστεύοντι is read by ℵ B C L N Δ.

Authorized Version, even though they are based on a superior manuscript tradition (τὸ εἰ δύνῃ, πάντα δυνατὰ τῷ πιστεύοντι), and are the result of great effort and ingenuity by translators who worked diligently to convey in all kinds of different ways (italics, capitalization, exclamation marks, question marks, dashes, etc.) the proper meaning of this saying of Jesus. One can while reading these translations still all too easily come to the conclusion that for Jesus the father is at fault for failing to believe!

But in my judgment, at this point in the narrative, Jesus' reply was not intended to place the blame on anyone for failure to cure the child—not on his disciples (he had already taken pains to do that), and certainly not on the father. By this reply Jesus is not telling the father that if only *he* can believe all things are possible (KJV). Rather, he is responding positively and with encouragement to the father's desperate words, 'If you can do anything, help us, have pity on us' (9.22).

Let me see if I can make this clear: the Greek definite article (τό) that is used to introduce Jesus' reply is at the same time both the problem and the solution to the problem, a truly important element in his answer that is impossible to translate properly except by a somewhat elaborate paraphrase. It is a word of introduction and in a construction such as this it acts as 'a combination of quotation marks and an exclamation'.[1] By its use Jesus is in effect saying to the father of the boy, 'So far as the "If you are able" is concerned I tell you all things are possible to the one who believes', or, 'What is this, "If you can do anything?" Don't you know that all things are possible to the one who has faith in God!'[2]

And by saying this or by asking this question in response to the father's plea I do not think that Jesus was *primarily* stating that everything can be done for anyone who has faith, thereby providing a general remark that is applicable to any and all Christian believers (although I do not wish to rule this out as a possible secondary meaning).

Nor, as suggested earlier, do I think that by his reply Jesus was turning the tables on the man—'You say to me, "If you are able to do anything, help us!" But I say to you, "If you are able to believe, you

[1]Mann, *Mark*, p. 370; Taylor, *Mark*, p. 399.

[2]BDF 267.1, and note Goodspeed's translation here: [The father said], '. . .But if there is anything you can do, take pity on us and help us!' Jesus said to him, '"If there is anything I can do!" Everything is possible for one who has faith'.

can help yourself!"'—for the father already has faith. He immediately responds with the words, 'I believe!' And although he adds, 'Help my unbelief!' he was not saying 'help me to turn my unbelief into belief', but 'help me out of my trouble, in spite of any unbelief that you may find in me'. The man already believes, but he does not rest his case there. 'He pleads the compassion of Jesus, instead of his own faith, and so unconsciously show[s] a genuine faith'.[1]

Rather, in this reply to the father's plea for compassion and help I hear Jesus, first and foremost, laying claim to being precisely that person who believes God and thus to being that person to whom nothing is impossible. When he said, 'So far as the "If you are able" is concerned I tell you that all things are possible to the person who has faith', he was in effect saying, 'What is this "If you are able" business?—Of course I am able! Of course I can cure your son! You have said it! And why is this so? Why am I able to do this? Because I have faith that God can heal him through me. I am trusting God to destroy the powers that are bent on destroying your son. I am the one who believes (τῷ πιστεύοντι) God, and all things can be done for the one who believes!' Professor Martin has it quite right to my thinking and has expressed it clearly and eloquently. He wrote,

> Normally we are quick to apply this tribute to the power of faith in reference to the Christian believer: if we believe, then all things are possible. I think that in its original setting it referred to Jesus, the man of faith who is claiming the confidence to see the boy healed on the ground that he trusts his heavenly Father to work through him. We get a fresh insight into Jesus' own life of trust here.[2]

The gospel writers tell us that Jesus' ministry was that of being God's servant in a wounded, broken, sick, impoverished, darkened world. He was sent by his Father into this world to preach God's good news to it, to mend its broken, to heal its sick, to bind up the wounds of its wounded, to open the eyes of its blind, to liberate its oppressed, to enrich its poor (cf. Lk. 4.18-19). And we look back over the record of that ministry, in a sense distilled for us in this story, to discover that he completed it successfully, that he fully accomplished what he was commissioned to do, not because he was God (though I believe the New Testament asserts that he was), but

---

[1]Gould, *St. Mark*, p. 170.
[2]Martin, *Mark*, p. 56.

rather because he was a truly human person who believed God to make his ministry effective.[1]

Jesus said to us, to his followers, 'As the Father has sent me, even so I send you' (Jn 20.21). Jesus thus calls us and sends us, as the Father had sent him, into this same broken world to continue his ministry of binding, restoring, healing, helping, building, saving. And he calls us to do this by sharing his faith in God and in the limitless energy of God. For like Jesus our ministry can only be effective by faith, by counting on God to do these totally impossible things through us. Faith was *the* essential ingredient for an effective ministry in the life of Jesus, in the life of the early Church, and so it is and will continue to be in ours.

---

[1]Perhaps it is necessary to be reminded from time to time that a statement of Jesus such as 'all things are possible to the one who believes' (Mk 9.23) must never be allowed to foster the idea that we can get anything, or do anything, simply by saying we believe, or that belief/faith is a device by which we can manipulate God so as to get what we may want, or even what someone else may want. Faith, rather, gives us the 'eyes' by which we see God, the 'understanding' by which we are able to comprehend who God is and what his program for the world is and how we fit into that program, and the 'will' by which we submit ourselves to him and to his vast program of restoration. The expression, 'The one who believes', envisions those who wholly trust God, completely depend on God, have total confidence in God, and trust that God is powerfully at work in and through them to effect his grand purposes of overthrowing the forces of evil and destruction. The saying, 'all things are possible to the one who believes', thus does not mean that 'faith can do anything', but rather that 'the one who has faith will set no limits to the power of God' (Rawlinson, *Mark*, p. 124). It is not a call 'to "put God to the test" by irresponsible prayer for what is our human desire but may not be His will. We are free to ask what we will, but only if it be what He wills (I Jn v. 14). This is no mere theological quibble: it is a statement in another form of the need for the "mind of Christ" in us. It is also a warning against taking a statement of Scripture in isolation, and basing presumptuous prayer on it' (R.A. Cole, *The Gospel According to St. Mark* [Grand Rapids, 1961], p. 147).

THE PRICE PAID FOR A MINISTRY AMONG GENTILES: PAUL'S PERSECUTION AT THE HANDS OF THE JEWS

Colin G. Kruse

Introduction

Paul's ministry among the Gentiles was one which, by his own confession, cost him dearly. It involved labours and imprisonment, physical danger and persecution, as well as anxiety for all the churches (2 Cor. 11.23-29). Persecution constituted a very large part of the price he had to pay for conducting a mission among the Gentiles, and he paid it throughout his ministry. His experience of persecution began when an attempt was made to arrest him in Damascus (2 Cor. 11.32-33) and continued through until his imprisonment(s) in Rome.

The persecution came from Jews, Gentiles and from false brethren (2 Cor. 11.26). But it was the persecution from fellow Jews which he mentioned most frequently in his letters, suggesting this was what he found the hardest to bear. He responded to it with hostility on one occasion (1 Thess. 2.14-16), but his more characteristic response appears to have been concern for those from among whom it emanated. His heart's desire for the Jews, he said, was that they might be saved (Rom. 10.1). He hoped that his ministry among the Gentiles might stir the Jews to jealousy and so lead to their salvation (Rom. 11.13-14). And while his own evangelistic efforts were directed primarily towards the Gentiles, that did not prevent him from engaging in a ministry to Jews as well. He became like a Jew to save Jews (1 Cor. 9.21). The salvation of his fellow countrymen, he said, was something for which he himself would be prepared to be accursed from Christ (Rom. 9.3).

The purpose of this essay is to document the extent of the references and allusions in the Pauline corpus to the price Paul paid in terms of persecution at the hands of the Jews, and to explore the clues available there as to why this price was extracted.

The Price Paul Paid

Virtually all the letters of the Pauline corpus contain some reference to the persecution he suffered in carrying out his mission to the Gentiles, and several contain either specific references or allusions to the persecution he experienced at the hands of fellow Jews.

1 Thessalonians

Several statements in the letter reflect indirectly the persecution experienced by Paul and Silas in Thessalonica. In 2.2 he reminded his readers that he preached the gospel in Thessalonica 'in spite of strong opposition', and in 2.3-12 we see that he felt the need to defend his good name against malicious slander there. Paul's abrupt and premature departure from Thessalonica may be reflected in his references to being torn away from them for a short time (2.17), his intense desire to see them again (2.17) and his inability to stand any longer the lack of news about them (3.1). In the light of Paul's outburst against the Jews found in 2.14-16 (see below), all the statements just mentioned probably reflect, in one way or another, the Jewish opposition that he experienced in Thessalonica.

In his hostile outburst against the Jews in 2.14-16, Paul highlighted four aspects of violent Jewish opposition to the gospel and its messengers: (i) they persecuted the churches of Judea; (ii) they killed the Lord Jesus (and the prophets); (iii) they drove out Paul and his colleagues, and (iv) they kept them from speaking to the Gentiles. It is the third and fourth aspects of persecution that call for further comment here.

They drove us out (2.15). The Acts 17.1-10 account of Paul's ministry in Thessalonica is the best explanation we have of what he might have meant by saying the Jews 'drove us out'. It tells us that his ministry was brought to an abrupt end by jealous Jews. They recruited ruffians to gather a mob to drag Paul and Silas from Jason's house and make them appear before the town assembly. When they failed to find them, they dragged Jason himself before the town magistrates instead, accusing him of harbouring men who flouted the emperor's laws. The magistrates required Jason to give security before they would release him. The net result was that Paul and Silas were forced to leave Thessalonica. Such an action on the part of the Thessalonian Jews, could well have been what Paul alluded to when he said they 'drove us out'.

They kept us from speaking to the Gentiles (2.16). This is one of two references Paul made in this letter to being hindered from doing what he wished.[1] In the second (which follows on immediately from the first) Paul spoke of Satan thwarting his repeated efforts to see the Thessalonians again (2.17-18). It may be that the reference to the Jews keeping him from speaking to the Gentiles, and the reference to Satan stopping him from making a return visit, are both connected with the security taken from Jason (Acts 17.9). He was accused of harbouring Paul and Silas, men believed to be defying Caesar's decrees (Act 17.7), and was only released when he gave 'security', i.e. paid a bond to guarantee that he would not harbour them again.[2] This would have meant that Paul and Silas could not continue their preaching in Thessalonica nor make a return visit there without placing Jason in an invidious position. If this was the case, Paul's hostile reaction towards the Jews in 2.14-16 is understandable, even though it might reflect a failure by the standards of Christian charity.

Galatians

The letter to the Galatians is concerned primarily with the opposition Paul experienced from Judaizers, not Jews. Nevertheless, it contains a number of statements which reflect Paul's attitude to his fellow countrymen, and in particular two statements which relate to persecution experienced at their hands.

---

[1]Different verbs are used (κωλύω in v. 16 and ἐγκόπτω in v. 18), but they overlap in their range of meanings. In both cases the range includes the idea of hindering in the sense of preventing or thwarting some desired action.

[2]The taking of security (ἱκανός) is generally interpreted by recent commentators as a reference to Jason's being bound over, with financial sanctions, to guarantee that Paul and Silas would leave and not return to the city. This may explain why they consented to leave and why Paul felt he could not return. Cf. e.g. Colin J. Hemer, *The Book of Acts in the Setting of Hellenistic History* (Tübingen: J.C.B. Mohr, 1989), p. 186.

The son born in the ordinary way persecuted the son born by the power of the Spirit (4.29). Paul concluded his theological arguments against the Judaizers' teaching with an allegorical interpretation of the Hagar-Sarah story (4.21-31). The two women, Hagar and Sarah, represented two covenants. Hagar represented the covenant from Sinai, which corresponded to the present Jerusalem which was in slavery along with all its children. Sarah represented (it is implied) the covenant from Zion, which corresponded to the Jerusalem above which is free (along with all its children).

Paul made two explicit applications of this allegory to the situation in Galatia. The first was to show that those who put their faith in Christ without any reliance upon works of the law were children of the promise like Sarah's son Isaac; they were Abraham's true children (4.28, 31). The second was to show that just as Hagar's son, born in the ordinary way, persecuted Sarah's son,[1] born by the power of the Spirit, so too the present day Jews were persecuting Paul and those who accepted his law-free gospel. It is true that the Judaizers were Paul's primary target in Galatians, but the logic within the allegory itself implies a comparison between unbelieving Jews and law-free Christians. The Judaizers who 'troubled' the Galatians were then being cast as virtually the same as unbelieving Jews who persecuted law-free believers. Thus Gal. 4.29 also reflects Paul's experience of persecution by the Jews.

Persecuted for not preaching circumcision (5.11). In response to claims made by the Judaizers, Paul asked the rhetorical question: 'If I am still preaching circumcision, why am I still being persecuted?' (5.11). This question is a *crux interpretum* for the exegesis of Galatians, and its implications for the understanding of the Galatian situation have been much debated.[2] However, one thing is clear:

---

[1]Gen. 16.4, 6 mentions Hagar's contempt for Sarah (and Sarah's harsh treatment of Hagar), but makes no mention of Ishmael persecuting Isaac. However, the Targums (esp. Targum of pseudo-Jonathan at Gen 22) speak of tension between Ishmael and Isaac. Cf. Michael G. Steinhauser, 'Gal 4,25a: Evidence of Targumic Tradition in Gal 4,21-31?', *Bib* 70 (1989), pp. 234-40; Lloyd Gaston, 'Israel's Enemies in Pauline Theology', *NTS* 28 (1982), pp. 406-07; Hans Dieter Betz, *Galatians: A Commentary on Paul's Letter to the Churches in Galatia* (Hermeneia; Philadelphia: Fortress, 1979), pp. 248-49. If Paul was using an *ad hominem* argument, picking up his opponents' own exegetical assumptions in order to turn them against them, then we should not necessarily assume that he accepted the truth of the targumic tradition he used.

[2]Cf. e.g. Peder Borgen, 'Paul Preaches Circumcision and Pleases Men', *Paul and Paulinism: Essays in Honour of C.K. Barrett*, eds. M.D. Hooker and S.G. Wilson (London: SPCK, 1982), pp. 37-41;

when Paul wrote Galatians he was still suffering persecution for not preaching circumcision. This is best understood as persecution emanating from Jews who were incensed at reports that Paul was relaxing the demands of the law in his preaching in the Diaspora (cf. Acts 21.28; 23.29).[1]

2 Corinthians

It is 2 Corinthians which reveals, more than any other Pauline letter, the price the apostle paid for his ministry among the Gentiles. The catalogue of sufferings in 11.23-33 is of particular interest in this respect. Not least among the sufferings Paul catalogued there were those he experienced at the hands of fellow Jews. Three references call for comment.

The forty lashes minus one (11.24). Claiming that he had been flogged more often than his opponents, Paul referred to beatings received at the hands of both Jews and Gentiles. He had been beaten three times with rods by the Gentiles, and received the forty lashes minus one five times at the hands of the Jews.[2] Nothing more clearly reflects the fact that Paul suffered persecution from his fellow countrymen than his admission that he had received the judicial synagogue flogging five times.[3] Of course, what Paul regarded as 'persecution'

George Howard, *Paul: Crisis in Galatia. A Study in Early Christian Theology* (SNTSMS 35; Cambridge: CUP, 1979), pp. 8-10; Francis Watson, *Paul, Judaism and the Gentiles: A Sociological Approach* (SNTSMS 56; Cambridge: CUP, 1986), p. 30.

[1]Martin Hengel, *The Zealots. An Investigation into the Jewish Freedom Movement in the Period from Herod I until 70 A.D.* (ET; Edinburgh: T. & T. Clark, 1989), pp. 197-200, shows how compulsory circumcision was part of the program of zeal for the law and the sanctuary of the Zealot movement of the period. Robert Jewett, 'The Agitators and the Galatian Congregation', *NTS* 17 (1970-71), pp. 204-206, builds on Hengel's work by suggesting that it was fear of the Zealot movement that motivated the agitators in Galatia to demand that Paul's converts be circumcised.

[2]Sven Gallas, '"Fünfmal vierzig weniger einen . . ." Die an Paulus vollzogenen Synagogalstrafen nach 2 Kor 11,24', *ZNW* 81 (1990), pp. 178-91, discusses the information available concerning scourging in the rabbinic literature (esp. *m. Mak.* 3.1-8), and provides details of the grounds upon which a person could be scourged, as well as the procedures, place, instrument and physical effects of scourging.

[3]When these floggings took place is a matter of debate. Did they occur in the early part of Paul's career, in the 'silent years' about which we know little? If so, it is unlikely that Paul's ministry was restricted at that time to Jews alone (contra Watson, *Paul, Judaism and the Gentiles*, p. 28), for Paul says his commission to preach to the Gentiles was received right back at the time of his conversion (Gal. 1.15-16). It seems, therefore, more likely that Paul carried on a limited mission to Jews alongside his primary mission to the Gentiles. Perhaps his reference to becoming like a Jew to win Jews in 1 Cor. 9.20 reflects such an ongoing ministry among Jews (along the lines described

on account of his loyalty to the gospel, the Jews would have seen as 'punishment' for his disloyalty to Judaism. The fact that he was so punished by them suggests that for their part the Jews still regarded him as one within the fold of Judaism, and so worth punishing. For his part it meant that he had not abandoned Judaism, despite the persecution he experienced.[1]

In danger from my own countrymen (11.26). Paul's constant missionary itineration involved him in many dangers. Among these was what he called 'danger from my own countrymen'. This needs little comment. It is simply one more piece of evidence of how heavy the burden of persecution by his own people was for him.

The flight from Damascus (11.30-33). Paul introduced his brief account of this experience with an oath formula, by which he emphasized the truthfulness of what he recounted (11.31). The modern reader might wonder why this little adventure received so much emphasis, and why Paul listed it among 'the things that show my weakness' (11.30). Did it not show rather how he was able to outwit those who wanted to seize him? But in Paul's day such an experience would be seen as humiliating retreat, and render him the object of ridicule.[2]

Perhaps the reason is that this experience of persecution had impressed indelibly upon Paul's mind just how vulnerable and weak he had now become. It was his first experience of persecution for the sake of the gospel. In his pre-conversion days he had persecuted the church of God; something which, more than anything else from his past, caused him to suffer remorse (cf. 1 Cor. 15.9; 1 Tim. 1.13). But with his conversion his persecution of believers ceased, and his own persecution by unbelieving Jews began. Immediately the shoe was on the other foot. Now, as the object of persecution, he was forced to flee from the city of Damascus which he had approached so boldly before.

in Acts). See discussion in Ralph P. Martin, *2 Corinthians* (WBC 40; Waco: Word, 1986), pp. 376-77.

[1]E.P. Sanders, *Paul, the Law, and the Jewish People* (Philadelphia: Fortress, 1983), p. 192, makes the point that *'punishment implies inclusion'*.

[2]Martin, *2 Corinthians*, pp. 371-72; 384-85, sees Paul's description of his ignominious escape from Damascus as an implied contrast with the dignity of the soldier who, in storming an enemy city, was the first over the wall, and was therefore awarded the *corona muralis*.

There are two accounts of the escape from Damascus, Paul's own account here in 2 Corinthians and another in Acts:

> In Damascus the governor under King Aretas had the city of the Damascenes guarded in order to arrest me. But I was lowered in a basket from a window in the wall and slipped through his hands (2 Cor. 11.32-33).

> After many days had gone by, the Jews conspired to kill him, but Saul learned of their plan. Day and night they kept close watch on the city gates in order to kill him. But his followers took him by night and lowered him in a basket through an opening in the wall (Acts 9.23-25).

The main similarities (lowered in a basket, through a window/opening in the wall) and differences (King Aretas sought to arrest; the Jews sought to kill) between the two accounts of what must have been one incident are well-known. Paul's first hand account in 2 Corinthians must take precedence over that of Acts. But if we allow the latter to inform the former,[1] we have further evidence of Jewish attempts on Paul's life; attempts which on this occasion came to nothing.

Romans

In ch. 8 Paul wrote generally about the sufferings experienced by the children of God in the present age (vv. 17-25, 35-36), and in ch. 15 he revealed something of his foreboding about further persecution at the hand of the Jews. He was about to make his journey to Jerusalem with the collection for the saints, and felt it necessary to ask the Roman believers to pray that he might be 'rescued from the unbelievers in Judea' (v. 31). The events which, according to Acts 21.27-36, took place there show that his fears were not groundless.

2 Timothy

In this letter Timothy is reminded of the persecutions which Paul endured in Antioch, Iconium and Lystra (3.11). According to Acts, in each of these three cities Paul suffered at the hands of the Jews. In Antioch they were jealous because of the crowd's attention to Paul, and so they spoke abusively against him (Acts 13.45). This had little effect upon the success of his ministry, for the word of God was

---

[1]By assuming, e.g. that the Jews had succeeded in getting the governor to take action against Paul, just as Jews in other cities were to try, and sometimes to succeed in, convincing the authorities to do the same on other occasions (cf. Acts 13.50; 14.5; 17.5-9; 18.12-13).

spreading through the whole region (Acts 13.49). So the Jews incited some of the leading citizens, who stirred up persecution against Paul and expelled him from their region (Acts 13.50-52). At Iconium unbelieving Jews plotted with some of the Gentiles to ill-treat and stone Paul so that he was forced to escape to Lystra (Acts 14.2-7). When he was working in Lystra, some of the Jews from Antioch and Iconium came and won over the crowds, and Paul was stoned and dragged outside the city, presumed dead (Acts 14.19).

In each of the letters referred to above there are, then, quite explicit references to persecution which Paul experienced at the hands of his fellow countrymen, as well as a few references which seem to imply the same. If Paul suffered so much at their hands, it is worth asking why this was so.

Why the Price was Extracted

It is one thing to document the evidence for the price Paul had to pay for his ministry among the Gentiles in terms of persecution at the hands of the Jews; it is quite another to determine the reasons why that price was extracted. However, Paul's own letters provide us with some clues.

Paul Preached the Faith He Once Sought to Destroy

In Gal. 1.13-24 Paul spoke of his 'previous way of life in Judaism'. It was a life marked by rapid advancement and extreme zeal for the traditions of the fathers (v. 14). This zeal manifested itself in intense persecution of the church of God with a view to its destruction (v. 13). But his conversion experience on the Damascus road produced a complete turn-around (vv. 15-16). As the report heard by the Judean churches put it, 'The man who formerly persecuted us is now preaching the faith he once tried to destroy' (v. 23).

There is a hint here of one of the reasons why Paul was persecuted following his conversion. He now preached *the faith* he once tried to destroy. Prior to his conversion Paul persecuted those who preached this faith. Following his conversion he began to preach it himself, and as a result became the object of the sort of Jewish persecution he formerly perpetrated against others.[1]

If Paul's former persecution of the church had the backing of the high priest, as Acts 9.1-2 indicates, it is little wonder that, following his conversion, the Jewish leaders felt great antipathy towards him. He had switched sides and now preached the faith which he had previously attacked on their behalf. It is easy to understand how this antipathy might have translated itself into active persecution of Paul.

Paul Regarded Cherished Elements of Judaism as Rubbish

Following his conversion Paul underwent a reversal of values, and this could have added fuel to the fire as far as his persecution by the Jews was concerned. The key text in this respect is Phil. 3.4b-8:

> If anyone thinks he has reasons to put confidence in the flesh, I have more: circumcised on the eighth day, of the people of Israel, of the tribe of Benjamin, a Hebrew of Hebrews; in regard to the law, a Pharisee; as for zeal, persecuting the church; as for legalistic righteousness, faultless. But whatever was to my profit I now consider loss for the sake of Christ. What is more, I consider everything a loss compared to the surpassing greatness of knowing Christ Jesus my Lord, for whose sake I have lost all things. I consider them rubbish.

In this text Paul listed those things which he formerly, and zealous Jews still, held to be so important: circumcision in strict accordance with the law, an impeccable Hebrew ancestry, a Pharisaic respect for the law, a militant zeal in punishing those who disregarded it, and a personal devotion to carrying it out in his own life. But all these things, he said, he now counted as 'rubbish'. If Paul was known to have such an attitude to these most cherished elements of Judaism, and was known to promote a similar attitude among others, it is little wonder that he drew down upon himself violent persecution from the Jews (cf. Acts 21.27-36).

---

[1] Arland J. Hultgren, 'Paul's pre-Christian Persecutions of the Church: Their Purpose, Locale, and Nature', *JBL* 95 (1976), p. 103, suggests that the early Christian messianic movement was persecuted, when other messianic movements were not, because: (i) It proclaimed as messiah one who had been crucified. This ran counter to Deut. 21.23 which pronounced a curse on such people. (ii) It proclaimed that the new age had been inaugurated and now fidelity to God and the Torah were tested in terms of belief in Jesus. (iii) It pronounced judgement on the Jews for apostasy. (iv) It proclaimed as messiah one who only recently had been condemned by the Sanhedrin.

Paul Encouraged Jews to Neglect the Law of Moses

In Galatians 2 Paul recounted an incident involving Cephas and himself which occurred at Antioch; an incident which reflects the fact that Jewish believers were persecuted by their unbelieving fellow countrymen for neglecting the law.

Before the arrival of the people from James, Cephas and certain other Jewish believers had been having table fellowship with Gentile believers in Antioch. But when the emissaries from James arrived they withdrew from this table fellowship, evidently feeling condemned by the newcomers, and by their own consciences, for transgressing the law. Paul then took Cephas to task for acting in a way which was inconsistent with the truth of the gospel (vv. 11-14).

In vv. 15-21 Paul offered a theological evaluation of the incident. This he did by highlighting two matters: (a) that about which he and Cephas agreed, i.e. that even Jewish believers knew that a person is not justified by works of the law, but by faith in Jesus Christ (vv. 15-16); and (b) that about which they disagreed, i.e. whether Jewish believers were required to observe the demands of the law as part of their ongoing Christian obedience (vv. 17-21).

The heart of the disagreement between them was summed up by Paul in the words, 'If, while we seek to be justified in Christ, it becomes evident that we ourselves are sinners, does that mean that Christ promotes sin?' (v. 17). This can be understood against the background of the Antioch incident. Cephas and the other Jewish believers, relying on Christ for justification, had felt free to share table fellowship with Gentile 'sinners'. But when the emissaries from James arrived they felt condemned as transgressors of the law. It seemed as if their faith in Christ had made them transgressors. Thus they felt they must observe the law lest Christ be blasphemously regarded as the promoter of sin. Paul rejected this line of thinking. In vv. 19-20 he argued that in Christ believers had died to the law, and from this it may be inferred that the law's condemnation was irrelevant. Paul thus expected Jewish believers to set aside the demands of the law when their observance would mean treating Gentiles saved by faith in Christ as if they were still 'sinners'.[1]

[1]Paul's encouragement to his readers in 1 Cor. 10.31-11.1 to emulate him in their response to the problems raised by εἰδωλόθυτα seems to imply that he expected them also to follow his practice of accommodation, i.e. to become like those under the law and those not under the law as

The matter of particular importance for our enquiry at this point is Paul's reference to the idea that, if Jewish believers did not observe the law, Christ must be a promoter of sin. It is possible that Paul was using the rhetorical ploy of *reductio ad absurdum* to brush aside such a notion as unthinkable. But it is also possible that he was reflecting a real fear on the part of Cephas and other Jewish believers. Had the emissaries from James reminded Cephas and the others that the new faith was already being criticized along these lines, and that their action would have the direst consequences if it were to become known in Jerusalem? In other words, were militant Jews persecuting the early Jewish Christian movement for its failure to observe strictly the requirements of the law, and were they the ones who were describing Christ as a promoter of sin? There is evidence that zealous Jews persecuted other Jews who violated the law,[1] and there is ample evidence that this persecution extended to Jewish believers as well.[2]

While it is impossible to be absolutely certain about the matter, Paul's reference in 2 Cor. 11.24 to his having received five times the forty lashes minus is probably further evidence that he was persecuted for neglecting the law and encouraging other Jews to do likewise.[3]

Paul Did not Preach Circumcision

The one explicit reference which Paul himself made to the reason for his persecution at the hands of the Jews is found in Galatians 5.11: 'If I am still preaching circumcision, why am I still being persecuted? In that case the offence of the cross has been abolished'. Three things may be inferred from this text. First, Paul's gospel was offensive to the Jews. Second, it was offensive because it denied the necessity of circumcision. Third, as a result of these things, Paul suffered persecution at their hands.[4]

---

the situation demanded. For the Jewish minority in the Corinthian church, to emulate Paul in this way would mean neglecting the law's demands.

[1]Cf. Hengel, *Zealots*, pp. 183-206.

[2]In Gal. 6.12 Paul said that the reason the Judaizers wanted the Galatians to be circumcised was so that they themselves might avoid being persecuted for the cross of Christ. This indicates that when Galatians was written Jewish believers were under threat of persecution from unbelieving Jews if they were in any way involved in advocating or condoning the neglect of the law. But the clearest proof is Paul's own repeated confession that in his pre-conversion days he himself had persecuted the church of God (1 Cor. 15.9; Phil. 3.6, cf. 1 Tim. 1.13), which Acts 9.1-2 says was done with letters of authority from the high priest in Jerusalem and the cooperation of local synagogues.

[3]Cf. Peter Stuhlmacher, 'The Theme of Romans', *AusBR* 36 (1988), p. 43.

[4]Sanders, *Paul, the Law, and the Jewish People*, p. 191, says that the only firsthand evidence from Paul's writings points to the mission to the Gentiles and 'circumcision' as the issue which led to

Paul Relaxed Ethical Demands

In the previous sections we saw that Paul suffered persecution at the hands of the Jews because he preached the faith he once sought to destroy, because he regarded cherished elements of Judaism as 'rubbish', because he encouraged Jews to neglect the law of Moses, and because he did not preach circumcision. Persecution on these grounds Paul accepted as part of the inevitable cost of his ministry among Gentiles. However, there is evidence that he was also accused of promoting unrestrained moral license, and this accusation he repudiated vigorously:

> Someone might argue, 'If my falsehood enhances God's truthfulness and so increases his glory, why am I still condemned as a sinner?' Why not say—as we are being slanderously reported as saying and as some claim that we say—'Let us do evil that good may result'? Their condemnation is deserved (Rom. 3.7-8).

It must be said that Paul's own letters indicate that some of his converts did approve immoral living, while being proud of their spiritual status as believers. For example, in 1 Cor. 5.1-2 Paul had to rebuke his readers for their pride in the face of a case of incest in the church. And in 1 Cor. 6.12-20 he had to counteract the view that Christian freedom enabled one to practise sexual immorality, in particular to patronize prostitutes, with impunity. So it would appear that Paul could not deny that those who put their faith in Christ may fall into sin, and may even believe that they could do so with impunity. What he did deny most vigorously (in Rom. 3.7-8 cited above) was that his gospel was an open invitation to do so.

Paul wrote Romans to believers, but his dialogical partner in that letter was the hypothetical Jewish objector to his gospel. Therefore, the blasphemous slander to which the apostle refers in Rom. 3.7-8 is to be taken as slander emanating from his fellow countrymen, who believed that he was guilty of dispensing with ethical standards altogether. This erroneous belief on the part of the Jews must also have contributed to the reasons why he was persecuted by them.

---

persecution. While Paul clearly suffered because of this issue, there do appear to be other reasons reflected in his writings for his persecutions at the hands of the Jews, as the present essay seeks to show.

Conclusion

Five reasons why Paul suffered persecution at the hands of the Jews are discernible from his letters. First, he was persecuted because he preached 'the faith'. Prior to his conversion he had persecuted those who preached it, and when he began to preach the faith he once tried to destroy, he became the object of a similar Jewish persecution.

Second, he was persecuted because his conversion had led him to devalue radically the things which most zealous Jews held to be so important. In fact he spoke of some of the most cherished elements of Judaism as 'rubbish'.

Third, Paul was persecuted because he encouraged Jews to neglect the law and the traditions. He strongly rebuked Jewish believers for not being prepared to free themselves from the law's demands for ritual purity which kept them from sharing table fellowship with Gentile 'sinners'. Thus he fell foul of the zealous Jews who persecuted other Jews who violated the law.

Fourth, he was persecuted because he did not preach circumcision. Most of the reasons why Paul suffered persecution from the Jews can only be inferred from hints found in his letters. For this fourth reason we have the evidence of an explicit statement by the apostle: 'If I am still preaching circumcision, why am I still being persecuted? In that case the offence of the cross has been abolished' (Gal. 5.11).

Fifth, Paul was persecuted because he was thought to be advocating the abolition of all ethical standards. While the apostle would have pleaded guilty to the charges lying behind the other reasons why he was persecuted, he strongly denied the charge lying behind this one. It was, as far as he was concerned, a piece of blasphemous slander. Nevertheless, because this was what his Jewish opponents believed, it would have also contributed to the reasons why he suffered persecution at their hands.

It is a great pleasure for me to offer this essay as a token, inadequate though it is, of my sincere gratitude to Professor Ralph P. Martin for his contribution to the academic study of the New Testament, and more personally, for his supervision when I was a graduate student and his encouragement and friendship ever since.

THE GOSPEL AND GODLY MODELS IN PHILIPPIANS

Peter T. O'Brien

The Significance of the Gospel

On an earlier occasion we surveyed the issue of the place and significance of the 'gospel' in Paul's Letter to the Philippians.[1] This present essay, dedicated to my former teacher, Ralph Martin, is intended to build on the results of those earlier researches in order to determine the relationship of the 'gospel' motif to the important notion of following or conforming to a godly model, a topic which turns up on a number of occasions in Philippians.

For the sake of convenience we shall summarize the main conclusions reached in the earlier article, since these serve as a basis of our present inquiry. We had noted that Paul, somewhat surprisingly, uses the noun εὐαγγέλιον ('news, good news, gospel') nine times in the space of four short chapters in Philippians and, apart from the occurrence in 1.27, employs it without any modifiers. The apostle does not explain the meaning of εὐαγγέλιον, presumably because it had become a technical term, the content and significance of which were already known to and accepted by the Philippians. εὐαγγέλιον turns up in a number of unique expressions (1.5, 7, 12, etc.) and almost always, as a noun of agency, denotes the act of proclamation or the activity of preaching the gospel. At 1.27, however, the content of this gospel is in view since the Philippians are exhorted to conform their manner of life to that εὐαγγέλιον of Christ.

In our earlier researches we observed that 'the advance of the gospel' (προκοπὴ τοῦ εὐαγγελίου, 1.12) was enormously impor-

---

[1] P.T. O'Brien, 'The Importance of the Gospel in Philippians', in *God who is Rich in Mercy. Essays presented to D.B. Knox* (ed. P.T. O'Brien and D.G. Peterson; Homebush West, NSW: Lancer, 1986/Grand Rapids: Baker, 1986), pp. 213-33.

tant to Paul. He subordinated his own personal interests to the wider concerns of the gospel and read his own personal inconveniences, sufferings and imprisonment in the light of its progress. The dynamic onward march of the gospel could be discerned by a number of observable results both outside the Christian community as well as within it: first, Paul's imprisonment was a demonstration of Christ's saving activity and thus contributed to the spread of the gospel among those who made up the praetorian guard as well as among other Gentiles (v. 13) and, secondly, the majority of the believers in Rome, having had their confidence in the Lord strengthened by Paul's example, had been encouraged to set forth the apostolic message more boldly (v. 14). The ultimate touchstone of the gospel's progress, as Paul makes plain through a number of synonymous expressions, is that 'Christ is being proclaimed' (v. 18). Even when some preach him from improper motives such as jealousy and selfish ambition, Christ is still being publicly announced, and in this Paul rejoices. Further, it is in the preaching of Christ (his death, resurrection and present lordship) rather than in the specific results of the preaching (e.g. conversions) that the progress of the gospel occurs.

But not only does Paul subordinate his own personal concerns to the wider interests of the kerygma (as an apostle 'set apart for the gospel of God' [Rom. 1.1] when he was confronted by the risen Christ on the Damascus road, we might expect this). He also desires that the Philippians—who were not commissioned to be apostles as he was and whose personal circumstances were different from his own—might bring their lives into conformity with the gospel. So he urges them to focus their attention on one highly significant demand (lit. 'now the important thing is this: see to it that you live lives worthy of the gospel of Christ', v. 27). This one admonition is both crucial and comprehensive for it covers every aspect of their lives. It would involve the readers standing fast or secure with a common purpose ('in one spirit') in the face of attacks upon that gospel progress so that, positively, they will continue to struggle for the faith which is based on the gospel (v. 27) and, negatively, they will not be frightened by those who oppose them (v. 28). By standing firm in the face of attacks made upon the gospel, Paul's Christian friends show that their goal is the same as his own, namely, the spread and growth of the faith which arises from this εὐαγγέλιον. Although their circumstances differ, Paul and the Philippians are engaged in the same 'struggle' (ἀγών, v. 30) for the gospel and its progress. Further, behaviour that is consistent with the gospel will mean that they demonstrate unity in humility among themselves (2.1-4) and shine like lights in the world (2.15).

Accordingly, we concluded that for both Paul and the Philippians issues of the gospel were of paramount importance. Paul subordinated his own interests to the wider concerns of the gospel, while he expected his Philippian readers, whatever else they did, to take note of one significant demand—to live lives worthy of that gospel of Christ (1.27).

Following Godly Models

It is rather surprising, then, to observe that cheek by jowl with this prominent emphasis on the dynamic, almost personal, character of the gospel, there are statements where the apostle calls upon his readers to follow or conform their lives to several godly models. The most important of these passages is clearly chap. 2.6-11 where Jesus' Lordly Example is set forth. Other references are chaps. 2.17, 20-22, 30; 3.15, 17; and 4.9. What functions do these different models serve? Are there any unifying factors that draw these functions together? And what is the relationship of this weighty theme of the gospel to Paul's admonitions to follow such models?

We turn first to the most important passage in the letter:

Jesus' Lordly Example: Ch. 2.6-11

This paragraph provides a marvellous description of Christ Jesus' self-humbling in his incarnation and death, together with his subsequent exaltation by God to the place of highest honour. The verses are difficult to interpret[1] and not all are convinced of the traditional view that the hymn presents Jesus as the supreme example of humble, self-sacrificing, self-giving service. Indeed, since the 1950s the majority scholarly opinion concerning Paul's use of the christological

---

[1]There is no agreement on the origin and authorship of the passage (is it pre-Pauline, Pauline or post-Pauline?), its form and structure (hymnic? the number of stanzas?), its conceptual background and function within the letter, as well as a number of key exegetical and theological issues. For a recent detailed treatment of these issues see P.T. O'Brien, *The Epistle to the Philippians* (NIGTC; Grand Rapids: Eerdmans, 1991), pp. 186-271.

hymn in vv. 6-11 has swung in favor of the view that the apostle is reminding the Philippians as to how they came to be in Christ—albeit for an exhortatory purpose. This 'kerygmatic interpretation', as it has been called, was argued brilliantly by Ernst Käsemann—in part as a reaction to an earlier Liberal interpretation—and capably supported by Ralph Martin.[1]

In spite of the powerful arguments presented in favour of the 'kerygmatic interpretation', we have concluded elsewhere[2] that the hymn presents Jesus as the Lordly Example, whose humble, self-giving service has been set before the Philippians as Paul urges them to show unity and humility in their relations with one another. Although this hymn is a christological gem unparalleled in the NT and may have been originally composed for christological or soteriological reasons, since it speaks about the real humiliation of the incarnation and the cross of the one who is himself God, Paul's object in using it here is not primarily to give instruction in doctrine but to appeal to the conduct of Christ and to reinforce teaching in Christian living. The hymn presents Christ as the ultimate model for Christian behaviour and action. It has been suggested that, because of the later connotations of the term, it is better to speak of Paul's ethics as having to do with 'conformity' to Christ's likeness rather than an 'imitation' of his example.

Verses 9-11, the second half of the humiliation-exaltation motif, indicate Jesus' actions of 2.6-8 received divine vindication and approval. These words are not simply an 'appendix' to the exhortatory material,[3] but have reference to both Paul and the Philippians themselves, albeit later in the epistle. There are significant connections between 2.5-11 and 3.20-21, where Paul spells out what will happen to Christians at the appearance of the Lord Jesus Christ. The apostle uses, what has been called the idea of 'interchange': Christ becomes what we are—so enabling us to become what he is. Phil. 2.6-8 sets forth the former idea; vv. 9-11 describe his exaltation. At 3.20-21 we learn that the power given to him will enable him to trans-

---

[1]E. Käsemann, 'A Critical Analysis of Philippians 2:5-11', *JTC* 5 (1968), pp. 45-88, and R.P. Martin, *Carmen Christi: Philippians 2:5-11 in Recent Interpretation and in the Setting of Early Christian Worship* (Cambridge: University of Cambridge Press, 1967; Grand Rapids: Eerdmans, 1983).

[2]P.T. O'Brien, *Philippians*, pp. 253-62.

[3]As the 'kerygmatic interpretation' of Käsemann, Martin and others claims. For a discussion of the issues involved and bibliographical details see P.T. O'Brien, *Philippians*, pp. 253-62.

form us into conformity with himself: we shall become like him. Jesus humbled himself under God's mighty hand and the Father has now highly exalted him. The Philippians are to be conformed to Christ's likeness in humility and they will be exalted when he transforms them into his own likeness.

How then does Phil. 2.6-11 function within its immediate context? At 1.27 Paul had urged his readers to focus their attention on one highly significant demand, viz. that of conducting their lives in a manner worthy of the gospel of Christ. This single exhortation is comprehensive, covering every aspect of the readers's lives. Furthermore, it stands as a heading to the whole section, 1.27–2.18, so that the subsequent admonitions and statements expand and explicate what is involved in living worthily of that gospel. The Philippians are to stand firm with a common purpose in the face of attacks from outside the congregation against the progress of the gospel (1.27-30), and steadfastly resist all kinds of internal division (2.1-4). This latter paragraph functions as a call to unity, love and humility within the closely-knit section of 1.27–2.18.[1] At 2.5, which forms a link between vv. 1-4 and 6-11, the apostle introduces Christ Jesus as the supreme example of self-abnegation and humility, and urges the readers to 'adopt towards one another, in [their] mutual relations, the same attitude which was found in Christ Jesus'.[2] The meaning of this right attitude to and regard for others, humility and compassion, which Paul calls for in vv. 1-4, are profoundly presented to the Philippians in this classic passage which sets forth Christ Jesus as 'the Lordly Example'. Immediately after the hymn (v. 12) and reinforced by its contents (ὥστε is an inferential conjunction meaning 'so then') Paul resumes his exhortation. Christ's obedience has been stressed (v. 8) and now serves as an encouragement to the readers. They are to shine as stars in the universe (2.12-18).

[1]Verses 12-18 are part of the larger whole 1.27–2.18. Thematic links with 1.27–2.11 are evident in the apostle's relationships with the congregation (1.27 and 2.12), the congregation's witness to the non-Christian world (1.27-28 and 2.15-16), and the eschatological perspective (1.28; 2.12, 16).

[2]So C.F.D. Moule, 'Further Reflexions on Philippians 2:5-11', in *Apostolic History and the Gospel: Biblical and Historical Essays Presented to F. F. Bruce* (ed. W.W. Gasque and R.P. Martin; Exeter: Paternoster, 1970), p. 265, who is followed by others. Note, for example, N.T. Wright, 'ἁρπαγμός and the Meaning of Philippians 2:5-11', *JTS* 37 (1986), p. 346.

Two Christ-like Examples: Timothy and Epaphroditus. Ch. 2.19-30.
In a paragraph (2.19-30) that has striking verbal parallels with the confession of vv. 5-11 and its related exhortations,[1] Paul presents Timothy and Epaphroditus as godly examples of the way the Philippians should imitate Christ.[2] Timothy had a genuine concern for the interests of the Philippians (τὰ περὶ ὑμῶν, 2.20) and had slaved selflessly in the gospel (2.22; cf. 1.1, 7), while Epaphroditus had risked his life in the *service* of Christ (2.30). The latter, in order to fulfil the responsibilities which he undertook on the Philippians's behalf, almost died: Paul deliberately echoes the language of Christ's self-humbling (he was 'obedient unto death', μέχρι θανάτου, 2.8) to show that Epaphroditus came 'close to death' (μέχρι θανάτου, v. 30). This representative of the congregation was a model of selfless service to the Philippians which Paul wants them now to emulate.

The apostle's intention, then, in writing 2.19-30 was not simply to inform the Philippians about his plans for Timothy and Epaphroditus, though it certainly had this function; it was also to set them forth as godly examples who followed the model of Christ Jesus and clearly illustrated a manner of life worthy of the gospel (1.27). Paul's referring to his colleagues in this way served to underscore the significance of his central proposition in 1.27-30.[3]

Paul himself as a Model: Chs. 2.17; 3.15, 17; 4.9
On four occasions in Philippians Paul calls upon his Christian friends to follow his own example in terms of either having the same attitude of mind in relation to their ultimate goals (3.15), being united and imitating him as well as paying careful attention to others following the apostolic pattern (3.17) or putting into practice the things which they had learnt and received from Paul (4.9; cf. 2.17).

The question immediately arises as to whether Paul's choice of himself as an appropriate model for Christian behaviour is truly consistent with Christian humility. The following points are pertinent. First, the apostle has already reminded his readers that Christ Jesus is

---

[1]See below. Note the discussion in R.A. Culpepper, 'Co-Workers in Suffering. Philippians 2:19-30', *RevExp* 77 (1980), pp. 350-51, and D.E. Garland, 'The Composition and Unity of Philippians. Some Neglected Literary Factors', *NovT* 27 (1985), p. 163.

[2]R.A. Culpepper, 'Co-Workers', pp. 350, 353; G.F. Hawthorne, *Philippians* (WBC; Waco: Word, 1983), p. 108, and D.E. Garland, 'Composition and Unity', p. 163.

[3]D.F. Watson, 'A Rhetorical Analysis of Philippians and Its Implications for the Unity Question', *NovT* 30 (1988), pp. 71-72.

the example par excellence (2.5-11) and that their attitude and behaviour should be like his. This is consistent with Paul's statement to the Corinthians that he was extremely careful about his conduct. He did not wish to become, either wittingly or unwittingly, a stumbling block to others and lead them into sin. He urged his Corinthian converts to be equally careful: 'Do not cause anyone to stumble, whether Jews, Greeks or the church of God—even as I try to please everybody in every way. For I am not seeking my own good but the good of many, so that they may be saved. Follow my example, as I follow the example of Christ' (1 Cor. 10.32–11.1, NIV).

Secondly, Paul was not placing himself on a pedestal, as though he was 'perfect' or had already arrived at the eschaton (contrast some at Corinth, 1 Cor. 4.7, 8). On the contrary, he disclaimed having reached perfection (Phil. 3.12-14) whatever others, who were having an adverse influence on the congregation at Philippi, might claim for themselves. He keeps on pursuing his long-cherished ambition of perfectly laying hold of Christ and he wants the Philippians to do the same. He is thus an example in his orientation and attitude (cf. 3.15) as well as his behaviour (v. 16).

Thirdly, the apostle includes others along with himself as the kind of example to imitate. He has already held up Timothy (2.19-24) and Epaphroditus (2.25-30) as godly models to follow—living examples of those who 'have the mind' of Christ Jesus. At chap. 3.17 he changes from the singular to the plural (ἡμᾶς) to include others along with himself: 'Be united in imitating me and pay careful attention to *those* who live according to the pattern *we* gave you'. Paul's was no arrogant claim which demanded that his readers should follow in his magnificent steps! In this context W. P. de Boer's remarks are worth quoting at length:

> The Christian walk was not merely one man's peculiarities, but the consistent pattern of Paul and his associates, seen both when they were all together, and when only various of the associates revisited Philippi. Hence, this Christian pattern had been held before them more than once. It had been stamped on their minds repeatedly and under various circumstances by Paul and his associates. There were presently leaders in Philippi who were themselves conforming to this Christian pattern. Paul directs his readers' attention to them . . . [he] is intent on appealing to the Christian pattern on as broad a base as possible.[1]

[1] W.P. de Boer, *The Imitation of Paul* (Kampen: Kok, 1962), p. 183.

Fourthly, it is clear from the following verses (3.18ff.) that there were, in fact, other models who were setting a bad example and having the wrong kind of influence on the Philippian church. Theirs was the absolute antithesis of the Pauline model. They showed by their behaviour (περιπατοῦσιν) that they deliberately repudiated all that the cross of Christ stood for (v. 18). Paul is obviously anxious that godly examples be clearly presented to the readers so that they will have a powerful influence on both their attitudes and behaviour.

In the light of these factors, then, we conclude that Paul's choice of himself as a model for Christian behaviour was not inconsistent with Christian humility. Our further remarks will serve to underscore this conclusion.

What function(s), then, do these references to Paul himself as a model serve? What points does the apostle make by using himself as an example? In order to answer these questions we shall examine each text in the order in which it appears in the letter.

(1) The reference to Paul's willingness to be 'poured out as a libation' over the Philippians's sacrifice (2.17) appears to play only a subordinate role as a model. He has already presented the example of Christ's lowly service (2.5-11) as a powerful corrective to the readers's undue concern about their own interests (v. 4). He now mentions his own example before passing on to the powerful models of Timothy (2.20-22) and Epaphroditus (2.30). As a result three instances of the self-renouncing attitude 'that Christ Jesus had' are set forth in the latter part of the chapter: (a) Paul himself, (b) Timothy for his unselfish service in the gospel and genuine concern for the Philippians, and finally (c) Epaphroditus whose devotion to his commission in the service of Christ was almost at the expense of his life. F.F. Bruce aptly remarks: 'all these display the unselfconscious care for others enjoined at the beginning of this chapter and reinforced by the powerful example of Christ's self-emptying'.[1]

(2) At chap. 3.15 Paul encourages his dear friends at Philippi in their progress as Christians. He recognizes that not all of them have the same attitude of mind (φρονέω) he has just mentioned, namely, of being filled with the burning ambition of fully gaining Christ. In the preceding context (3.12-14), perhaps in order to counter the danger of 'a doctrine of obtainable perfection based on Judaizing practices',

[1] F.F. Bruce, *Philippians* (GNC; San Francisco: Harper, 1983), p. 73.

Paul has shown that Christian perfection is a goal to strive for. He has presented his own example, not in any arrogant way for he knows what it is to struggle against difficulties, and paints the picture of a runner who presses on determinedly, aiming to finish the race and win the prize (vv. 12-14). He then effectively applies these words to the Philippians's lives, for he wants them to be equally determined to fulfil the same ultimate aim that he has. He is an example in orientation and attitude as well as in his behaviour (v. 16). The presentation of himself as a model, therefore, serves the function of placing before the Philippians the highest of goals and of urging them to pursue it.

(3) The apostle calls upon the Philippians to be united in imitating his own example and that of others like him (3.17). Having written about his readers's attitude (v. 15), he then urges them to move forward together in accordance with the same rule that they have already followed, that is, consistently with the guidelines for Christian living that he regularly passed on to his converts (v. 16). Here as in the earlier references of the letter an appropriate model for Christian behaviour follows a series of admonitions and is set before the Philippians to imitate. To the call for Christian living (3.15-16) the exhortation to follow Paul's own example is immediately added (v. 17). His admonition is urgent because (γάρ, v. 18) the apostle is well aware that sinister and destructive patterns from elsewhere present themselves to the Philippians. Here at v. 17 Paul himself is clearly a 'model' (τύπος).[1] But the shift from the singular 'me' to the plural 'us' shows that the other members of the apostolic band, as well as Paul himself, collectively provide a pattern for the Philippians.

What, then, is the function of this 'model' (τύπος) in the present context? In part, the apostolic example is intended to stand over against and in stark contrast to those false models of Christian behaviour in which there was a deliberate repudiation of all that the cross of Christ stood for (v. 18). Paul had warned the Philippians about these false Christians on a number of occasions previously and he does so again because of the potential threat they were to the congregations where they were active. The issues are momentous since they have to do with a person's ultimate destiny—either eternal destruction (ἀπώλεια, v. 18) or a commonwealth in heaven (τὸ

[1] τύπος as an ethical 'pattern or model' describes the Christians at Thessalonica (1 Thess. 1.7), Timothy as a godly leader (1 Tim. 4.12; Tit. 2.7), Peter and his fellow-elders (1 Pet. 5.3) as well as Paul and his colleagues (2 Thess. 3.9).

πολίτευμα ἐν οὐρανοῖς, vv. 19, 20). Paul and his colleagues's example is thus intended to reinforce the serious warning not to be influenced by the enemies of the cross of Christ. It thus functions to reinforce Paul's call to perseverance which was clearly spelled out in 1.27-30.

(4) At the conclusion of his final exhortations (4.1-9) the apostle urges his converts to live by the teaching and example he has given to them (v. 9). Using terms that were known in popular moral philosophy, he lists several positive ethical qualities ('whatever is true, noble, just', etc., v. 8), then summarizes them and describes comprehensively the characteristics that they are to reflect upon in order to shape their conduct ('yes, whatever is morally excellent [ἀρετή], whatever is praiseworthy [ἔπαινος]—let your thoughts continually dwell on these things [so that your conduct will be shaped by them]'). These excellent characteristics, described in general terms, had been presented clearly and specifically in Paul's teaching and instruction as well as by his exemplary behaviour ('these things which you learned and received from me, . . . that you heard about me and saw in me', v. 9). The Philippians had appropriated these qualities for themselves, and they are now urged to 'put them into practice continually' (πράσσετε).

Again we ask the question: What function does Paul's example serve in this context? The apostle wants to reinforce most vividly the points that he has made in his exhortations. These admonitions of vv. 2-9 are only loosely related to one another; however, they appear in the paragraph headed by the exhortation to 'stand firm' (στήκετε, v. 1; cf. 1.27), and this is itself a repetition of his call to perseverance in 1.27-30. That call to stand firm is an essential element in the comprehensive injunction for the readers to 'live [their lives] in a manner worthy of the gospel of Christ' (1.27). So in chap. 4, as Paul addresses his dear friends with some of the most affectionate and endearing terms he ever uses in his letters ('My beloved brothers, whom I long for greatly, my joy and crown', v. 1) and concludes his exhortations (vv. 1-9), he uses himself as a model to reinforce the points of the admonitions in a vivid way and therefore to remind them of what constitutes a life worthy of the gospel of Christ.

Conclusions

Our concern to explain the links between the motif of the 'gospel' and the important notion of following godly models has led us to make an examination of seven passages in which Christ Jesus, Timothy and Epaphroditus—Paul's colleagues—as well as the apostle himself are presented as examples to which the Philippians are to conform their lives. Our study has led to the following conclusions:

1. In each case the model follows and serves to underscore one or more of the preceding apostolic exhortations and so to reinforce the instruction in Christian living. It is as if Paul is saying, 'Here is the way to put these instructions into practice; follow this godly example!'

2. Christ Jesus is not only the *first* model mentioned in the letter (at 2.6-11); he is also the *archetypal* example to whom all others are to conform their lives. His self-humbling in his incarnation and death provides the ultimate pattern for Christian attitudes and behaviour. Further, other models, whose lives the readers are to emulate, do in fact conform to this Lordly Example, and Paul goes out of his way to show that this is so in the cases of Timothy, Epaphroditus and himself. The apostle's examples are patterned on the model of the Lord Jesus Christ. So Timothy is like the Lord Jesus because he had a genuine concern for the interests of others, in this case the Philippians, and had slaved selflessly in the gospel (2.20, 21). Epaphroditus had come 'close to death' (2.30; note the same wording μεχρὶ θανάτου with reference to Jesus at v. 8), for he risked his life in the service of Christ, while Paul himself is prepared, like his Master, to be 'poured out' for the sake of the congregation (2.17). The apostle calls on his readers to 'Follow my [and others'] example, as I [and they] follow the example of Christ' (1 Cor. 11.1).

3. Furthermore, the Lord Jesus as the archetypal model reinforces the *central exhortation* of the letter, 'Now, the important thing is this: live as citizens of heaven in a manner that is worthy of the gospel of Christ' (1.27), which is itself part of the leading proposition to persevere and stand firm (vv. 27-30). Others like Timothy and Epaphroditus reinforce this crucial proposition, while Paul himself as a model (2.17; 3.15, 17; 4. 8-9) underlines the points of the preceding admonitions in a vivid way and thus reminds his readers of what it means to stand firm and live this worthy life.

4. At the heart of the letter (1.27-30), then, godly models are closely integrated with the motif of the gospel. Paul expects his readers, as well as himself, to be caught up with the ongoing dynamic of the gospel, so that they are wholly committed to its continuous advance. They had already shown their active participation in the εὐαγγέλιον from the first day until the present (1.5), and this involved, not simply their monetary support or generosity towards the apostle, but also their active commitment to the message and its mission in the broadest sense. Paul's glowing thanksgiving to God (vv. 3-6) implies that he wishes this dynamic participation to continue. At the same time it is vital that the Philippians's lives be conformed to and consistent with this authoritative announcement (v. 27). This will involve them standing fast and persevering in the face of common attacks upon the gospel, so that they continue to struggle for the faith based on it and are not frightened by their opponents. The circumstances of Paul and his Christian friends differ; but both are engaged in the same 'struggle' for the gospel (v. 30). And the model of the Lord Jesus Christ, who is the centre and substance of this apostolic announcement, reinforces Paul's comprehensive admonition and provides the supreme example for it. The regular proclamation of the word of the Lord and a commitment to its ongoing advance is to be matched by a lifestyle that is in full harmony with it and, therefore, in conformity with the Lord Jesus Christ himself.

In some contemporary churches progress in the Christian life is understood wholly in terms of imitating Christ, while in other traditions it is the 'proclamation of the word' that dominates and the notion of conformity with Christ hardly rates a mention. A sharp wedge is driven between the two; but the apostle's words to the church at Philippi do not endorse such a dichotomy. Rightly understood, the gospel, its mighty advance and a personal commitment to it should go hand in hand with the following of godly models, especially the Lordly Example of Jesus Christ himself who is the heart of the gospel.

THE PRIESTHOOD OF ALL BELIEVERS: 1 PETER 2.1-10

Eduard Schweizer

In his book on *Worship in the Early Church* Ralph Martin refers to 1 Pet. 2.9, or rather to the whole section 2.1-10, as the text that sets the stage for his studies.[1] Later on he quotes Rev. 1.6; 5.10, where the same Old Testament passage as in 1 Pet. 2.9 is reapplied as a description of the church's worship.[2] In 1 Peter 2 he detects the church as a spiritual temple, a holy priesthood, summoned in its being by God in order to be a worshiping community.[3] Since he is obligated to read my essay, it might be as well to try a short analysis of this text which is so meaningful to him.

1. *The Structure of 2.1-6*

Similarities

It is questionable whether we should limit the section to 2.1-10 in this way. Some interpreters combine vv. 1-3 with 1.22-25 and start a new section in 2.4.[4] Usually, however, 2.1-10 (or 12) are taken as a

---

[1]R.P. Martin, *Worship in the Early Church* (London: Marshall, Morgan and Scott, 1964), p. 9. 'Biblical Theology', i.e. an honest and carefully worked out exegesis with a 'theological' and even 'spiritual' aim, is what R.P. Martin has richly given us in his books and articles. Thus, a short essay in this field, such as I try to present here, would seem still to be welcomed by him according to his remark in *TLZ* 116 (1991), p. 37 (in a review of J.M.G. Volf, *Paul and Perseverance*).

[2]Martin, *Worship in the Early Church*, p. 23.

[3]Martin, *Worship in the Early Church*, p. 10.

[4]L. Goppelt, *Der erste Petrusbrief* (KEK 12/1; Göttingen, 1978), pp. 127, 138; E. Best, *First Peter* (NCB; London: Oliphants, 1971), pp. 99: 1.22-2.3 behavior/2.4-10 nature of the community. Cf. J.R. Michaels, *1 Peter* (WBC; Waco, TX: Word, 1988), p. 49: 2.1-3 is a metaphor of growth, 2.4-10 of building (which is closely associated), shifting also from an individual to a corporate focus.

unit.[1] The structure of vv. 1-6 certainly speaks in favour of the latter decision. On the one hand, the imagery of a new birth in v. 2 is the same as in 1.23 and οὖν ('so') in v. 1 refers back to the preceding verses. Yet v. 1 begins a new development of the thought contained in the preceding verses, drawing the conclusions from them. On the other hand, v. 4 is closely connected with v. 3 by a relative pronoun. More important in its theological as well as grammatical implications is another fact. Verse 1 begins with a participle, leading to an imperative in v. 2a, on which a final clause depends (v. 2b). Finally, v. 3 grounds the whole unit on a Biblical quotation introduced by a causal conjunction.[2] Exactly the same happens in v. 4 (participle), v. 5a (imperative),[3] v. 5b (εἰς . . . followed by a final clause in the form of an infinitive), and v. 6 (the word of the Bible).

In both cases, the *logical* structure starts from the Biblical truth (at the end), which incites the church to do what the imperative clause voices (position 2), and to do it in the way described in the participle clause (position 1), in order to reach the goal defined in the final clause (position 3). Actually, it is the truth of God's graceful acts, revealed in the scriptures, that sets everything in motion. The *rhetorical* structure starts both times from our situation, picks up the readers where their experiences, problems, and questions might be lurking, defines the task lying before them (both times calling to a being rather than a doing, suggesting that God has performed and is performing the essential change in our lives), shows the goal, and lastly proclaims in the form of a Biblical word the basic power that will work in and through them.

Differences.

Verse 1 begins with an aorist participle, pointing to a definite act to be done once for all, namely the final separation from all wrong-doing,[4]

---

[1] C. Bigg, *The Epistles of St. Peter and St. Jude* (ICC; 2d ed.; T & T Clark, 1902; reprint ed., 1961), p. 129; J. Michl, *Die katholischen Briefe* (RNT; Regensburg: F. Pustet, 1953; 3d ed. 1968), p. 117; Bo Reicke, *The Epistles of James, Peter, and Jude* (AB 37; New York: Doubleday, 1964), p. 88. Strangely, J. Moffatt, *The General Epistles: James, Peter and Judas* (MNTC, London: Hodder & Stoughton, 1928; 8th ed. 1963), pp. 109-119: 1.22-2.1/2.2-5/2.6-10.

[2] εἰ is not an open condition ('if'), but means 'since' (cf. the textual variant εἴπερ in C etc.).

[3] The parallel to v. 2a speaks in favour of this, though an indicative understanding would be possible.

[4] Typically, only sins that may occur within the church are mentioned (as e.g. in 2 Cor. 12.20), not the sins of Gentiles (immorality, greed, idolatry: cf. 1 Thess. 4.3-6; 1 Cor. 5.10; 6.9; Col. 3.5; Eph. 5.5; 1 Pet. 4.3). For a combination of both types cf. Gal. 5.19-22; Rom. 13.13; 1.29-31;

while the one in v. 4 describes a still present action. The (negative) 'turning away from . . .' becomes a (positive, and therefore on-going) 'turning to . . .'. At the same time, the focus of v. 1 is on the individual members of the church, who distinguish themselves from their fellow men, as the selection of vices shows.[1] Verse 4, on the contrary, calls the readers to become one with Christ as a corporate person so that the individuals become a 'spiritual house', the church, as v. 5 shows. Again, the imperative of v. 2 is put in the aorist tense stressing the moment of decision;[2] the one in v. 5 describes a continuing event in the present tense. The final clause in v. 2 speaks of 'growing up to salvation', i.e. to a goal in which our personal lives will find their perfection. Contrariwise, v. 5 speaks of what will be given to God by our lives. The Biblical reference in v. 3 bases the summons on our personal experience, the one in v. 6 on the 'objective' reality revealed in the scripture.

Thus, there is a movement detectable in the text. Though both sections lead the readers in three steps from their situation to a new act (or being) in view of a definitive goal, and then base this in a fourth step on God's action, the first section (vv. 1-3) speaks of a beginning of the motion towards the final goal, whereas the second one (vv. 4-6) takes up with its first two words the last word of vv. 1-3 ('the Lord'), which now becomes the keyword and speaks of what has happened to *him* and has definitively changed our existence to that of a holy priesthood founded on him, the corner stone.

2. *The Theological Intentions in 2.1-6*

Participle and Main Verb.

No doubt v. 1 expects some radical change of position, and participles may be equivalent to imperatives.[3] Yet the formal parallel in vv. 4-6, where again the participle leads to the main verb in the imperative (or indicative?) form, seems to prove that this change is consciously

---

Col. 3.5-8 and E. Schweizer, 'Gottesgerechtigkeit und Lasterkataloge bei Paulus', in *Rechtfertigung* (FS E. Käsemann; Tübingen: Mohr, 1976), pp. 461-77; also *idem*, 'Traditional Ethical Patterns in the Pauline and Post-Pauline Letters and Their Development (List of Vices and House Tables)', in *Text and Interpretation* (FS M. Black; Cambridge: University Press, 1979), pp. 195-201.

1 Cf. the preceding note and the fourth note of this essay.

2 Here rather *aoristus ingressivus*, while the one in v. 1 is *effectivus*.

3 BDF § 468.2 (cf. 1 Pet. 3.7!); D. Daube in E.G. Selwyn, *The First Epistle of St. Peter* (2d ed.; Oxford: Blackwell, 1947; reprint ed. 1974), pp. 467-88.

made. It does not mean that the main verb is subordinated to the participle;[1] on the contrary, the latter rather states in what way the action intended by the main verb should happen, i.e. in such a way that the readers will get really engaged. Precisely because all the following verbs describe what *happens* to them, this must be said expressly.[2] For the imperative of v. 2 actually says 'be hungry!' To be hungry is no spectacular achievement, it is the very nature of a 'newborn babe'. Thus, the imagery emphasizes the 'indicative' connotation of the imperative. Birth has happened to the newborn babe. It would be senseless to command 'be born!', nor are there laws to be observed by the babe when being born. Thus, the imperative means simply, 'be what you really are, be as hungry as a newborn babe is!' No detailed programs of a birth to be followed by the babe exist (as some prescribe for a genuine rebirth of a believer). If a midwife insisted (like spiritual midwives often do) on exactly the same pattern for every birth she would find herself in prison for manslaughter within a short time. It is God alone who decides how the birth shall come about. Again, as a babe would not know of any other food than the milk of her mother, as a babe would not ponder whether to choose a Chinese or Mexican or Indian restaurant, so the newborn member of the church is naturally driven to the λογικόν—the 'logogeneous', the 'word-like'[3]—milk that comes to him/her in the form of the Word. Similarly, v. 4 mentions our active engagement in 'going to' Christ. That he is 'rejected by men' reminds the readers of their distinguishing themselves from other people, but the emphasis lies on their turning to the one whose life, election and preciousness they shall share. The imperative is actually in the passive (or, at least, middle) voice: 'be . . . built' (parallel to 'be hungry'). Thus, even reading the verb as an indicative would not change its message very much, though the idea of the conscious acceptance of what happens to them would not be expressed equally clearly.

---

1. Thus, F.W. Beare, *The First Epistle of Peter* (Oxford: Blackwell, 1947), p. 93.
2. For the same reason, R.P. Martin pleads for the authenticity of 2 Cor. 6.14-7.1 (*2 Corinthians* [WBC; Waco, Texas: Word, 1986], p. 211): the church, as the temple of God (2 Cor. 6.16; cf. 1 Pet. 2.5), has necessarily to sever decidedly from the world, 'not to be mismated with the unbelievers' (2 Cor. 6.14), as 1 Pet. 2.7 contrasts those 'who believe' to those 'who do not believe' and 'to go (ἐξέρχεσθαι) out of their midst' (2 Cor. 6.17), as 1 Pet. 2.4-5 summons the church 'to go (ἔρχεσθαι) to the living stone' in order to become 'a spiritual house'.
3. Cf. now also Dan G. McCartney, 'λογικός in 1 Peter 2.2', *ZNW* 82 (1991), pp. 128-32.

Whither and Whence.
The final clause of v. 2b underlines both that there is a future definitive salvation and that this has to do very much with our present lives. The situation of today is clearly connected with this goal, but the stress lies rather on its character as a beginning that is not yet the end of the way. The Biblical reference in v. 3 reminds the readers of what they have already received on this way, namely the 'milk' that they have tasted and that they should taste time and again in order to grow to their final state. Verse 5b rather describes what they are already: the ones who are in direct contact with God by offering him what he will accept, not because it is valuable in itself, but because Jesus Christ has accepted them and their achievements. The word of the scripture in v. 6 lays the emphasis on what God has done once and forever, and on the certitude that they 'will not be put to shame'. Thus, God's acts both in the past (at the beginning of believers' lives and in the Christ event) and in the future (in their final salvation and acceptance by God) form the frame of what the imperatives call the church to, the participles providing the details.

3. *The Structure of 2.7-10*

The Four Steps.
The sequence of participle, imperative, final clause and Biblical foundation is no longer observed. Yet, the progress from v. 7 to v. 10 follows still in its content, if not in its grammatical form, basically the same pattern of the four steps. (1) Verses 1a/4a summoned the readers to turn away from evil-doers and to turn definitively to Christ. This is taken up in vv. 7-8. Since Isa. 28.16 quoted in v. 6 is already in the tradition of the church interpreted by Isa. 8.14 (Rom. 9.33!), this passage replaces the two participles. What vv. 1a/4a formulated as a call to the readers takes now (in vv. 7-8) the form of a statement: Christ is the watershed, the 'divide' between believers and unbelievers, between those from whom they are to turn away, and the church to which they are to turn. In this way, he is foundation stone and stumbling block at the same time. (2) The main verbs in vv. 2a/5a spoke of the nourishment of the babe (the believer) and the building up of the spiritual house (the church). Verse 9 varies the imagery

again to express the same thought: the readers are (or should be?)[1] 'a chosen race, a royal priesthood, a holy nation, God's own people'. (3) The final clause in vv. 2b/5b pointed to spiritual growth up to the point of final salvation, and to offering spiritual sacrifices. This is now specified as the church's missionary preaching of God's 'wonderful deeds', who called them 'out of darkness into his marvelous light'. (4) The section also closes with a Biblical substantiation, in which, again, the imagery of a people replaces that of food tasted by them for their growth or of the foundation stone laid by God for their upbuilding.

The Differences Compared with 2.1-6.

Similarly to vv. 1-3/4-6 the section 2.7-10 starts from the situation of the readers ('you who believe'), from their everyday problems of living together with 'those who do not believe'. It is the life of the 'exiles of the dispersion' (1.1), which is dealt with throughout the whole letter. However, vv. 7-8 state a definitive fact rather than a movement (away from all malice towards Christ) as in vv. 1/4. It assures them of their new state. Whereas v. 2 uses the imperative form and v. 5 an ambiguous one that could be imperative or indicative, v. 9a seems to express this in an indicative way. The final clause is cognate to that in v. 5b, because 'the spiritual offerings' consist, very probably, of praise and thanksgiving to God. Differently, however, from vv. 2b/5b the emphasis is on the transposition from darkness to light, which has happened definitively. At the same time, the focus has moved from the church's own growth (v. 2b) or even its thanks to God (v. 5b) to its responsibility to the world, to which it is to preach what has happened. The word of the Bible in v. 10 refers neither to the church's experience, which should be repeated (as in v. 3), nor to the Christ-event, which happened 'outside' of the church before their time (as in v. 6), but to what is true of the church itself now and forever: the change from a no-people to God's people has taken place and cannot be changed back. Thus, the message of the gospel has reached its climax. No imperative is left concerning a movement of the church towards its own fullness. Yet, a new imperative, of another dimension, takes its place now. The church is being God's people precisely in its living, which retells to their fellow men the gospel that they have heard themselves and that is unchange-

---

[1] The verb is lacking, perhaps deliberately wavering between indicative and imperative (as in v. 5a).

ably true for them. Thus, the character of the message of 2.1-10 becomes gradually clearer, it is the 'gospel', not 'law', and yet engaging us totally.

4. *The Theological Intentions in 2.7-10*

'Royal Priesthood'?

Exod. 19.6 (repeated in 23.22 LXX) is the only passage in the Old Testament that attributes priesthood to all members of Israel.[1] Rev. 1.6 and 5.10 show that the reference to this text has become traditional in the church. In 1 Pet. 2.9 it is framed by passages that are also quoted in Rom. 9.25-26/32-33. Thus, the author follows traditional trains of thought. But what does it mean for him? All the New Testament books know that the ardent desire of Moses, 'Would that all the Lord's people were prophets, that the Lord would put his Spirit upon them!' (Num. 11.29), has been fulfilled in the church.[2] Thus, it is not surprising that this text from Exod. 19 turns up here. Unfortunately, how it should be translated is uncertain. Certainly 'priesthood' does not serve as the designation of an abstract idea, but means, in the parallel to 'chosen race' and 'holy nation', something like 'a body of priests'. In v. 5 the same term explains what a 'spiritual house' is and designates clearly those who are offering spiritual sacrifices, i.e. 'priests'. Moreover, Rev. 1.6 and 5.10 use 'priests' instead of 'priesthood'. But what about the first expression (βασίλειον)? There are good arguments to take it as a substantive, parallel to 'body of priests' and to translate 'a royal palace (household?)'.[3] This would well correspond with the juxtaposition of 'a kingdom' and 'priests' in Rev. 1.6; 5.10, and this seems to be the original understanding in Exod. 19.6. Yet the arguments are not decisive. Lexicographical dates are ambiguous; as a substantive ('royal palace') the word is usually put in the plural, but the adjective is rather rare (especially in the LXX). Admittedly, the position of the adjective before the substantive would be difficult to explain, but the

---

[1]Rabbinic Judaism limits this to Israel before its idolatry of the golden calf and to Israel in the messianic age (J. H. Elliott, *The Elect and the Holy: An Exegetical Examination of 1 Peter 2.4-10 and the Phrase βασίλειον ἱεράτευμα* [NovTSup 12; Leiden: Brill, 1966], pp. 104-105; for Exod. 19.6 LXX cf. 120-21).

[2]πνεῦμα (referring to God's Spirit) is missing in James, but cf. 3.15-17.

[3]Elliott, *The Elect and the Holy*, pp. 149-53; also N. Brox, *Der erste Petrusbrief* (EKK 21; Zürich: Benziger, 1979; 2d ed., 1986), pp. 103-104, and others.

three other designations of the church always combine substantive and adjective (or, in the last case, a circumscription for an adjective). Thus, the rhythm of the verse would rather commend reading it as 'a royal body of priests'. If we had to deal with two substantives, one might argue that in a royal palace (or household) there is but one king, and that, therefore, the same reasoning forbids to speak of every member of the church as a priest.[1] This, however, is what ἱεράτευμα (which must mean something like 'a body of priests') says. Thus, the parallel of 'royal palace' and 'body of priests' would not be very convincing. Furthermore, the same term in v. 5, also combined with an adjective, though without any connotation of royalty, describes people that perform priestly functions. This (and, to a lesser degree, also the final clause of v. 9) shows that the emphasis lies clearly on the priestly character of the church. Nonetheless we are certainly not allowed to press the imagery too much.

The Priesthood of All Believers.

What then is the priestly character of all believers? It does not mean a total uniformity in which nobody would be leading and nobody led. There are in the church of 1 Peter elders to tend the flock, probably even recompensed for that task (5.1-3); there are different functions according to everybody's special gifts (4.10-11). What then is the priestly function given to all members? According to 2.9b it is 'proclaiming the wonderful deeds of God'. Would this exclude a special ministry of preaching? The context shows that the proclamation of v. 9 is focused on the situation of the church among the Gentiles, who will 'see the good deeds' of their Christian companions and 'glorify God' (2.12). This is relevant in two ways. First, what 2.9 has in view is not the relations within the church, so that any church order would be suspect. It should certainly be the order of the Holy Spirit, a 'charismatic'[2] order, but order it should be. The function of these 'priests' is not an intrachurch one; it is turned towards the non-Christian world. Second, v. 12 speaks of 'deeds' to be 'seen', not of words to be heard. This means that the most important service of 'proclaiming the wonderful deeds of God' is the one described in the following section 2.13-3.17. To be sure, there are situations in which

---

[1]Cf. Brox, *erste Petrusbrief*, pp. 104-105.

[2]4.10 is, in the New Testament, the only passage outside of the letters of Paul and his school to use χάρισμα and to equate it, as Paul does, with χάρις θεοῦ (Goppelt, *erste Petrusbrief*, p. 198).

words are needed (3.15!), but there are also, and even more often, situations in which the proclamation of the gospel 'without a word' (3.1!) is decisive. It is the slaves that are merely suffering, the wives with their 'reverend and chaste behaviour' who are the best witnesses of Christ to the world. They are the most active and effective *'Verbi Divini Ministri'* (ministers of the word of God).

Doubtless, we should reformulate what is said here. What we read here is language of the first century, and we have to translate it in the language of our century. It is with language as it is with water. Chemically pure, distilled water no longer quenches the thirst. Even water melting from some snowfield in the mountains does not really help before it has passed through the ground and become enriched by its minerals (one could even say, its dirt). Similarly, a 100% pure word of God, which has not touched the ground with all its dirt, does not quench the thirst of the soul. This is why we have to replace the 'minerals' of the first by those of the twentieth century. 'Integrating oneself' under 'everybody' (2.13!),[1] under one's master or husband, should not exclude critical reflections nor express itself in blind obedience to all edicts of the authorities in a perpetually silent and slavish suffering of injustice or in an unreflected acceptance of traditional male/female patterns. Notwithstanding this, in all the examples of 2.13-3.17 it is the usually unnoticed, weak, even suffering partner that is the really essential person, the 'priest' that 'proclaims the wonderful deeds of God'. And they are so 'among all peoples', as Exod. 19.5 already describes the position and role of Israel among the Gentiles. The examples of behaviour may look different today, but basically the understanding of the priesthood of all believers remains the same. It still is, first of all, the weak and suffering members of the church that preach, often silent or silenced, by their very lives more effectively than the learned scholars and pastors do by their words.

1 κτίσις certainly cannot mean 'institution', but 'creation' or 'creature'; thus v. 13 is to be understood in line with Phil. 2.3b and Rom. 12.10, and the following verses specify this with regard to the emperor and his governors.

THE INTERPLAY OF MINISTRY, MARTYRDOM AND DISCIPLESHIP IN IGNATIUS OF ANTIOCH

Michael J. Wilkins

Throughout his distinguished career Professor Ralph Martin has illuminated the life of the early church by spotlighting its place within Judaism and the broader Greco-Roman world. Further, he has provided additional illumination by tracing the evolution of NT themes and practices in the church into the period following the NT era. My early study of discipleship within Jesus' ministry and the life of the early church was directed by Professor Martin, who mentored my doctoral program.[1] In that research I explored the classical, Hellenistic, and Judaistic forms of discipleship in the ancient world, in addition to the NT teaching.[2] In this present essay I would like to take the study one step further by exploring forms of discipleship as found in the apostolic fathers.[3] The study will examine the general concept of discipleship, with special emphasis upon the intriguing interplay of ministry and martyrdom amid discipleship found in the church in the period following the NT era.

'The blood of the martyrs is indeed the seed of the Church. Dying we conquer. The moment we are crushed, that moment we go forth victorious'. This valiant declaration of the Latin church father Tertullian voices a rallying cry which echoes throughout church his-

---

[1]My initial interest in discipleship in Matthew's gospel was stimulated in part by two of Professor Martin's many insightful articles: R.P. Martin, 'St. Matthew's Gospel in Recent Study', *ExpTim* 80 (1969), pp. 132-36, and *idem*, 'Salvation and Discipleship in Luke's Gospel', *Int* 30 (1976), pp. 366-80.

[2]My doctoral dissertation, supervised by Professor Martin, was published in the *Novum Testamentum* Supplements series: Michael J. Wilkins, *The Concept of Disciple in Matthew's Gospel: As Reflected in the Use of the Term Μαθητής* (NovTSup 59; Leiden: E.J. Brill, 1988).

[3]The research undertaken for this essay contributed background for a chapter in my biblical theology of discipleship: see Michael J. Wilkins, *Following the Master: Discipleship in the Steps of Jesus* (Grand Rapids: Zondervan, 1992), ch. 16: 'Apostolic Fathers: Martyrs for the Name', pp. 311-36.

tory.[1] Tradition records that most of the first disciples of Jesus were martyrs for their faith in the risen Christ. The English word 'martyr' descends from the Greek word μάρτυς, witness. From its earliest days, the church has honored individuals who have witnessed to their faith in Christ by choosing to die rather than compromise their faith. Jesus gave a call to discipleship in his earthly ministry which set the tone for that sentiment when he said,

> If anyone would come after me, he must deny himself and take up his cross daily and follow me. For whoever wants to save his life will lose it, but whoever loses his life for me will save it. What good is it for a man to gain the whole world, and yet lose or forfeit his very self? If anyone is ashamed of me and my words, the Son of man will be ashamed of him when he comes in his glory and in the glory of the Father and of the holy angels (Lk. 9.23-27).

Since the days of the early church, men and women have responded to Jesus' radical summons, and many have received the strength and courage necessary to follow Jesus all the way to death. Persecution marked the fate of the early church, yet this suffering did not dim the passion for following Jesus. Luke captures the attitude of the apostles after they had experienced beatings: 'The apostles left the Sanhedrin, rejoicing because they had been counted worthy of suffering disgrace for the Name. Day after day, in the temple courts and from house to house, they never stopped teaching and proclaiming the good news that Jesus is the Christ' (Acts 5.41-42).

The same readiness to suffer for the name of their Master, Jesus Christ, reverberates in the writings of the earliest church fathers. The author of the *Martyrdom of Polycarp* declares, 'Blessed and noble, therefore, are all the martyrdoms that have taken place in accordance with the will of God . . . For who could fail to admire their nobility and patient endurance and loyalty to the Master' (*Mart. Pol.* 2.1-2[2]). Polycarp, one of the early church fathers who experienced a martyr's death, when speaking of Christ's suffering on the cross for our sake, says, 'Let us then be imitators of His endurance, and if we suffer for

[1]H. Workman concludes his classic study of persecution in the early church by citing this famous declaration by Tertullian: see Herbert B. Workman, *Persecution in the Early Church* (1906; rpt.; Oxford: Oxford University Press, 1980), p. 143.

[2]Unless otherwise noted, all translations of the Apostolic Fathers are from either Kirsopp Lake, *The Apostolic Fathers, with an English Translation* (2 vols.; LCL; 1912; rpt.; Cambridge, Mass.: Harvard, 1977), or from Michael Holmes' revision of J.B. Lightfoot and J.R. Harmer, *The Apostolic Fathers*, ed. and rev. Michael W. Holmes (1891; 2d ed.; Grand Rapids: Baker, 1989).

His Name's sake let us glorify Him. For this is the example which He gave us in Himself, and this is what we have believed' (Pol. *Phil.* 8.1-2).

The writings designated the *Apostolic Fathers* are important because they are a primary source for the study of early Christianity, especially the period after the majority of apostles have passed from the scene (c. AD 70-150). They provide significant and often unparalleled glimpses of and insights into the ministry and life of Christians and the Christian movement immediately following the apostles.[1] At the time when the Fathers wrote, the churches they addressed had been established for at least a half-century. The early flush of conversion had passed for many of these churches, a mounting danger from heresy was exerting itself upon them, and increasing persecution from the Roman empire was threatening their very existence. What was discipleship like under these conditions?

Our study will focus on specific terms, teachings, and concepts which reveal attitudes about discipleship. In addition, we will compare our findings with the biblical data to look for similarities and differences of discipleship life. Many of the same terms and concepts of discipleship which occur in the NT also occur in the Fathers.[2] The writings that will anchor our study are those of Ignatius, bishop of the church at Antioch in Syria. Ignatius uses discipleship terminology more frequently than any apostolic father, revealing the most information about the development of discipleship in the days of the early church. Virginia Corwin observes, 'The Ignatian letters have more references to imitation and discipleship than all the other apostolic fathers together'.[3] Ignatius will anchor our study, but we will touch briefly on the writings of the other apostolic fathers as they contribute to a more complete understanding of our subject.[4]

---

[1]For an excellent discussion of the significance, historical setting, and texts of the apostolic fathers, see Michael Holmes' revision of Lightfoot and Harmer, *The Apostolic Fathers.*

[2]Through the search capabilities of the computer data base of *Thesaurus Linguae Graecae* (TLG), housed at the University of California, Irvine, I examined all of the extant writings of the apostolic fathers, even the spurious writings, for the following terms: 'disciple' (μαθητής) and 'I make disciples' (μαθητεύω), 'follower' and 'I follow' (ἀκολουθ– stem), 'believer' (πιστεύοντος; πιστός), 'brother/sister' (ἀδελφ– stem), 'Christian' (Χριστιανός), 'imitator' (μιμητής), 'apostle' (ἀπόστολος), and 'saints' (ἅγιοι).

[3]Virginia Corwin, *St. Ignatius and Christianity in Antioch* (Yale Publications in Religion 1; New Haven: Yale University Press, 1960), p. 228 n. 9.

[4]Later church fathers speak frequently of disciples and the life of discipleship (e.g. Irenaeus and Eusebius), but the apostolic fathers reveal the earliest attitudes about the concept of discipleship in the church following the passing of the apostles.

Ignatius of Antioch

'Just as we become aware of a meteor only when, after travelling silently through space for untold millions of miles, it blazes through the atmosphere before dying in a shower of fire, so it is with Ignatius, bishop of Antioch in Syria'.[1] This famous description captures the brilliant influence of the early church leader, Ignatius, bishop of the church at Antioch. Ignatius is not a figure well-known to many modern-day Christians, but his influence has been significant throughout church history. We know virtually nothing of his early life. His apparently long ministry in the region of Antioch in Syria goes unrecorded in church annals. We meet him for the first and only time a few weeks shortly before his death as a martyr in Rome early in the second century. But in those few weeks Ignatius left a legacy which has had a remarkable impact upon the church. His legacy is in the form of seven brief letters.

Ignatius was arrested during a time of persecution in Antioch and sent to Rome to be tried and executed. He travelled from Syria to Rome in the company of ten Roman soldiers in approximately AD 110.[2] Along the route he wrote letters, five to churches located in cities along the way (Ephesus, Magnesia, Tralles, Philadelphia, and Smyrna), one to his friend Polycarp, bishop of the church at Smyrna, and one to the church in Rome, alerting them to his impending arrival there.[3] In these seven brief letters Ignatius left a powerful mark upon church history. Ignatius is important because of the early date of his writings, reflecting unparalleled light upon conditions at a crucial

---

[1]Lightfoot, Harmer, and Holmes, *The Apostolic Fathers*, p. 79.

[2]The majority of scholars follow the suggestion of Eusebius that the general time of Ignatius' martydom was during the reign of Trajan, c. AD 98-117 (Eusebius, *Hist. Eccl.* 3.21-22), but debate the exact date. The date of AD 110 is an approximation. Cf. Lightfoot, Harmer, and Holmes, *The Apostolic Fathers*, p. 82. For somewhat later dating see Klaus-Gunther Essig, 'Mutmassungen über den Anlass des Martyriums von Ignatius von Antiochien', *VC* 40 (1986), pp, 105-117; Charles Munier, 'A propos d'Ignace d'Antioche: observations sur la liste épiscopale d'Antioche', *RSR* 55 (1981), pp. 126-31.

[3]The middle recension of seven letters as the authentic corpus appears to be the firmly held consensus of the majority of modern scholars. Cf. William R. Schoedel, *Ignatius of Antioch: A Commentary on the Letters of Ignatius of Antioch* (ed. Helmut Koester; Hermeneia; Philadelphia: Fortress, 1985), pp. 3-7; Lightfoot, Harmer, and Holmes, *The Apostolic Fathers*, pp. 82-83. For an extended, older discussion, see J.B. Lightfoot, *The Apostolic Fathers: Revised Texts with Introductions, Notes, Dissertations, and Translations*, Two Parts in 5 volumes (1889-1890; rpt.; Grand Rapids: Baker, 1981), part 2, vol 1, pp, 233-430.

time of church development. But, and this is the focus of our study, he is also important because of the impact of his attitude toward Christian life, ministry, and discipleship.

Ignatius was a complicated person. On the one hand, scholars suggest that he was full of self-doubt, attributable to the fact that he had lost control over warring factions in his church in Antioch. On the other hand, some scholars say that he had an inappropriately authoritarian attitude, which is displayed toward his own church and toward other churches and church leaders. Some point to his regular self-effacement and suggest that he had a low personal self-esteem. Others say that he had a naturally vigorous, impulsive, and energetic personality.[1] But all scholars point to Ignatius' remarkable attitude toward his impending martyrdom, even though they may point with differing interpretations of his attitude. Ignatius' attitude toward his martyrdom has unfailingly disturbed readers. However, what disturbs readers the most is that he longs for his martyrdom, even begging his readers not to interfere with the Roman government's process. One observer notes, 'The vivid, almost macabre eagerness with which Ignatius apparently anticipates his death has repelled many readers, and a good deal of unwarranted criticism (e.g. labeling him "neurotic") has been directed toward him . . .'[2] It is in this very attitude toward martyrdom that we encounter a unique element of Ignatius' understanding of discipleship, an element that has had a profound impact upon the church's notion of discipleship ever since. I quote here a long, classic passage from Ignatius' letter to the Roman church. In its raw power and emotion this passage describes the utter horror of his impending martyrdom. But it also demonstrates Ignatius' attitude toward that martyrdom and what it meant for him as a disciple of Jesus Christ.

> I am fighting wild beasts from Syria to Rome, through land and sea, by night and day, bound to ten leopards—which is a company of soldiers—who when well treated become worse. *By their mistreatment I become more of a disciple,* but 'not for that reason I am justified'. May I have the pleasure of wild beasts that have been prepared for me. I will even coax them to devour me promptly, not as they have done with some, whom they were too timid to touch. And if when I am willing and ready they are

[1]For background to these views, see Schoedel, *Ignatius*, pp. 10-15. See also Corwin, *St. Ignatius*, p. 21ff. and Lightfoot, Harmer, and Holmes, *The Apostolic Fathers*, pp. 79-82.

[2]Lightfoot, Harmer, and Holmes, *The Apostolic Fathers*, p. 81.

> not, I will force them. Bear with me—I know what is best for me. *Now at last I am beginning to be a disciple*. May nothing visible or invisible envy me, so that I may reach Jesus Christ. Fire and cross and battles with wild beasts, mutilation, mangling, wrenching of bones, the hacking of limbs, the crushing of my whole body, cruel tortures of the devil—let these come upon me, only let me reach Jesus Christ! (Ign. *Rom*. 5.1.4-5.3.3; italics added for emphasis).

What lies behind Ignatius' attitude? Is this attitude to be found in other apostolic fathers? What is Ignatius' understanding of discipleship, and how does it relate to the New Testament conception?

Discipleship Terminology

Ignatius uses many of the same discipleship terms found in the NT. The other apostolic fathers use some of this terminology, but not to the extent as Ignatius.[1] Ignatius uses the word 'disciple' (μαθητής) and related terms fourteen times, while in all the other apostolic fathers combined the word disciple occurs less than a dozen times.[2]

Ignatius uses the noun 'disciple' (μαθητής) nine times,[3] the verb 'I make/become a disciple' (μαθητεύω) four times,[4] and the rare noun 'lesson' (μαθητεία) once.[5] Categories of usage will be discussed below more fully, but a few observations at this point will indicate the signficance of 'disciple' terminology for Ignatius. First, Ignatius uses disciple-terms in three seemingly contradictory ways. In some passages the word disciple simply designates a Christian. In other passages the word seems to designate the person who is a more committed Christian than other Christians. And in a number of other passages the word disciple seems to designate the person who is a martyr. Surprising usage indeed, which has caused much debate and confusion among students of discipleship over the years. Second, when Ignatius uses the verb 'I make/become a disciple (μαθητεύω), the same verb

---

[1] Although Ignatius' abundant use of discipleship terminology causes him to stand out prominently, he shares several common discipleship themes with the other apostolic fathers. For other discipleship terms in Ignatius and the other Fathers, see Wilkins, *Following the Master*, pp. 320-23.

[2] μαθητής occurs in the *Martyrdom of Polycarp* (*Mart. Pol.* 17.3.2, 5; 22.2.1) and the anonymous letter to Diognetus (four times in *Diogn.* 11.1-2).

[3] Ign. *Eph.* 1.2.4; Ign. *Magn.* 9.1.6; 9.2.3; 10.1.3; Ign. *Trall.* 5.2.4; Ign. *Rom.* 4.2.4; 5.3.2; Ign. *Pol.* 2.1.1; 7.1.5.

[4] Ign. *Eph.* 3.1.3; 10.1.4; Ign. *Rom.* 3.1.2; 5.1.4.

[5] Ign. *Trall.* 3.2.5.

used in the Great Commission of Matthew's gospel, he provides a unique link with the writings and activities of the early church.[1] A direct line is drawn from Matthew's record of the commission of Jesus (Mt. 28.19) to Luke's record of the activities of the apostolic church (Acts 14.21) to Ignatius' record of the life of the churches of the second century (Ign. *Eph.* 3.1.3; 10.1.4; Ign. *Rom.* 3.1.2; 5.1.4). Third, in some contexts Ignatius seems to draw upon the 'learner' aspect of the noun μαθητής (Ign. *Rom.* 3.1.2). Although the semantic range of the noun certainly included the meaning 'learner', in common New Testament and Hellenistic secular usage the 'adherent' factor was more in view.[2] The 'learner' aspect in Ignatius may be illustrated by his use of the rare noun 'lesson' (μαθητεία, Ign. *Trall.* 3.2.5), formed from the same stem as the noun 'disciple' (μαθητής). μαθητεία occurs neither in the NT nor anywhere else in early Christian literature. Fourth, although Ignatius refers to himself as a disciple, he does not consider himself to be an apostle (Ign. *Trall.* 7.1.4; Ign. *Rom.* 4.3.2). For Ignatius, 'apostles' are the special and limited group that were the foundation of the church (cf. Ign. *Magn.* 6.1.5; 7.1.2; 13.2.3; Ign. *Phld.* 5.1.6; 9.1.5; Ign. *Smyrn.* 8.1.2). The 'council of apostles' appears to be limited to the Twelve and Paul (Ign. *Rom.* 4.3.2).

The use of disciple-terms in the *Martyrdom of Polycarp* (written approximately AD 160, some fifty years after Ignatius) is also quite interesting. First, μαθητής is used to designate those persons who found martyrdom as 'disciples and imitators of the Lord' (*Mart. Pol.* 17.3.2). This is similar to the martyr-theme that we find in Ignatius. Second, the term is also used to designate a mentor relationship between a Christian leader and a novice-trainee. For example, the author refers to Irenaeus as a 'disciple of Polycarp' (*Mart. Pol.* 22.2.1).[3] Ignatius agrees with the concept of learning from and following the example of other Christians, but he does not use the term to designate a formal mentor relationship between two Christians.[4]

---

[1]A search of the apostolic fathers through the TLG data base indicates that the verb does not occur elsewhere in these writings. Cf. also BAGD, p. 486.

[2]See Wilkins, *The Concept of Disciple in Matthew's Gospel*, esp. chs. 1 and 3.

[3]The term also occurs in the longer conclusion found in the Moscow manuscript.

[4]One textually debated passage reads 'that I may be found to be your disciple at the resurrection (ἀναστάσει)' (Ign. *Poly.* 7.1.5). Lake (*The Apostolic Fathers*, p. 274 n. 3 and p. 275 n. 2) and Corwin (*St. Ignatius*, p. 228 n. 8) prefer this reading. Lightfoot (*The Apostolic Fathers*, p. 304) and Schoedel (*Ignatius*, p. 278 n. 4) prefer the reading, 'that I may be found to be a disciple by

Third, 'fellow-disciple' (συμμαθητής) occurs as a compound form in *Martyrdom of Polycarp,* but it does not occur in Ignatius. The author points to the martyrs, especially Polycarp, and prays that he too may join them as fellow-disciples in martyrdom: 'God grant that we too may be their companions and fellow-disciples' (*Mart. Pol.* 17.3.5). This is an interesting phenomenon, because 'fellow-disciple' is quite rare in Hellenistic and early Christian usage. But it does occur once in the New Testament, when John records, 'Thomas, called the Twin, said to his *fellow disciples,* "Let us also go, that we may die with Him"' (Jn 11.16 NRSV). Interestingly, this is also in a martyr context.

The word 'disciple' also occurs in *The Epistle to Diognetus,* one of the latest in the collection of the apostolic fathers (c. AD 150-225), and called by J.B. Lightfoot 'the noblest of early Christian writings'.[1] In this anonymous apologetic tract to an unbeliever the author uses the word disciple four times, all in one provocative passage.

> I am not talking about strange things, nor am I engaged in irrational speculation, but having been a *disciple* of Apostles, I am now becoming a teacher of the Gentiles. To those who are becoming *disciples* of the truth I try to minister in a worthy manner the teachings that have been handed down. Indeed, does anyone who has been rightly taught and has come to love the Word not seek to learn exactly the things openly made known by the Word to *disciples*? To them the Word appeared and revealed these things, speaking quite plainly as He did so; though not understood by unbelievers, He explained them to *disciples,* who, being regarded as faithful by Him, learned the mysteries of the Father (*Diogn.* 11.1-2[2]; emphasis added).

Several issues arise from this intriguing passage. First, since 'disciples' are used opposite of 'unbelievers', the phrase 'becoming *disciples* of the truth' indicates conversion to Christianity. Second, as a '*disciple* of apostles' the writer was one who had been instructed by the apostles,[3] and who, in turn, is now a 'teacher of the Gentiles'. This expression indicates acquisition of the truth of the gospel, as the phrase 'those who are becoming *disciples* of the truth' reveals. As we

means of your prayer' (αἰτήσει). Schoedel argues convincingly against the former reading on the basis that a disciple in Ignatius is always a disciple of Jesus.

[1]Lightfoot, Harmer, and Holmes, *The Apostolic Fathers*, p. 291.

[2]Lake concludes that this and the following chapters belong to a different document; cf. Lake, *The Apostolic Fathers*, II, p. 349.

[3]Whether the writer was taught personally or through their writings is debated.

observed in Ignatius and the *Martyrdom of Polycarp,* this usage emphasizes the 'learning' aspect. Third, this 'learning' aspect is intimately linked with conversion. As one is taught the meaning of Christianity and receives it as one's own, that person becomes a 'disciple of the truth', a Christian.

Discipleship Characteristics

The apostolic fathers use many of the same discipleship terms as do the NT writers.[1] When using the word 'disciple' the fathers, especially Ignatius, use the term in a restricted manner. In the gospels, and to a lesser degree in Acts, the word disciple was used as a title in narrative material simply to designate those who were believers. Many times the term could be used without special significance. On the other hand, a growing technicality surrounded the word disciple as Jesus developed his particular form of discipleship. That technicality implied a personal relationship with Jesus and an assumed progress of growth, especially in the goal of imitating and becoming like the Master. By the time of the early church, this technical understanding of what it meant to be a disciple of Jesus was firmly attached to the term. We can see that in the book of Acts the term is used somewhat unceremoniously as a title for a confessing Christian.[2] However, the apostolic fathers do not use the term in this unceremonious manner. They tend to use 'disciple' in a reverent sense which emphasizes in context the technicality of the discipleship life of the Christian. This may be influenced by a growing reverence for the those disciples who walked with Jesus in his earthly ministry, but it almost certainly is influenced by the persecution which the church was experiencing.

Overall, discipleship is understood as the development of the Christian life. However, the most perplexing feature of discipleship in Ignatius and some of the other apostolic fathers is the relationship to martyrdom. We noted above that Ignatius seems to imply that the

---

[1]For other discipleship terms in the Fathers, see Wilkins, *Following the Master*, pp. 320-323.

[2]See F.F. Bruce, *The Acts of the Apostles: The Greek Text with Introduction and Commentary* (1951; 1952; 3d. ed.; Grand Rapids: Eerdmans, 1990), p. 180; Charles H. Talbert, 'Discipleship in Luke-Acts', in *Discipleship in the New Testament*, ed. Fernando F. Segovia (Philadelphia: Fortress, 1985), p. 62; Ernst Haenchen, *The Acts of the Apostles: A Commentary* (1965; ET; Philadelphia: Westminster, 1971), p. 260 n. 1; Richard N. Longenecker, 'The Acts of the Apostles', (EBC, 9; Grand Rapids: Zondervan, 1981), p. 493; Rengstorf, 'μαθητής', *TDNT*, IV, p. 458; David John Williams, *Acts* (GNC; San Francisco: Harper & Row, 1985), p. 102.

word 'disciple' is a common referent for 'believer' or 'Christian'. In several passages discipleship is simply the outworking of the Christian life. Yet we also noted that as he approached martyrdom Ignatius saw himself finally 'becoming a disciple'. In several passages discipleship seems to be a more advanced stage of the Christian life. What are we to make of these seemingly contradictory expressions of discipleship? In order to answer that question adequately we must take a closer look at both kinds of passages.

Discipleship as the Christian life.

Ignatius indicates that a person enters into and advances along the life of discipleship through conversion and Christian growth. When pagans 'find God' they 'become disciples' (Ign. *Eph.* 10.1.4). Once a person becomes a disciple, growth in discipleship transpires by living one's life in accordance with the characteristics of Christ and His teachings. Ignatius tells the church that, 'having become His disciples, let us learn to live in accordance with Christianity. For whoever is called by any other name than this does not belong to God' (Ign. *Mag.* 10.1.3). Here Ignatius draws a contrast between the Judaizers, those who would lead the church back into legalism, and true disciples, those who 'live in accordance with Christianity'.

While Ignatius strongly emphasizes that conversion results from faith, initiating the life of discipleship, he just as strongly emphasizes that endurance in the life of discipleship is the evidence of belief. When Ignatius writes to the Magnesians he indicates that those who believe in the death and resurrection of Christ are disciples. He even points to the Old Testament prophets and calls them 'disciples in the Spirit' because they were awaiting Christ. The Christian life is centered on and flows from the mystery of the cross.

> If, then, those who had lived in antiquated practices came to newness of hope, no longer keeping the Sabbath but living in accordance with the Lord's day, on which our life also arose through Him and His death (which some deny), the mystery through which we came to believe, and because of which we patiently endure, in order that we might be found to be disciples of Jesus Christ, our only teacher, how can we possibly live without Him? (Ign. *Magn.* 9.1.1-6).

The cross and resurrection determines the shape of Christian existence. Christ is the only teacher of those who would call themselves disciples, because he provided the ultimate example of endurance in his obedience to the point of death.[1] '"Endurance" is a sign of discipleship precisely because, for Ignatius, Christ's teaching consists of his enactment of his Father's will in being obedient to the point of death'.[2] Belief must be proven by endurance. Only those who are obedient prove to be disciples, and the conclusive proof is obedience to the point of death (cf. Ign. *Magn.* 9-10). As Ignatius saw the threat to the church from the Roman government and from the Judaizers, he declared that endurance and obedience is the proof of true belief/ discipleship. Conversion is the point at which one becomes a disciple, but true disciples will continue to grow in discipleship.

However, this is not to say that disciples will always obey perfectly. At times disciples will be wayward and will need to be brought back into line. When Ignatius advises Polycarp how to deal with wayward members of his church, he says, 'If you love good disciples, it is no credit to you; rather with gentleness bring the more troublesome ones into submission' (Ign. *Pol.* 2.1.1). Ignatius is as realistic as are the NT writers. Obedience and endurance are the expected signs of discipleship, but perfection is not demanded as one traverses the path.

Developmental discipleship.

Discipleship in the apostolic fathers is clearly developmental. Although a person becomes a disciple/Christian through conversion, the life of a disciple (i.e. discipleship) is not a static phenomenon. Discipleship means growth and progress toward the goal of becoming more like Jesus. Simply by using the term 'disciple' the authors conjure up an image of the Christian who is a committed follower of Jesus. To be a true disciple means that a person has made a definite conversion commitment to follow Jesus, and it is expected that the person who makes that commitment will carry it through to completion. This is especially significant for those who were experiencing persecution. During this time of persecution if persons were charged with being Christians they could simply deny the name of Jesus and they would be set free. Those who continued to claim the name of Jesus demonstrated the reality of their faith. This was the ultimate

---

[1] Cf. William R. Schoedel, 'Ignatius and the Reception of Matthew in Antioch', in *Social History of the Matthean Community: Cross-Disciplinary Approaches* (ed. David L. Balch; Minneapolis: Fortress, 1991), p. 165.

[2] Schoedel, *Ignatius of Antioch*, p. 124.

demonstration that they were true followers, their vindication of faithfulness to the Name, to the reality of the Christian life, to Christian ministry.

Therefore, the time of conversion was a significant moment for considering the hardship that lay ahead. To claim the name of Jesus as Savior meant that one would surely experience persecution for the sake of the Name. This is an unmistakable illustration of Jesus' teaching on counting the cost of discipleship. Counting the cost not only meant the cost of what becoming a disciple meant, but also the cost of what the life of discipleship might entail. In the parables of counting the cost of discipleship, Jesus plainly pointed out the cost of what completing the process of discipleship would take (Lk. 14.28-32). Jesus wanted people to recognize that discipleship was not simply the moment of conversion, but it included the life that would follow. It is this ongoing life that Ignatius, in particular, emphasizes. The closer Ignatius gets to the time of completing his life, the closer he was to being a completed disciple.[1]

Someone has said that 'a disciple is always becoming more fully a disciple'. That is similar to the developmental process which Ignatius emphasizes. At the moment of conversion he became a disciple, but as he grows he becomes more like his Master, and the more like Jesus he becomes the closer he comes to the realization of the completed task of being made into the final likeness of Christ. This theme also continues the 'already/not yet' tension which NT writers develop. An example of this is found especially in Paul, who emphasizes that although he *already* counted the cost of knowing Christ for salvation, he does *not yet* know Him fully. That knowledge is expanded through the life that he now lives, and will be perfected at the time of death.

> But whatever was to my profit I now consider loss for the sake of Christ. What is more, I consider everything a loss compared to the surpassing greatness of knowing Christ Jesus my Lord, for whose sake I have lost all things. I consider them rubbish, that I may gain Christ and be found in him, not having a righteousness of my own that comes from the law, but that which is through faith in Christ—the righteousness that comes from God and is by faith. I want to know Christ and the power of his resurrection and the fellowship of sharing in his sufferings, becoming like him in his death, and so, somehow, to attain to the resurrection from the dead.

[1]Cf. Demetrios Trakatellis, '"Ἀκολούθει μοι/Follow Me" (Mk 2:14): Discipleship and Priesthood', *GrOrthThR* 30 (3, 1985), see pp. 283, 285.

> Not that I have already obtained all this, or have already been made perfect, but I press on to take hold of that for which Christ Jesus took hold of me. Brothers, I do not consider myself yet to have taken hold of it. But one thing I do: Forgetting what is behind and straining toward what is ahead, I press on toward the goal to win the prize for which God has called me heavenward in Christ Jesus (Phil. 3.7-14 NIV).

As with Paul, so with Ignatius. Ignatius writes at a critical point in his life. For him, being a disciple was not a convenience. It would cost him his life. But this did not cause him to cringe from the challenge. In fact, facing martyrdom brought him into the stark realization that he was coming closer and closer to the fulfilment of his life of discipleship. He was closer to the end. Closer to being with his Lord. And, in addition, as he faced martyrdom he realized that he was walking the same path of suffering and death that his Lord had walked, and that most of the Twelve and Paul had walked.[1] He saw in his own martyrdom not a horror, but a privilege to walk as his Master had walked.

Later in church history this attitude would be taken to an extreme where men and women would seek out martyrdom in an ascetic fashion in order to gain meritorious salvation or a higher level of Christianity, such as sainthood.[2] Such a conception is not biblical discipleship. In Ignatius, on the contrary, we find an example of discipleship which closely follows the model Jesus and the apostles developed.

Imitation and discipleship.

We noted above that discipleship and imitation converge in Ignatius' thinking. The two notions are not precisely the same, but they have kindred meaning. Discipleship implies devotion to Christ and following His pattern. Imitation emphasizes the pattern, but assumes the devotion. Corwin explains,

---

[1]For a discussion of the view that readiness for martyrdom was a NT theme, see George Dragas, 'Martyrdom and Orthodoxy in the New Testament Era—The Theme of Μαρτυρία as Witness to the Truth', *GrOrthThRev* 30 (3, 1985), pp. 287-96.

[2]For a recent discussion of the interplay of asceticism and martyrdom in the early church during the second through fourth centuries see Maureen A. Tilley, 'The Ascetic Body and the (Un)Making of the World of the Martyr', *JAAR* 59 (1991), pp. 467-479. Tilley rightly emphasizes that the tendency toward romanticization and idealization of martyrdom for sainthood increased with Contantinian Christianity, c. AD 350, when persecutions within the Roman Empire ceased (p. 467 n. 1).

> The key to Ignatius' view of the Christian life is an understanding of the twin conceptions of imitation and discipleship, for they are central to his thinking. They give content to the choice that he urges, and in following the path that they indicate the Christian life is grounded securely, for it is provided both with an effective motive, in devotion to the Lord, and a pattern for life, in a general sense at least.[1]

Although some suggest that Ignatius adopted his imitation theme from Hellenistic philosophy,[2] close comparison of Ignatius' teaching with NT teaching indicates that Ignatius shaped his teaching after the model of Scripture, not Hellenism.[3] When Ignatius expresses his desire to be allowed to imitate the Lord to the point of being executed, we hear reflections of NT usage: 'Allow me to be an imitator of the suffering of my God. If anyone has Him within himself, let him understand what I long for and sympathize with me, knowing what constrains me' (Ign. *Rom.* 6.3.1). Here Ignatius expresses what he says every Christian should understand, the desire to be completely obedient, even if it means to suffer as did Christ. The context reveals clearly that Ignatius is very much in line with the NT authors for whom following Christ's example of submission implies suffering. The apostle Peter says, 'To this you were called, because Christ suffered for you, leaving you an example, that you should follow in his steps' (1 Pet. 2.21).

We can also see discipleship and imitation merging in relationships between believers. Believers are to provide an example of godliness for pagans to follow (Ign. *Eph.* 10.1.4), and believers are to learn from one another (Ign. *Rom.* 3.1.2). The author of the *Martydom of Polycarp* suggests that in following the example of another believer one is said to be a disciple of that person (*Mart. Pol.* 22.2.1). Only one time does the NT speak of a believer having disciples (Acts 9.25: Saul's/Paul's disciples), but the theme of learning from and following the example of other believers is a thoroughly NT theme. The exam-

---

[1]Corwin, *St. Ignatius and Christianity in Antioch*, p. 227.

[2]E.g. Michael Atkinson, 'Body and Discipleship', *Theology* 82 (1979), pp. 279-87, who follows the highly influential article by Karl H. Rengstorf, "μαθητής," *TDNT*, IV, pp. 415-461, esp. p. 460.

[3]Cf. Corwin, *St. Ignatius and Christianity in Antioch*, pp. 227-237; H.H. Henrix, 'Von der Nachahmung Gottes: Heiligkeit und Heiligsein im biblischen und jüdischen Denken', *Erbe und Auftrag* 65 (3, 1989), pp. 177-87. While Henrix touches only briefly on Ignatius' attitude toward the Jewish heritage (pp. 186-87), the article is valuable for tracing the continuity of the imitation of God in the Jewish-Christian tradition.

ple often has to do with the way in which prior believers endured suffering. The writer to the Hebrews exhorts his readers to look back upon OT saints who suffered in faith and to follow Jesus' example of suffering (Heb. 12.1-3), and Paul commends the Thessalonians, 'For you, brothers, became imitators of God's churches in Judea, which are in Christ Jesus: You suffered from your own countrymen the same things those churches suffered from the Jews' (1 Thess. 2.14).

Some have suggested that in his emphasis upon imitation of Christ's suffering and martyrdom Ignatius is leaning toward a later church doctrine of 're-enactment of Christ's passion'. In later church doctrine a distinction was made between discipleship and imitation. Discipleship meant following after Christ, whereas imitation meant replicating Christ-like qualities in order to attain sainthood. Following after Christ was seen as a category of faith and obedience which is stimulated by the grace of God, whereas imitation assumed the accomplishments of the dedicated person, the saint.[1] But the theme of imitation is not the same in Ignatius as is found in later church tradition. For Ignatius, imitation of Christ, even in suffering, is not a special saintliness. Rather, it is the calling of Christians in general.[2]

Discipleship, Ministry, Martyrdom.

While Ignatius indicates that a person enters into and advances along the life of discipleship through conversion and Christian growth, he startles modern readers with language which seems to indicate that those approaching martyrdom experience discipleship in a unique manner. For example, Ignatius expresses an eagerness for 'fighting with beasts at Rome, that by so doing I might be enabled to be a true disciple' (Ign. *Eph.* 1.2.4). As he considers imminent martyrdom by being devoured by wild beasts, he says, 'Coax the wild beasts, that they may become my tomb and leave nothing of my body behind, lest I become a burden to someone once I have fallen asleep. Then I will

---

[1]See Schoedel, *Ignatius*, p. 30. Cf. Hans von Campenhausen, *Die Idee des Martyriums in der alten Kirche* (2d ed.; Göttingen: Vandenhoeck & Ruprecht, 1964). This distinction is still seen in scholarly studies under the technical terms *Nachfolge* and *Nachahmung*: e.g. cf., Hans Dieter Betz, *Nachfolge und Nachahmung Jesu Christi im Neuen Testament* (BHT 37; Tübingen: J.C.B. Mohr/Siebeck, 1967); Anselm Schulz, *Nachfolgen und Nachahmen: Studien über das Verhältnis der neutestamentlichen Jüngerschaft zur urchristlichen Vorbildethik.* (SANT 6; Munich: Kösel, 1962).

[2]Trakatellis, "'Ἀκολούθει μοι/Follow Me"', pp. 283, 285. For a discussion of 'imitation' in the light of one of the most difficult passages of Ignatius' letters (Ign. *Rom.* 6.3.1), see Schoedel, *Ignatius*, pp. 183-84.

truly be a disciple of Jesus Christ, when the world will no longer see my body' (Ign. *Rom.* 4.2.4). Ignatius exults in the spiritual benefit martrydom will finally bring, because through it he will finally become a disciple.

> May I have the pleasure of wild beasts that have been prepared for me. I will even coax them to devour me promptly, not as they have done with some, whom they were too timid to touch. And if when I am willing and ready they are not, I will force them. Bear with me—I know what is best for me. Now at last I am beginning to be a disciple (Ign. *Rom.* 5.3.2).

What are we to make of this kind of language related to discipleship? Some students of the early church have found here in Ignatius a two-level form of discipleship. That is, they suggest that, for Ignatius, it was only in experiencing martyrdom that he attained discipleship. If we take only one or two passages, this indeed might be the conclusion we reach. However, upon close examination of the seven passages in which Ignatius discusses discipleship and martyrdom, we can see that in each Ignatius reflects two thoroughly NT themes: 1) the Christian life is a developmental process which will be completed only at death and union with Christ, and 2) vindication of the reality of our Christian life and ministry is realized at death when we stand before the Lord. For example, as Ignatius contemplates the circumstances of his chains, which are producing great spiritual blessing, he gives us a unique perspective of his idea of discipleship: in facing imminent martyrdom he will finally 'attain God' and in so doing finally become a disciple. 'For I myself, though I am in chains and can comprehend heavenly things, the ranks of the angels and the hierarchy of principalities, things visible and invisible, for all this I am not yet a disciple. For we still lack many things, that we might not lack God' (Ign. *Trall.* 5.2.4). Schoedel comments, 'Thus Augustine speaks of martyrs who "endured so much to acquire God", a future-oriented form of the theme of "having" God' (cf. Ign. *Magn.* 12).[1] A disciple in this sense is one who has attained spiritual fullness of God by being obedient to the point of death.

In a passage cited above, as Ignatius considers imminent martyrdom by being devoured by wild beasts, he says, 'Coax the wild beasts, that they may become my tomb and leave nothing of my body behind, lest I become a burden to someone once I have fallen asleep. Then I

[1]Schoedel, *Ignatius*, p. 145.

will truly be a disciple of Jesus Christ, when the world will no longer see my body' (Ign. *Rom.* 4.2.4). The disappearance of his body means that he will no longer be a burden to anyone (a remarkably Pauline theme) and will also mark his complete transformation. He goes on to say that, 'if I suffer, I will be a freedman of Jesus Christ, and will rise up free in Him. In the meantime, as a prisoner I am learning to desire nothing' (Ign. *Rom.* 4.3.4). In passing from this world Ignatius realizes that he will finally attain true freedom, true perfection, which means true discipleship.[1]

A combination of the developmental and vindicational aspect is clearly evident in a passage where Ignatius draws directly upon a Pauline statement. 'I am fighting wild beasts from Syria to Rome, through land and sea, by night and day, bound to ten leopards—which is a company of soldiers—who when well treated become worse. By their mistreatment I become more of a disciple, but "not for that reason I am justified"' (Ign. *Rom.* 5.1.4). Here Ignatius equates discipleship with justification, and draws upon 1 Cor 4.4 to provide an illustrative principle. Ignatius sees his travel to Rome for martyrdom as a victory campaign against opposing forces.[2] The Roman power is going down to defeat, but in a paradoxical way. Ignatius' victory will take the form of dying in the amphitheater and thus attaining God. His present sufferings are teaching him to become a disciple and are readying him for his justification. Citing Paul's words serves to emphasize the fact that Ignatius' justification is still future, the time when his perfection will be realized.[3] As Ignatius continues speaking of his imminent martyrdom, he exults in the spiritual benefit it will finally bring: he will finally become a disciple.

> May I have the pleasure of wild beasts that have been prepared for me. I will even coax them to devour me promptly, not as they have done with some, whom they were too timid to touch. And if when I am willing and ready they are not, I will force them. Bear with me—I know what is best for me. Now at last I am beginning to be a disciple. May nothing visible or invisible envy me, so that I may reach Jesus Christ. Fire and cross and battles with wild beasts, mutilation, mangling, wrenching of bones, the hacking of limbs, the crushing of my whole body, cruel tortures of the devil—let these come upon me, only let me reach Jesus Christ! (Ign. *Rom.* 5.3.1-3).

---

[1]See Schoedel, *Ignatius*, p. 176.

[2]Cf. Schoedel, 'Igatius and the Reception of Matthew in Antioch', p. 133-137.

[3]See Schoedel, *Ignatius*, p. 179.

This is perhaps the most extreme statement in his letters, but it once again shows Ignatius' eagerness to undergo any suffering to attain discipleship, which here means final attainment of being with Jesus Christ.

The same theme surfaces in Ignatius' letter to Polycarp. Since his church in Antioch is at peace as a result of the prayers of the Smyrnaeans and Polycarp, Ignatius is now free from anxiety. He can face his coming martrydom with a heart which is free from the concerns of this world. Therefore, he covets their effective prayers for himself as well. For what does he want them to pray? '. . .that through suffering I reach God, that I may prove to be a disciple by means of your prayer' (Ign. *Pol.* 7.1.5). Schoedel comments, 'the end of troubles in Antioch is evidently taken to indicate that Ignatius may expect his own troubles to be over; or more precisely, vindication of Ignatius in Antioch is taken to mean that the bishop may now have higher hopes of God's final approval'.[1]

One other passage clarifies Ignatius' attitude toward discipleship in connection with martyrdom. When writing to the Ephesian believers Ignatius gives strong admonitions based upon his authority as a bishop. However, he also points to the imperfection in his life, an imperfection which will be rectified only through growth as a disciple and through death.

> I am not commanding you, as though I were somebody important. For even though I am in chains for the sake of the Name, I have not yet been perfected in Jesus Christ. For now I am only beginning to be a disciple, and I speak to you as my fellow-students. For I need to be trained by you in faith, instruction, endurance, and patience (Ign. *Eph.* 3.1.1-3).

Ignatius does not place himself above the Ephesian believers, even though he has the authority of a bishop. And he does not place himself above them because he is now 'beginning to be a disciple'. Discipleship does not place him in a higher category of sainthood. Rather, it simply shows that he is in the process of actualizing his final goal of being with Christ after death. Indeed, these believers are his 'fellow-learners'.[2]

---

[1] Schoedel, *Ignatius*, p. 278.

[2] συνδιδασκαλίτης ('fellow-learners') is a *hapax legomenon* in Greek literature, most likely coined by Ignatius to indicate his unity with the church. See Schoedel, *Ignatius*, pp. 48-49 n. 5.

Therefore, martyrdom is seen by Ignatius as the time when he will attain final development of the discipleship process, and when he will be fully vindicated as one who was a diligent and faithful servant of Jesus Christ. In that sense, true discipleship is when Ignatius attains union with Christ through martyrdom. This desire does not deny the reality of present earthly discipleship, however. We saw above that Ignatius indicates elsewhere that a disciple is simply a Christian. What Ignatius shows us is that following Jesus into death brings the disciple into the final realization and proof of the reality of his or her relationship with Christ. In a powerful passage Ignatius contrasts those who are simply 'Christian' in name with those who are 'really Christians' and indicates that it is only in death that true Christians will prove the reality of their faith (Ign. *Magn*. 4.1.1).

> For just as there are two coinages, the one of God, the other of the world, and each has its own stamp impressed on it, so the unbelievers bear the stamp of this world, and the believers the stamp of God the Father in love through Jesus Christ, and unless we willingly choose to die through him in His passion, His life is not in us (Ign. *Magn*. 5.1-2).

Willingness to be obedient, even unto death, was for Ignatius the evidence that a person was a Christian, a true believer, a disciple.

Implications

What of us? This issue of martyrdom for many of us seems so removed from our modern setting. How can we learn from these early believers who faced death so radically as a natural consequence of their true faith? In the past two millennia the church has taken both the biblical data and the teachings of the apostolic fathers to unwarranted extremes.

On the one hand, we can see that some later church fathers, and even some modern-day Christian leaders, misunderstood the radical commitment to discipleship displayed by Ignatius and others to be possible only for the spiritually elite within the church. Phillip Schaff notes that later church fathers referred to a special class of self-denying Christians (called ἀσκηταί) who were held in high esteem by the church, who had special seats at worship, and who 'were considered the fairest ornaments of the church'.[1] This later practice is often read back into earlier conceptions of discipleship. Origen 'attached the notion of holiness to perfection and, therefore, to a certain group of Christians, a spiritual elite'.[2] Throughout the Middle Ages this theme was echoed by monastic writers such as Bernard of Clairvaux (AD 1091-1153), who looked on the monastic life as an imitation of the poverty, humility, and charity of the earthly Jesus.[3] But as we have noted, nowhere does Ignatius or the other apostolic fathers indicate that discipleship is an elitist conception. All Christians are disciples, hence, the radical nature of discipleship displayed by Ignatius is a personal extension of his own Christian life. As Schoedel states, 'It is one-sided to find here [Ign. *Rom.* 6.3] decisive evidence that Ignatius has moved beyond the conception of following Christ in the New Testament and exalted the achievement of a special saintliness above the commitment to the Christian mission and its concern to illuminate the whole of human existence in light of the cross'.[4] Although later fathers would find in Ignatius a seed-bed for elitist teaching, such was not the intention of Ignatius.

On the other hand, we can see in a related way how some later church fathers misunderstood the apostolic fathers' attitude toward martyrdom to be an indication that the calling to suffering or martyrdom creates a special saintliness. Soon after Ignatius' and Polycarp's martyrdom, the influential church father Irenaeus suggests that martyrdom was the highest form of spirituality. Irenaeus speaks of 'the true and perfect disciple of Christ as the one who is ready to go with him to the cross. True spirituality always involves some form of death. The ascetic and the martyr are for this reason the true spirituals of the church'.[5] In the fourth century Antony and the Desert Fathers saw the monastic and hermetical life as an 'unbloody martrydom' and thus as perfect discipleship.[6] Ignatius saw God's will for his life to include martyrdom, but this calling does not make him an eli-

[1]Philip Schaff, *History of the Christian Church* (Grand Rapids: Eerdmans, 1910), II, pp. 388, 391. Some of the later fathers who referred to the ἀσκηταί were Athenagoras, Tertullian, Origen, Eusebius, and Jerome, among others.

[2]John D. Zizioulas, 'The Early Christian Community', in *Christian Spirituality—Origins to the Twelfth Century*, eds. Bernard McGinn and John Meyendorff (New York: Crossroad, 1985), p. 39.

[3]Avery Dulles, 'Discipleship', *The Encyclopedia of Religion*, Mircea Eliade, ed. (New York: Macmillan, 1987), IV, p.363.

[4]Schoedel, *Ignatius*, p. 183.

[5]Zizioulas, 'The Early Christian Community', p. 39.

[6]Dulles, 'Discipleship', p. 363.

tist, and this calling is not for all others. As Cyril Richardson says, 'Others may reach the divine through their own particular sufferings, which may not include marytrdom. The will of God may not be the same for all believers'.[1] Ignatius appears comfortable with a tension between discipleship as a present reality and as a future hope made perfect through martrydom.

In our day we find those who go to these same extremes when interpreting the biblical data and the apostolic fathers. We find those who speak in elitist terms of disciples as a special category of committed Christians. We also find those who speak of a special saintliness for those who suffer martyrdom.[2]

On the other hand, we find those in our day who display a radical commitment to Christ in the most difficult circumstances, even those who suffer martyrdom on account of the Name, yet who see their actions as a natural extension of the Christian life. They understand that their life of discipleship includes a challenge to count the cost of yielding their comfort, their careers, their families, even their lives, for the sake of the Name of Jesus. They have renounced all in counting the cost of becoming a disciple and of carrying out that life, and they see their calling as simply an extension of the Christian life. The call to martyrdom which Ignatius faced is a startling reality even in our day.

In those days of persecution by the Roman empire, the theme of following the example of Christ in suffering was a necessary stimulus to the faith of all those in that early, harried church. The *Martyrdom of Polycarp* concludes with an exhortation to his readers which is reminiscent of the diverse expressions of ministry and discipleship found in the NT:

> We bid you farewell, brothers, as you walk by the word of Jesus Christ which is in accord with the gospel; with whom be glory to God for the salvation of the holy elect; just as the blessed Polycarp was martyred, in whose footsteps may we also be found in the kingdom of Jesus Christ (*Mart. Pol.* 22).

May Christ's example in suffering, and the example of his disciples, whatever the era, be a stimulus to our faith as well.

---

[1]Cyril Charles Richardson, *The Christianity of Ignatius of Antioch* (New York: Columbia, 1935), p. 24.

[2]See Dulles, 'Discipleship', p. 363; Wilkins, *Following the Master*, pp. 27-30.

With this essay I pay special tribute to Professor Ralph P. Martin, my mentor in my doctoral studies at Fuller Theological Seminary. It was Professor Martin who first introduced me to the world of formal scholarship and who guided my academic studies of discipleship in the ancient world. No person has had more influence on my scholarly endeavors than Professor Martin. In addition, his endurance in the middle of personal suffering, his pastoral heart extended to students, and his gracious spirit when interacting with opposite points of view has provided me an example of the true Christian scholar. However humble the attempt, my gratitude and appreciation is extended with this essay and Festschrift for his influence on my career.

INDEXES

INDEX OF BIBLICAL REFERENCES

I. OLD TESTAMENT

II. OLD TESTAMENT APOCRYPHA

III. NEW TESTAMENT

IV. THE PSEUDEPIGRAPHA

V. QUMRAN

VI. Tractates of the Mishnah and Talmud

VII. Philo

VIII. Josephus

IX. Christian Authors

X. OTHER ANCIENT AUTHORS

INDEX OF MODERN AUTHORS